AF560108

BIOLOGY OF BIRDS

By

Dr. D.R. Khanna
Reader in Zoology
Gurukul Kangri University
Haridwar (Uttaranchal)

&

Dr. P.R. Yadav
Lecturer
Department of Zoology
D.A.V. College
Muzaffarnagar (U.P.)

DISCOVERY PUBLISHING HOUSE
NEW DELHI-110002

First Published [illegible]

ISBN 81-7141-933-X

Published by

DISCOVERY PUBLISHING HOUSE

[illegible]

[illegible]

[illegible]

E-mail: [illegible]

Printed at: [illegible]

[illegible] Delhi [illegible]

Contents

1

INTRODUCTION

Scientists divide the animal kingdom into several major groups for classification purposes. By far the largest group is the invertebrates: it contains about 95 percent of the millions of known species of animals, including sponges, mollusks, arthropods, and insects. Groups of vertebrates, or animals with backbones, contain the other 5 percent of known species. They can be divided roughly into fishes, amphibians, reptiles, birds, and mammals. The class Aves—birds—consists of approximately 9,000 species, grouped (in the classification system adopted by this book) into 24 orders. One order, the Passeriformes (known as passerines or songbirds), contains more than half of the known bird species. The remaining orders are known collectively as non-passerines. Birds come in all shapes and sizes, from the ostrich *Struthio camelus*, standing about 2.5 meters ($8^1/_4$, feet) tall, to the bee hummingbird *Mellisuga helenae*, which measures less than 6 centimeters ($2^1/_3$ inches) from tip of bill to tip of tail and possibly is the smallest bird. There are large birds that cannot fly, small ones that can hover or fly backwards, and just about every conceivable intermediate. But it is the possession of feathers that immediately differentiates birds from other animals. All birds have feathers.

Plumage

Feathers constitute the plumage of a bird. As well as providing mechanical and thermal protection, the plumage assists in streamlining the body, thereby reducing friction during flight, or when moving on the ground or through water.

There are several types of feathers, but the most important are contour feathers, which constitute the ordinary visible plumage, and comparison to poor fliers or those that fly only short distances. Like mammals, birds are "warm-blooded". Although this capability of maintaining body temperature above that of the surroundings was acquired independently by the two groups, the physiology of thermoregulation for mammals and birds is remarkably similar, and is a striking example of parallel evolution.

Birds have a highly specialized respiratory system. The small lungs comprise only about two percent of the body volume, but connecting airsacs are well developed, and in total may be up to 20 percent of the body volume. These air-sacs are located in various parts of the body, and they play an important role in the through passage of air.

The digestive tract of a bird is basically the same as that of other vertebrates and consists of a coiled tube or gut leading from the mouth to the anus. Food passes from the mouth into the gullet and then to the crop, which is a thin-walled distensible pocket of the gullet where food is stored for subsequent digestion or feeding of the young by regurgitation. The crop is well developed in grain-eating and many flesh-eating birds, less developed in other species, and absent altogether in some insect-eating birds. The proventriculus and the ventriculus or gizzard together correspond to the stomach in mammals, and again are well developed in grain-eating species. From the gizzard food passes to the duodenum and intestines, where digestion is completed before waste is excreted through the anus. Birds have no urinary bladder, so nitrogenous wastes are excreted in the form of urea, a semi-solid paste-like substance, after water has been absorbed in the cloaca. The cloaca is a common opening through which the products of the reproductive, digestive, and excretory systems are passed. Some birds, such as owls, eliminate the indigestible components of their food in the form of pellets regurgitated through the mouth.

The Sense

The general structure of the bird eye is similar to that found in all vertebrates. However, the extremely well-developed, efficient eyes possessed by almost all birds, especially the large eyes of some birds of prey and nocturnal species, lead ornithologists to conclude that vision is of the utmost importance.

Attempts to ascertain the level of hearing possessed by birds have met with only partial success, but the few auditory functions that have been measured are almost as sensitive as they are in humans. A higher proficiency was detected in the ability to recognize different sounds repeated so rapidly that to the human ear they become inextricably fused. Birds apparently possess adequate olfactory organs, but in some species the sense of smell seems to be poorly developed and plays little part in their lives.

How Birds Reproduce

All birds lay eggs, within which development of the embryo subsequently takes place, but of course this form of reproduction is prevalent in other groups of animals. As in the majority of vertebrates, the adult male has testes and the female has ovaries. although in nearly all bird species, only the ovary on the left side is functional. During copulation the cloaca of both sexes is everted so that sperm can transfer from male to female, but in some birds (for example, many ducks and the ratites) part of the cloaca of the male is modified to form a penis. Fertilization of released ova takes place in the upper oviduct, then as each egg passes along the oviduct, layers of albumen are deposited on it. In the wider and greatly distensible uterus, the shell and pigment are added to complete the egg, which finally passes through the vagina and cloaca to be expelled into the nest.

The egg must be kept at the correct temperature for embryonic development. This is usually brought about through contact with the

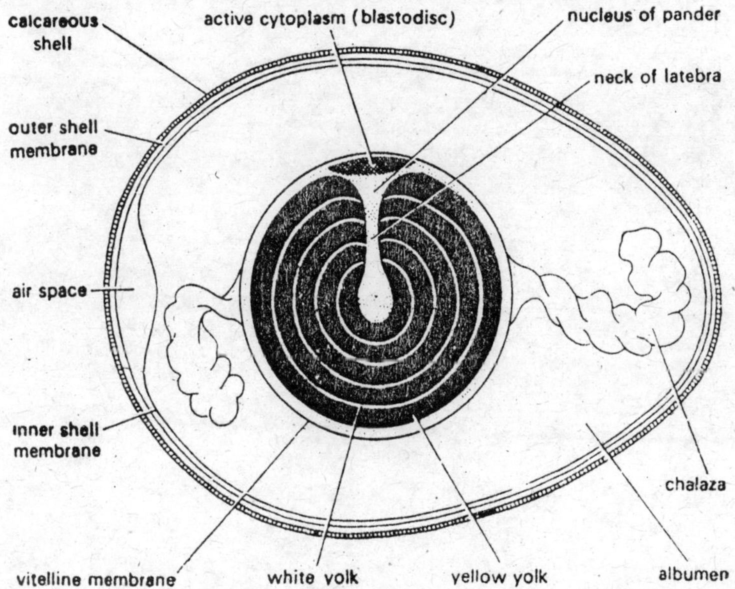

Fig. 1.4. Diagrammatic longitudinal section of a bird's egg.

body of a parent, and the adults of many species develop brood-patches—areas denuded of feathers and richly supplied with blood vessels. The parent bird settles on the nest so that its brood patch or patches cover the egg or eggs; and with regular changeovers of the parents or short breaks away for feeding, the eggs are incubated until the chicks hatch. Incubation periods vary from 80 days for a large albatross, to 10 days for some small passerines. Some species do not incubate their own eggs but parasitize other birds by laying their eggs in the host's nest, and the megapodes make use of natural sources of heat such as sunlight or the fermentation of decaying vegetation to maintain the temperature of eggs buried in a mound or sand.

2

CLASSIFYING BIRDS

The diversity of a group of animals such as birds could not be covered easily in this book without the use of a well-established classification. It enables biologists to summarize a vast amount of biological information in an efficient fashion. For example, categorizing birds as members of the animal kingdom, the phylum Chordata, the subphylum Vertebrata, and the class Aves informs us that each individual bird possesses, among other things, gill slits, a dorsal hollow nerve cord, a vertebral column, a neural crest, feathers, and forelimbs modified into wings.

Avian Classification

The class Aves is divided into orders—24 in the classification adopted for this book, although there are additional orders containing only extinct birds. Knowing that a bird is an owl, order Strigiformes, informs us that it possesses a bony arch on its radius bone, among other features. And if a bird is a hornbill, family Bucerotidae, we know that the first two cervical vertebrae are fused into a single unit. Each order is subdivided into families (about 165), each family into genera (slightly over 2,000), and each genus into species (slightly over 9,000).

It must be emphasized that considerable disagreement still exists about the limits of some groups and the relationships between orders and between families included in an order. However, most of the family-level groups covered in this book are well substantiated and will retain their identity even when we learn more about the relationships of birds to each other.

What is a Species?

A species is defined as a group of actually or potentially interbreeding populations of organisms, which are genetically isolated from other such groups. Species maintain their separation from each other by the possession of intrinsic isolating barriers which prevent the exchange of genetic material among them.

The scientific name given to a species is made up of two words derived from Greek or Latin—for example, *Falco peregrinus*. This name is used by ornithologists around the world, no matter whether they are Dutch taxonomists working in Egypt, Russian researchers in Siberia, or Spanish-speakers in South America. However, the vernacular or common name that people give to this species can vary from place to place; thus the peregrine falcon may also be called the black-cheeked falcon in English, and different names in many other languages, but they all refer to one species, *Falco peregrinus*.

Where populations of a species are separated geographically they may develop slightly different details of size or plumage colour, and can be identified as separate races or subspecies. A third word is then added to the scientific name. For example, *Falco peregrinus tundrius* is one of the North American subspecies, and *Falco peregrinus calidus* one of the European subspecies. An adult female should be able to breed successfully with an adult male of a related subspecies where their geographic ranges overlap and the habitat conditions are suitable.

From time to time biologists have to decide whether geographic representatives should be considered as subspecies of a species or as separate species. Such decisions are largely arbitrary, as there are no objective tests for judging the specific status of geographic representatives whose ranges do not meet.

The Basis of Classification

Biological classification, the work of systematists, has two main goals. The first is recognition of the basic units or biological diversity—species and their subunits (mainly subspecies); this then establishes the extent of diversity throughout all organisms, living and extinct. The second is the arrangement of these basic units into a system of increasingly higher-level groups, providing the foundation for summaries of biological knowledge. When two or more species are quite similar in their morphology, physiology, behaviour, and ecology, they can be classified in the same genus; all species in a genus are presumed to be descendants of a common ancestor.

Biologists are interested in a single natural classification suitable for all comparative analyses, one which reflects the past evolutionary history of organisms by summarizing the amount of evolutionary change along each lineage and the splitting of lineages. These aspects would be revealed by the number of taxa (groups) at successive levels—such as species, genus, family, order, class—indicating the degree of relationships among species and higher-level taxa.

Several different types of biological classification have heen used in recent years. One type is known as phenetic. The only aspect of evolutionary change reflected in such a classification is the amount of evolutionary change expressed as the similarity among taxa. A second type is cladistic (from the Greek *klados* meaning "branch"). The only evolutionary aspect reflected in this type of classification is the splitting of phyletic lineages (branching patterns). A third type, evolutionary classification, attempts to summarize both the amount of evolutionary change in phyletic lineages and the splitting of these lineages; however, these two evolutionary aspects are not absolutely correlated with each other, so evolutionary taxonomists must decide which aspect should be given greater importance in particular cases. The order Passeriformes, for example, includes more than half of the known species of living birds, for its members show much less diversity than the rest of the orders of birds combined. In contrast, the order Coliiformes (mousebirds) contains a single genus with only six species but it is quite distinct from other orders. Evolutionary classifications contain the greatest amount of information for biologists, and provide the best all-purpose general reference system. The evolutionary classification used in this book follows closely the system advocated in the 16 volumes of the recently completed Peters' *Check-list of Birds of the World*.

Establishment of a Classification

The establishment of a biological classification is a two-step process. First is the formulation of hypotheses about the classification of groups—for example, that the kingfishers (family Alcedinidae) and the horn bills (family Bucerotidae) are members of the same group, the order Coraciiformes. This hypothesis is tested scientifically against taxonomic properties of characters, of which the most important is homology. The second step is the formulation of hypotheses about the taxonomic properties of characters—homology, for example—which are tested against empirical observations. This second step, character analysis, is the most important part of classifying organisms into higher-level groups.

The words homology, homologous and homologue come from the Greek *homologos* meaning "agreeing, corresponding". In biological usage a homologue is a feature in two or more organisms that stems phylogenetically from the same feature in the immediate common ancestor of these organisms. Thus the hypothesis that the fused first and second cervical vertebrae are homologous in species of hornbills means that this feature was inherited from such fused vertebrae in the immediate ancestor of all known horn bills. Hypotheses about homologous features are tested by comparing them and ascertaining their similarities. These similarities are assumed to be paternal ones—descriptive of the feature in the immediate common ancestor and remaining unchanged during the evolution to each descendent organism. Thus, homology of the fused cervical vertebrae in hornbills would be tested by establishing similarities in the structure of this feature in diverse hornbill species. This is the only available valid way to test hypotheses about homologies.

Unfortunately this test is frequently not very robust and often does not provide correct answers. Hence further analyses are needed to establish a degree of confidence in each homologue. This involves functional and adaptational analyses of the postulated homologues, and estimates of the probability that two similar features evolved independently ("convergent evolution").

The possibility of being fooled by independent evolution of unrelated organisms subjected to similar demands from their environment can be reduced by studying various features so that at least some of the features will be independent of similar selective demands. For this reason, the scientist will attempt to use a diversity of features, choosing them carefully to include those associated with different aspects of the life of the organisms. So although both grebes and loons have webbed feet, the presence of different types of webbing suggests that these two groups are not closely related despite being foot-propelled diving birds. Systematists are more confident in the correctness of a classificatory hypothesis if it is supported by a variety of homologous features. But each feature must be carefully and independently analysed.

Ornithologists have used this approach, but with varying success. The major problem appears to be a great emphasis placed on finding new taxonomic characters—biochemical ones during the past two decades—but in the absence of functional/adaptational analyses to establish how much confidence should be given to taxonomic characters in different groups of birds.

Moreover, the tendency has been for each systematist to emphasize the classification supported by the characters he or she used. After all, most of the classic morphological characters used to establish the currently accepted classification have never been properly analysed.

And neither have the newly established biochemical and genetic (DNA) characters.

What is a Sequence?

What is a classification and what is a sequence? Why does the sequence of birds vary in different books? Before addressing these questions, we should consider the difference between a classification and a sequence.

Classifications are systems expressing the evolutionary relationships of taxonomic groups arranged in an inclusive, non-overlapping hierarchy. In anyone taxon, all members descend from a single common ancestor. The taxa in this type of hierarchy are arranged in a series of categories at different levels; for birds, the class Aves is the highest categorical level, followed by orders, families, genera, and species. Intermediate levels such as superfamilies, subfamilies, and tribes are also used.

Sequences are arrangements of the taxa to suit books and other data banks with similar linear restrictions. Rules do exist for the establishment of sequences—such as more primitive groups being listed before more advanced groups—but other equally valid sequences could be established from the same classification. Broadly accepted standard sequences are important because they permit greater ease of communication. For this book we have adopted not only the basic classification but also the general sequence used in Peters' *Check-list* because it is the most standard recent sequence for birds of the world.

Rules for Scientific Names

The International Code of Zoological Nomenclature is concerned with names for groups at different levels, from subspecies to families, with the goal of establishing a stable universal set of taxonomic names for all animals.

Priority means that the valid name of any taxon, is the oldest name applied to it. If new studies reveal that two species are members of the same genus but were formerly classified in separate genera, they should both be given the generic name that was published first. However, priority is only one of the rules used to achieve stability and universality in zoological nomenclature. Long-term established usage regulated through plenary powers of the International Commission on Zoological Nomenclature is another.

Special care has been used in this volume to use the valid name for each avian taxon, especially those advocated in the recently developed list of names for bird families.

3

BIRDS THROUGH THE AGES

The biology of living birds is better known than for any other group of vertebrates. Our understanding of the evolutionary history of birds is not as far advanced, however, in part because fewer fossils have been found. But many spectacular fossil finds in recent years, along with comparative studies of the anatomy and genetic structure of species alive today, are providing valuable evidence with which to reconstruct the pattern of avian evolution, especially the early history of birds.

"Feathered Dinosaurs"

Although birds arose more than 150 million years ago, the first 50 million years of avian history has yielded relatively few fossils. Those that do exist have provided important information about the modernization of the avian body plan, especially as it pertains to the evolution of flight.

During the past decade, paleontologists have reassessed the relationships between birds and two-legged theropod dinosaurs, a group that includes perhaps the most famous dinosaur of them all, *Tyrannosaurus rex*. The realization that birds are "feathered dinosaurs" arose as a result of the discovery of new specimens of the oldest known bird, *Archaeopteryx lithographica*. Indeed, the two beautiful, nearly complete specimens of *Archaeopteryx* now housed in museums in London and Berlin were among the very first fossil birds to be described.

All six specimens of *Archaeopteryx* were found in the Solnhofen limestones of Bavaria, in southern Germany, and had lived during the late Jurassic period, 200 to 145 million years ago. The close relationship of *Archaeopteryx* and other birds to theropod dinosaurs is significant,

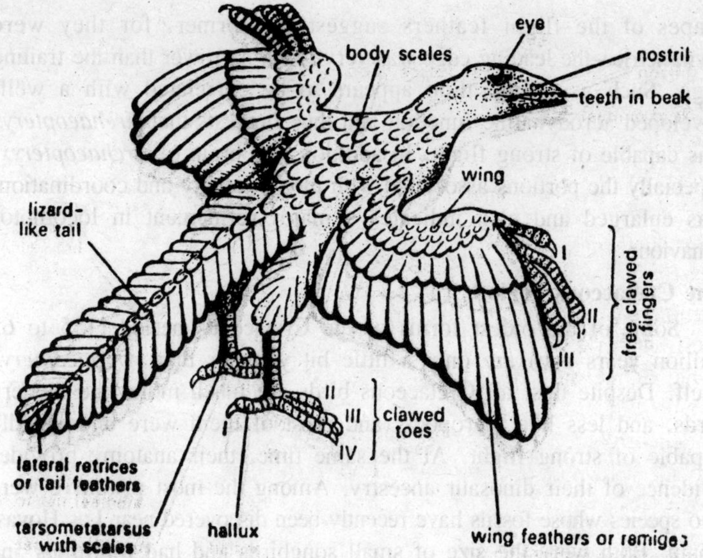

Fig. 3.1. Archaeopteryx. Restroration showing detailed structure.

because it means that the most distinctive characteristic of birds—flight, and all the structural modifications necessary for flight—arose in ancestors that were swift two-legged predatory creatures designed to exploit terrestrial environments rather than trees.

Although *Archaeopteryx* is very clearly related to birds, much of its skeleton recalls that of a theropod. Most of the bones of the forelimb, for example, had none of the special modifications developed in modern birds, such as the fusion of the bones in the wrist and hand facilitating the attachment and fine manipulation of the flight feathers. The bones of the shoulder girdle—the scapula and coracoid—were like those of theropods, and the two clavics were fused into a U-shaped furcula, or "wishbone". It was long thought that the furcula was a distinctive avian feature, bracing the two shoulder girdles during flight, but we now know that it was present in some advanced theropods, where it also probably functioned as a brace, but for arms used in prey capture not flight.

From the days of its discovery in 1861, *Archaeopteryx* was considered a bird because its body was covered with feathers arranged in feather tracts similar to those of modem birds. Yet despite the presence of feathers, paleontologists have debated whether *Archaeopteryx* was capable of powered flight or was simply a glider. The detailed shapes of the flight feathers suggest the former, for they were asymmetric—the leading edge was very much narrower than the trailing edge. Such a configuration appears to be correlated with a well-developed aerodynamic function and thus suggests that *Archaeopteryx* was capable of strong flight. In addition, the brain of *Archaeopteryx*, especially the portions associated with motor activity and coordination, was enlarged and also indicates a major refinement in locomotor behaviour.

The Cretaceous Period

Some of the oldest forms of the Cretaceous period (145 to 65 million years ago) are only a little bit younger than *Archaeopteryx* itself. Despite this, all Cretaceous birds are much more like modern birds, and less like theropods, and most of them were undoubtedly capable of strong flight. At the same time, their anatomy provides evidence of their dinosaur ancestry. Among the most primitive were two species whose fossils have recently been discovered near Las Hoyas, Spain. Both were the size of small songbirds and had forelimbs and shoulder girdles that were relatively similar to modern birds, whereas the skeletal elements of the pelvis and hindlimbs were more similar to *Archaeopteryx* and theropods. These birds also had a pygostyle—a fusion of the most posterior caudal vertebrae, providing a central point of attachment for the tail feathers—and an ossified sternum, which indicate improvements in the ability to fly.

Several other early Cretaceous birds are interesting because they suggest that anatomically more advanced forms had already evolved by this time. One of these, *Ambiortus*, found in Mongolia, was the size of a small crow. *Ambiortus* possessed a well-developed keel on the sternum and a very modern shoulder girdle, and (unlike the Las Hoyas fossils) the bones of the wrist were fused to form a single element, the carpometacarpus, just as in modern birds. Although nothing is known about the pelvis and hindlimbs of *Ambiortus*, another early Cretaceous bird fills in some of the gaps in our knowledge. This form, named *Gansus* after the Gansu Province of China where it was discovered, is known only from the distal part of the leg, but those bones are of an entirely modern aspect and thus are much more advanced than the Las Hoyas birds. *Gansus* was apparently a small shorebird-like species.

Perhaps the most famous of all Cretaceous fossil birds were *Hesperornis* and *Ichthyornis* from the late Cretaceous of North America. Hesperornithiform birds are also known from the early Cretaceous of

Englarid and the late Cretaceous of South America, which suggests they were successful and widespread. *Hesperornis* and *lchthyornis* are notable because they retained the primitive theropod condition of having teeth on their upper and lower jaws, as did *Archaeopteryx*. Although many other Cretaceous birds probably had teeth, no evidence for this has yet been found. *Hesperornis* and its allies were flightless, foot-propelled divers. As such they had lost the keel on the sternum, greatly reduced the size of wing, and developed nonpneumatic bones. *Ichthyornis*, in contrast, was a strong flier, reminiscent in some respects of modem gulls, but much more primitive and unrelated to them.

The Rise of Modern Birds

Modern birds, called the Neornithes ("new birds"), are divisible into two well-defined groups. The first of these is the paleognaths ("ancient jawed", in reference to their somewhat primitive skull) including the tinamous of South and Central America, and large flightless ratite birds such as the ostrich of Africa, the rheas of South America, the emu and cassowaries of Australia-New Guinea, and the kiwis of New Zealand. Paleognaths have had a long history that predates the breakup of Gondwana and the drift of the southern continents. Several fossils from the late Cretaceous period have been found in Mongolia and Europe. In the Paleocene (65 to 57 million years ago) of Europe and North America there existed numerous species of relatively small paleognaths, most of which were capable of powered flight.

The second group of modern birds is the neognaths ("new jawed", in reference to their more advanced skull anatomy). More than 99 percent of all species alive today are neognaths. We know that most of the major groups were represented in the Eocene (57 to 37 million years ago) and Oligocene (37 to 24 million years ago), but few of them have a fossil record from as early as the Cretaceous, primarily because of the scarcity sediments containing fossils. Paleontologists are probably justified in inferring that many of these groups, or their ancestors, extended well into the Cretaceous.

One of the more primitive lineages of neognaths includes the galliform birds (chickens, pheasants, quails) and the anseriform birds (ducks, geese, swans). Both are first known from fossils in the Eocene, and each apparently had a worldwide distribution by that time. This radiation also included a small group of very large birds, some more than 2 meters ($6^1/_2$ feet) tall: the flightless diatrymas of the North American, European, and Asian Eocene. Although it was assumed for a long time that they were fierce predators, recent studies suggest they were herbivore., which would be consistent with their apparent relationship to anseriforms. It is also possible that another group of flightless giants, the dromornithids or "Mihirung birds" of Australia, are members or this lineage.

Recent evidence suggests that waterbirds such as penguins, loons, grebes, pelicans, cormorants and their allies, and the albatrosses, shearwaters and their allies comprise a distinct evolutionary lineage. Many of these groups have fossil representatives in the Eocene, and so it is reasonable to assume this radiation had its beginnings in the Cretaceous. Penguins are well represented in the fossil record of Australia, South America, and New Zealand, where they live today, and even in the Eocene they were already specialized for "flying" through water.

Few lineages of birds have as interesting a fossil record as the pelecaniforms. The must bizarre group was the pseudodontorns ("false-toothed birds"), a diverse assemblage of albatross-like gliders. Ail had

Fig. 3.2. Milvus migrans.

jaws with teeth-like bony projections, which were presumably used for capturing prey while skimming the ocean's surface. Some pseudodontorns were truly gigantic, with a wingspan of as much as 6 meters (20 feet), far larger than any living albatross.

The most fascinating order of birds from a paleontological perspective is the Gruiformes, which includes rails and cranes, as well as a number of morphologically distinct families. The gruiforms have perhaps the best fossil record of any order of birds. One lineage now represented only by the trumpeters and seriemas of South America was much more diverse; it included several closely related families that radiated extensively in Europe and North America during the Eocene and Oligocene. Another lineage radiated in South America as the spectacular phorusrhacoid birds. These included a large number of gigantic species, most, if not all, of which were flightless and roamed the savannas and pampas as fierce predators. They survived to the end of the Pliocene (5 to 2 million years ago). Inexplicably, one of the largest members of the group, *Titanis walleri*, has also been discovered

Fig. 3.3. Rhea americana.

from Pliocene fossil records in Florida, the only certain record of these birds north of Brazil.

Because they inhabit aquatic environments, charadriiform birds—shorebirds, gulls, terns, and their allies—are well represented in the fossil record. At least four extinct families of the late Cretaceous of North America are tentatively placed in this order, thus attesting to the ancient origins of this group. Many contemporary families, including sandpipers, plovers, avocets, puffins, and auks, were present by the Eocene.

Another lineage of aquatic forms includes flamingos, storks, and ibises, and they too have a relatively good fossil record. All three were present and widely distributed by 45-50 million years ago.

The two great groups of raptorial birds include the falconoforms (hawks, eagles, falcons, and vultures) and the owls. Whether they are all closely related has been the subject of intense debate. Although

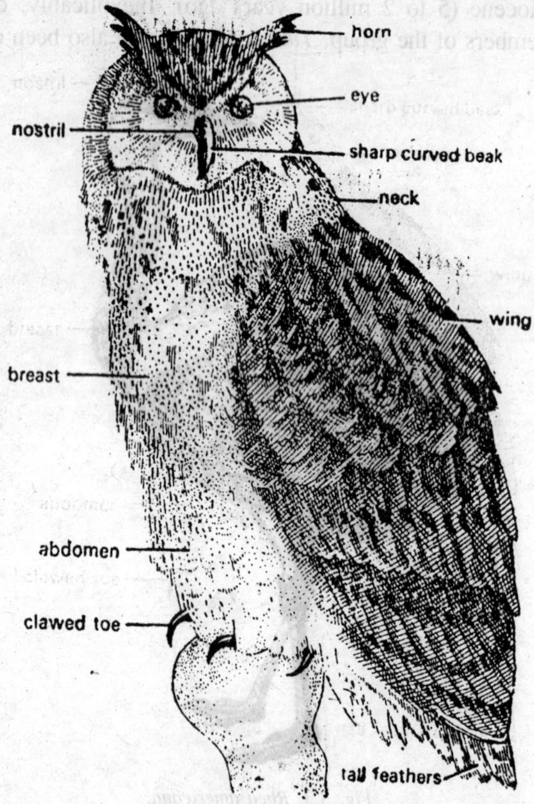

Fig. 3.4. Bubo bubo (Owl).

the fossil record does not help solve this problem, it documents that both groups have been in existence for at least 50 million years. Hawks and eagles had diversified on most continents by the Eocene, and other falconoform groups such as ospreys and secretarybirds are nearly as old. The "New World" cathartid vultures, whose evolutionary relationships are still uncertain, also have an excessive fossil record, including a number of forms in the Eocene and Oligocene of Europe and Asia as well as in North and South America. But unquestionably the most spectacular vulture-like birds—their relationships are also obscure—were the teratorns ("wonder birds") of the Miocene (24 to 5 million years ago) and Pliocene (5 to 2 million years ago) of South America and the Pleistocene (2 million to 10,000 years ago) of North America. *Teratornis merriami* found in the Rancho La Brea tar pits in California was quite large, having a wingspan of perhaps 3.8 meters ($12^1/_2$ feet). But soaring across the Miocene skies of the South American pampas was *Argentavis magnificens*, the largest-known flying bird. *Argentavis* had a wingspan that may have reached 7.5 meters ($24^1/_2$ feet) and a body weight of 80 kilograms (176 pounds). Present evidence based on skull morphology suggests this giant was largely a predator rather than a scavenger like most vultures.

The second group of captors, the owls. was remarkably diverse: no fewer than three families, now extinct, arc known from the Paleocene and Eocene of North America and Europe, and numerous extinct genera of barn owls are known from the same deposits. Owls in the modern family Strigidae are first known from the early Oligocene, and since then have radiated nearly worldwide.

Other orders and families of birds, while not having as extensive paleontological records as the preceding groups, are represented by fossils which indicate they too had their origins more than 50 million years ago. Included among these are nightjars and their allies (Caprimulgiformes), cuckoos (Cuculiformes), parrots (Psittaciformes), swifts (Apodiformes), and kingfishers, rollers, and their allies (Coraciiformes).

The largest order of birds is the Passeriformes, or songbirds. More than 70 families and thousands of species are alive today, but because virtually all of them are small tree-dwelling birds, their fossil record is relatively poor; the fossils that have been found are only tens of thousands of years old at most. Although a small number of species have been described from deposits that are at least 40 million years old, their relationships are not clear. But genetic distances among their most divergent families are much greater than among many non-passerine groups that were present 50-60 million years ago. This suggests that songbirds arose long before that time.

All the evidence suggests that most orders and many families of living birds probably originated in the Cretaceous, more than 65 million years ago, and then subsequently radiated. It may be difficult to document this conclusion directly until we find more fossils in non-marine sediments of the late Cretaceous. Nevertheless, recent years have seen a significant growth in the field of avian paleontology, which is certain to expand our knowledge of avian evolution in the very near future.

4

HABITATS AND ADAPTATIONS

The habitat of a bird can be loosely defined as the environment it occupies, particularly the climate and vegetation. Its habitat must provide food, foraging sites, cover from predators and the weather, and nesting sites. Birds have adapted to habitats as diverse as the Arctic tundra, the Sahara Desert, the Amazonian rainforest, and the middle of the oceans. They have carved out niches from the available resources. Most have survived ice ages and periods of great aridity, causing the expansion and contraction of their favoured habitats. It is true, that some became extinct, but others evolved to take their place. Each habitat has a characteristic array of species, many of which will display morphological adaptations to that particular habitat.

Habitat Requirements

A bird's habitat may be restricted by geographical barriers; for example, numerous families of songbirds such as cotingas, manakins, antbirds, and woodcreepers are restricted to South and Central America; bowerbirds, fairy-wrens, and lyrebirds are found only in the Australia-New Guinea region. More often, habitat restriction comes about because a species requires a particular resource to be present. This may be food, such as the seeds of spruce trees for the common crossbill *Loxia curvirostra* in Scandinavia, or protea flowers for the Cape sugarbird *Promerops cafer* in South Africa. Often it is a safe nesting site, such as a hole in a living pine tree for the red-cockaded woodpecker *Picoides borealis* in southeastern United States, and termite mounds for the golden-shouldered parrot *Psephotus chrysopterygius* in northern Australia.

Birds may be generalized or specialized in their habitat. The peregrine falcon *Falco peregrinus* and the barn owl *Tyto alba* occupy a wide range of habitats around the world. Kirtland's warbler *Dendroica kirtlandii* is an example of a highly specialized species, living only in jack pine woodlands recovering from fire that burnt through them six to thirteen years previously. Some species occupy different habitats in different parts of their range. The horned or shore lark *Eremophila alpestris* breeds in the high Arctic, the cold deserts of Central Asia, and the mountains of the Balkans, Morocco, and the Middle East. In North America the species is widespread in tundra, mountains, and deserts, as well as fields and grasslands. There is even a small isolated population in the Andes.

In many regions the presence of other animals, particularly predators, parasites, and competitors, may deter birds from an otherwise

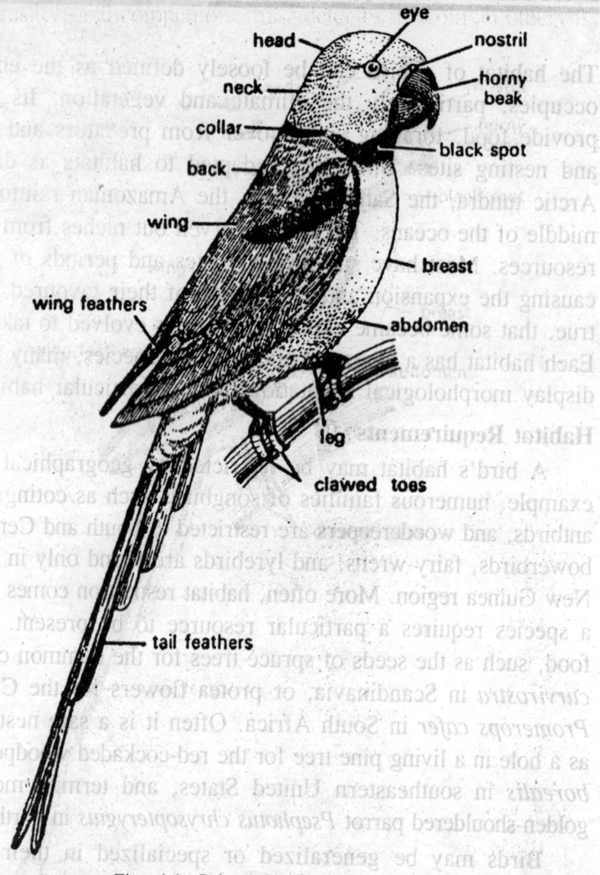

Fig. 4.1. Psittacula (Parrot).

suitable habitat. Introduced predators such as stoats and rats have eliminated many native birds from the main islands of New Zealand, so the stitchbird *Notiomystis cincta* and the saddleback *Philesturnus carunculatus*, for example, are now restricted to tiny offshore islands. An introduced mosquito which carries avian malaria has forced the endemic honeycreepers of the Hawaiian Islands to retreat to the mountain forests of each island. Evidence for competitive exclusion is more difficult to find, but many species expand their habitat in the absence of a similar species. For example, the horned lark is probably so widespread in North America because there are no other true larks there.

Many migratory birds occupy quite different habitats in the breeding and non-breeding seasons. Seabirds roam across the oceans but breed on islands and cliffs. Perhaps the most remarkable is the marbled murrelet *Brachyramphus marmoratus* which nests in the crowns of forest trees 50 meters (150 feet) high, inland from the Pacific coast of North America.

Ecological Niches

The ecological niche is the role an animal occupies in its habitat—its relation to food, shelter, and enemies. Generally it is the feeding behaviour that tends to determine a species' niche. For example, the great spotted woodpecker *Picoides major* of Eurasia is a forest-dwelling,

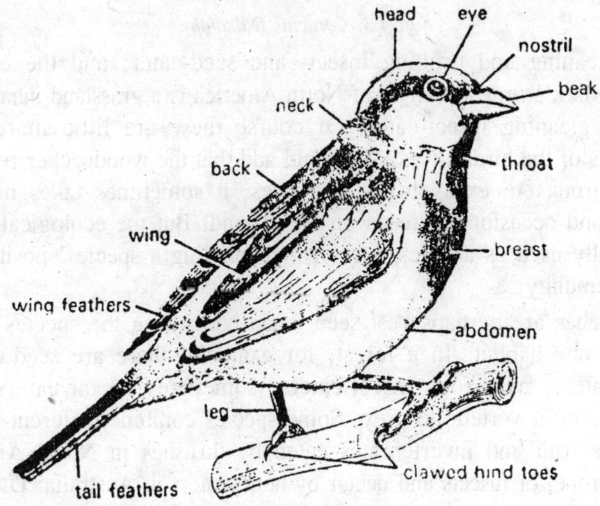

Fig. 4.2. Passer domesticus (House sparrow).

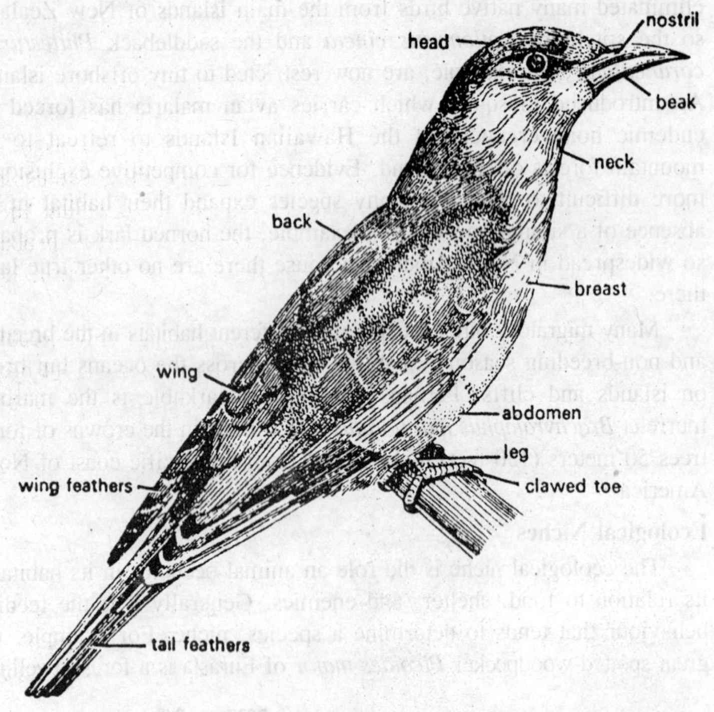

Fig. 4.3. Coracias (Nilkanth).

bark-gleaning and probing insect- and seed-eater; and the eastern meadowlark *Sturnella magna* of North America is a grassland-inhabiting, ground-gleaning insect-eater. Of course these are little more than sketches of the birds' lives. We could add that the woodpecker requires rotten trunks to excavate its nest sites, it sometimes takes nestling birds, and occasionally feeds on the ground. But the ecological niche is usually used as a quick way of pigeonholing a species' position in its community.

Niches are perhaps best seen when comparing the species living in any one habitat. In a forest, for example, there are seed-eaters, fruit-eaters, numerous insect-eaters, sometimes nectar-eaters, and consumers of vertebrate prey. Some species combine different foods, such as fruit and invertebrates eaten by thrushes in North America and Europe, or insects and nectar by honeyeaters in Australia. Different species taking the same type of food often forage on different levels within a habitat, known as microhabitats; for example, among insect-eaters there are different species feeding on the ground, among foliage, on bark, and capturing prey in the air. Species may take similar foods in the same place but of different sizes.

Scientists studying the ways in which birds share or partition the resources in similar communities around the world have noticed two things. First, there are often similar-looking (but possibly unrelated) birds filling similar niches on different continents; this is known as convergence. Second, there are differing numbers of species present in any given habitat.

Specific Diversity

A birdwatcher in spring in a North American, European, or southern Australian forest might expect to see 40 or 50 bird species on a good morning. More could be added in subsequent visits, but an observer would be very pleased if their bit of forest attracted as many as 100 species during the year. However, a small area of rainforest in New Guinea may be the home of more than 200 bird species, and the best parts of Amazonia may support 300 to 500 species. Why are tropical rainforests so rich? It seems that there are several answers. Rainforests hold a greater variety of resources, such as a vast array of fruits and flowers and large insects, and foraging opportunities in vine tangles and palm fronds. Birds such as parrots, fruit-doves, jacamars, motmots, and oropendolas exploit these niches. In South America there is a whole range of species that follows army ants, capturing the insects they displace.

Islands typically have fewer kinds of birds than continents. Generally the smaller the island and the more distant it is from the mainland the fewer species it possesses. The reason that larger islands have more species is because they have more habitats and hence more ecological niches. Also each species that finds a suitable niche can become common enough to be reasonably safe from extinction. Remote oceanic islands may have few species partly because not many birds have reached them. However, recent research on fossil remains on the Pacific islands has revealed that they had many more species when they were settled by Polynesians than when Europeans arrived. So their impoverished wildlife today is partly because the island peoples exterminated many local forms.

Adaptive Radiation

Island birds include some remarkable forms. These have evolved as a result of long periods of isolation from mainland relatives in a strange environment, but also because many other mainland forms are absent. Frequently one kind of bird has diversified in ecology and appearance, so that there are now many, and these occupy different ecological niches.

This can be seen best in Darwin's finches of the Galapagos Islands. There were probably no other land-birds when the first finches arrived from the neighbouring South American mainland. But there were insects, fruits, flowers and buds, as well as the seeds that make up the main diet of finches. Some of the finches continued to occupy seed-eating niches, so the larger islands have large-, medium-, and small-billed species (*Geospiza magnirostris*, *G. fortis* and *G. fuliginosa*), which eat large, medium, and small seeds respectively. One species evolved a longer bill and feeds on cactus flowers and fruits as well as seeds (*G. scandens*). Another evolutionary line led to the tree-dwelling finches

Fig. 4.4. Darwin's finches of the Galapagos Islands.

(genus *Camarhynchus*), which feed on fruit, buds, seeds, and insects. The woodpecker finch exploits insects from beneath bark and in rotten wood; it does this by using a small stick or cactus spine to locate and dislodge prey from inaccessible positions. A further species, the warbler finch *Certhidea olivacea*, adopted the way of life of a warbler and gleans small insects from foliage and twigs. Perhaps most remarkable of all, one of the finches, the ground or sharp-billed finch *Geospiza difficilis*, now feeds on blood from seabirds. It perches on nesting boobies, pecks at the base of their wing and tail feathers, and laps up the blood that oozes out.

The differences in appearance of the finches on this arid, remote archipelago led Charles Darwin to the belief that species were not immutable, but can change over time—in other words, evolve. The process by which a single species diversifies into a whole array of forms exploiting different niches is known as adaptive radiation. It can be seen on many groups of oceanic islands. The Hawaiian islands provide perhaps the supreme example. Again, a finch arrived some millions of years ago, perhaps from Asia, and found an environment with endless opportunities. The result was about 40 species of honeycreepers or sickle bills (family Drepanididae), which exploited all sorts of seeds, insects, and nectar over all the main island. Sadly, the familiar story of extinction under the impact of Polynesian and European settlement followed; direct predation, habitat clearing and burning, and introduced predators and parasites have severely depleted the number of honeycreepers.

Just as adaptive radiation can occur on islands, so too it can occur on continents. Mountain ranges and deserts may act as barriers that isolate populations, allowing them to diverge.

Bills, Feet, Wings, and Tails

Birds have characteristic sizes and shapes of their body parts, which have been adapted to suit their feeding behaviour and the niches they occupy. Birds' bills display adaptation best. The long dagger-shaped bill of the herons, the huge pouches on the pelican's bill, the hooked bill of predatory birds, and the deep, heavy bills of seed-eating parrots and finches are all adaptations to their food. Differences between bills of related species reflect differences in ecology. The blue tit *Parus caeruleus* in Europe has a deeper bill than the coal tit *P. ater* as it takes insects from broad-leaved trees, while the latter feeds in conifers; a fine bill offers an advantage when probing into pine needles. A similar pattern is shown in North America, with the plain titmouse

P. inornatus having a deeper bill for deciduous trees and the chestnut-backed chickadee *P. rufescens* having a finer bill for coniferous trees.

Feet, too, show adaptations to a bird's feeding behaviour and environment. The talons of raptors for gripping large prey, the webbed feet of ducks for swimming, and the extremely long toes of the jacana for walking on waterlilies are good examples. Ground-feeding birds usually have long legs and toes, whereas tree-creeping birds have very long toes and claws but short legs. Aerial birds such as swallows and swifts have small feet; indeed the scientific name for one group of swifts is *Apus*, meaning "no feet". Legs may also be short in birds in very cold climates, to reduce heat loss; the tundra-dwelling ptarmigans (genus *Lagopus*) have very short; feathered legs and feet.

Wings and tails can be important too. Long wings provide economy during night. The house martin *Delichon urbica* uses far less energy when flying than similar-sized but more terrestrial birds. Short wings give maneuverability, however, and are found in birds living in dense habitats or those that indulge in aggressive aerobatics. A comparison of two species, of which one is a migrant and the other is not, shows that the former invariably has longer wings. Long tails can also provide maneuverability and are shown by most flycatching birds. They can also be important in display, as in pheasants.

Of course, many birds change their diet and even their habitat during the year, so their bills, legs, and wings have to be compromises. Many birds eat seeds and insects, but the former require a deep bill and the latter a fine bill. It seems that birds are adapted morphologically to the time when food is in shortest supply. The chaffinch *Fringilla coelebs* and the great tit *Parus major* feed on insects in summer but nuts and seeds in winter. They have fairly deep bills, adapted to when food is scarce. The long bills of many waders are poorly adapted for insects, which they eat in the breeding season, but are ideal for probing estuarine mud in winter.

Natural selection operates on birds' bills, legs, and wings by favouring those with the most efficient size and shape. These birds will survive best and leave the most offspring, who will have inherited their parents' advantageous characteristics. Natural selection takes place in this way over thousands and millions of years, and this evolution allows species to adapt to changing conditions.

5

BIRD BEHAVIOUR

The behaviour of birds is governed primarily by their senses of vision and hearing. In this respect they are very like humans, which probably goes part of the way—along with their beautiful plumage and striking songs—toward explaining why birds are so attractive to us. Although the behaviour of birds is wonderfully varied, all of them must find their way from one place to another, find food, avoid being eaten by predators, breed with a mate of their own kind, and rear young which are well equipped to achieve all these feats in their turn. The senses play an important role in all of these activities.

Eyes and Ear like Humans

The eyesight of most birds is rather like our own, although recent evidence suggests that some of them see very much better in ultraviolet light than we do. Likewise, their hearing range is similar to ours, but some, such as owls, have special abilities that are remarkable. The barn owl can home in on and kill a mouse in a pitch-black room within seconds because its ears are adapted for extremely accurate sound location. Most birds also resemble us in having a poor sense of smell, but again there are some exceptions: the New Zealand kiwis are noted for their ability to smell out prey.

The other main factor to be considered as a background to discussing bird behaviour is their movement patterns. Birds are extremely mobile. The power of night enables them to travel long distances in pursuit of food or mates. Those that breed in higher latitudes need not hibernate or eke out a precarious existence during the short and cold winter days, when many foods are absent or in short supply. They can travel to more equable climates where living is easier.

Finding Food

The ability to find a reasonably constant supply of food is obviously very important to a flying animal that must be light and therefore cannot store large reserves. Whether they are diving for fish, probing at the water's edge for crabs, gleaning insects from the forest canopy, or searching for seeds in the undergrowth, most birds spend a high proportion, of their waking hours in pursuit of food.

Not many birds cooperate in the search for food. They may be solitary hunters, like hawks or owls, or they may gather in groups where food is in abundant supply, as do finches or penguins, but they do not often assist each other to catch it. Pelicans swimming in formation, and cormorants diving in synchrony, probably help to round up fish shoals, but close cooperation to track down and kill a single prey, like that of wolves or lions, is rare among birds. The social hunting displayed by Harris's hawks, where several birds combine to catch large prey such as a rabbit, may be an example. Members of a mated pair may forage together, and there is evidence that some birds that roost together at night may benefit by gaming information from each other about where best to feed. But, when feeding, most birds look after themselves alone.

Small birds, which do not have extensive food reserves, must feed very actively through most of the daylight hours. Indeed, some very small ones, such as hummingbirds, have so little in reserve that they lose heat overnight and rely on the warmth of the sun to get them going again in the morning.

It is of great benefit to birds to find food as quickly and economically as possible, especially if they feed in the open where their searching may expose them to the danger of being eaten themselves. A good deal of evidence suggests that birds do indeed feed in this way. A thrush that has just found a worm will search in the same area more carefully—a good strategy, given that worms usually occur in groups. A flycatcher, which eats small insects in the treetops early in the day, moves closer to the ground later on when large flies become active, as these yield more energy for the work expended in catching them.

Individual birds may also develop different feeding skills and concentrate on the foods to which they are best adapted. Some gulls may feed on the shore, eating crabs and other invertebrates, while others search for food on agricultural land, and yet others specialize in the spoils to be found on rubbish dumps. Even with a single type of

Fig. 5.1. Showing feeding behaviour in Birds.

food, techniques may differ. It is not easy to prize apart the two shells of a mussel and so gain the meal inside, but oystercatchers have various different ways of doing it. Some specialize in "stabbing", inserting their bill between the valves and cutting the muscle that holds them together. The favoured technique for others is "hammering", by which they break their way in through the shell. Some gulls and crows have yet another method: they fly up into the air and drop the mussel repeatedly until it breaks. They may even choose hard surfaces on which to do this, so that it is more likely to be successful.

Dropping shells onto a hard surface is just one stage removed from the use of tools. Song thrushes use special stones, their "anvils", on which they repeatedly smash snail shells until they break. Egyptian vultures take the opposite approach to break the very thick-shelled eggs of ostriches, gaining access by hitting them with a heavy stone

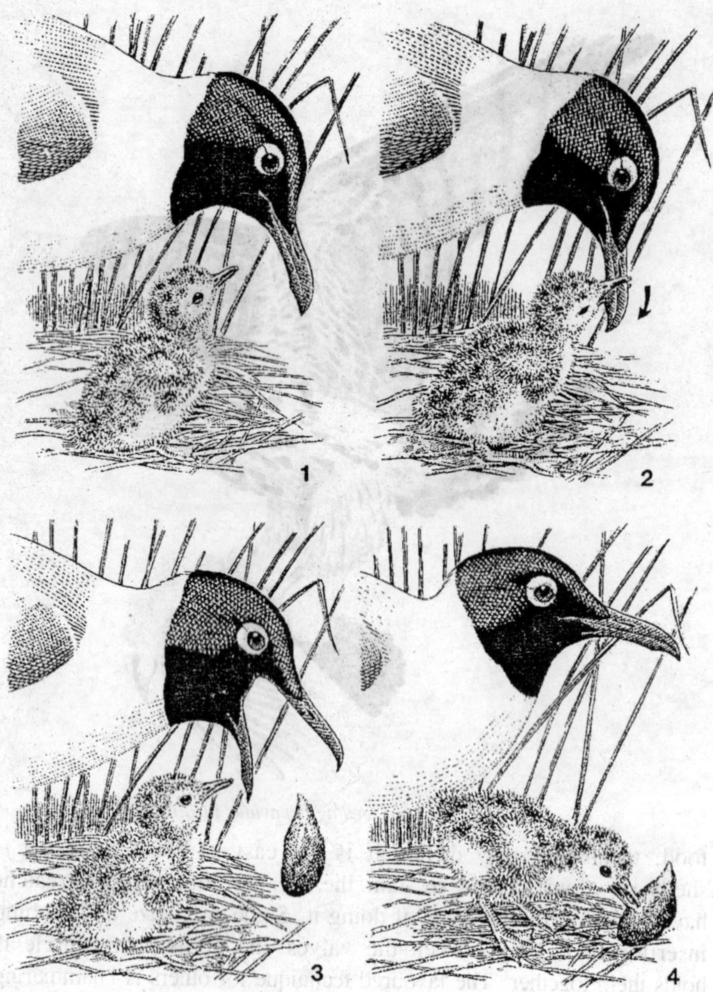

Fig. 5.2. Showing parental care in Goose.

thrown from their bill. Even more subtle is the behaviour of the woodpecker finch from the Galapagos Islands. It uses a cactus spine held in the bill to extract grubs from holes in trees.

Some birds have overcome the lack of a constant food supply by storing it. A marsh tit that finds a rich supply of seeds will hide them one at a time in the surrounding area, remembering their locations and returning to eat them one at a time during the next couple of days. Other birds, such as the acorn woodpecker, use food storage as a longer-term strategy to tide them over the months when the nuts that they eat are scarce.

Avoiding being Eaten

As well as feeding, birds must avoid being fed upon. A lone finch foraging in the open is easy prey to a cat or hawk. It is probably largely for this reason that many small birds feed in flocks where they can benefit from the warning provided by more pairs of eyes. In a large group one of them is bound to have its head up, looking around for danger. The first to spot a predator often produces an alarm call and so warns the others. Each bird may be able to spend more time feeding and less looking out for predators simply because of the safety in numbers. An ostrich, for example, feeding on its own, will raise its head and look around more often than when it is in a group.

Solitary birds have several ways of avoiding being preyed upon. The snipe, a secretive wading bird, sits tight until one is almost upon it, and then darts into the sky with a zig-zag flight that would be very hard for a predator to follow. Its plumage, streaked in various shades of brown, matches the long grass of the marshes where it lives, and like many cryptically coloured birds its main defense comes from the difficulty predators have in detecting it. The burrowing owl in North America has an even better trick. It lives down the burrows of ground squirrels, and if one of these should chance upon it, it has a call that closely resembles that of a rattlesnake. The squirrel does not stay around to find out who produced the call!

Courting and Mating

The breeding behaviour of birds is wonderfully diverse. Most birds are monogamous, and the male often defends a territory in which sufficient food may be found for the pair and their young. In songbirds the male may sing to attract a mate and to keep rivals out of his territory; he will threaten male intruders and court female ones with displays that often show off brightly coloured parts of his plumage. But this general picture hides a wealth of variety. For example, in some species, such as phalaropes, which are small waders nesting high in the Northern Hemisphere, it is the female that courts the male. In some species that are colonial, such as gannets, the territory is only large enough to contain the nest, and feeding is done elsewhere. In some species males form "leks"—groups of very small territories on which they display to attract females to mate, then the females themselves nest elsewhere. Some males may mate with several females

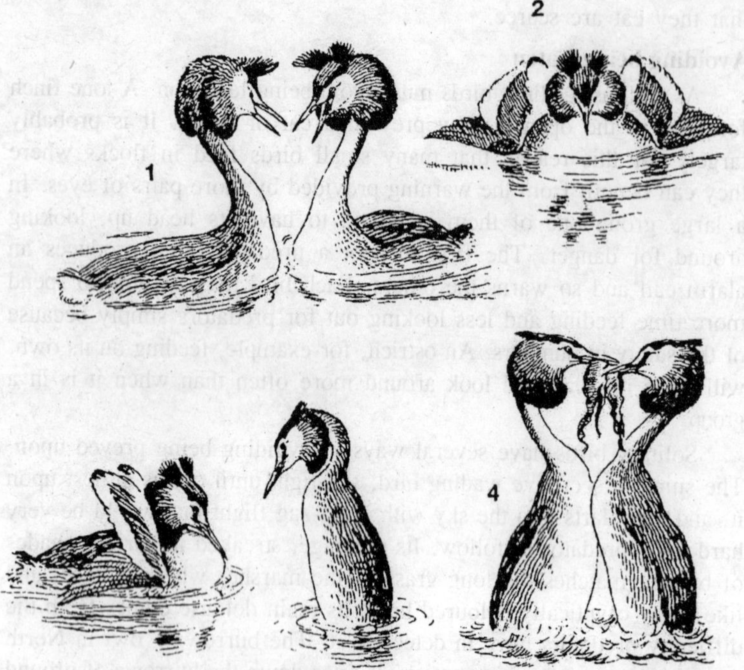

Fig. 5.3. Showing mating behaviour.

on the same territory, some may have several territories with a different female on each. In some songbirds, such as the house sparrow, the male has no real song, whereas in others, such as the superb lyrebird, the nightingale, or the brown thrasher, he may have hundreds or even thousands of phrases. These lavish songs, like the tail of a peacock, are thought to have evolved because females find the variety attractive, and the bigger and better the display the more mating success the male achieves.

After pairing comes nest-building, mating, and egg-laying. The nest may be an elaborate affair, such as those made by weavers, whose construction involves a complex sequence of movements and carefully chosen materials, or it may be a simple scrape. Some birds build no nest at all, whereas others create a vast pile. The mound of vegetation, several meters across, amassed by the male brush turkey is the most notable, especially as the eggs are incubated by the warmth of its fermentation rather than by either of the parents. In more conventional cases incubation may be by the male, by the female, or by both. Either or both of the sexes may carry out care of the young as well, with the added variant that many species have now been round to have helpers at the nest: additional birds, often the offspring from earlier broods, which help the parents to feed their chicks and so to raise more young. Helping like this is perhaps at its most bizarre in the white-rumped swiftlet, where the female lays two eggs several weeks apart. By the time the second is laid the first has hatched and is old enough to incubate it.

Birds with young or eggs have a particular problem in keeping predators away from their brood. Special alarm calls produced when a hawk is spotted may serve to warn the mate and young so that they keep quiet and still until the danger has passed. Some small birds on the nest hiss and rattle their wing feathers in frightening similarity to a nasty predator such as a snake. Wading birds often produce distraction displays. When a dangerous intruder such as a human comes near the nest, they run away with wings dragged along the ground as if badly wounded. When the predator has been tempted to chase them far from the nest, they rise in the air and fly strongly away. The predator is distracted from one meal by the prospect of another, and as a result loses both.

Predators may also be driven off. The fulmar, a seabird from the North Atlantic which eats foods such as squid and jellyfish, as well as offal thrown from trawlers, defends its nest by spitting its last oily and half-digested meal at an intruder. It can score a hit at up to 2 meters (61/2 feet), and its aim is deadly, so intruders are best to keep away. They are also well advised to keep clear of the territories of skuas. These gull-like seabirds dive-bomb large animals that stray near their nests, swooping down from above to approach at high speed. Though they seldom hit, only those with a steely nerve remain close by.

Growing Up

In some birds (for example, songbirds and birds of prey) the young hatch small, naked, and helpless, and must be fed in the nest until they have developed sufficiently to fledge. This can often be several weeks. In other birds (for example, ducks and gulls) the young are well developed at birth, can stand within a short period, and leave the nest within a day of hatching. They rapidly learn to feed themselves, and the parents provide them with only shelter and protection.

Experience plays an important role in the development of all birds, particularly after they leave the nest. A young gull learns the call of its own parent and will perk up to beg only when it hears the call of that particular adult returning to the colony. It also learns to peck at its parent's bill to obtain food. In chickens and ducks, where the young follow the mother in search of food, they learn her features also. At first a young chick will follow any large object it sees, but after a few days it has imprinted on its mother and will follow only her. Other large objects are now frightening to it and if one should appear, instead of following it the young bird will run to its mother for safety.

By experience with their parents and their siblings young birds also learn the more general features of their own specks, and, when they are more mature, it is for these that they look when seeking a mate. This is true of songbirds too, even though they remain in the nest for longer. If a young male zebra finch is reared by a pair of Bengalese finches, it will prefer to court and mate with a Bengalese when it becomes adult.

As they grow, young birds develop many of the skills required to survive and reproduce by trial and error and by interactions with their parents and others around them. Young mammals, particularly predatory ones such as cats, often romp around in rough-and-tumble play. Play is less obvious in birds, but young predators such as falcons will often fly at each other and grapple in dazzling aerobatic displays. One theory is that such predators, in their play, are learning the complex skills required to capture and subdue their prey.

Bird Brains

Much of the learning shown by birds is more a case of special abilities matched to a way of life than a sign of wide-ranging intelligence. A brown thrasher will master more than a thousand song phrases; a marsh tit can memorize the locations of hundreds of hidden seeds. But neither could manage the other task, nor many other tasks that to us seem simple. Natural selection has endowed them with special abilities where they need them.

This is not to argue that birds are stupid. They have large brains like those of mammals, and their behaviour is elaborate and varied. The evidence for their learning by imitation is as good as that for any mammal besides ourselves and our closest relatives. This is just one of the many striking features of bird behaviour that make it a fascinating subject.

6

Reproductive Organs

Reproduction is a cyclic phenomenon, and the majority of avian species are seasonal breeders whose physiological mechanisms regulating gametogenesis are synchronized by environment stimuli ensuring that young are produced at the time of year best suited for their survival. Only in some domesticated species, or in those species inhabiting an environment showing little seasonal variation in food availability, has this ancestral cyclic pattern sometimes been lost. Generally, the reproductive organs of most birds undergo a great annual variation in size and functional activity; the whole reproductive process from copulation through the fledging of the young is usually crowded into a few weeks, particularly in those birds that undergo long migrations to highlatitude breeding grounds.

The reproductive system of birds repeats the basic vertebrate pattern. Thus, the seasonal fluctuations in gonadal activity are produced by the environment stimuli exerting their influence through a central nervous mechanism that leads to gonadortropin release from the adeno-phypophysis. This is mediated, as appears to be common throughout the vertebrates, by the liberation of neurohumoral substances from median eminence of the neurohypophysis, these being transported by portal vessels to the pars distalis. The neuroendocrine system, therefore, constitutes a finely integrated and balanced coordinating link between the organism and its environment. The system has evidently had a long evolutionary history, since neurosecretory cells have been identified in primitive coelenterates, platyhelminths, annelids, mollusks, and arthropods, as well as in all the verterbrate classes. The avian neuroendocrine system in discussed in considerable detail in later chapters, and a further elaboration is not necessary in this chapter. Therefore, we have restricted our dissertation to a consideration of the primary sexual organs, the accessory sexual structures, and the associated behavioral aspects that are concerned with the process of reproduction. We have also excluded any extensive consideration of the phenomenon of intersexuality, which is common in certain avain species.

In common with those of all other vertebrate groups, the avian gonads are responsible both for the proliferation of gametes and also for the secretion of the steroid sex hormones that control the development and functional activity of the accessory sexual structures and secondary sexual characteristics. In mammals, these two functions are known to be regulated by the secretion of two distinct gonadotropic hormones from the pars distalis of the anterior pituitary gland, germinal epithelium, and the luterinizing hormone (LH), which in the namely, the follicle stimulating hormone (FSH), which is primarily responsible for the regulation of gametogenetic activity of the male regulates the secretory activity of the interstitial Leydig cells and in the female induces ovulation and the formation of ovarian corpora lutea. In birds, it has sometimes been suggested that the gonads may be regulated by only one type of gonadotropic secretion, but pituitary cytology distinguishes two gonadotropic cell types as in the mammalian situation, and distinct FSH-like and LH-like fractions were earlier obtained by Fraps *et al.* (1947) from chicken pituitaries using a method previously applied to ovine glands. More recently, more purified samples of these two gonadotropic hormones have been separated from the chicken pituitary gland, and their specificity has been established by biological assay. There is also evidence of two anatomically distinct areas in the hypothalamus of the Japanese Quail responsible for the regulation of secretion of FSH and LH, respectively. Thus, electrolytic or radio frequency lesions in the anterior regions of the infundibular nuclear complex result in regression of the seminiferous tubules without any apparent depression of interstitial cell activity, whereas lesions placed in the medial, ventral, and posterior regions produce, in males, a regression of both gametogenesis and interstitial cell activity, and in females, a cessation of ovulation but no regression of the ovary or oviduct. Similarly, there is good evidence in cockerels, too, that the posterior infundibular region controls the release of an avian LH, whereas the release of FSH is associated with an anatomically separate region.

The male and female gonads are derived from a pair of sexually undifferentiated primordial associated with the intermediate mesoderm (nephrotome). The primordianl germ cells within these structures are derived from the embryonic splanchnopleur and migrate in the blood to be housed in these locations and become the presumptive germinal epithelium. The sink below the surface into the connective tissue (stroma). The left presumptive gonad receives a greater compliment of primordial germ cells than the right, and thus establishes as asymmetrical gonadal development which generally persists throughout life. Initially, proliferation of the germinal epithelium in both presumptive gonads in either sex forms a potential testis (medullary tissue). In the female a second proliferation of cells gives rise to a cortex in the left gonad which then becomes the potential ovary. In some species, particularly the domestic hen, a few cortical cords may also sometimes be laid down in the embryonic right gonad as well.

In males, the embryonic gonadal primordial develop into paired testes, but in the female of many species only the left organ develops into a functional ovary, and the right generally remains in an ambisexual state. When the left ovary is removed, or when it becomes non fun functional due to some pathological condition a compensatory-development of the rudimentary gonad may take place under the influence of the increased circulation of gonadotropin. In the large majority of cases in which this occurs the rudiment develops into a testis or ovotestis. The experimental induction of this condition in chickens has demonstrated that age can be a modifying factor on the result; full spermatogenesis can develop in the resultant ovotestis if the operation is done at an early age, but if performed in older birds full spermatogenesis is rarely achieved, but ovulations can take place. Under natural conditions, many old domestic hens suffering from senile changes become masculinized, assuming the cock plumage and the capacity to crow, because the rudiment of medullary (testicular) tissue becomes functional. Such sex reversal is also relatively common and often spectacular in pheasant species in which, for example, a somber colored female Goledn Pheasant (*Chrysolophus pictus*) can, as a result of such changes, assume the resplendent plumage of a male. A high incidence of intersexual individuals may also occur in strains of the domestic pigeon, in which apparently a delay in the degeneration of the embryonic cortical tissue causes genetic males to develop with an intact right testis but a left testis in which the cortical component persists and differentiates into ovarian tissue.

Occasionally, adult birds are found with two functional ovaries, particularly among members of the Accipitridae, Falconidae, and Cathartidae, but even in these specimens it is sometimes unaccompanied by a corresponding development of the associated right oviduct. Functional right ovaries are also frequently found in pigeons and in the Herring Gull (*Larus argentatus*).

Individuals without gonads are also sometimes found. Usually these lack both right and left Mulerian ducts and exhibit a general masculine appearance, thus resembling subjects experimentally castrated as embryos. Taber (1964) points out that in man gonadal agencies or the Turner syndrome is accompanied by loss of one of the sex chromosomes, producing a neuter genotype resembling the female (genetic composition XO which resembles XX). Since males are the homogametic sex in birds, it may be significant that birds lacking gonads resemble the male.

Anatomy of the Male Reproductive System: Passage and Storage of Sperm

Anatomy

The reproductive system of the male consists of paired testes, the epididymi, the vasa deferentia (which transport the spermatozoa to the penis), and the penis. The testes are near the cephalic end of the kidneys and ventral to them. The weight of the testes in chickens comprises about 1% of the total body weight, or about 9-30 g per single testis at sexual maturity, depending on breed, state of nutrition, and other factors. In old cocks testis weight may approach 40-60g.

In wild species the tests weight less but are greater in terms of total body weight. The epididymi in birds are small in comparison to those in mammals. The birds, unlike mammals, has no Cowper's gland or seminal vesicle. The avian testis is without septa and lobules, and consists of seminferous tubules, the rate tubules, and vas efferentia.

The penis of chickens is quite small and when erected is engorged with lymph from the lymph folds. This lymph fluid is added to the semen in the vas deferens and both are ejected simultaneously along the longitudinal groove of the phallus. The reproductive organs of turkey are similar to those of the chicken. Ducks and geese have well-developed aphelia, which are spirally twisted and which serve as intromittent organs. Penislike organs have been reported in certain ratatie birds.

Nerves to the ductus deferens and penis include pelvic nerves (lumbosacrals 8-11), some of which are involved in erection of the penis, and probably symptherit fibers (hypogastric), which are most probably involved in ejaculation.

Passage and Storage of Sperm

From the seminiferous tubules, the sperm pass to the rate tubules and then to the was efferentia, *epididymis*, and vas deferens. Normally, at least in the chicken, sperm are stored not in the epididymis but in the vas deferens.

In passerine birds, the terminal part of the vas deferens is enlarged and is often referred to as the seminal vesicle; however, Marshall (1961) states that structurally this organ has nothing in common with the seminal vesicle of mammals, and he prefer the designation "seminal sac". Sperm, however, may be stored here.

Development of the Testes, Spermtogenesis and Semen Production

The growth and development of the testes and spermtogenesis have studied in detail by number of workers. Detailed studies of spermatogenesis in ducks have been made by Clermont (1958) and more recently by Johnson (1966).

The testes of all species undergo marked changes during the development of spermatogenesis and these are essentially similar in most species. Details of these changes have been studied by Kumaran and Turner (1949a, b) and Blivaiss (1947) as follows; during the first 5 weeks of age the tubules are organized and multiplication of the basal layer of cells, the speremategnia, occurs. The primary spermatocytes begin to appear at about the sixth week. During the next 2 or 3 weeks, growth of the primary spermatocytes takes precedence over the further multiplication of the spermatogonial layer.

The secondary spermatocytes begin to appear at about 10 weeks of age as result of the reduction division of the primary spermatocytes. Spermatids (immature spermatozoa) begin to appear in the seminiferous tubules at about 12 weeks of age and by the twentieth week are usually present in all of the tubules.

The seminiferous tubules of prepuberal males are small and are lined with a single layer of cells. The mature testis has multilayered epitherlium representing the various stages of spermatogenesis. From the wall of the tubule to the lumen may be found spermatogonia, primary spermatocytes, secondary spermatocytes, spermatids, the nutritive cells (cells of Sertoli) to which the spermatids are attached, and the spermatozoa.

The time involved in the completion of all stage of permatogenesis and sperm transit has been estimated (Japanese quail) to be approximately 25 days based on the use of spermatogonial chemicals (Myleran and cycolhexane). The time necessary for sperm to pass through the epididymes and vas deferns of cocks (chickens) was 4 days, and the time required for primary spermatocytes to become mature spermatozoa was 12 days.

Spermatozoa

Mature spermatozoa (SZ) to birds, exhibit a great deal of variation in size and shape, depending on the species. Romanoff (1960) has described and shown photographs of spermatozoa from many avian species. Electron microscopic studies of fowl spermatozoa have been conducted by Grigg (1951) Lake *et al.*, (1968), and Hrris *et al.*, (1973). In the chicken, the spermatozoon has a long headpiece with a pointed acrosome and a short midpiece, to which is attached the long tail.

Avain spermatozoa are small compared to those of mammals; their average volume is 9.2 μm^3. Based on the ultrastructure, the following description is from Lake *et al.*, (1968) and Lake (1971). The acrosome is simple, the midpiece is a cylindrical distal centriole surrounded by sheath of mitochondria. The chicken acrosome is about 1.75 μm in length, the head is about 12.5 μm long, the midpiece is 4 μm long, and the principal tail piece is 80 μm long.

Rapid freezing and the wing produce pronounced changes in the ultrastructure of SZ. The fate of SZ retained in the vas deferens after its ligation was studied by electomicrocopy. The spermatozoa showed signs of disintegration mainly in the head region, and there was an uptake of SZ by the epithelil cells lining the male sperm ducts that was increased after ligation of the vas deferens. These observations

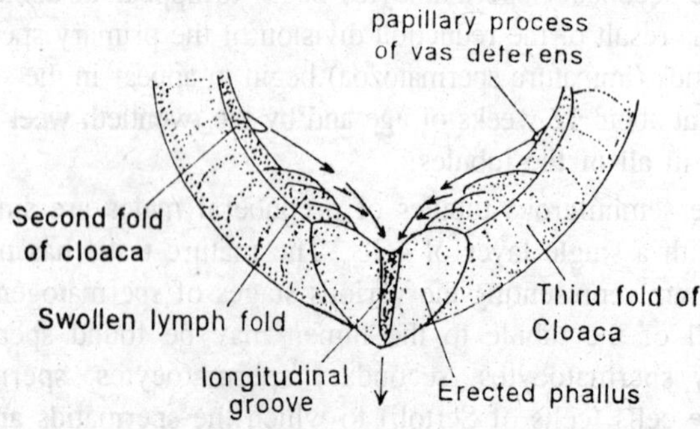

Fig. 6.1. Diagram showing the ejaculation of the semen of the cock.

(according to the authors) may indicated a route for disposal of unejaculated SZ in male chickens.

Chemical Composition and Physical Properties of Semen

Lake (1966, 1971) has described in detail chemical and physical properties of semen and it is clear that avian semen is different in important respects from that of mammals. These differences are attributable to the absence of seminal vesicles and prostate glands and the presence of a rudimentary epididymis. Fowl seminal plasma is almost completely lacking in fructose, citrate, ergothionene, inositol, phosphoryl choline, and glyceryl phosphoryl choline. The chloride content of avian semen is low, and potassium and glutamate content are high. The source of the large glutamate content may be the seminiferous.

"Results are average values (range in parenthese) expressed in mg/100 ml fluid or cells unless otherwise stated.

Semen from the cock is usually white and opaque but may be clear and watery, particularly when the concentration of spermatozoa is low. The pH of cock semen is 7.0-7.6 depending on the amount of transparent fluid present in semen (Lake 1971).

Number of Spermatozoa and Amount of Semen Produced

The volume of semen of given ejaculation has been measured by a number of workers; some of the variation reported may be attribution to the methods of collection. Some have collected the semen from the cloaca of the hen after a normal mating, and some have collected it directly from the male, obtaining it artificially by massaging the abdomen after the technique of Burrows and Quinn (1937).

Parker (1949), who reviewed the subject, compiler the results of a number of investigators, including his own. The volumes reported (averages) range from 0.11 ml (collected form the cloaca of the hen) to 1 ml (collected from the male directly). Spermatozoa per cubic millimeter of semen average about 3.5 million. In a given ejaculate (0.5 to 1 ml volume), therefore, the number of spermatozoa ranges from 1.7 to 3.5 billion. Lake (1957) reported averages of 7 billion and a maximum of 8.2 billion in Brown Leghorn cocks.

Marini and Goodman (1969) reported great differences in SZ concentration of volumes of semen of chickens selected and bred for high and slow growth rates. These numbers ranged from 4.9 million SZ per cubic millimeter in the slow growing strain to 2.3 million in the rapid growth line. There were also differences in the numbers of abnormal SZ between the strains.

Turkeys produce less semen the chickens, but the concentration of spermatozoa (SZ) is much greater. The amounts average about 0.2 ml per collection, and the concentration varies from 6.2 to 7 million per cubic millimeter, depending on breed. The amount of semen obtained from Phasianus colchicus (pheasant) is 0.1 ml or less.

Factors Affectings Fertility in the Male

A minimum of 100 million spermatozoa must be inseminated to obtain optimum fertility according to Parker et al., (1942). However, Wekley and Shaffner (1952) reported little changes in fertility when semen was diluted 1:10 and each insemination supplied less than 100 million sperm; optimum fertility was obtained by Nishiyama et al., (1968) with 70 million.

Maturing of Spermatozoa

Munro (1938) demonstrate that spermatozoa of the chicken must be ripened or matured in the epididymis before they are capable of fertilization. Spermatozoa taken directly from the testes to not fertilize ova, and those taken from the epididymis fertilized only 13% of the females inseminated. When semen was taken from the lower vas deferens, 74% of the inseminated females laid fertile eggs. The duration of the ripening period apparently is not long, because it was shown

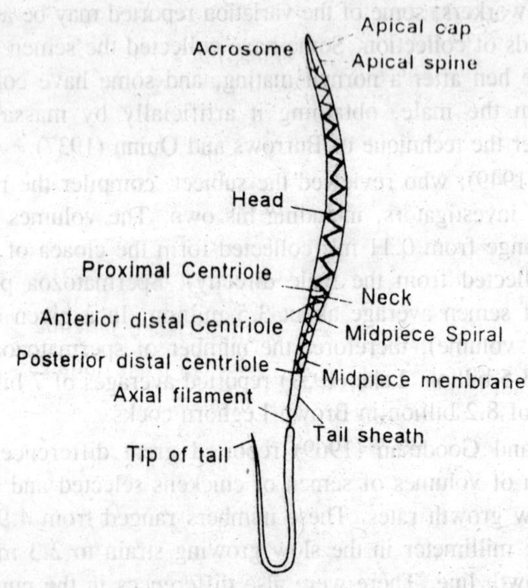

Fig. 6.2. Diagram of the spermatozoon of the chicken.

that spermatozoa could pass from the testes through the vas deferens to the cloaca within 24 hours.

Number of Matings

The number of matings or ejaculations per day influence the volume of semen produced and the concentration of spermatozoa. Both deceres with the frequency of mating, and after three or four successive ejaculations the concentration of spermatozoa is very low in some mailes.

The number of times male chicken male may range from 25 to 41 per day according at early workers, but more recent work of Guhl (1951) suggests that males may mate still more frequently than this. Guhl made studies on individual male placed in pens with from 30 to 40 females, where mating behavior was observed for 21 min/day for periods as long as 84 days. The observations were made during the first 21 min that the male were introduced to the female. The actual observation times was 29 her and 24 min. The number of treteding for three males during this period were 410, 788, and 853, or 13.9, 26.7 and 29.0 matings per hour, respectively. It was shown, however, that when males are first introduced into a pen, they mate most frequently during the first 3-6 min. Guhl et al., (1945) and Guhl and Wrren (1946) demonstrate that the social order or "peak order" of the hens to which male are introduced affects their mating behavior. Males, regardless of their social standing, tend to mate most frequently not with the highest or lowest ranking hens, but with the "middle-class" hense. When three or more males are introduced together in a pen of females, both the frequency of matings and the fertility are highest for the top-ranking male. The lowest ranking male mates with few females because of interference form the higher ranking males.

The number of White Leghorn females to which one male may mate and still obtain optimum fertility is approximately 15. This ratio is narrower for heavy breeds.

Light

Natural daylight or artificial light initiates the production of semen in males by stimulating the release of gondotropic hormones of the interior pituitry (FSH and LH). FSH stimulates growth of seminiferous tubules and spermatogensis, and LH stimulates the interstitial cells of testes (Leydig cells) to produce androgens.

Usually 12-14 hr of light are required to stimulate the growth and development of the testes maximally in young cockerels and most wild species. When 14 or more hours of light are combined with high ambient temperature, as is normally experienced in the summertime, fertility may decline because there is usually a decrease in sperm concentration caused mainly by the high temperature. Testes sized and growth, however, although delayed by less than 12-14 hr of light (8 hr), eventually reach normal size and activity.

Similar results were reported by Siegel *et al.*, (1969). Clark and Srakoon (1967) have made a detailed study of the effects of different environmental temperatures on fertility.

Wavelenths and intensity. Red and orange lights have a greater stimulating effect on the pituitary and gonads, particularly testes, than do green and blue lights. Light intensity within wide limits (2-50 lux) is not and important factor in gonad stimulation, but dim light may retard sexual development.

Oishi and Lauber (1973a) studied the stimulating effects of different intensities and wavelengths on goand size (testes) of Japanese quail under continuous illumination (24-hr light). The thereshold for incandescent light intensity to maintain maximal gonad size was between 1.6 and 15.7 $\mu W/cm^2$ for male with intact eyes and for those blinded. In intact birds both red (625 nm) and green (500nm) were effective at low intensity (4.0$\mu W/cm^2$ for red and 9.6$\mu W/cm^2$ for green), but only red light was effective at either of the low intensies. In blinded birds only red light was effective at low intensity.

Orange-red radioluminescent pain (15 mg) placed beneath the skill immediately over the pineal body elicited a marked gonadal response, but green pain did not. After pinealectomy there was no response to red pain, suggesting that the pineal may be an auxiliary photoreceptor or a director of red light to the hypothalamus. The pineal and eyes may be removed. However, without affecting the main response to light.

Light and Wild Species

In many wild species the reproductive system is alternately photosensitive or photorefractive to long days during the annual cycle. This is true of a number of passerine species, including sparrows, juncos, and starting. The testes of these species regress spontaneously even when the initial effective stimulatory period is continued. The sensitive period usually begins in the winter and continues until after the breeding season in late summer or early fall. In birds in the temperature zone photorefractoriness usually lasts until late fall or winter when the photoperiod is not long enough to be stimulatory.

Some species, such as bobwhite quail, Japanese quail, wood pigeon, common pigeon, and weaver bird, are not refactory to light. These species respond when day length is sufficiently long. Many investigators believe that the mechanisms controlling synthesis and release of pituitary gonadotropins are involved in photorefractivity, but others think gonad sensitivity is also involved.

It is essential to distinguish between the function of light as a cure for synchronizing endogenous circadian rhythms and the function of light as a stimulus for the production of hormones by the pituitary. According to an Tienhoven and Shally (1972). Long photoperiods may stimulate the production of pituitary hormones. The occurrence and properties of circadian rhythms is another matter, (this has been reviewed by van Tinhoven and Shally, 1972). Evidence has been presented that indicates circadian rhythms in responsiveness to light in certain species.

Other Factors

Other factors affecting the production of semen and fertility of the male and female are season, age, state, of nutrition, and health.

Diurnal and Seasonal Variations

There is a diurnal variations in the production of spermatozoa by the fowl, with the greatest spermatogenic activity at 3 a.m. According to Riley (1940) and at midnight according to Macartney (1942). However, lake and Woodgush (1956) reported a diurnal rhythm in semen production of Brown Leghorns in Scotland in May and June with the greatest concentration of spermatozoa in the collections in the evening at 17-18 hr.

Male chickens vary in their production of semen and fertility with season. The amount of semen and the number of spermatozoa increase from December through April and then decline, to reach a low in July and August in chickens. Fertility also declines in the summer.

Age

It is generally conceded that fertility declines in male and females in the second and third years of life.

Enzymes and Hormones

There is evidence that a trypsin-like enzyme, which acts on the acrosome of avain SZ, is necessary for optimum fertility. Poly-a-glutamic acid has been isolated from the oviduct of the laying females and it extends the life of SZ *in vitro*. Oxytocin added to semen decreased the motility of SZ and decreased fertility, and injection of oxytocin also decreased fertility (Hughes and Parker, 1970); injections of oxytocin and arginine vasopressin to laying hens also decreased fertility.

Behaviour

Whether or not male are aggressive or not has little effect on semen production and quality. Male that were houses singly in cages produced the most semen and when two males were house together semen production was least.

Storage of Semen

Avian semen retain its fertilizing capacity *in vivo* for as long as 35 days in chickens and longer in turkey. Attempts to store semen *in vitro* without impairing fertility have generally been unsuccessful. Semen can be quick frozen and then thawed immediately without reducing motility but when stored for longer periods fertility is impaired.

Storage at 0°-5°C for 4 hr reduced motility of fresh sperm considerably, but when the sperm were diluted with hypertonic fructose solution, motility after cold storage was good. Tanaka and Wilcox (1966) have also studied the effects of different hypertonic solutions on sperm motility. Diluted chicken semen was cooled with liquid nitrogen at cooling rates from 1° to 6.7°C/min, from 30°C until frozen, and was stored for 12 days in liquid nitrogen. Highest fertility (77%) was obtained in semen in a special diluent that was cooled at 6°C/min. The reason for the differences in the effects of storage of avain and mammalian semen is not known and is still being sought. One of the major differences in the composition of avain and bull semen is the high concentration of glutamate in avian semen. It has been reported that a diluent containing a high concentration of glutamate increased the fertilizing capacity of chicken semen to some extent. Storage of semen for 48 hr decreased motility and fertility of SZ, but the duration of fertility even more. Storage decreased aminopeptidases, fumarase, aconitase and glutamic oxaloacetic transminase activity of SZ. There was an increase in lactic dehydrogenase and in aldoalse activity.

Genetic Differences

There is considerable variations in fertility of different breeds and strains of chickens. The lower than average fertility reported in White Wyandotte chickens is well known.

Fertility in natural matings of White Plymouth Rocks was higher than in Cornish chickens and the difference was inherited but it was not attributable to amount of semen produced and motility. The difference disappeared after artificial insemination. Likewise, Parker (1965) reported that fertility from natural matings was not related to amount of semen produced, which averaged 1.43 ml per male for the high semen producers and 0.63 ml for the low producers.

Siegel (1963) reported heritability estimates on semen concentration, semen volume, and motility in an unselected line of chickens as 0.01, 0.14 and 0.29, respectively. Soller et al., (1965b), in a line of chickens selected for the semen characteristics shown above, reported hertibility values of 0.79, 0.78 and 0.83 for the same three characteristics, respectively.

Marina and Goodman (1969) reported highly significant difference in amount of semen and concentration of SZ between lines of chickens selected for rapid and slow growth rates, and the differences were highly heritable.

Fertility and Time of Mating or Insemination

A number of workers have studied the relation of time of mating or artificial insemination to fertility. Most investigators reported higher fertility if inseminations occurred in the afternoon, when a soft-shelled egg was usually in the uterus, and lowest when a hard-shelled egg was present however Parker (1950) and others found little difference in fertility between these groups. Hoshon and Parker (1970) again found highest fertility with afternoon inseminations when a soft-sheeld egg was present but they reported that factors other than the presence of hard or soft shell are also involved. Their results indicate that has inseminated 4 hr before laying (hard shell) or 1 hr after laying showed poor fertility.

Maximum fertility in chickens is usually obtained 2 or 3 days after matings. Good fertility is obtained as long as 5 or 6 days after the last matings, and then declines rapidly, but a few fertile eggs may be obtained as late as 35 days after the last mating. Seventy-two hours after the last mating, however, spermatozoa are found only in the infundibulum according to Van Drimmelen (1945, 1951). In turkeys high fertility is obtained 20 days after insemination; it then decreases slowly with some fertiles eggs obtained 10 weeks after insemination. Spermatozoa are stored in the infudibulum and uterovaginal glands. Lorens et al., (1967), Van Krey *et al.*, (1966), and Lorenz and Ogasawara (1968) have shown that when spermatozoa are introduced into the infundibular region or the magnum of the oviduct (Where sperm storage glands are located) fertility is prolonged, but there was a high incidence of early embryonic mootaility as compared to results when insemination was in the uterovaginal region. Likewise, Schindler and Hurwitz (1966) demonstrate that when spermatozoa were injected into different sites of oviduct, their motility was maintained in all sites for at least 4 hr. The ultrastructure of the uterovaginal glands of the hen has been studied by Burke *et al.,* (1972).

Artificial Insemination

Burrows and Quinn (1937) and Parker (1939) developed a technique for obtaining semen artificially from the male. By this technique it is possible to dilute semen as much as ten times and inseminate a large number of females. To ensure good fertility, inseminations should be made every fourth or fifth day in the chicken. Turkey hens remain fertile after matings much longer than do chickens (as long as 30 days). The duration of fertility and life of a spermatozoon in the body of the female is influenced by sperm nest in the infundibulum and uteroaginal glands.

In a more recent review of the subject, Lorenz (1959) stated that the most satisfactory results (fertility) had been obtained with freshly collected and undiluted semen at 0.05 ml per insemination at 5 to 7 day intervals for chickens and 0.025 ml at 3 week intervals for turkeys. Difficulty, however, is often experienced in successfully inseminating such small quantities. For further details of insemination of turkeys, see Nestor and Brown (1968) and Ogasawara and Rooney (1966).

Sterility

Ingestion of mestranol by quails induced irreversible sterility in females and sterilized many males. Abnormal spermatozoa may cause sterility, but apparently very few males produce sufficient numbers of abnormal spermatozoa to produce this effect.

The annual cycle can broadly be classified into three phases:

1. The regeneration, or preparatory (Wolfson 1959 a.b, phase come immediately after reproduction in singhbrooded species, and after the final ovulation of the season in multibrooded forms. Morophologically, it is marked by the rapid regression of the tests, which can be attributed to a changed and possible diminished gonadotropin release from the anterior pituitary. In many species, this takes place at a time of year when the environmental photoperiod is still highly stimulatory but the neuroendocrine apparatus no longer responds. The bird is said to be in the refractory period and remains sexually quiescent even when artificially subjected to long photoperiods. Such postnuptial refractoriness is a feature of nearly all species so far submitted to

controlled and cricital photostimulation experiments, and it has been tacitly assumed or inferred that it is a phenomenon of universal occurrence among avian species. However, recent photoexperimentation on the Wood Pigeon (*Columba palumbus*) has shown this species, and probably others as well, to be without a photorefractory phase. The Wood Pigeon, like the Stock Dove (*Columba oenas*), is multibrooded with a breeding season extending into early autumn where agricultural grain harvests provide abundant food for rearing the latter broods. Reproductive activity ceases when autumn day lengths fall below a stimulatory level, and the bird then enters its regeneration phase. Spermatogenesis can, however, be immediately reactivated by artificially prolonging the photoperiod. A refractory period is not therefore a necessity for gonad rehabilitation as previously supposed.

The regeneration phase is characterized by rehabilitation of both the interstitial tissue and seminiferous tubules and is a period of sexual quiescence during which the bird displays little or no sexual behaviour. In many species, infiltration of the interstitial tissue by large numbers of leukocytes takes place during the early stage, and the replacement of the weakened testis tunic, and sometimes also the postnuptial molt, occurs during this phase. In the White-crowned Sprraw, for example, a rapid and intensive postnuptial molt is inserted between the breeding period and the onset of autumnal migration. However, the Wood Pigeon molts throughout the breeding season when the gonads are fully active, while the European Turtle-Dove (*Streptopelia turtur*) exhibits a partial molt immediately as it enters the refractory phase but defers the molt of its primaries until it reaches its African wintering grounds. The duration of the regeneration phase varies from species to species, and its termination is probably marked by the completion of the interstitial cell rehabilitation, which may sometimes manifest itself in the form of an autumnal resurgence of sexual behavior seen in many species. In birds that have a refractory period, the end of the regeneration phase is also heralded by the restoration of photosensitivity.

2. The acceleration, or progressive, phase succeeds the regeneration phase and is a period marked by the intersitial cell and seminiferous tubules responding to gonadotropic secretions from the adenophypophysis. The postnuptial molt is usually completed. A recrudescence of gametogenetic activity occurs under favorable environmental conditions but becomes retarded or stimulated by a variety of environmental inhibitors or accelerators that are mutually antagonistic. Thus, the cycle hastens, slows, or sometimes stops altogether, depending upon

the factors currently presented to it by the changing environment. Temperature is perhaps the most important modifier of the testicular cycle during this stage, and its effect has been demonstrated experimentally by a number of investigators. In addition, there are many field data that indicate a correlation between temperature and speed of testicular development. Low temperatures will inhibit the cycle of most species, and anusally cold spring will often nullify the accelerating effects of long sunny days. Among temperate zone birds, some species begin their acceleration phase in late summer or early autumn, but generally this becomes depressed or even halted by the onset of winter conditions until after the winter solstice. In some tropical or xerophilous species, the absence of rainfall may similarly retard the gemetogenetic progress during this phase (Marshall, 1970), whereas among waterbirds and many others, a frequent inhibitor is the lack of a safe and traditional nesting site.

The acceleration phase is a period marked by increasingly intensive sexual activity and song, during which gametogenesis leading to the production of spermatozoa occurs. In some species, the winter feeding flocks begin to disintegrate as individuals start territorial selection and defensive displays. The phase varies enormously in duration, both interspecifically and intraspecifically. An interesting example of this is shown by the differences displayed by the resident British population of European Starlings (*Sturnus vulgaris*) and the continental starlings that migrate to Britain for the winter. Spermatogenetic activity begins in the British population in late September, but does not usually progress beyond the proliferation of spermatogonia and occasional primary spermatocytes until February, when a burst of activity populates the seminiferous tubules with secondary spermatocytes and later stages. Continental birds, on the other hand, show no spermatogonial division in autumn, the first mitoses are not seen until late December or early January, and primary spermatocytes not until early March. Thus, both populations respond to January and February photoperiods, though this marks a beginning of spermatogenesis for continental birds but a resumption of the acceleration phase already started in the British population. Unlike continental birds, the British population shows earlier and more intensive interstitial cell activity in the autumn and winter, which is evident by the earlier changes in bill coloration and development of the vas deferens. This early elevation of androgen titer is also responsible for autumnal sexual displays and even winter breeding in exceptionally mild winters, events virtually absent in the life history of the continental population.

3. The culmination phase, during which actual ovulation and insemination occur, may be regarded as a distinct component of the annual cycle, since a species-specific requirement is generally necessary before the cycle can culminate in oviposition. By the end of the preceding phase, the male bird has reached a fully reproductive condition with expanded testes containing seminiferous tubules charged with masses of spermatozoa. Nevertheless, although the internal physiology may be now wholly prepared for reproduction, many complicated behavioral factors may influence the final culmination. The male generally assumes this reproductive state before the female, and the final timing of oviposition then depends on the female receiving the appropriate psychological stimuli, both from her mate and the environment. The appropriate habitat and interpair displays are often essential to stimulate final oocyte development, ovulation, and insemination. The action of stereotyped behavior in causing specific hormone secretion is now well appreciated, and conditions of captivity, for example, have been shown to inhibit gonadotropin secretion in the Pintail (*Anas acuta*), thus preventing breeding.

Interstitial Cells

There is an extensive literature concerning the seasonal changes observable in the avian interstitial, but many of the early reports are contradictory, often being based on unsatisfactory and now outmoded histological procedures. Because of their dispersal by seasonal tubule expansion, the Leydig cells have sometimes been stated to be absent from the gonad at certain times of the year, and an inverse relationship between sexuality and interstitial (Leydig) cell activity has sometimes been claimed. This, of course, is not ture and the more recent histochemical and electron microscopic observations discussed in Section II, A have clearly established the close relationship between these cells and the androgen dependent sexual structures. Furthermore, the selective destruction of the germinal epithelium of cockerel by roentegen radiation, which leaves the interstitium and secondary sexual characters apparently unaffected also indicate this tissue as the site of androgen production. Tumors of the interstitial cells result in an increased production of androgens and 17-ketosteroids.

In birds, as in the majority of seasonal vertebrates, the interstitial cells undergo well defined seasonal secretory cycles involving a rhythmic accumulation and depletion of cholesterol positive lipoidal material. The interstitial cells of young birds are generally heavily impregnated with such material. Then, at the approach of the sexual season and consequent buildup of spermatogenetic activity in the seminiferous elements, they become rapidly depleted of their lipids and cholesterol and become strongly fuchsinophilic. In a species such as the Northern Fulmar (Fulmarus glacialis), in which the young do not begin breeding until 7 years old. The interstitial cells of newly hatched birds are less lipodial but become more heavily impregnated when the birds are just over 2 years old. In adults, the interstitial cell of the sexually quiescent winter gonad are generally small and often sparsely lipodial with numerous fuchsinophilic elements that are more easily seen after dissolution of the lipids in wax-embedded material. During the acceleration phase, these cells rapidly increase in size and there is a buildup of the lipoidal inclusions, so that the interstitial tissue is seen to consist of compressed aggregations of heavily lipoidal and cholesterol-rich cells. They also react positively to tests for 3 HSDH. Then, as in juveniles, the lipoidal content rapidly diminishes at a time when androgen-dependent sexual displays reach their maximum intensity. During this period, the cholesterol reaction also becomes weaker, and may disappear altogether, although * HSDH activity remains strong. The nuclei of Leydig cells also attain maximum diameter at this time, reflecting an increase in secretory activity. In migratory waders (Charadriiformes), this depletion of interstitial lipids is often evident just before the birds leave their African wintering grounds on their north-bound migration.

With the advent of the regeneration phase, the now exhausted interstitial cells have reached the end of their secretory cycle, and it has been reported that they distengrate so that ultimately their total number is drastically reduced. It may be that the massive invasion by leukocytes that takes place at this time clears the spent Leydig cells by phagocytic action. However, there is a need for further investigation by electron microscopy to confirm this point, and the possibility that the spent Leydig cells return to an inconspicuous fibroblast-like form should not be excluded. Concomitant with the atrophy of the exhausted generatio, a new generation of juvenile interstitial cells begins to arise, presumably by their differentiation from fibroblast-like progenitors, and gradually begin to mature.

This seasonal replacement by new interstitial cells at the end of each breeding period is not unique to avian testicular cycles. A similar phenomenon has also been recorded in some snakes and in the common frog (*Rana temporaria*). Marshall (1961b) suggests that the sequence is part of an endogenous rhythm that can occur even in the absence of any gonadotropic rhythm. Thus, even after complete removal of the adenohypophysis, Coombs and Marshall (1956) have reported that the interstitial cells of domestic cockerels still renew then mselves and develop a new generation of Leydig cells with some lipoidal and cholesterol-positive material. It is doubtfull, however, whether such cells would ever become secretory in the absence of gonadotropins.

The length of time necessary for interstitial cell rehabilitation probably varies from species to species, but there is evidence that in some birds at least it may be fairly rapid process. Thus, Lofts and Marshall (1957) have recorded that the newly arisen interstitial cells of fifteen different migratory species were already beginning to manufacture small cholesterol-positive lipid droplets in their cytoplasm when they were autoposed at the time of their departure from Britain on their southward migration.

The cyclical waxing and waning of cellular lipids, which although in itself is insufficient to implicate unequivocally a steroid secreting role, is a useful index of the functional activity of the tissue. The lipids are both cholesteriol-positive and strongly birefringent, reactions that are probably indicative of precursor material involved in androgen biosynthesis. The prenuptial buildup in birds often precedes the hypertrophy of the accessory sexual apparatus and behavioral activities thought to be dependent on androgen secretion. In young chicks, for example, the increase in concentration of birefringent material in the interstitial tissue is in close agreement with the gradual hypertrophy of the comb, and in the House Sparrow (*Passer domesticus*) the level of 17 hydroxylase activity in the interstitial tissue has been shown to increase rapidly between February and March, a time when the interstitial cells are losing the lipodial material accumulated earlier in January and February.

The sudden depletion of lipids and cholesterol at the high of the breeding activity has also been noted in a number of reptilian species, and it has been suggested that it is probably indicative of a rapid utilization or precursor material at a time of high androgen release.

The observations of Jones (1970) that the height of the epididymidal epithelium in the California Quail (*Lophortyx Californicus*) attains its maximum thickness at the time when the interstitial tissue is showing this phenomenon are in agreement with such an interpretation. Certainly 3b HSDH activity is high at this time. In the Department of Zoology, University of Hong Kong, we have been attempting to correlate these histochemical events with the seasonal fluctuations in androgen production, measured by *in vitro* methods. For this, portions of testicular material have been taken at monthly intervals from the migratory Green-winged Teal (*Anas crecca*) throughout the year and incubated with radioactive pregeneolone as an added precursor. The biosynthetic activity of the tissue has been determined by standard chromatographic analysis of the steroids produced, and the percentage conversion of the added [16-^{3}H] pregnenolone to testosterone per unit weight of tissue has been calculated. Because of the seasonal dispersal of interstitial tissue during testicular expansion, fewer Leydig cells will be contained in the tissue from the sexually mature testis compared with the same weight of tissue taken from the regressed testes of winter birds. The conversion figures have therefore been multiplied by the mean testicular weight to give a truer picture of the seasonal pattern of steroid production by the whole gonad. Some preliminary results showing the seasonal variation are shown. They support the hypothesis outlined above. Thus, the gradual elevation in androgen production from mid-February to early June coincided with the appearance of lipoidal inclusions in the interstitial tissue. Lipid depletion was observed in early July at a time when androgen biosynthesis reached a peak and the subsequent rapid decline marked the bird's entry into the postnuptial refractory period.

Sertoli Cells

As well as the interstitial tissue, the Sertoli (sustentacular) cells of the tubule also undergo cyclic seasonal changes involving an accumulation and depletion of cholesterol-positive lipoidal material. Furthermore, ultra structurally these cells show the fine structure normally associated with a steroid-producing tissue and also react positively to tests for 3 HSDH. The enzyme 17 B HSDH can also be demonstrated in the tubules of the European Trees Sparrow (*Passer montanus*) at the height of spermatogenetic activity. An endocrine role is perhaps also suggested by the feminization effects seen in the plumage of cockerels suffering from Setoli cell tumors.

Generally, when the germinal epithelium has advanced beyond the production of primary spermatocytes in the early acceleration phase, there is an absence of lipoidal material from the intratubular components. But as this phase draws toward its termination, and bunched spermatozoa are seen to be radially arranged around the tubule lumen, sections stained with sudan dyes show a light scattering of fine lipoidal granules concentrated in the region of the sperm heads. The small dropletsare a component of the sperm heads. These small droplets are a component of the residual bodies that form part of the spermatid protoplasm. The residual bodies subsequently become sloughed off from the spermatid during the end stage of spermateleosis and remain behind in the seminiferous tubules after evacuation of the spermatozoa. They are a common feature of the spermatogenetic process of probably allamniotic vertebrates and have been extensively studied in the rat, where they are known to be subsequently phaocytized by the Sertolic cell. In addition to their lipid inclusions, the residual bodies also contain a large amount of RNA, clusters of mitochondria and Golgi remnants and, in the rat at least, it has been suggested that they may be instrumental in maintaining the radial coordination of the associated germ cell population.

In contrast to the slight scattering of intratubular lipids observed in the fully mature testis, a dramatic metamorphosis into a condition of heavily sundanophilic and strongly cholesterol-positive tubules takes place during the postnuptial regeneration phase. In sectioned material the seminiferous tubules appear to become filled with a dense amorphous mass of lipid and cholesterol, completely occuluding the lumen, but with the better resolution provided by the electron microscope, the lipid is generally seen to be within the Sertolic cell cytoplasm. While some of this lipid might be contributed by the lipoidal inclusions of the phagocytized residual bodies, much of it is probably produced by the Sertoli cell cytoplasm. Steroid dehydrogenase activity ceases to be demonstrable in these cells at this time. The tubules remain in this heavily lipoidal state for sometime; then, concomitant with the recrudescence of spermatogenetic activity in the adjacent stem spermatogonia, the sudanophilic material rapidly disappears. The duration between the sudden accumulation in the Sertoli cell cytoplasm and the start of lipid depletion varies from species to species and may be as long as several months. For example, in the migratory Whimbrel (*Numenius phaeopus*), the seminiferous tubules have already become heavity lipoidal by the time the animals leave Britain and head south to their African wintering grounds. The gonads remain in this condition for about 5-6 months, and the Sertoli lipid clearance and spermatogenetic recovery begin just before the birds leave the contranuptial are and return north to breed. By the time they arrive in Britain, tubule lipids are absent and testes are reaching sexual maturity. In columbid species, such a massive postnuptial tubule steatogenesis does not occur, and the quantity of Sertoli lipid is very much less.

In view of the fine structure and histochemical evidence, the question arises as to whether this seasonal waxing and waning of cholesterol-rich lipoidal material in the Sertoli cells is indicative of a seasonal endocrine function as in apparent in the adjacent interstitial tissue. Tentative evidence for this has been provided by Lofts and Marshall (1959), who chromatographically analyzed testicular lipids extracted from birds with regressed gonads containing heavily lipoidal tubules but a lipid-free interstitium. The results showed the presence of progresterone, which also correlated with a positive progestogenic reaction in the blood subjected to a parallel bioassay. A similar analysis on birds with gonads with expanded nonlipoidal tubules but heavily lipoidal interstitial cells resulted in an absence of demonstrable progestogenic activity in the blood, and only androgenic steroids were identified in the testis extracts. By present-day standards, the above data would require more rigorous criteria for specific identification of the steroids, but so far as the authors are aware, no further confirmation of these data has yet been attempted. However, there is strong evidence in favor of this hypotehesis in mammals and also in reptiles, in which a separation of seminiferous tubules and interstitial tissue has been achieved by microdissection. By incubating seminiferous tubules with labeled precursors, their steroid biosynthetic capacity has been clearly established. Furthermore, in reptiles, Lofts (1972) has shown that testosterone is a major steroid being produced by this tissue, and that the production varies on a seasonal basis.

Anatomy of the Female Reproductive System

The reproductive organs of the avain female include the left ovary and left oviduct. Although the right ovary and oviduct are formed in the embryonio stages, they usually do not persist in adult life. A persistent right ovary and oviduct have been reported in some avain species and in rare instance in ducks and chickens where both ovaries and oviducts were functional.

Ovary

The left ovary is situated on the left side of the body at the cephalic end of the kidneys and is attached to the body wall by the mesovarian ligament. The ovary consists of an outer cortex, made up of follicles containing ova, and an inner medulla.

The ovary of the immature bird is made up of a mass of small ova, at least 2000 of which are visible to the naked eye in the chicken, there are also about 12,000 ova of microscopic size. Only a relatively few of these (200-300) reach maturity and are ovulated in certain domesticated species and considerable fewer do in wild ones.

Ovarian follicle

The individual follicles vary is size depending on the species and the size of egg laid, but in the sexually nature chicken they attain a diameter of approximately 40 mm before ovulation. Histologically the structure of the avian ovarian follicle is very much like that of mammals. The follicle encircles the ova, which is made up of an innermost lawyer, zona radiata, the ganulosa lawyer, the theca internal, and the theca external.

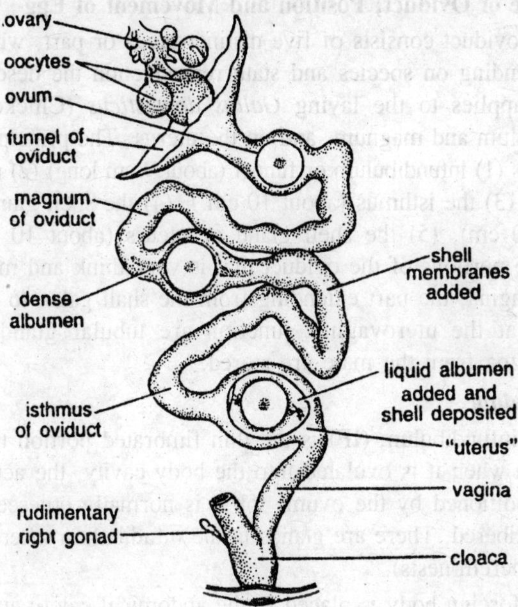

Fig. 6.3. The egg in the oviduct of the hen.

The ovarian follicle is highly vascular except for the stigma, which to the naked eye appears a vascular, although microscopy examination shows that small arteries and veins extend across it, according to Nalbandov and James (1949). The ovary receives its blood supply from the short ovarian aureately, which usually arises from the left renolumbar artery but may branch directly from the dorsal aorta. The ovarian artery divides into many branches, and usually from two to four separate arterial branches lead to a single follicular stalk. A few a arteries immediately surround the ovum; after branching, they pass through the theca, become arterioles, and form a capillary network peripheral to the basement membrane.

The venous system of the follicle is more prominent than the arterial, and forms three layers or beds; (1) the innermost, located in the theca; (2) a middle layer; and (3) the outer or peripheral layer, consisting of a few large veins that encircle the follicle and leave via the stalk. Eventually all of the veins from the ovary unite into the two main anterior and posterior veins, which empty into the posterior vena cava. The follicle is intensely innervated and contains both adrenergic and cholinergic fibers.

Structure of Oviduct; Position and Movement of Egg

The oviduct consists of five distinct areas or part, which vary in size depending on species and state reproduction the description that follows applies to the laying *Gallus domesticus* (Chicken); on the infundibulum and magnum, and on the uterus. The principal parts are so follows (1) infundibulum or funnel (about 9 cm long) (2) the magnum (33 cm); (3) the isthmus (about 10 cm.); (4) the shell gland or uterus (about 10 cm), (5) the shell gland or uteurs (about 10 cm long, a pouchlike portions of the oviduct that is very think and muscular and (6) the vagina, the part extending from the shall galen to the cloacla. Located at the uterovaginal junction are tubular glands in which spermatozoa from the male are stored.

Infundibulum

The infundibulum (IF) is the thin fimbrated portion that engulfts the ovum when it is ovulated into the body cavity, the activity of the IF is conditioned by the ovum, for it is normally quiescent until the ovum is libered. There are glands in the infudibulum where sperm are stored (sperem nests).

If a foreign body is placed in the abdominal cavity at the time of ovulation and the ovum is removed, the if will engulf the foreign body. If this is done at some time before or after ovulation, the if remains inactive. Thus, the activity of If is conditioned by ovulation. Occasionally the ovum is not picked up and the hen appears to be laying but never does so. The cause of the defective IF is not known but may be related to certain respiratory disease. The ovum, when not engulfed by the if, can be absorbed in the body cavity in 24 hr or less.

Magnum

The ovum passes to be magnum, the largest single portion of the oviduct (hence its name), measuring 33 cm in length. Here most of the protein of the e.g. (albumen) is formed. Histologic studies by a number of workers reveal that the magnum is highly glandular and contains two types of glands, tubular and unicellular. The tubular glands are composed of nongoblet cells that are not ciliated, but the unicellular glands are of the goblet type.

Isthumus

The peristaltic movements of the magnum force the ovum into the isthmus. The line of demarcation between it and the magnum is distinct; the folds of the glands in the isthumus are not as large and numerous as those in the magnum. The inner and outer shell membranes are formed in the isthmus. Some researchers have believed that some albumen is added to the egg here, but the data of other workers suggest that no albumen and only insignificant amount of water are added.

Uterus or shell gland

The uterus is pouch like, thick, and muscular. It contains tubular and unicellular glands, the function of which is unknown. It is presumed that they form the watery uterine fluid which is added to the albumen through the shell membranes. Whether or not these glands are concerned in shell formation is unknown.

The ovum receives the shell in the uterus and water and salt are added to the albumen. The pigment of the shell is formed in the uterus during the last 5 hr before the egg is laid. The brown pigment, porphyrin, is synthesized by the shell gland in chickens from s-amino levulinic acid. The pigment is evenly distributed throughout the shell but is absent from the shell membranes; in quail egg, which is more deeply pigmented, the pigment is more prominent in the cuticle and pigment is deposited 3.5 hr before the egg is laid.

Motility of the genital tract has been studied in vitro by Chen and Hawes (1970). Spontaneous activity was observed; a gradient was reported highest in the fimbrial region and lowest in the vaginal region, and particularly so in the uterovaginal junction.

Duration of egg passage down tract

The average time of passage of ovum through the various part of the tract are as follows; Infundibulum, 18 min (1/4-1/2 hr); magnum, 2 hr and 54 min (2-3 hr), isthmus, 1 hr and 14 min (11/4 hr). The time elapsing from the ovum's engulfment by the funnel to its reaching the uterus therefore average 4 hr and 26 min. The egg remains in the uterus for approximately 20 hr and 46 min. These figures are for chickens but the figures for turkeys (22-24 hr) and *Coturnix cotunix japonica* (19-20 hr) are approximately the same.

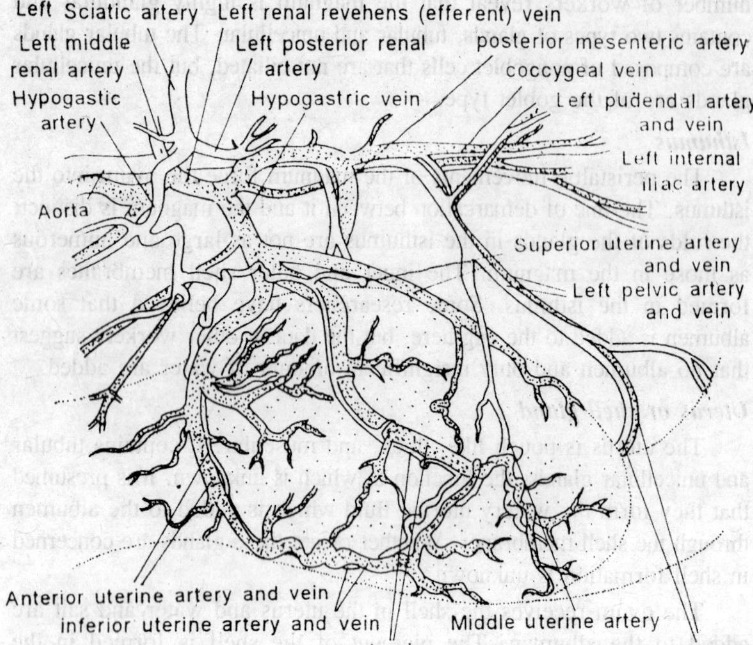

Fig. 6.4. Lateral view of the blood vessels to the uterine portion of the hen's oviduct.

Vagina

The vagina is the part of the oviduct leading from the uterus to the cloaca; it takes no part in the formation of the egg but may be involved in the explosion of the egg. A sphincter is situated at the border of the uterus and vagina and the uterovaginal glands are located here, where spermatozoa are stored.

Blood and Nerve Supply

The early literature has been reviewed by Freedman and Sturkie (1963a,b) and Stukie (1965). Early research described nerve plexuses and blood vessels in the oviduct but without sufficient details as to differentiation of region. Freedman and Sturakie (1963a,b) reported in detail on the blood vessel and nerves, particularly to the shell gland, and most of these details have been confirmed by Hodges (1965).

Blood is supplied to the hen's uterus by three arteries, all of which originate from the left side of the body. The hypogastric artery bifurcates into an anterior uterine and superior uterine artery. Lateral and inferior uterine arteries originate from the anterior uterine artery on both surfaces of the uterus. For blood vessels to other part of the tract from the work of Hodges (1965).

Nerves have been described by Freedman and Sturkie (1963a,b) Bennett and Malmfors (1970), and Freedman (1968). The parasympathetic pelvic nerves originate from the pelvic visceral rami of spinal nerves 30-33 or lumbosacral nerves (LSN) 8-11, but the principal contribution is from LSN 8 and 9. LSN 8 represents the first pelvic nerve in the chicken. The pudendal nerve, homologous to that in mammals, arises mainly from LSN 8 and 9. Only the left pelvic nerve innervates the uterus of the hen, via branches that accompany the middle and posterior uterine arteries; this is probably related to the fact that only the left mullerian duct persists in the chicken. Where the oviduct is bilateral, as in mammals, the pelvic plexus is also bilateral.

The sympathetic innervation to the uterus is from the hypogastric nerve, which represents a direct continuation of the aortic plexus. This nerve (present only on the left side) courses along with the hypogastric artery. The uterovaginal junction is abundantly innervated.

Histophysiology

General Histophysiology

Literature on the cyclic changes of the avian ovary is sparse, and very little is known beyond the follicular activity of domestic species, Data on the histophysiological changes in the ovary of the seasonally breeding bird throughout the year are almost nonexistent and have been reported, in any sort of detail, only in one species, the Rook (*Corvus frugilegus*). In this bird, the follicles of the December ovary are too small to be observed on the surface macroscopically, but histologically, sectioned material shows some oocyte development to be taking place internally, and follicles up to 1 mm diameter occur in association with numerous smaller ones. Marshall and Coombs report that the largest follicles at this time of year have distended, sudanophilic, glandular cells incorporated in the theca internal, and that the granulose layer of some of the biggest follicles disappear as such, as proliferation of this tissue fills the structure with large lipid-free cells, which later on apparently become secretory. There is relatively little lipoidal atresia at this time of year.

In temperate-zone species, the advent of the spring weather is, as in the male, generally accompanies by a recrudescence of gonadal activity, and developing follicles become increasingly obvious, macroscopiclaly, over the ovarian surface. In Corvus frugilegus, follicular recrudescence begins in late January and early February, and from, then until the first ovulation in March the whole organ becomes studded with cholesterol-positive lipoidal structures, as increasing numbers of the smaller follicles start developing and become atretic. The stromal interstitial cells also become heavily charged with lipids at this stage and react positively to histochemical tests, both for cholesterol and 3*HSDH. In the Rook, by March some follicles have enlarged enormously and a few enter the final vitellogenic stage and become ovulated. In a species such as the Band-tailed Pigeon (*Columba fasciata*), on the other hand, no more than one such enlarged follicle is found in the breeding ovary, and this can be correlated with the fact that such species lay only a single egg per clutch. Generally, a species that lays several eggs per clutch will have an ovary containing several large follicles filled with yellow yolk.

After extrusion of the egg, the follicular wall collapses and becomes spotted with lipoidal material. In the hen, the granulose cells become inflated with lipids and remain conspicuous for about 72 hours after ovulation, but luteinization does not occur and no corpus luteum develops. In seasonal breeders the completion of the last clutch is succeeded by a rapid regression of the gonad, and individual follicles become increasingly difficult to distinguish by the naked eye, though internally great numbers of follicles continue to undergo a slow development followed by lipoidal atersia. According to Marshall and Coombs (1957), a differentiation of a new generation of interstitial tissue, a phenomenon analogous to the testicular interstitial cell rehabilitation during the regeneration phase, takes place in the Rook ovary during the autumn.

There is unequivocal evidence that the avian ovary, like its mammalian counterpart, is a source of androgenic, estrogenic, and also progestogenic secretions, even though a true corpus luteum is lacking. Chromatographic studies have clearly established that this organ, both in its embryonic stage and in the adult bird has the capacity to produce these hormones, and androgenic, estrognic, and progestational steroids have all been extracted from the plasma of the domestic fowl. The respective intraovarian sites of biosynthesis of these various steroids, however, is still somewhat speculative. We have already noted that the thecal and granulose tissue of the prevulatory follicle, the postovulatory follicle, the atretic follicle, the interstitial cell of stromal origin, and also the exfollicular gland cells of Marshall and Coombs, at some stage all contain cholesterol-rich lipoidal inclusions and also have other glandular characteristics that might suggest every one of them to be possible loci of endocrine function, and this is confirmed by the fact that a positive reaction for * HSDH activity has been reported for all these tissues. Furthermore, electron microscopy has shown that all these tissues at some stage possess the fine structure normally attributed to steroidogenic tissue.

Interstitial Cells

Because of their apparent homology with the testicular Leydig cells, the ovarian interstitial cells arising from the stormal tissue are generally regarded to be the most likely source of androgenic secretion within the female gonad. Techniques for displaying steroid dehydrogenase activity have indicated that in the hen the steroidogenic potential in this tissue develops early in the embryogenesis of the organ and not just in the post -hatching period, as had previously been supposed, and this has also been shown to be the case in *Coturnix*. In a seasonally breeding bird, such as the Rook, the cyclic development of these cells closely parallels the development of the sexual activity heightens in the spring and autumn. In the hen, too, the * HSDH activity in these cells increases in intensity as the follicular phase wanes. The work of Taber (1951) also strongly suggests that a stomal cell is responsible for and rogen production. The comb of the domestic fowl is in both sexes under androgenic control and is sometimes used as a bioassay for androgenic analysis. Taber recorded a reappearance of foamy lipoidal interstitial cells concomitant with the decline of androgen production (comb regression) in hens after the cessation of gonadotropic stimulation and decline in androgen synthesis, the rapid accumulation of cholesterol-rich lipoidal precursor material in these cells resulted in them becoming more prominent. The more recent methods for the visualization of androgenic steroids by means of fluorescent antibody techniques confirm that the interstitial tissue is the primary locus of androgen secretion, though the thecal and granulose layers also produce a weak reaction.

Boucek and Savard (1970) have recently investigated steroid formation in the hen's gonad at different stages of the ovarian cycle, by a chromatographic analysis of the bioconversion of [^{14}C] acetate into progesterone, androstenedione, testosterone, and estradiol-17* in an *in vitro* incubation. A parallel analysis of the distribution and intensity of 3* HSDH and 17* HSDH activity was also carried out to provide data on the intravaorian location of the sites of activity. It is discovered that whereas the same spectrum of radioactive steroids was manufactured, the relative ratios of one steroids to the other varied significantly with the state of the ovarian cycle. Thus, a relatively large proportion of androgenic steroids was synthesized by the gonad of the molting hen, whereas the steroid profile produced by the ovarian tissue of the laying hen showed equivalent amounts of progesterone, androgens, and estrogenic hormones. In the broody hen, chiefly progesterone and estrogen were synthesized with very little androgen. Significantly, the histochemical studies demonstrated that the high androgenic production by the molting hen coincided with an intense 17* HSDH activity in the stromal cells, and also the thecal tissue, where only race reactions were produced by these cells during the laying stage.

Developing Follicle

In mammalian overian histophysiology, current opinion generally credits the thecal cells of the developing follicle with the secretion of estrogens, and the granulose cells with the secretion of progesterone after they metamorphose into the granulose lutein tissue of the corpus luteum. Support for this latter observation is also provided by the data showing that granulose cells grown in tissue culture manufacture progesterone. In birds, the evidence is more conflicting, but the tremendous increase in the size of the oviduct which is coincident with sexual maturity is known to be an estrogen-dependent effect and indicates that estrogen secretion appears to be a consistent consequence of follicular development, as is the case in mammals. In a seasonally breeding species, the marked annual fluctuations in oviduct development closely parallel the activity of the ovary. Thus, in *Corvus frugilegus* the oviducal epithelial height in the sexually inactive winter condition is 8 *m, but cellular proliferation begins in early February as the vernal acceleration of follicular development starts, and the epithelial layer rapidly expands to a maximum height of about 40 *m by the end of the month. When follicular development diminishes, the oviducts become constricted again. Estrone, estradiol-17b, and estriol have all been found in avian ovarian tissue, and the former two substances have also been identified in the plasma of the laying hen. In addition to their vitally influential role in the seasonal preparation of the oviduct, estrogens have many effects on a wide variety of somatic and physiological processes in birds, and the reader is directed to the extensive reviews that have been published for details on these various aspects of estrogenic influence.

The seasonal histochemical changes described to Marshall and Coombs (1957) in *corvus frugilegus* seem to support the hypothesis that the avian thecal cells may similarly be the site of estrogen synthesis as they apparently are in the mammal. Thus, an accumulation of cholesterol-positive lipoidal material builds up in the glandular cells of the theca internal in the largest follicles during the winter month, and then rapidly becomes depleted as estrogen titers are reaching their peak and the mature follicles are undergoing their culminating vitellogenic phase prior to ovulation. By the time yellow yolk appears in the oocytes, only slight traces of sudanophilic material remain in the cytoplasm of the greatly distended thecal cells. Vitellogenesis, and the consequent deposition of large quantities of yolk within the developing oocyte, is an estrogen-dependent phenomenon and the rapid depletion of the thecal cholesterol and lipids at this stage of the seasonal cycle may be indicative of a rapid utilization of precursor material at a time of high steroid synthesis, as has been suggested to be the case when a similar depletion occurs in the testicular Leydig cells. Certainly, the fine structure of the thecal cells and their possible site of steroid synthesis, and the more recent demonstration that isolated thecal tissue from growing follicles of the hen's ovary has the capacity to convert cholesterol to estrogens provides strong support for the suggestion that this tissue may be the locus of estrogen production in the avian ovary. Sayler *et al.,* (1970) have investigated the effects of photo stimulation on the distribution of * HSDH in the ovary of young Japanese Quail and have attempted to express changes in steroidogenesis by expressing the intensity of * HSDH histochemical reaction by means of an arbitrary scale based on the density of the formazan granulation deposited by the different steroidogenic tissues. In *Coturnix* that were raised from hatch to maturity under a stimulatory (16L:8D) light cycle, 3* HSDH activity increased in all the ovarian steroid producing tissues, but from day 35 onward, the index of 3* HSDH activity in the thecal tissue in creased very rapidly from an average value of 1.3 to 4.3, whereas the enzyme activity in the granulose tissue was less intense, rising from an average of 1.0 to 2.9 in the same period. Interestingly, the enzyme activity in the thecal tissue of birds kept under a short day length (8L:16D) was also much higher than that of the granulose tissue.

According to Chieffi (1967) the granulose cells are the probable site of estrogen biosynthesis, since 17* HSDH is limited to this tissue. This enzyme catalyzes the transformation of testosterone in the androstenedione and of estradiol into estrone. Arvy and Hadjiisky (1970) have also recorded a greater dehydrogenase activity in the granulose cells both in the hen and in the quail. However, Marshall and Coombs (1957) point out that the granulose cells in the seasonally breeding

Rook are the only prominent ovarian cells that do not contain cholesterol during follicular development, and electron microscopy studies of the hen ovary have shown that granulose cell start development abundant a granular endoplasmic recticulum, mitochondria with tubular crisfae, cholesterol, and sudanophilic granules, only at a time when the follicles are ready to ovulate, thus suggesting that their steroidogenic activity has been relatively slight up to this time.

Boucek and Savard (1970) have confirmed Chieffi's earlier observations of the localization of 17B HSDH in the granulose cells of the laying hen, but have also shown that in the molting bird the reverse situation develops and 17B* HSDH activity now becomes intense in thecal tissue but absent from granulose cells, even though in vitro incubation and chromatographic analysis of the ovarian tissue show that there is a considerable bioconversion of radioactive acetate into estradoil-17B during this time. The same investigation has also shown that there was little or no progesterone production in these molting hens. In view of the absence of 17* HSDH in granulose tissue in these birds, and also the very marked reduction in the intensity of the 3* HSDH as well, it seems not impossible that the granulose cells might be involved in the synthesis of progesterone. The ovarian steroid profiles of the laying and broody hens both show considerable progesterone biosynthesis and, in both groups, steroid dehydrogenase activity occurs in the granulose tissue, being particularly intense in the laying hen. These observations are also supported by the data of Furr (1969a), which show that progesterone occurs in the blood or ovaries of molting birds. Furthermore, the highest levels of progesterone are found in the follicles and only negligible amounts occur in the ovarian stroma.

Post Ovulatory Follicle

The postovulatory follicle has sometimes been suggested as the source of ovarian progestogenic steroids, and the ruptured follicles have been shown to contain progesterone and have the capacity of synthesizing steroids in vitro. Furthermore, the experimental removal of recently ruptured follicles influences the retention time of eggs in the oviduct. Conner and Fraps (1954) have established that there appears to be a quantitative relationship between the amount of postovulatory tissue and oviposition, so that the greater the proportion removed, the greater the retardation in oviposition. It has also been established that when the next-to-last ruptured follicle is removed it has no effect, suggesting that whatever endocrine activity the postovulatory follicle

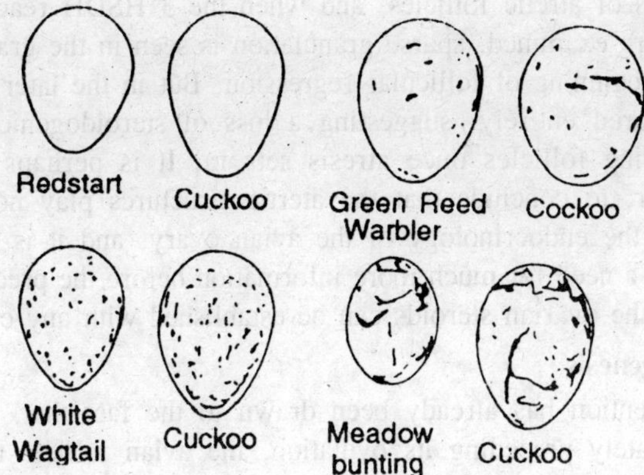

Fig. 6.5. The delay or lag in hours between the laying of successive egg in a cycle.

possesses, it is rather short-lived, and this is also indicated by the rapid degeneration that generally occurs in most avian species.

The very transient endocrine phase of postovulatory follicles outlined by the experiments of Fraps and his colleagues is also supported by the electron microscopic studies of Wyburn and his co-workers, who have recorded anextensively developed arangular endoplasmic reticulum in the granulose cells of the recently ovulated follicle, together with an increase in sudanophilia and cholesterol content. There is also a very intense reaction to tests for 3* HSDH, but this rabidly diminishes with the degeneration of the postovulatory structures. It seems likely that this very abbreviated postovulatory steroidogenic capacity in these cells is probably a hangover from the activity of the granulose tissue during the period of high progesterone production immediately preceding the ovulatory process.

Atretic Follicle

Cholesterol is abundant in the thecal tissue of the atretic follicles, and during the initial stages of atresia in the granulose cells. In both layers, a positive 3* HSDH activity has been reported. The latter investigators also report 17* HSDH in the granulose layer. Marshall and Coombs (1957) have suggested that the atretic follicles may be involved in progesterone production, since great numbers of follicles undergo such lipoidal atresia, and, in a seasonal breeder, this phenomenon builds up a considerable reservoir of cholesterol by the time of the seasonal ovulation period. However, Sayler *et al.*, (1970) have established that when young Coturnix are reared to maturity under nonstimulatory light conditions (8L:16D), there is an increase in the numbers of atretic follicles, and when the 3 HSDH reactions in the ovary are examined, sparse granulation is seen in the granulosa cells at the beginning of follicular regression. But in the later stages, this disappeared entirely, suggesting a loss of steroidogenic activity in developing follicles once atresis sets in. It is perhaps premature, however, to conclude that the atertia structures play no significant part in the endocrinology of the avian ovary, and it is evident that there is a need for much more information before the precise locus of any of the ovarian steroids can be established with any certainty.

Vitellogenesis

Attention has already been drawn to the fact that, in the days immediately preceding its ovulation, the avian follicle undergoes a very rapid expansion in size due to the storage of large quantities of yolk in the maturing oocyte (i.e. vitellogenesis). For example, in the chicken, the mass of yolk can increase form 100 mg to as much as 20 gm in the 7 days before ovulation. Although experiments using radioisotopes leave no doubt that protein synthesis can, and does, occur within the growing oocyte, this accounts only for a minor portion of materials synthesized during this short time interval, and current evidence indicates that the greatest portion of the yolk lipids and proteins laid down in vitellogenesis arise elsewhere in the organism. Basically, the process can be divided into three successive stages, all of which are causally related. These are (1) the synthesis of the yolk proteins and lipids (2) their transportation to the ovary and uptake by it, and (3) the incorporation of the serum proteins into the yolk elements.

In the avain oocyte, the yolk contains relatively more lipid (33% wet weight) in relation to protein (16%) than is the case in many other vertebrate eggs. In fine structure, it is seen to consist of two major components, namely, the yellow and white yolk granules which appear to be freely suspended in the second component, the yolk fluid. The granules often have discrete limiting membranes and, internally, may contain osmophilic subgranules that are larger in the white granules than they are in the yellow ones. The yellow and white granules are laid down in alternating concentric layers that reflect a diurnal variation in carotenol deposition. Very few mitochondria are observal within the matural yolk mass, except during the early stages of yolk-granule formation, nor is there much evidence of an endothelial recticulum. Much of the protein, together with some of the lipid, largely occurs in the granules, whereas the yolk fluid contains large quantities of lipid globules and a smaller proportion of proteins. Although there are slight differences in their detailed chemistry, the major yolk proteins consist, as in all other groups of oviparous vertebrates, of lipovitellins and phosvitin.

Evidence for the extraoocyte origin of most of these constituents stems from the earlier observations that phosphoprotein appear the plasma of the laying hen. In view of its chemical similarity with the yolk protein vitellin, it was suggested that plasma phosphoprotein might be a precursor of the latter, which eventually became translocated into the egg. The role of blood proteins in yolk formation was further emphasized by the demonstration, by immunological techniques, that even foreign proteins after being injected into the circulation could be detected in the yolk. Other changes in the constitution of the blood that have been observed to occur as a prelude to vitellogenesis are a very sharp elevation in the level of plasma calcium and also of lipids.

More recently, Schjeide and co-workers (1963) have been able to show that, at the onset of laying, two new serum proteins appear in the hen which are chemically and immunologically similar to the three major egg yolk proteins - phosvitin and * and *-lipovitellin. The same investigators also confirmed the transference of serum lipovitellin into the egg yolk by means of radioactive tracers. In this experiment serum lipovitellin was first extracted and labeled with ^{14}C, then injected into a laying hen. Within 10 hours, much of the radio-active protein was lodged in the yolk proteins, indicating its transference from the circulation across the egg cell barriers into the yolk. The mechanism of the transmission of such blood proteins into the oocyte is far from clear, but it may be by micropinocytotic activity at the oocyte surface. The follicular epithelium certainly seems to play a significant part, and Patterson *et al.,* (1961) have clearly demonstrated a preferential transfer of serum *-globulins by the follicular tissue to developing ova and have found that its concentration in the yolk is many times that in the serum. Gonadotropins appear to be important for stimulating the mechanism of this final transference of blood proteins into the oocyten, and in some of the lower vertebrate groups, an increase in serum protein transmission and yolk deposition has been shown to result from FSH treatment, possibly by a stimulation of the process of micropinocytosis.

The liver appears to be the extraoocyte locus of the synthesis of yolk protein and lipid, and hepatectomy has been shown to prevent the typical plasma changes associated with the onset of the vitellogenic phenomenon. Furthermore, radioactive phosphate injected into the wing vein of laying hens has been shown to becomes incorporated first into a protein-bound component in the liver which then becomes circulated in the plasma as a phosphoprotein, before finally being transferred into the oocyte and localized in the egg yolk. Confirmation is also provided by the demonstration that the in vitro incubation of liver slices from laying hens can synthesize phosvitin, which is similar to the yolk phosphoprotein, and Hawkins and Heald (1966) have similarly demonstrated the *in vitro* synthesis of triglycerides and established that it is much greater in laying hens than in the liver of immature pullets. These triglycerides are mainly transported to the oocyte as *-lipoproteins in the plasma, and eventually become concentrated within the fluid yolk compartment of the egg as lipid globules. Although * lipoproteins occur in the plasma of immature as well as mature birds, there is a pronounced lipemia at the onset of vitellogenesis in the latter.

Oviposition or Laying, and Brooding Habits of Birds

In their laying and brooding habits birds vary in (1) the number of eggs laid in a given time, (2) the sequence in which the eggs are laid, (3) the intervals or breaks in the sequence, and (4) whether or not they incubate their eggs.

Wild birds usually lay one or more egg in sequence and then stop laying and sit on them (clutches). The number of clutches and the number of eggs in the clutch vary with the species and the season. Some birds, such as the auk and pengiuin, lay only one egg before sitting; the pigeon usually lays two and the partirideg as many as 12-20 eggs before sitting. Removal of eggs from the nests of some birds prolongs the laying time or number of eggs laid (indeterminate species), but is without effect in others.

Some birds are continuous breeders and lay and mate at anytime of year (domesticated chickens, ducks, turkeys, quails); some are multibrooding. Particularly when kept in equitable environments and others are seasonal and breed once or twice a year. During these seasonal and mutlibrooding cycles the ovary undergoes periods of growth and regression.

The weight of the European starling ovary may fluctuate from 8 mg during the regression phase to 1400 mg at the height of breeding season. In the domesticated species (a continuous breeder) the ovary usually remains well developed most of the year except when the bird is molting or, more, rarely, when it is not laying for extended periods of time. After ovulation the ruptured follicles regress and finally degenerate. The postovulatory follicles of the chicken are usually resorbed within days or weeks, whereas those of the pheasant and mallard duck may persist for months. There is no corpora lutea in birds.

In some wild species mating or copulation is related to nest building, which begins at about the time the female is sexually receptive. Nest building in some species is also related to the time the first egg is laid, usually beginning a few days before hand.

Laying Cycle and Rate of Laying

Many of the domesticated species, botably the chicken, quail (*Coturnixm*), and duck, lay a number of eggs on successive days (a swquence): then the sequence is interrupted for one or more days before laying is resumed; such birds usually do not incubate their eggs. The terms "cycle" and "clutch" have been used to designated such behavior. Neither of these terms, however, adequately describes the rte and rhythm of laying by domesticated birds. Strictly speaking, "cycle" means a regularly recurring succession events applied to laying, it involves a sequence and the time intervals interrupting the sequence. Thus, a hen with a three-egg laying cycle would lay three eggs on successive days, before skipping a day or more, and then repeat the performance.

Some of the variations in rhythm or pattern of laying exhibited by chickens or other continuous layers may be illustrated as follows:

xx-xx-xx	Two-egg cycle
xxx-xxx-xxx	Regular sequence irregular skip
xx-xxx-x-xxx	Irregular sequence regular skip
xxxxxxxxxxxxx	Long sequence

The rate of lay, or laying frequency, is the number of eggs laid in a given period of time, without regard to the pattern or rhythm of laying. For example, a hen laying 15 eggs in 30 days lays at a rate of 50%. More details concerning sequences and cycles are reported by Fraps (1955). Selected hens of the better laying laying breeds of chickens lay between 250 and 270 eggs per bird per year. The number of successively laid eggs for most good laying hens ranges from four to six, but some lay for many days without an interruption in the sequence. Some breeds of domesticated ducks and Japanese quail also are high rate layers.

Cycle and sequence are terms frequently used interchangeably c1, c2cT refer to ovulation and oviposition sequences in a cycle, C1 represents first egg or ova of a cycle or sequence and CT, the terminal egg of cycle.

The interval between eggs laid on successive days by most hens ranges from 24 to 28 hr, depending on the length of the laying sequence. The lag or the interval between eggs is greater in short than in long sequences, and the intervals between the first two and the last two egg of the sequence are greater than for intervening eggs, regardless of the length of the cycle. These difference in lag represent mainly difference in time of ovulation. Lag represents not the interval between successive ovipositions but the temporal difference in time of day of one oviposition with respect to its predecessor. Most of the laying sequences of Coturnix are two, three, and four eggs, in that order.

Lag between C1 and CT eggs is much greater in chickens (4-5 to 8 hr, depending on sequence) than in Japanese quail (15-2 hr). the mean interval between eggs of chickens and Coturniz are about the same but there is less variation in Coturnix with variable sequence; the interval is slightly longer in turkeys.

The interval between successively laid eggs of the pigeon is 40-44 hr, but the number of clutches and the interval between clutches varies with the season. Records from the New Jersey pigeon test show that the number of clutches laid by pigeons aveaes eight a year, and that the interval between clutches is approximately 45 days is the fall and winter and from 30 to 32 days in the spring and early summer.

Ovulation in chickens usually occurs soon after the onset of light; in *Coturnix* however, it occurs about 8-9 hr after the onset of light. Twelve or more hours of light (either natural or artificial) are required in order to obtain maximum lay in domesticated species.

The actual time of day when eggs are laid depends on the length of the sequence and position of the egg in the sequence, and also on the length of the day (hours of daylight). Although hens may lay eggs during any of the daylight hours, most of them lay in the forenoon, and they tend no lay earlier when the days are longer.

The laying and breeding seasons of some birds are influenced by climatic conditions, such as temperature and rainfall, and by the availability of food. For more details on the relation of behavior and reproduction in wild birds, consult Marshall (1961), Lehrman (1961), and Lofts and Murton (1973). For details on laying behavior of bobwhite quails.

The differences observed in the laying and brooding habits among different species of birds suggest differences in the release or pituitary hormones concerned in the growth and maturation of the follicles and in vouation and broodiness.

Control of Oviposition

Little is known concerning the immediate causes of uterine contraction and oviposition, but there is evidence that the time of laying is influenced by the ruptured ovarian follicle from which the egg is ovulated. Although recently ruptured follicle influence laying time, older ruptured ones also influence it, suggesting the release of some inhibitory factor from the ruptured follocile. However, no such factor has been isolated.

Neurohypophyseal hormones

There is good evidence that arginine vasotocin, the hormone from the posterior lobe of the pituitary, may initiate the contraction of the uterus that leads to oviposition. Work by Munsick et al., (1960) demonstrated conclusively that the avian posterior pituitary lobe contains this hormones and that the chicken uterus is considerably more sensitive to it than it is to oxyytocin.

Assays of the posterior lobe by Tanaka and Nakajo (1962) revelaed the least amount of vasotocin coincident with laying, suggesting that it was released at this time into the blood. Sturkie and Lin revealed that the posterior lobe releases this hormone. Prior to oviposition the concentration in the blood was low (150-167uU/ml) and immediately prior to and during oviposition, the level increased to 7059 uU. Similar results were reported by Niezgodda et al., (1973). Gilbert and Lake (1964) revealed a decrease in a blood amino peptidase that normally deactivates oxytocin and vasotocin, coinciding with the increase in these substances at time of oviposition.

Other agents, such as acetylcholine, Nembutal, and uterine, distension, which may cause premature oviposition, did not causes the release of vasotocin. Stimulation of the preoptic area of the brain caused a release of vasotocin into blood and premature oviposition. although hens continue to lay after surgical removal of the posterior lobe, the median eminence is still intact and it contains vasotocin; so dies the anterior lobe of the pituitary.

Pure synthetic arginine vasotocin (available from Sandoz), containing 250 pressor units per milligram, is very effective at dosaes of 0.1-0.4 ug/kg in inducing premature oviposition in chickens. Synthetic oxytocin (Sandoz), containing 450 oxytocic units per miligram, was effective also in causing premature oviposition at dosages from 1.0 to 4.0 ug/kg. Both substances increased intrauterine pressure considerably but vasotocin and the greater effect.

Earlier work on the effects of posterior hormones dealt with mixtures of oxytocic and pressor factors; injections of these were effective, particularly the latter, in inducing oviposition. Obstetrical pituitrin, containing mainly the oxytocic factor, when injected at a level of 0.1 to 0.2 ml is effective intravenously in most birds within 3-4 min; it causes contraction of the uterus and premature oviposition. The sensitivity of the uterus to oxytocin and vasopressin increases at normal oviposition time.

Drugs and other hormones

Morash and Gibbs demonstrated that histamine, acetylcholine, and ergotoxine produced contraction and that epinephrine produced relaxation of the uterus. Atropine blocks the effects of acetylcholine. Acetylcholine and histamine cause premature oviposition, and ephedrine retards laying from 4 to 24 hr in the intact hen. Sodium pentobarbital at an anesthetic in about 33% of birds, if injected a few hours before normal oviposition.

Epinephrine retarded oviposition in the intact chicken, inhibited the motility of uterine strips, and caused the circular muscels of the vagina to contract; however, it had no effects on longitudinal muscles. Polin and Strukie (1955) observed a hen that habitually laid soft shelled eggs. After administration of ephedrine sulfare, which relaxes uterine muscle, the hen laid normal shelled eggs. Hypothermia causes hens to expel eggs prematurely. Permture oviposition was induced in quail (*Coturnix*) by intrauterine injection of prostaglandin, PGE (0.01 ug dose) by Hertelendy (1974).

Neural control

Because the shell gland receives sympathetic and parasymparthetic innervations, one might expect the motility of the gland to be influenced by these nerves. However transition of the pelvic nerves or of the hypogastric sympathetic nerves had no effect on oviposition. Studies involving cohoinestrease stains indicate that the pelvic nerves are cholinergic. Administration of a cholinergic blocker (atropine) did not influence ovipsition time. The results of these studies indicate that the sympathetic and parasympathetic innervation of the uterus has little influence on oviposition.

Sykes reported that the "bearing down" reflex is initiated by cloacal or vaginal stimuli, such as occur when an egg enters the vagina, or it can be evoked by other stimuli; it causes the hen to squat. Evocation of the reflex leads to an increase in respiratory rate and strong contraction of the abdominal muscles. He concluded that the contraction of both uterus and vagina is necessary for laying, and that "bearing down" aids greatly in the expulsion of the egg. Sturkic *et al.*, (1962) abolished the activity of abdominal and cloacal skeletal muscle by administering curare, which paralyzes skeletal muscle but not smooth muscle. Their results demonstrated that abolition of the abdominal press did not prevent oviposition, although it delayed it slightly.

Opel (1964) reported that electrical stimulation of certain areas of the brain, particularly the preoptic area, caused premature oviposition in a high percentage of birds, most of the eggs being laid 2-6 hr before the expected time of oviposition. Even insertion of electrodes without stimulation was effective, and the author presumed that the premature ovipositions were caused by immediately release of neurohypophysial hormone (vasotocin) following the stimulations.

Orientation of the Egg in the Oviduct

The orientation of the egg in the oviduct and its movement and rotation have been subjects of controversy. Early workers, including Purkinje in 1825, Von Baer in 1828, and some others since, observed that the egg in the uterus of the opened hen lay with its pointed end caudad. Oisen and Byerly (1932) in an extensive study, observed that the pointed end appeared first in from 66 to 82% of the eggs laid. These results have in general been confirmed by Wood-Gush and Gilbert (1969), although in one group of hens 46% of eggs were laid blunt end first. Bradfield (1951), by fluoroscopic examinations of the egg in the uterus of the bid, showed that during most of the 18-20 hr that the egg was in the uterus it remained in the same position, with the pointed end directed caudally, but that just prior to laying the egg was rotated through 180° and most were laid with the blunt end caudad.

Other Factors and Oviposition

Foreign bodies. Sutures (thread) placed in the uterus cause hens to expel eggs prematurely. Insertion of a glass catheter in the shell gland resulted in the premature expulsion of eggs and the cessation of laying.

Shelles eggs. The mechanism responsible for the laying of shelless eggs is not known. They may he the result of premature contraction of the uterus and expulsion of the egg before calcium deposition has occurred, or there may be some defect in the mechanism of calcium deposition. Most of the shelless eggs are laid by young pullets in the early laying stage and between the hours of 5 and 9 p.m.

Oviposition and body temperature. At oviposition the body temperature of the laying hen reaches its peak.

Fistulation. A technique of fistulation of hens oviduct through the abdominal wall has been described by Gilbert and Wood-Gush (1963), such that ovulated ova were picked up by the infundibulum and shunted through the fistulated portion through the body wall to the exterior.

Formation and Growth of Ova

As the female approaches sexual maturity, the immature ova begin growing at a rapid rate; in the chicken they reach maturity within 9-10 days. The weight of the ova and yolk during the 7 days preceding ovulation increases approximately 16-fold and in a regular and straight-line manner. The final weight of the chicken ovary is approximately 16 g. This rapid growth phase, however, has been reported as variable and ranging from 5 to 11 days, according to most investigators. The rate of growth in wild species is similar to that in the chicken, with the final period of rapid growth ranging from 4 to 11 days preceding ovulation, depending on the species.

Using Sudan Ill, a fat dye, Conrad and Warren (1939) found that, during the growth period the yolk material is laid down in concentric rings. However, Bohren et al (1945) found no such concentric rings in birds fed diets rich in xanthophylls pigments. Shenstone (1968) also doubted the deposition of yolk in concentric layers. For further details on the formation and composition of yolk, consult Gilbert and WoodGush (1971) and Gilbert (1971 c, d).

There is some controversy about whether yolk deposition continues up to the time of ovulation. Some workers have suggested that no yolk is deposited in the last 24 hr preceding ovulation, and the work of Gilbert (1970), based on fat dye deposits, indicates that in about 20% of the eggs (ova) of the first sequence (C,) there was no yolk deposited in the last 24 hr.

Follicular Hierarchy

There is a gradation in maturation of developing ovarian follicles (hierarchy). The hierarchy usually involves four to six follicles in the chicken, but the number varies among individuals and the number of graded follicles is usually larger in those with longer laying sequences. The control or regulation of this follicular hierarchy is not understood. It is true that the growth of the follicle is in response to the endogenous elaboration of follicular stimulating hormone (FSH) and luterinizing hormone (LH), and it may be that the ovary itself controls or influences the hierarchy. However, this does not explain the facts that the administration of FSH and LH in chickens prevents the hierarchy and that there are multiple maturations and even ovulations. Moreover, in ovarian transplants with no intact nerves the follicles respond to endogenous FSH with multiple maturations and no gradations. In some wild birds, however, the follicular hierarchy occurs even after the administration of FSH.

The administration of FSH does not mimic in kind or quantity the release and action of endogenous FSH. Mitchell (1967a, b), by careful administration of FSH, was able to maintain an almost normal follicular hierarchy in hypophysectomized hens.

Warren and Conrad (1939) reported that the first egg of the sequence had a larger yolk than succeeding ones, but more recent data indicate that this is incorrect. The size of ova in a sequence is purely random. In white-crowned sparrows the ovary develops in the spring, and there is a hierarchy of ova only in laying sparrows. Kern describes the ovaries and types of ateritic follicles in wild sparrows and those kept in captivity, and there are differences.

Ovarian Hormones

The principal ovarian hormones are estrogens and progesterone.

Progesterone

In the mammalian ovary progesterone is produced by the corpora lutea, which is absent in birds; progesterone is produced by the ova of Aves. The granulose cells of mammal produce progesterone and this is probably true also of Aves, although the evidence is conflicting. These cells probably are also the site of estrogen synthesis, but other data suggest that the theca cells may also be involved.

Progesterone is formed in the ovary as follows:

Cholesterol —* pregnenolone → progesterone

The liver is a major site of progesterone metabolism.

Assays and levels. Progesterone has recently been determined in chicken plasma at different stages before ovulation by a sensitive radioimmunoassay method. Their results follow:

Hours before ovulation	Progesterone (ng/ml)
27-24	2.68
23-20	2.56
19-16	2.69
15-12	2.75
11-8	4.39
7-4	6.47
3-0	4.6

Similar results were reported by Kppauf and van Tienhove (1972; competitive protein-binding method), with the highest levels occurring 4-7 hr before ovulation; there was no peak concentration on day when ovulation did not occur. At comparable stages, however, these absolute levels were lower than those of Furr et al., (1973); the latters figures compare favorably with those of Arcos and Opel (1971), who employed gas liquid chromatography. It is presumed that the variable blood levels reflect variable release of progesterone from the ovarian follicle. Apparently the avian ovary does not store appreciable quantities of progesterone, based on the uptake of radioactive progesterone.

Plasma progesterone levels in male ring doves determined by radio-immunoassay averaged 1.27 ng/ml and varied little, where as in females the levels were influenced by sexual behavior. While they were incubating eggs and brooding, the level averaged 1.13 ng/ml, 5 days after courtship began, however, the level rose to 3.01 ng/mg and there was a significant correlation between follicle development and progesterone.

Effect of progesterone. When administered in large doses, progesterone causes follicular atresia, and inhibits ovulation in chickens and quails. Molting may also be induced by large doses of progesterone. Other effects of progesterone are discussed under ovulation.

Estrogen

The principal naturally occurring estrogens in the urine, blood and ovaries of aves are estrone (E1), and 17 b-estradiol (17B-E2), and 17a-estrodiol (17a-E2). Present also in the hens urine are four estriol epimers of 14-keto 17b-estradiol. These steroids are probably derived from and rogens as in mammals, and are formed in the ovary and liver as shown above.

O'Grady and Heald (1965) reported E1 and 17b-E2 in the plasma of hens' based on an isotope dilution technique, but their values for estrone and those of others were higher than these reported by Layne et al., (1958) and by Peterson and Common (1972). The latter workers employed the radioimmunoassay for E2, which measures 17b-estradiol, principally, and estrone.

It is apparent that both estrogens increase significantly 6-2 hr before ovulation. Senior (1974) also determined estradiol (E2) by the radioimmunoassay in chickens at different stages before and during sexual maturity as follows:

7 weeks before first egg	94 pg/ml
2-3 weeks before first egg	355 pg/ml
After laying	138 pg/ml

The very high level 2-3 weeks before laying is probably related to the rapid formation and growth of ova (egg yol) and the synthesis of Ca and proteins.

Chan and Common (1974) also demonstrated that 17a-estradiol is a major phenolic steroid of hens blood. 17b-Estradiol levels of plasma of ring doves (by radiommunoassya) vary according to their sexual stage and behavior as follows:

Females, isolated	40 pg/ml or less
Females, male introduced	85 pg/ml
Females, nest building	67 pg/ml
Females, incubating eggs	not detectable

Estradiol was not detectable in the plasma of males at any of those stages. A number of synthetic estrogens are available, including diethylstibesterol, dianisylhexene, and dienstrol.

Assays. Most biological assays for estrogen are based on changes in oviduct weight, but the treatments of data vary among investigator.

Effect of estrogen

A part from the role that estrogens may play in growth and development of the ovarian follicle, and possibly in the releases of the ovulating hormone, it has many other functions, many of which are mentioned elsewhere and later in this chapter. Endogenous estrogen is responsible for the increase in plasma lipids, calcium, and proteins that occur at the time of sexual development and also for the tremendous increase in size and growth of the oviduct at this time.

Estrogen and secondary sexual characteristics

Estrogen influences certain secondary sex changes, particularly color of feather plumage and shape of feathers, in breeds that exhibit plumage dimorphis, such as the Brown Leghorn chicken and many wild species. The plumage of the Brown Leghorn female castrate reverts back to the more brilliantly colored male plumage but the plumage of the castrate male in unchanged, so estrogen is responsible for the changes. In African weaver finches the female has the natural type of plumage. In black breeds of chickens, the intensity of the black pigment in the feathers is usually greater in the female.

Estrogen and differentiation of sex

When estrogen in injected into incubating egg and, before sexual differentiation in embryos, into genetically determined (zygotic) females, the right oviduct, which normally is small or degenerated at hatching time, persists and is hypertrophied. Estrogen administered to zygotic male embryos causes the development of an ovotestis on the left side and sometimes on the right side. With large doses, ovarian follocles may be present on the left side. The right testis is much less responsive.

Effects of estrogen on output of pituitary gonadtropins

Administration of large doses of estrogen or androgen depresses the output of pituitary of gonadotropins.

The influence of estrogen on the output of other pituitary hormones is less clear.

Effects of estrogen, fat deposition, and fat storage in tissues

Estrogen administration increases the blood lipids and the deposition of fat in tissues, possibly of this practices has been tested by a number of investigators, with varying results. The results have been reviewed in detail by Stukie (1954, 1965).

Ovariectomy

Castration in the female is termed ovarectomy. The effect of sinistral and bilateral ovariectomy are different. Usually two operations are required for bilateral ovariectomy. In the first operation, the left ovary is removed (sinistral). Then a hypertophy of the rudimentary right gonad produce and ovtestis and rogen first. Soon after the sinistral operation and following the next molt, the new plumage is like that of the male in color and structure; later, after the right gonad has further developed and begun to secret estrogen however, the new plumage following the next molt may reverts to the female type. The right gonad is then removed and the plumage to the male type which is retained. Development of the rudimentary right gonad in castrates can be inhibited by the administration of estrogen.

Ovulation

The release of ovu from the ovarian follicle (ovulation) is caused by the rupture of the follicular membrane at the stigma, a relatively avascular area of the follicle. Ovulation occurs in most domesticated species within 15 to 75 in after oviposition, and within 4 to 5 hr after the first egg is laid in pigeons. The internal between oviposition ovulation of the next egg in a sequence is similar in those species that lay eggs daily in sequence, such as chicken, duck, turkey, and quail.

Hormonal effects

LH

Ovulation is caused by the cyclic released of the ovulating hormone (luteinizing hormone in mammals, LH) from the enterior pituitary. This hormone is released 6-8 hr prior to ovulation. When the anterior pituitary was surgically removed (hypophysectomy) 2 hr prior to ovulation. It did not effect ovulation time; when the operation was performed 8 hr prior to normal ovulation time however, olvulation was inhibited in most cases. Factors affecting the release of LH and its releasing hormone are discussed.

The LH content of pituitaries and blood have been determined and related to time of valuation. Later determinations involving more sensitive assay methods indicate that there is at least one peak of LH concentration in the blood occurring 4-8 hr prior to ovulation and coinciding in general with the lowest level or pituitary LH. This peak in concentration is probably the one related to ovulation. Others have reported a second peak at 18-20 hr, the significance of which is not known.

Premature ovulation can be induced by the injection of the ovulating norm one or by progesterone or other substances that cause the release of the hormone. For example, certain adrenocotrical hormones may either block or induce ovulation, depending on the amount administered. Time of ovulation is not influenced by time of oviposition because neither premature oviposition, which can be induced by certain drugs, nor retarded oviposition, which can be produced by administration of epinephrine, influence ovulation. The prematurity of ovulation extends from 17 to 30 hr in some instance, depending on the does of LH, but the ovarian follicle is most sensitive to LH-6-8 before normal ovulation.

Progesterone and estrogen

Neher and Fraps (1950), by injecting progesterone or LH, were able to increase the number of eggs laid in a 12-day period significantly. The yolk of the laid eggs was smaller than normal, however, suggesting that ovulation occurred before all ova were matured. Injection of small amounts of progesterone into the preotpic region of the hypothalamus caused premature ovulation, but not injections into the hypophysis.

Progesterone is also ineffective in the hypophysectomized chicken, indicating that it normally stimulates the pituitary to release LH. Does endogenous progesterone play a role in LH release? Determination of plasma progesterone at different stages of the ovulatory cycle revealed a peak concentration at form 4 to 6 hr prior to ovulation, or at about the same time as the main LH peak. It then declined but was still above basal levels at ovulation time. There was no peak on days when there was no ovulation.

Similar results were reported by Furr et al., (1973), who employed radiommunoassys for both progesterone and LH. An increase in the level of progesterone either preed that of LH or the two increase simultaneously. Never did the increased level of LH occur before the rise in progesterone. The latter results suggest that progesterone causes or influences the LH peak and is somehow involved in the feedback that may be involved in the release of LH.

Fraps (1955) postulated in diurnal variations in the threshold of a neural components (probably the LH-releasing factor) concerned with LH release, which he considered was sensitive to an "excitation" hormone secreted by the ovarian follicle. This might suggest that progesterone is the excitation hormone of Fraps. However, this excitation hormone may also be estrogen, because Senior and Cunningham (1974) have reported that the plasma LH peak occurs about 2 hr after the peak concentration of plasma estrogen (estradiol) is realized, suggesting an LH releasing role for estrogen. However, implants of estrogen into the hypothalamus or hypophysis prevented LH release and ovulation in Japanese quail.

LH-releasing hormone

Synthetic porcine LH-RH (NIH), injected at a does of 15-20 ug per chicken (i.v.) caused premature ovulation in a high percentage of cases.

LH and FSH preparations

Most of the data on premature ovulations induced by pituitary preparations involved mixtures of LH and FSH. Recent data on pure synthetic LH and FSH, single and in combination, have been reported by Kamiyoshi and Tanaka (1972) (Table 16-1). It is apparent that the addition of FSH to LH increased its effectiveness in causing ovulation.

Imai (1973) compared mammalian (ovine) FSH and LH (NIH-FSHS7; LH-S-15) and other preparations, including bovine pituitary preparation (BAP) and avain preparations (CAP), in inducing ovulation in hens pretreated with pregnant are serum (PMS). The higher doses caused multiple ovulations. Adding FSH to the LH did not increase the effect of LH appreciably. Moreover CAP was more effective in causing multiple ovulations than was NIH-LH.

Open (1966a) induced ovulations in Japanese quail with mammalian LH (available from Armour) and dried chicken pituitary. Premature ovulations were produced within 5-9 hr in 94% of the cases in birds that were preated with (PMS), which tends to suppress ovulations, however, only 81% ovulated.

Ovulation in Vitro

Olsen and Neher (1948) demonstrated that excised ova can be made to ovulate *in vitro* by placing them in Ringer's solution at a temperature of 107°F. Excised follicles where made to ovulate *in vitro* by applying proteolytic enzymes directly to the follicles. Ogawa and Nishiyama (1969) studied ovulation *in vitro* following removal of ova at different stages before expected ovulation and treating them with (1) saline alone, (2) chorionic gonadotropin (HCG) alone, (3) HCG plus blood plasma and (4) HCH, blood plasma, and pregnant mare serum (PMS). Treatments (1) and (2) were ineffective, but treatment (3) was very effective in ovulating ova removed 2-3 hr before the expected time of ovulation. Treatment (4) caused ovulation in follicles removed 24 hr or more before the expected time of ovulation. The authors conclude that some substance in the blood other than circulating LH (probably proteins) acting with the other agents was involved.

Interruption of Ovulation

Ovulation is more easily interrupted or inhibited than induced this applies to birds ore than to mammals. It may be inhibited in a number of ways. Subcutaneous injections of such substances as ovalbumen, casein, peptone, desiccated brain, muscle, and other tissue delay ovulation in the chicken from 6 to 10 hr when small dosages are administered, but large doses produce prompt and extensive follicular atresia.

Abdominal operations usually cause a temporary cessation of ovulation in the chicken. Rothchild and Fraps (1945) found that the incidence of follicular atresia and the time before resumption of ovulation following operations were inversely proportional to the rate of ovulation preceding the operating.

Progesterone-induced ovulation can be blocked by administration of adrenergis blocking agents, such as SKF 501 and dibenamine, and of atropine an anticholinergic agent.

Electrical stimulation of the hypothalamus of certain mammals causes a release of LH, but such attempts have been unsuccessful in the chicken. Lesions produced in the preoptic region of the hypothalamus prevent progesterone-induced ovulation in the hen. The latter workers showed that stimulation with stainless steel electrodes was effective but that stimulation with platinum electrodes was ineffective as have been reported in mammals.

Ovulation can also be inhibited by intrauterine insemination involving trauma to the uterovaginal junction.

Large doses of prolactin (100 IU) were effective in preventing prematre ovulatin, normally induced by LH.

Calcium-Deficient Diets

Many years ago, Titus showed that when hens were fed a diet low in calcium they would lay about one or two normal eggs per month; then they stopped laying and ovulating until enough calcium was mobilized for the shell of another egg. Recent studies by Gilbert and co-workers have confirmed and further extended the observations by Tirus. They conclude that calcium may act to affect the response of the target tissue or influence the gonadotropin output of the pituitary.

Effects of Light on Ovary and Ovulation

The stimulating effect of light on ovulation, laying, and testes growth is well known and has been reviewed more recently by Farner and Follett van Tienhoven and Planck (1973), Meier and McGregor (1972), and Oishi and Lauber (1973a). It is also known that light (natural or artificial) causes birds to start laying earlier than usual and to lay more intensely during the fall and winter months if they are continuous layers; however light do not usually increase average annual egg production. Maximum stimulation is produced in chickens by continuous

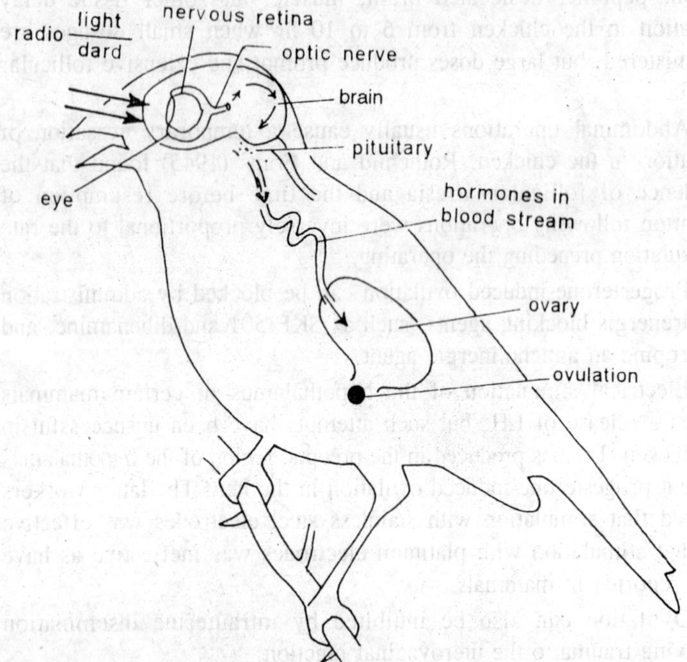

Fig. 6.6. Steps in stimulation of ovulation by light in a bird.

light is not necessary, however if the light is interrupted with periods of darkness. The fact that some hens may continue to lay even if kept in complete darkness, indicates that light is not the only factor that affects the release of the ovulating hormone. Intermittent light and flashing light have been used, but these did not increase laying rate significantly. Darkness appears to influence the time at which ovulation occurs, even thought it may not increase the ovulation rate; this was demonstrated by Lanson (1959). Who showed that a minimum of $1^1/_4$ hr showed or more of darkness were imposed beginning at 5 p. and extending to midnight, most of the birds laid their eggs during the hours of 5-7 a.m. If the birds were held in darkness from midnight to 7 a.m. however most of the hens laid their eggs in the afternoon (2-3 pm.). Similar results week obtained by Wilson et al., (1963). Van Tienhoven and Ostrander (1972) imposed a light - dare regime of 8 hr L: 10D : 2L: 4D. or a total of 12 hr of light interspersed with darkness, and found that egg production was as good if not better than birds with 14L: 10D.

Morris (1967) revelated that age at sexual matutiry in chicken varied inversely with hours of light exposure. The response was roughly linear and inverse after 2-12 hr of light exposure (with decreasing age and with increasing light) but after 12 hr the response was curvilinear, exhibiting a slight increase with increasing light. However as the bird approaches sexual maturity, the response to eight Tents to increase. Variations in light cycles at time of ovulation and oviposition have been reported by Rosale *et al.*, (1968) and by Faster (1969). Combination of 14 hr light, followed by 9, 11 or 3 hr of darkness, yielding cycle of 23, 25 and 27 hr., were tried and it was found that increasing cycle length beyond the normal inherent cycle length tended to increase number of eggs laid. Similar results were obtained by Fostres (1969) but the increase in eggs laid was much less.

Wave lengths and intensity

Red and orange lights have a greater stimulating effect on the pituitary and gonads, particularly testes, than green and blue light.

Formation of Albumen and Shell Membranes, and Shell

The components of the egg are shell, shell membranes, albumen, and yolk. A number of investigators have studied the formation of the egg components.

Albumen

There are four distinct layers of albumen in the laid egg: (1) the chalaziferous layer, attached to the yolk; (2) the inner liquid layer; (3)

the dense or thick layer; and (4) the outer thin or fluid layer. Approximately one-fourth of the total albumen is found in the outer layer and one-half in the dense, thick layer. The inner layer comprise 16.8% and the chalaziferous layer 2.7% of the total.

An egg taken from the hen just before it enters the isthmus contains only one layer of albumen, thick and jellylike in consistency. At this time the egg contains approximately one-half the amount of albumen of the laid egg and about twice the amount of protein per given volume. The presence of the different strata of albumen an the relative decrease in the proteins and solids of the laid egg therefore suggest that after the egg leaves the magnum mainly water is added to the albumen and that this change, plus other physical changes resulting from rotation and movement of the egg down the oviduct, is responsible for the stratification of albumen.

About 60% of the total albumen is found in the thick white layer, 25% is in the outer thin layer, and the remainder is in the inner thin white and chalazae. Shortly after the albumen is secreted in the magnum, water is added to it mainly in the uterus and the albumen is diluted considerable. Actually, the quantity of albumen in the laid egg is approximately twice what it was when it was first secreted.

Types and concentration of proteins in albumen

This has been studied by a number of workers. Egg albumen is made up a number of different proteins, including (1) ovalbumen, 54% (2) ovotransferrin (conalbumen), 13% (3) ovomucoid, 11% (4) ovoglobulin 3%, (5) lysozyme, 3.5% and (6) ovomucin, 2%. The functions of several of these are not known.

The lysozyme of egg albumen is an important enzyme that is well characterized. Its main biologic property is its lytic activity against bacterial cell walls it also hydrolyzes polysaccharide.

Ovmucoid is a protein enzyme inhibitor (or proteases). Chicken ovomucoid inhibits only trypsin but the from other avain species inhibits trypesi and chymotrypsin. Ovomucin is an insoluble, fibrous, acidic glycoprotein and it probablv is responsible for the gel-like qualities of egg white, particularly the thick white.

Hughes and Scott (1936) determined the amount of mucin, globulin, and albumen in the different layer of laid and oviducal eggs and the percentage of the total nitrogen contributed by the different types when the oviducal eggs had been in the utreus about 4-5 hr and most of the albumen had been formed. Ovomucin concentration was highest in the middle thick layer and chalazae and lowest in the inner thin layer of both laid and oviducal eggs, but it was higher in all layer of the oviducal egg than in the laid egg. The amount of mucin is responsible for the higher viscosity of the thick white layer, yet this layer contains slightly more water than the outer thin white layer. Ovoglobulin, however, is higher in all layers of the laid eggs than that in oviducal eggs. Globulin is highest in the inner thin layer and lowest in the outer thin layer. There is little or no difference in the relative amounts of ovoalbumen in the laid and oviducal eggs with respect to a given layer of albumen, but the highest amount is found in the outer thin white layer.

Formation of albumen: layers

The chalazae are the paired twisted stands of albumen attached at opposite poles of the yolk, and parallel to the long axis of the egg. The chalazae are formed by the mechanical twisting and segregation of the mucin fibers from the inner layer if albumen. The chalazae are twisted clockwise and counterclockwise at the large and small ends of the egg, respectively, suggesting that the egg is rotated on its long axis, suggesting that the egg is roated on its long axis, so as to produce the twisting of the strands. Conrad and Phillips (1938) were able to produce clalazae artificially by placing isthmian eggs in a mechanical roater.

Sturkie and Polin (1954) removed oviducal eggs from the uterus 2-3 hr after they had left the magnum, where albumen is secreted, and compared the condition of the albumen with that of freshly laid eggs, which varied greatly in albumen quality. It was concluded that albumen deteriorates in quality (becomes thinner) before the egg leaves the magnum and enters the uterus and that poor quality in the albumen (thinness of the white) is caused mainly by changes taking place in the uterus rather than by secretory activity in the magnum.

Rate of albumen formation

The weight of the albumen of the egg leaving the magnum and entering the uterus is approximately one-half of the laid egg. During the first 6-8 hr in the uterus, the increase in weight of albumen is rapid and fairly constant; after this time there is little change in weight, however, and most of the albumen is formed.

The formation of the inner and outer thin layer begins as the egg enters the uterus; this is at the expense of the thick or gel-like layer. After the egg has been in the uterus for 18-20 hr, the volumes of the outer and inner thin albumen approximate 5 and 9 ml, respectively. The final volume of the thick albumen is now only 58% of what it was when it left the magnum. An increase in the outer thin layer implies a decrease in the volume of the thick layer, but such a decrease does not occur until about the twelfths hour. This suggests that while the egg is in the uterus, water is added at a more rapid are than its diffusion into and through the thick white.

The great decrease in thick albumen occurring during the first 5-6 hr in the uterus is caused mainly by the addition of water, the slight but progressive decrease thereafter particularly after shell is formed, is mainly a result of the breakdown of mucin, the constituent that makes albumen thick. With the addition of water through the shell membranes to the thick albumen, there is a corresponding decrease in the percentage of solids, mainly protein, during the first 4-6 hr there is no change thereafter.

Stimulation of albumen formation

The stimulus for the magnum and other parts of the oviduct to elaborate albumen, shell membranes, and shell is believed by many to be a reflex reaction to the passage of a body or object through the oviduct. The pressure of the yolk stimulate the magnum to secrets albumen, and the amount formed is believed to be related to the size of the yolk. There are cases on record, however, of the secretion of albumen by isolated loops of the oviduct while an egg passed through the intact portion of the tract and of yolkless eggs containing albumen. Stimuli other than mechanical therefore appear also to be concerned in the secretion of albumen.

Nervous control of and the effects of drugs on albumen formation

That the ovary and oviduct are innervated by autonomic system has been noted, but the role of these nerves in albumen secretion has not been determined. Sturkie et al. (1954) studied the effects of sympathomimetic and parasympathmimetic drugs on the secretion of albumen. Among the drugs they used were ephedrine sulfate (sympathomimetic) and acetylcholine (parasympathomimetic). The drugs produced minor but insignificant changes in most instances. The result suggest that sympathetic and parasympathetic nerves play a minor role in albumen formation in the magnum.

Effects of disease, environment, and heredity on formation and deterioration of albumen

High environment temperature decreases the amount and viscosity of the albumen of laid eggs. Respiratory ailments, such as Newcastel disease and bronchitis, cause deterioration of the thick albumen in laid eggs. The duration of the effect of bronchitis irus on albumen quality apparently depends on the type and ivrlens of the strain, because some birds recover fairly soon after an attacks of bronchitis, whereas other persist in laying poor eggs indefinitely.

By selective breeding strain of chickens have been developed that differ markedly in the amount of thick and thin white produced in the egg.

It is well known that the thick albumen of normal freshly laid eggs deteriorates with age, length of storage, temperature and other factors. This suggests that freshly laid eggs containing albumen of low viscosity (thin, watery albumen) may result also from the breakdown of mucin in the isthmus and uterus. Results obtained by Sturkie and Polin (1954), discussed in the section on albumen layer formation, support this view.

Shell Membranes

There are two shell membranes, an inner one and an outer one. Each consists mainly of the protein keratin, with minute amounts of carbohydrates of various sort. Hydroxproline is in both membranes. For details of ultrastructure of the membrane.

The inner membrane is formed first. An egg partly extending into the isthmus can be observed to have the membrane (inner) formed on that part of the egg. By the time all of the egg is in the isthmus, the outer membrane is believed to have been formed. Data from other sources tend to support this view.

The amount of membrane formed in relation to the time the egg moves into the isthumus and the time it remains there has been studied by a number of workers. The relation of the rate of protein formation in the membranes to the distance that the center of the egg has traversed in the isthmus is a linear one, according to Burmester (1940). The membranes are semipermeable and permit the passage of water and crystalloids.

Copulation and Fertilization

Copulation in birds consists of the transfer of semen from the cloaca of the male to the cloaca of the female. In most male birds, only a very small, erectile phallus occurs, and coition involves nothing more than close apposition of cloacas of the two sexes. In a few groups such as ratites, tinamous, and ducks and geese, a fairly large, erectile, and grooved penis occurs to aid in copulation. In the ostrich this organ may be as long as 20 cm. Perhaps because of the relative inefficiency of sperm transfer in most birds, the semen contains a high concentration of spermatozoa. It has been reported that as many as 8.2 billion sperm per ejaculate are produced by some domestic roosters.

Once deposited within the female's cloaca, the semen may be stored in a sac within the vagina. Although fertilization may occur just several hours after copulation, in many species peak fertility occurs several days after copulation. Because of their ability to store viable sperm, females can remain fertile for periods of several weeks following copulation. One of the events that occurs at the time of fertilization is sex determination. The sex determination system of birds is the reverse of that found in other vertebrates. Female birds produce two types of eggs, ones with a male sex chromosome and ones without. All sperm contain the male sex chromosome. The egg with a male sex chromosome with produce a male when fertilized; the egg without the male sex chromosome will produce a female when fertilized. Thus, the female gamete is the one that determines the sex of the offspring.

The sex organs of both male and female also contain several endocrine glands in the interstitial tissue surrounding the germ cells that produce sex hormones that affect both development and behaviour. We shall discuss these further when we look at the timing and synchronization of breeding events.

Egg Laying and Incubation

Egg laying

Once a female has reached the egg-laying stage, an egg is laid each day in most species until the clutch is complete. Larger birds such as geese, swans, herons, hawks and owls may lay eggs at about two-day intervals, while some species lay in even longer intervals. Eagles and condors exhibit four to five days interval between eggs, and five to seven days may elapse between the first and second eggs of some seabirds. Most species lay their eggs in the morning, presumably because the shell has formed and formed and hardened overnight when the hen is not active, but there is a great deal of variability in the time of laying both within and between species.

The number of eggs in a clutch is also quite variable both within and between species. Most species within a particular region exhibit a typical clutch size, although this varies somewhat with age and time of nesting. Young birds in general lay smaller clutches than older birds, and first clutches during the breeding season are generally larger than second clutches. For example, the Great Tit (*Parus major*) has an average clutch size of ten eggs in April nestlings, and only seven eggs in June nestlings.

The mechanisms that determine when the bird will stop laying and start incubating are not fully known. Some species are determinate layers; that is, a certain number of follicles mature within the ovary each spring, and once these have been laid, the clutch is complete, regardless of the number of eggs actually in the nest. Other species are indeterminate layers, because they have the capacity to keep laying eggs well beyond the number in a typical clutch. Normally; these species must use visual or tactile cues in concert with hormonal adjustments to stop laying. If eggs are removed from the nest, though, they will lay eggs for long periods. Unfortunately, so much variation occurs among birds that one cannot clearly classify all species as either determinate or indeterminate layers.

Incubation

When the clutch is completed, incubation of the eggs commences. The heat required to raise egg temperature to the optimal levels for embryonic development is usually provided by the parents through incubation. Little heat is produced by the embryo, except at the end of incubation. Only in rare cases is the incubation provided by a non-parent, or even, as in the case of the megapodes, by decaying vegetation. Developing embryos are quite sensitive to fluctuating temperatures, so the parent bird must control the thermal environment of the egg through various behavioural and physiological adjustments. Optimum temperatures for development in 37 species averages 34°C. Temperatures above 43°C for just 1 hour are lethal for embryonic Heerman's Gulls (*larus heermanni*), and development of most avian embryos ceases below 25°C. Several studies have shown how the amount of incubation by the parents is directly related to ambient temperatures. In general, incubating birds adjust the heat delivery to their eggs by varying the time spent in direct contact with them, not by raising their own heat production to warm the eggs. In order to maintain egg temperature at about 35°C, parental attentiveness (i.e., sitting on the eggs) increases with decreasing air temperature below 25°C and with increasing air temperatures above 35°C. At air temperatures between 250 and, 35°C, parents allow the eggs to passively heat or cool. The result of these adjustments is a surprisingly uniform thermal environment for the developing embryo. This is more easily managed when both parents share incubation responsibilities, so that while one is on the nest, the other can leave to forage and rebuild its

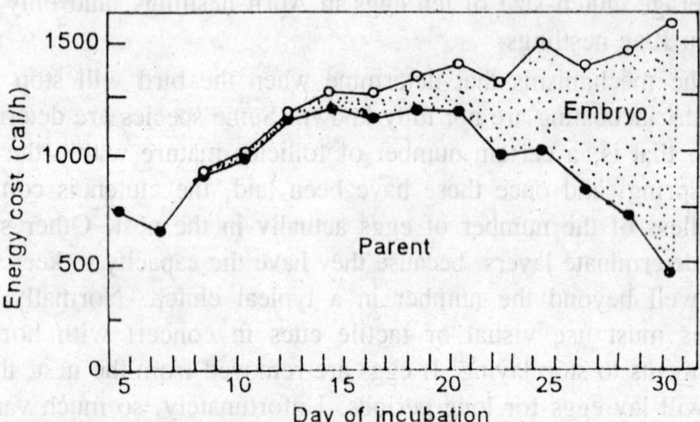

Fig. 6.7. Contribution of parental and embryonic heat to the regulation of egg temperature during incubation of Herring Gulls.

own energy stores. The eggs of single sex incubators are much more likely to vary in temperature over the course of the day when parent must leave the nest to forage. The amount of time spent incubating also varies with the stage of development. Parental attentiveness (as measured by the per cent of time spent incubating) increases during the first one third of the incubation period in *Herring Gulls* (*Larus argentatus*). In this case, external heat supplied by the parent plus the heat generated by the embryo itself help maintain the embryo temperature between 37° and 38°C. Only in larger birds do embryos generate more heat through growth late in development than they lose through evaporation, and consequently, less incubation is required at this time. In similar eggs, such as those of the House Wren (*Troglodutes aedon*), heat produced by the embryo does little to elevate egg temperature.

Heat is probably more threatening to embryonic development than chilling temperatures, and overheating by direct solar radiation of the nest can occur in any climate. Some species have developed means of regulating eggs temperature under hot conditions. In cases where external temperatures are warm but no extreme, parent bird may not incubate but will simply shade or perhaps fan the eggs. In more extreme cases, though, the contact between eggs and incubating bird can be used to cool the eggs, or at least to prevent them from reaching a lethal temperature. Heat from the egg is transferred to the parent who dissipates it through radiative, convective, or evaporative means. Studies with the Double-banded Courser (*Rhinoptilus africanus*), a ground nester of the *Kalahari Desert of Africa*, showed that parent birds shaded but did not incubate eggs when temperatures were between 30°C and 36°C, but employed constant incubation for maintaining egg temperature at air temperatures above 36°C. Similarly, White-winged Doves (*Zenaida asiatica*) nest is open desert and despite intense solar radiation and air temperatures up to 45°C maintain egg temperatures at 39.2°C by constant incubation. Interestingly, these doves accomplish this without resorting to panting or gular flutter; the means by which they dissipate heat during incubation is not known. In extreme case, a few open-habit, ground-nesting species bring water to the eggs by wetting their feathers. This both cools the nest and provides a moister environment for development. The Egyptian Plover (*Pluvianus aegyptius*) incubates its eggs at night but covers them with sand as the air warms in the morning. During the heat of the day it drops water onto the sand from its soaked ventral feathers, and evaporation keeps the egg temperatures at about 37.5°C, compared to nearby sand temperatures of 46°C.

In cold habitats, birds must incubate continuously to maintain the large thermal gradient between egg temperature and air temperature. Cold climate creates energetic problems for incubating adults because of the restriction of their foraging time. Several adjustments are made by species that regularly nest under these circumstances. Some species of hummingbirds, which are small, single-sex incubators, employ temporary hypothermia at night when ambient temperatures fall below 0°C. This, is course, slows down embryo development. Other small-bodied birds circumvent the potential energy drain of thermoregulation at night by utilizing the nest microclimate to buffer the decline in air temperature. The air temperature in nests placed in cavities, caves, or even within dense conifers, which can greatly diminish the heat lost by radiation and convection from the surface of an incubating bird, may be as much as 10°C warmer than air outside the nest. In other single-sex incubators, such as the Great Horned Owl (*Bubo virginianus*), which nests during the middle of winter in the temperature zone, the male brings food to the female both during incubation and during the early nesting stages. Sometimes, however, the parent is forced to abandon its eggs in order to forage at great distances from the nest, leaving the eggs to chill in the nest. Some species of procellariiforms, for example, neglect their eggs for hours or even days while they are foraging. Their embryos tend to be very resistant to chilling, but the effect of this intermittent incubation is reduced hatchability and a greatly prolonged incubation period.

Incubation depends on intimate contact between the incubating birds and the eggs, so that the heat generated by the adult is passed to the eggs. This interaction can be viewed as though the eggs were simply an additional appendage and the parent and eggs were a single unit. The site of heat transfer between parents and eggs is the incubation or brood patch which is usually found on the lower breast and abdomen of the bird. The area is generally characterized by a lack of feathers edema leading to flabbiness of the superficial skin and thickening of the epidermis, and an increase in the number and size of blood vessels and the musculature around these vessels. All of these modifications increase the efficiency of heat transfer between egg and parent by allowing closer contact of the skin with the egg and by increasing the amount of heat present at the surface of the well-vascularized brood patch.

In most species, the brood patch develops through the hormonal influence of prolactin, which is secreted by the anterior pituitary gland, and estrogen, which is secreted by the ovary.

Prolactin causes defeathering of the region, and estrogen produces epidermal thickening and vascularization. In many water-fowl the brood patch is actually plucked by the bird, and the downy feathers are used to insulate the nest. In pigeons, the brood patch occurs in a region without feathers (a trait possible in part because all pigeons and doves have clutches of only one or two *eggs*). In some species, the brood patch consists of distinct regions that are egg-sized and arranged as the clutch is arranged. For example, gulls have three distinct brood patches to match their typical three-egg clutches. In many species both sexes develop brood patches to aid in incubation; among these are the grebes, albatrosses and relatives, pigeons, woodpeckers, shore-birds and cranes. Only the female has a brood patch in the galliforms and owls; only he male has a brood patch in phalaropes, jacanas, and some sandpipers. In these latter cases, occurrence of a brood patch reflects the type of mating system in which the female defends the territory and the male incubates. Among the hawks and passerines, there is great variation in the occurrence of brood patches, with many species having patches in both sexes and many with only the female incubating. Much of this variation may also reflect mating and parental care characteristics. Only the pelecaniform seabirds, some of the auklets, and the Bank Swallow (*Riparia riparia*) do not develop a brood patch. Many of these are burrow nesters, and the insulative properties of the burrow may preclude the need for a brood patch. At least some of the pelecniform species use their very large, webbed feet as the heat exchange organ in place of an abdominal brood patch.

Through the interaction of incubation and the thermal environment provided by the nest, the parents attempt to provide the nest, the parents attempt to provide the proper developmental environment for the eggs. At the same time, through both properties of the nest and various behavioural patterns, the parents also attempt to keep predators away from the eggs and the nestlings.

Egg Structure and Embryonic Development

Once an egg has been laid, the parents are unable to provide any nutrients to the young bird until the egg hatches. How is the egg constructed so that it can provide the proper medium for development of a young bird? What can or (in most cases) must the parents do to aid the proper development of the embryo within the egg until it hatches? How much variation occurs in the processes of egg development and the final product, a baby bird?

As we attempt to answer these questions, we must remember that a bird egg starts out as a single cell composed of all the appropriate nutrients needed for development but with very little structure. The process of growth within the egg consists largely of the incorporation of these nutrients into the embryo.

Egg structure

Since the whole purpose of an egg is the production of a young bird, let us start our look at egg structure with the embryo. When the egg is laid, the embryo is a tiny spot called the germinal disc, which sits on top of the yolk mass. The embryo remains at this location even when the egg is moved, because the yolk floats freely within the egg. The yolk of a chicken egg has a definite structural organization. A whitish layer of yolk within the center of the mass is highly proteinaceous. Yellow yolk is stratified in concentric layers around this core and is composed largely of lipoprotein and proteins that are the main nutrient source of the embryo. The yolk mass makes up 20% - 65% of the egg, depending in part on the type of development (altricial or precocial).

Surrounding the yolk are the 'whites,' or albumen. Albumen makes up about 65% of the egg mass inprecocial species and is composed entirely of protein and water. It is arranged into three compartments. Immediately surrounding the yolk is the chalaziferous layer, a thick, viscous layer that forms twisted fibrous strands (chalazae) that anchor

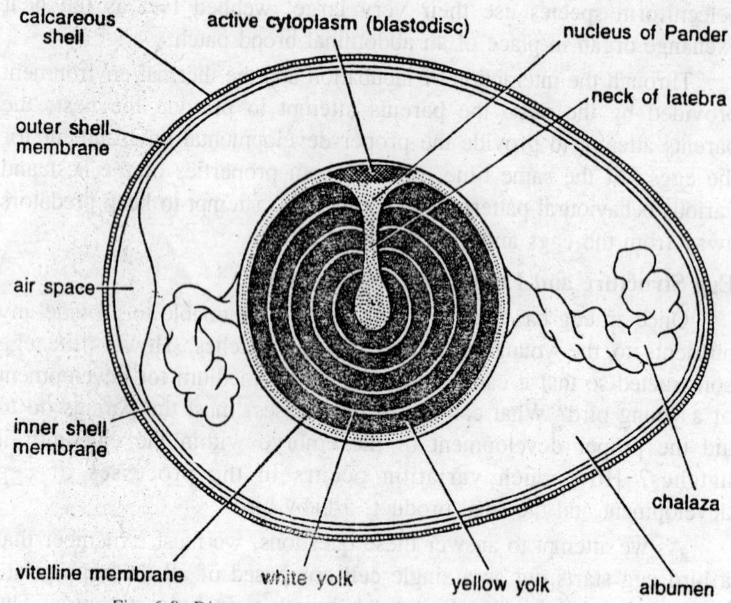

Fig. 6.8. Diagrammatic longitudinal section of a hen's egg.

the yolk to the poles in the long axis of the egg. Next is an inner, thin, watery layer of albumen around the yolk, and then a middle layer that is much thicker and more viscous, and finally an outer, thin, watery layer. The differences in the various layers lies only in the amount of water or fibrous ovomucin protein they contain. The yolk is suspended in these layers of albumen yet anchored so that, as the egg rotates, the embryo stays on top of the yolk. The albumen is also important for several other reasons; it provides an aqueous environment for development, it retards desiccation, it has some antibacterial properties, and it provides an additional nutrient source for the embryo.

Surrounding the albumen are two fibrous shell membranes made of another protein, keratin. The inner membrane rests on the surface of the albumen and holds this watery layer of the egg together. The outer layer is about three times thicker and has elements of the external shell anchored in it. The two layers separate at the blunt end of the egg, where they create an air space that enlarges during development, as yolk is absorbed by the embryo, and provides the first air to the baby bird prior to hatching.

The calcareous shell is the external barrier, and it serves a variety of functions that require some compromises in structure. For example, the shell should be hard enough to keep the egg from breaking easily under the weight of the incubating parent, but not too hard for the hatchling to break through. It must be porous enough for diffusion of oxygen into the egg and carbon dioxide out of it, but not so porous that the embryo desiccates or that bacteria can enter the egg. To accomplish all this, an organic (protein) framework serves as a skeleton for deposition of inorganic minerals, 98% of which are crystalline calcite (C_2CO_3). The mineral is arranged in vertical columns, between which are minute air spaces that open to the surface as oval or cimular pores. There are thousands of these minutes pores over the surface of the shell; estimates range from 6000-17,000 in a chicken egg. Apparently these pores function in gas exchange, because recent studies have shown that the number and sizes of pores varies with altitude and climatic conditions. The pore size and density greatly influence the rate of gas exchange (O_2, CO_2, and water vapor) across the egg shell and are a measure of the shell's conductance or diffusivity. Eggs laid under hurnid or hypoxic (low O_2) conditions, such as in burrows, or under vegetation (megapodes) often have elevated conductance in order to facilitate movement of O_2 to the embryo (and CO_2 from the embryo). The greater potential for water loss from the egg is not realized in this case because of the higher humidity surrounding the egg.

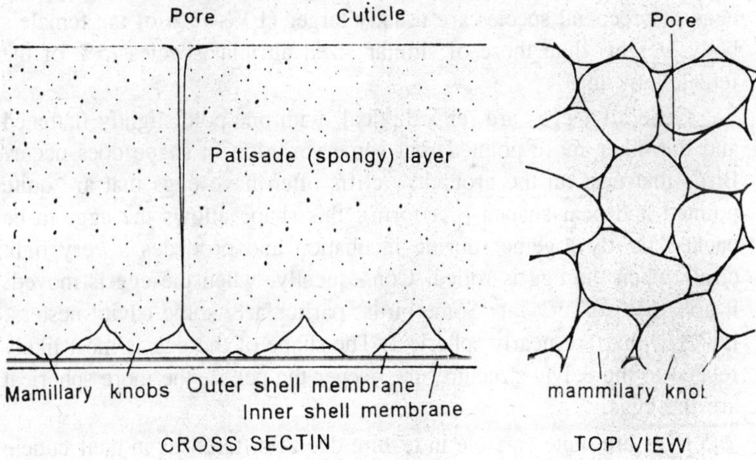

Fig. 6.9. Structure of an avian eggshell and location of the pores.

The outermost covering of the egg is the cuticle, which imparts the characteristic surface texture of the egg. The adaptive significance of the various outer coverings of eggs (glossy, greasy, chalky, ridged, powdery) is not known. The cuticle has been most thoroughly examined in chickens, in which it is a thin, continuous layer of glycoprotein over the entire shell, including the pores. It imparts water repellent properties to the egg surface, and impedes both water loss through the shell and bacterial entry. All of the above structures results in an eggs that is, at the time of laying, about 65% water, 12% protein, 10% lipid and 11% mineral.

Egg size and shape varies with the type of bird that lays the egg. The larger egg known to man was that of the Elephant Bird (*Aepyornis Maxima*) of Madagascar, which had a capacity of more then 9% and measured 34 by 24 cm. The smallest egg known is that of a hummingbird, the Jamaican Emerald (*Melisuga minima*); the egg is only 1 cm by 0.65 cm and its mass is 0.5 g or about 1,50,000 of an Elephant Bird egg. Many factors influence the size of bird eggs. Generally, larger birds lay larger eggs, but the size of the egg relative to its parent decreases with increasing size of the bird. For example, an ostrich lays an egg that is about 1.8% of its body weight, while a wren lays one that approaches 14% of its weight. Many exceptions to this general trend occur, though. For example, the kiwi lays an egg that is about 18% of its body weight, rather than the 3% expected for a bird of that size. Birds lay larger eggs as they get older, and the eggs of precocial species are usually larger (10%-15% of the female's body weight) than those of similar sized altricial species (5% of the female's weight).

Generally, eggs are semielliptical, with one pole slightly flattened and the other more pointed, but some variation in shape does occur. Birds that nest on the ground or cliffs often have eggs that are quite pointed and pear-shaped (pyriform); this shape allows the eggs to be packed tightly together during incubation and produces a very tight circle when the egg is rolled. Consequently, when the egg is moved, it does not go very far. Some birds, particularly some cavity nesters, lay eggs that are nearly spherical. The shape of the egg is most likely related to the pelvic structure, the deeper the pelvis, the more spherical are the eggs.

Eggs are quite variable in texture due to differences in their cuticle layer, as discussed above. Egg colour is also highly variable. While it has been suggested that these colours are merely a means of excreting metabolic waste products, it is more likely that their primary function is a protective one – to camouflage the eggs and so shield the developing embryos from incident UV radiation. Support for the latter view is the fact that egg colour of hole-nesting species, which typically experience lower predation and little to no incident solar radiation, is usually white. The colour and pattern of markings on the eggs of the Common Murre (*Uria aalge*) is extremely variable and may aid the parent in locating its single egg within the densely populated nesting colony on rocky ledges. *Oniki* (1985) proposed that the brightly coloured eggs of the tinamou allowed the parents to find all the eggs after they had been protectively camouflaged with leaf litter. However, the main benefit of egg colour is protection against predation, accomplished by camouflage. For example, blue eggs in dark nests that are placed in isolated areas receiving partial sun seem to imitate the sports of light on green leaves in a forests. Buff-coloured eggs occur in birds that lay them in leaf little or on other dull but well-lighted substrates. Spotted white eggs occur in thinly formed nests. In poorly lighted spars foliage, where the egg tends to vanish against its speckled background.

Table 6.1. Egg Weight as a Proportion of Female Body Weight

Species	*Adult female body weight*	*Egg weight*	*Egg weight body weight (%)*
Ostrich	90,000	1600	1.8
Emperor	30,000	450	1.5
Mute Swan	9000	340	3.8
Snowy Owl	2000	83	4.1
Peregrine Falcon	1100	52	4.7
Mallard	1000	54	5.4
Herring Cull	895	82	9.2
Puffin	500	65	13.0
Robin	100	8	8.0
House Sparrow	30	3	10.0
House Were	9	1.3	13.7
Vervain	2	0.2	10.0

Embryonic Development

The development of the embryo begins with cell divisions almost immediately after fertilization. The second meiotic division of the voum occurs after penetration of the sperm. The male and female pronuclei fuse to form the zygote nucleus, and the first cleavage division occurs three to five hours after fertilization while the egg is in the magnum and the inner layer of albumen is being added. The second cleavage division coincides with the laying down of the shell membranes in the isthmus. By the time the egg reaches the uterus, it has reached the 16-,cell stage, and when it is laid, the embryo consists of a double-layered blastula oriented at right angles to the long axis of the egg. In most cases, embryonic development is suspended after an egg is laid, then resumes with the regular application of heat to the egg through incubation. It is beyond the scope of this book to examine the many details of embryonic development, but we do want to look at general patterns of development and the requirements for them.

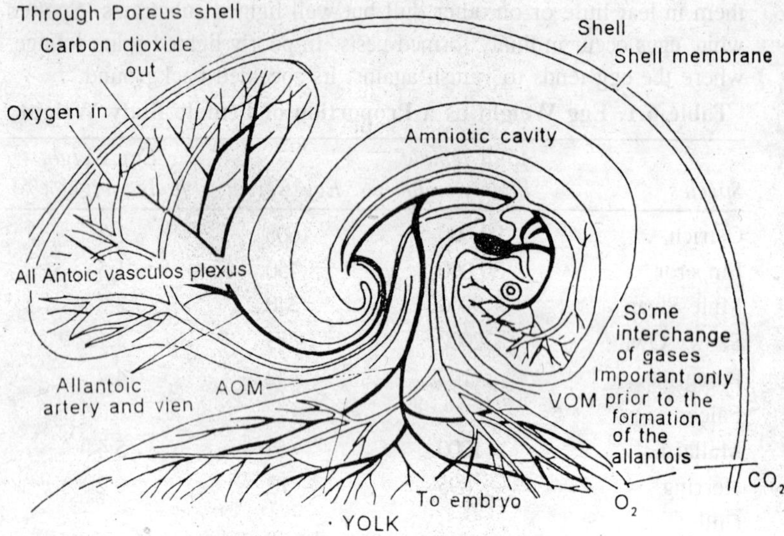

Fig. 6.10. Embryonic membranes and circulation.

Early in its development, the embryo becomes enveloped in the amniotic layer, which forms a fluid-filled chamber around it and protects it. Next, cells grow downward and envelop the yolk, forming a yolk sac; veins develop on the surface of the yolk sac which transport nutrients from the yolk to the embryo. Shortly before hatching the yolk sac is drawn into the body so that stored nutrients are still available after hatching. In many species, hatchlings can live for several days on stored reserves from the yolk. Finally, in the early development of the embryo a third membrane develops, the allantois. This grows out as a pouch from the hindgut to line the inner surface of the shell membrane, where it serves as both a bladder, or waste depository, and as a respiratory organ. A rich supply of blood vessels develops in the allantois in close proximity to the shell and facilitates gas exchange. The arantois also serves as a depository for nitrogenous wastes, generally in the form of uric acid salts. By excreting uric acid into the allantois, the avian embryo can avoid the potential toxicity of accumulated nitrogenous waste and conserve water at the same time. (See the discussion of water conservation by uric and excretion). The uric acid salts form crystals, which are simply stored outside the embryo until hatching.

The optimal development of an embryo requires the appropriate gaseous environment, an external source of heat, and he proper egg position, including in most cases, turning of the egg. The gaseous environment is controlled by gas exchanged through eggshell pores. The outward diffusion of CO_2 and inward diffusion of O_2 is of primary importance movement of water vapor from the saturated interior of the egg to the less humid microclimate of the nest must also be regulated. Variation in the construction of the eggshell between species enables all avian embryos to be exposed to roughly the same conditions. In fact, experiments on domestic fowl have shown that levels of oxygen less than 15% or greater that 40% (normal is 21% of atmospheric air) or CO_2 levels greater than 1% (normal is 0.03%) greatly retard embryonic development. As a consequence, despite large variations in egg mass, incubation period, climate, geography, and so forth, avian embryos complete their development with similar water losses (about 16% of the initial egg mass). Similar gas pressure gradients across the shell, and similar O_2 and CO_2 content in the air cell before hatching (Carey 1980b). Hatchability depends on the consistency of these parameters during development.

Development also requires parental (or other) input of external heat energy in order to maintain egg temperature at an optimal 37°-38°C. We have pointed out that temperature tolerances of embryonic development are rather narrow, and it should be noted that the optinial development temperature is very close to the lethal temperature for avian embryos (above 43°C). In addition, tolerance to temperature extremes declines with development; embryos close to hatching cannot stand the extremes that a freshly laid egg can.

Not only must parents provide the heat for incubation but they must manipulate the eggs so that each receives uniform heat. A temperature gradient of as much as 5.6°C was measured between the central and peripheral eggs in the clutch of the Mallard (*Anas platyrhynchos*). Turning the eggs is also important to prevent adhesion of the membranes to the shell early in development. Repositioning of eggs also aids the development of its equilibrium position. At first, the yolk mass is free to revolve in the shell and the embryo remains uppermost because it floats on a lighter portion of the yolk. Later, however, the extrembryonic membranes fuse with the shell membrane, and the embryo position becomes fixed in the shell with the head oriented toward the blunt pole and the air space. The egg then becomes asymmetric in weight, and will always assume a certain orientation, embryo uppermost, when it is rolled in the nest.

The time required for embryonic development is variable among birds, even among birds of similar size and taxonomic affiliation. Generally, large birds lay larger eggs and have longer development times than small birds. However, other factors affect the length of incubation and embryonic development. Young birds at hatching are not equivalent developmentally. Woodpeckers, for example, hatch at an early stage, compared to small passerines, and although their development time would appear short, they are not as mature as other altricial nestlings with longer development. The same is true when comparing precocial and altricial young. Precocial young have much longer development times than altricial young do, but their organ systems are much better developed, and they can essentially feed and take care of themselves soon after hatching. It has also been suggested that birds exhibit some ecological adjustment of embryonic development, such that open nesting birds have shorter development times than hole nesters. This may occur because of the higher predation pressures on open nesters, and the need to hurry the developmental as well as the subsequent nestling growth process.

Hatching

Hatching is obviously a critical stage in the development of a baby bird, for it involves escape from the confinement of the shell and conversion from the embryonic to adult form of such physiological processes as breathing, excretion, and so forth. The shift been functional systems must be done fairly quickly.

Hatching success is highly dependent upon the proper position of the embryo within the egg. During the days before hatching, the embryo assumes, what is known as the "tuck" position, with the head between the right wing and the body and with the bill pointed toward the blunt end of the egg. From this position, the first act of hatching involves

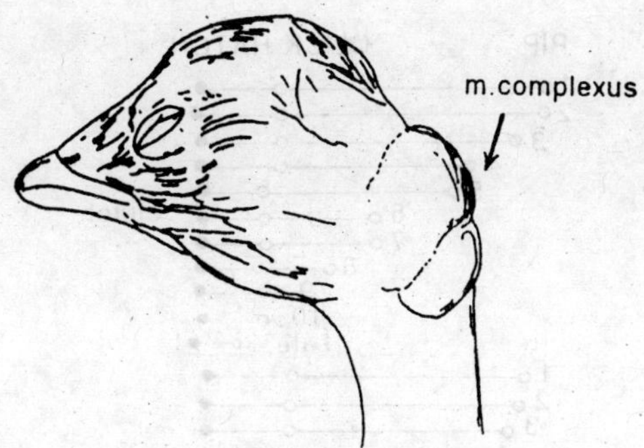

Fig. 6.11. The hatching muscle in a chicken on the day of hatching.

puncturing the air sac and the initiation of lung breathing by the embryo. This stage occurs a day or two before actual hatching. Pipping, or shell breakage, also occurs from this position. The first pip may occur ten hours or more before hatching as the result of a random movement of the embryo. At some point, this movement becomes much more active and involves strong thrusts of the beak into the shell accompanies by propulsive movements of the entire body by pushing with the feet. In the process, the embryo rotates within the shell causing a ring of cracks near the blunt end. This process is aided by specialized structures in the full-term embryo: a horny knob or egg tooth on the upper mandible, and hatching muscles on the back of the head that are responsible for the vigorous back thrust of the head during pipping. Both structures either fall off or regress shortly after hatching. Usually one rotation within the egg will sever the cap of the egg, although two or three rotations have been observed in some birds. Eventually, the embryo will break off the cap and the thrusting motion will push the baby bird out of the shell, but this may take several hours to even several days in albatross chicks.

Embryonic development is a series of chemical processes whose rates are a function of the external heat provided. However, if heat were the only factor that affected development, one would expect to find variation in hatching times of the eggs in a clutch that reflected differences in their laying times. This is not the case. For example, eggs taken from a Mallard nest, shortly after completion of the clutch, were incubated and hatched over a span of 16 hours. In the wild, a clutch of Mallard eggs usually hatches over a period of only two to eight hours. The male Rhea (*Rhea Americana*) incubates the eggs of several females, and although eggs may be deposited in a nest over a two-week period, or even added after incubation is started, the entire

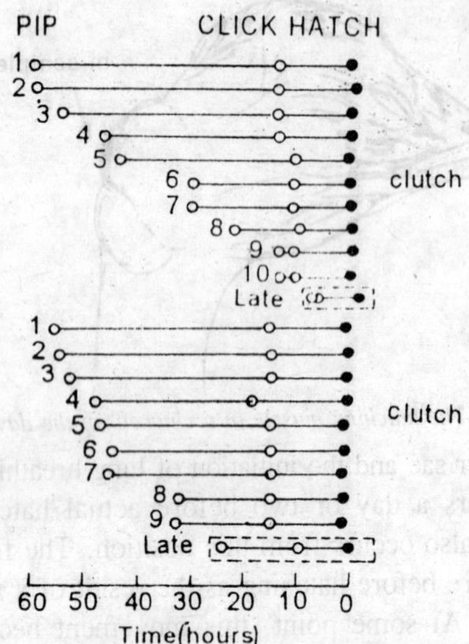

Fig. 6.12. Events which may determine hatching synchrony in two-clutches of the Bobwhite Quail (Colinus virginianus).

clutch usually hatches within two to three hours. It is obvious from these observations that some sort of behavioural modification by the embryos synchronizes the final hatching process. Studies of how this might be accomplished have focused on gallinaccous birds and waterfowl, where the hatching synchrony is critical because the parents lead the young from the nest soon after hatching. All young birds emit a clicking noise just prior to hatching and shortly after they develop the ability to breathe. The clicking apparently synchronizes the hatch by speeding up the final development of nestlings that are somewhat behind in the hatching process and perhaps by retarding the movements of the more advanced individuals. Thus, through acoustic communication between the embryos, hatching of the entire clutch occurs in a minimal period of time.

Stage of Development at Hatching

Up to this point, we have looked at a general pattern of development, but most everyone knows that baby chickens are different from baby robins in how thy behave and in the amount and type of care they require. While baby chicks or ducts may be good pets for children, one would not want to give a child a clutch of recently hatched robins or bluebirds as pets! Obviously, the extent of development during incubation varies among birds.

Recently, hatched birds have been classified into several developmental categories. *Precocial* young are those that hatch with their eyes open, are downy-covered, and have the ability to leave the nest in a matter of a few hours or a day or two. Some precocial chicks actually grow up independently of their parents, but others follow their parents (walking and or swimming) and are either fed / or shown food by the parents. Ducks, chickens, grebes, and many sandpipers have precocial young; they are also described as *nidifugous*, or nest fugitives, for their behaviour of leaving the nest. *Altricial* birds are those at the other extreme; they hatch with their eyes closed, have little or no feathering, and require great amounts of care and feeding. Most passerines and other small birds fit into this category; these young are also termed *nidicolous*, or nest dwellers, because of their prolonged occupancy of the nest.

Within these groups two other categories are regularly recognized. *Semi-precocial* birds hatch with their eyes open and have a downy covering, but, although able to walk, they do not leave the nest and are generally fed by their parents. Included among these are gulls and terms. *Semi-altricial* birds are somewhat less developed than the above; they are down-covered but are not able to leave the nest. The semi-altricial nestlings of hawks and herons hatch with their eyes open, while those of owls have their eyes closed.

The difference in the product that hatches reflects differences in egg composition between precocial and altricial birds; eggs of precocial young often have larger yolks than those of attricial young, and much of the yolk remains at hatching as an internalized yolk sac. More important, however, is how growth is apportioned to the various organs

Mode		Down	eyes	Mobility	Parental nourishment	Parantal attendance	Examples
Precocial	1	○	○	○	○	○	Magapodes
	2	○	○	○	○	●	Duckc chorebirds
	3	○	○	○	○	●	Quail, grouce
	4.	○	○	○	◓	●	Grebes rails,
Semi-Precocial		○	○	◓	●	●	Gulls terns
Semi-altricial	1	○	○	●	●	●	Herons howks
	2	○	●	●	●	●	Owis
Altricial		●	●	●	●	●	Passeriness

Fig. 6.13. Variation in the characteristics of precocial, altrical, and two intermediate types of nestlings.

of the body during embryonic development of precocial and altricial young. Altricial nestlings hatch with still relatively immature organ systems. Only the digestive tract is well-developed at hatching, enabling them to maximize their assimilation of food. In contrast, the precocial hatchling is a minimize adult with relatively mature organ systems that allow even a new hatching to stand immediately, to run from predators, and to seek its own food.

Nesting Development

Growth of Altricial vs. Precocial Nestling

Most young birds grow rapidly at first, but their growth rate slows as they approach adult size. The pattern for most birds is one of a sigmoidal-shaped growth curve. Although the shape of the curve and the actual daily growth rates may vary greatly between species, this is a consistent pattern of growth in all birds.

The gradual diversion of food energy from primarily growth to maintained and activity during development is the basis for the signoidal shape of the growth curve. The illustrate this point, we shall describe some characteristic features of the nestling development of altricial young and compare their development with that of precocial young.

After hatching, altricial nestlings are totally dependent on their parents for food and for maintaining their body temperature. During the first third of the nestling period, the young move about very little but begin to have better control of their head and neck; feathers emerge

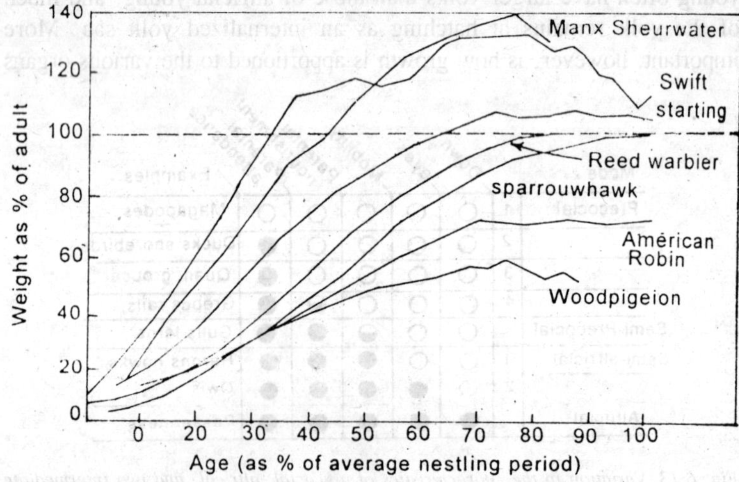

Fig. 6.14. A comparison of growth curves of young of several species.

and begin to grow but the body is still largely devoid of insulation. The nestling have little control of their body temperature when exposed to cold at this early stage. Because most of the energy ingested goes into building tissue, they young can achieve very high growth rates. During the next third of the nestling period, feathers cover more of the bare skin and they young begin to shiver and to move around in the nest. With better insulation and more heat production from the musculature, the young now exhibit better control of body temperature during cold exposure. They are alert to external cues and exhibit appropriate innate behaviours (e.g., begging from the parent, crouching in fear). During the final third of nestling development, feather development is completed, temperature and sensory responses become acute, and the young exercise in the nest, preparing themselves for flight. More intensive foraging efforts by the parents for these large and voracious nestlings means that they young must expend more energy regulating their own body temperature. Consequently, the ingested energy channeled into growth decreases and the growth rate slows. Increased activity of older nestlings is another source of energy diversion away from growth, but most nestlings are close to adult size at this time.

Although the growth curve of precocial nestlings is sigmoidal, the growth rate is only about one-third that of altricial nestlings. As we have discussed, precocial young can walk, see, and feed themselves soon after hatching. They also are able to thermoregulate with limits. This means that they must apportion more of their daily energy to maintenance and less to growth; the further development of their relatively advanced organ systems leaves even less energy for overall growth. Finally, these young must move around ton feed and to escape predation, and some energy must be diverted away from growth and into activity costs.

The marked differences in developmental rates between attricial and precocial nestlings suggest two major options in reproductive strategies among birds. Those with altricial young can produce offspring rather rapidly due to their high growth rates, but these young require extensive amounts of care, including brooding to keep them warm, and must be provisioned with high energy foods. This strategy also carries a higher risk of predation, and the parent risks losing all of its reproductive investment during the nesting period.

In contrast, precocial young are at risk from predation only during the incubation period, because nestlings can usually avoid predators from time of hatching on, and rarely are whole clutches lost. Precocial young do not require as much care as altricial young, since they often need only to be guided to appropriate feeding locations and protected (often just through warning) from predators. The primary cost in such a seemingly easy strategy is a longer embryonic and nestling development period than that of altricial young; as a consequence, it is more difficult to rear more than one brood per breeding season. Young precocial birds require access to prey that is fairly easy to capture, but their reduced growth rates also mean that they can survive on somewhat lower-quality foods than altricial young. The above factors both tend to release the parents from some of the constraints of care that are related to the number of young, so that bids with precocial young tend to lay larger numbers of eggs in a clutch.

Factors Affecting Growth Rate

After hatching, the development of most baby birds is dependent on various features of parental care and a set of external and internal constraints that limit growth; diet and food availability, predator pressure, climate, internal allocation of energy in the young, even biochemical processes all have an impact on growth rate. Generally, small birds grow more quickly than large ones, young in open nests grow faster than those in cavities, temperature zone birds mature faster than their tropical counterparts, species at high altitudes mature faster than those at sea level, and young fed insects develop more quickly than those fed a fruit diet.

Explanations for the intraspecific variation in growth rates among young birds focused on several of these constraints. British ornitholotgist *David Lack* (1968) regarded growth rate as a balance between predation pressure selecting for rapid growth and food supply selecting for slower growth. Lack proposed that young birds exposed to high risk of predation should grow as fast as possible in order to outgrow this possible mortality factor. The Lack hypothesis is supported by the slower growth rates found in hole or cavity nesters (low predation pressure) compared to that in open nesting birds (high predation pressure) in similar areas. In addition, Lack hypothesized that growth rate of the young is adjusted to the food the parents can provide. A slower growth rate in hole nesters means that less food is required per young per day, which in turn implies that parents can therefore raise larger broods of young. In fact, hole nesters do have larger broods. Other groups exhibition slow growth include those that live on predator-free islands and those whose young can run away from predators, all of which support the Lack hypothesis.

American ornithologist *Robert Ricklefs* (1969) was not convinced by Lac's arguments and retested the hypothesis that growth rates were optimized by mortality patterns of each species. A clear correlation of growth rate and mortality was absent in the many species be examined. Ricklefs further countered that food requirements do not increase proportional to increases in growth rate. For example, doubling the growth rate of the slow-growing Leach's storm-petrel (*Oceanodroma leucorhoa*) would increase the energy required for growth only 5%.

The Lack hypothesis also does not explain why most tropical birds with high nest predation have slower growth rates than their temperate counterparts, with comparatively lower nest predation. Lower inetabolic rates of tropical species and the lower nutritional quality of their diet could be responsible. In fact, tropical birds that feed their young fruits, which may be of poor nutritional quality, tend to have slow-growing offspring.

In contrast, nestlings fed highly nutritious food, such as insects, grow more rapidly. The protein deficient diet of young petrels fed an oily regurgitant by their parents has been proposed as one of the reasons for their slow growth. However, parental choice of highly nutritional items for their young should generally rule out the nutrition hypothesis for all but a few species.

Organismal constraints on growth rate may be set by the young bird's ability to assimilate the ingested food. The size of the digestive tract is proportionally larger and is more mature in altricial young than in precocial young. This disparity of development between the two groups leads to the conclusion that altricial young can assimilate more energy and thus can grow faster than precocial young. *Perrins'* (1976) feeding experiment on Blue Tits (*Parus cacruleus*) also supports this hypothesis. To demonstrate that the slower growth of late broods of this species was related to the high concentration of oak leaf tannins in their prey, Perrins compared the growth rates of young reared on plain mealworms with that of young fed mealworms contaminated with tannic acid. The uncontaminated young gained weight faster and exhibited more intense begging activity and interest in food.

Ricklefs (1979) has proposed that two types of physiological constraints limit growth rates of birds. Biochemical and molecular constraints limit the extent to which functionally mature tissue can continue to grow and proliferate. Thus, growth rates are determined by a balance between the mature and embryonic functions of tissues. Generally, growth and differentiation are two competing and mutually exclusive processes in tissue development. That is, maturation of nerve and muscle tissue into a more refined locomotory system cannot be accomplished while muscles are growing in size and developing neuronal connections. This is the reason that growth slows as tissue matures and explains why, in altricial young, we see a rapid growth phase first, followed by a maturation phase of slower growth.

The second physiological constraint is a consequence of maturation of the tissues. Mature organ systems have higher maintenance costs, and a greater percentage of the assimilated energy must be diverted away from growth into maintenance. Similarly, on an oganismal level, as the young mature, more of their assimilated energy is diverted into thermoregulation and activity, leaving less for growth.

Fledging

The growth and development process generally stops when the offspring reaches adult size. In most species, at or near this point the process of fledging occurs when the young bird leaves the nest, learns to fly, and fends for itself Parental care often is terminated shortly after the young leave the nest; parents may refuse to feed a begging youngster, forcing it to look for food itself. Eventually the young learn to follow the adults and search where they are feeding, until finally they become completely independent. In some species, such as blackbird sand sparrows, large flocks of young birds form at the end of the breeding season; they roost together and may migrate together, separately from their parents. However, in some owls, the fledgling period is prolonged for months, as the young learn where and how to find their food under limited light conditions. Birds receiving extended parental care probably benefit either from avoiding food shortages while sill inexperienced, or from learning how to forage.

Timings of Reproductive Products

In an evolutionary sense, birds should breed at the time when they can produce the most offspring that can survive to breed in the future. In the temperate zone, this is usually during the spring or summer when temperatures are moderate and food is abundant. Even in the tropics, the wet-dry seasonal cycles affect nesting seasons. Rather than focus here on the ultimate, evolutionary factors affecting the timing of nesting (many of which we shall discuss later), we shall address the proximate factors that determine breeding time. Given that evolution mandates that June, for instance, is the time to nest, how do birds synchronize the many changes necessary to initiate the breeding process and advance from one stage of reproductive behaviour to the next?

The synchronization of the stages in the reproductive cycle is complex. Initiation and termination of one stage are requisite for proceeding to the next: arrival of spring migrants is followed by establishment of territory which leads to courtship of the female, ovulation, completion of the clutch, incubation, and so forth. This sequencing is rather rigid in birds; that is, individuals at one hormonal stage in the cycle may be unresponsive to external stimuli associated with another stage. For example, during the nest-building stage, adults may be completely unresponsive to the begging stimuli of nestlings placed in their nest.

Photoperiod Control of Reproduction

In the temperate zone, the external cue that most often initiates the development of the reproductive organs and start of the breeding process is an increasing photoperiod, that is, an increase in the amount of light each day. Factors such as rainfall, social conditions, or food supply may also affect the initiation of breeding, but often these serve as final cues for the fine tuning of the reproductive response. In some species, however, these factors may be the primary cues used to initiate reproduction. For example, in the Red-billed Quelea Finch (*Quelea quelea*), rainfall and green vegetation seem to be the proximate inductive factors. These birds migrate across Africa following the rains

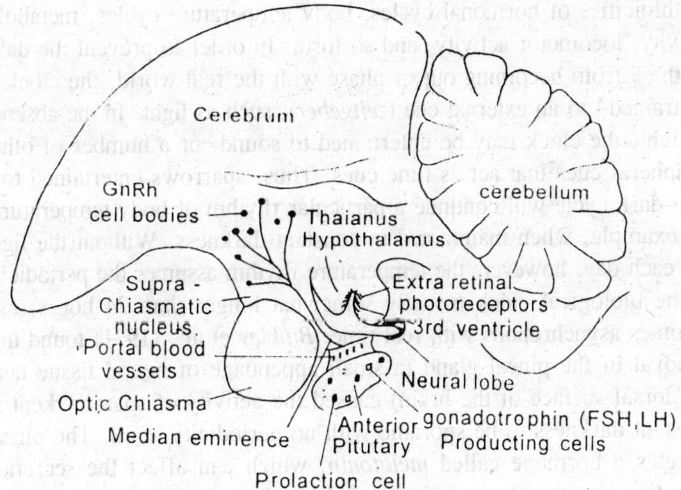

Fig. 6.15. Sagittal section of the avian brain showing the structure of the hypothalamus and pituitary, external area of photosensitivity (hatch lines), and location of neurons which manufacture GHRH and other releasing factors for pituitary hormones.

and stop to breed wherever and whenever the females can store enough energy reserve to produce a clutch of eggs.

To use day length to regulate reproductive function, birds must have photoreceptors and some means of measuring time. The eyes are the most logical photoreceptor, but it has been demonstrated by many investigators that the eyes are not essential, at least in testicular development. In a classic experiment, *Benoit* and *Ott* (1944) used a quartz rod to direct light of various wavelengths directly to the brain of blinded mallards and found that the maximal testicular growth occurred with red light directed toward the hypothalamus. In fact, the hypothalamus was 100 times more sensitive to photostimulation than was the retina. Other researchers have used luminescent beads or optic fibers to deliver light to selective areas within the brain and have found that stimulation of the ventromedial hypothalamus with light produced the greatest response of gonadal (testis) growth.

The existence of a biological clock for measuring day length, or even longer periods of time up to a year, has been documented for both plants and animals, beginning with Bunning's experiments in the 1930s. The structures that comprise the clock are the pineal, the suprachiasmatic nucleus (located in the hypothalamus above the optic chiasm), and perhaps the retina as well. The biological clock is responsible for maintaining the internal (endogenous) daily (circadian) rhythmicities of hormonal cycles, body temperature cycles, metabolic activity, locomotor activity, and so forth. In order to prevent the daily rhythms from becoming out of phase with the real world, the clock is "entrained" to an external cue (*zeitgeber*), such as light. In the absence of light, the clock may be entertained to sound, or a number of other peripheral cues that act as time cues. Thus, sparrows entertained to a light-dark cycle will continue a particular rhythm of body temperature, for example, when maintained in constant darkness. Without the light cue each day, however, the temperature rhythm assumes the periodicity of the biological clock (usually somewhat longer than 24 hours) and becomes asynchronous with real time. *Binkley* et al., (1971) found that removal of the pineal gland (a small appendage of neural tissue near the dorsal surface of the brain) caused the activity of sparrow kept in constant darkness to be sporadic with no periodicity at all. The pineal secretes a hormone called *melatonin*, which can affect the secretion or action of other brain hormones. Even in culture and in darkness, the pineal gland releases melatonin rhythmically, with peaks with peaks occurring about every 24 hours.

In addition to the endogenous circadian rhythms already mentioned, there is a circadian rhythm of photosensitivity. A particular physiologic event may be induced when light is received during the photosensitive period. Based on this, it is easy to see how changing day length might initiate the entire cascading series of events in the reproductive cycle. At present there are two theories that explain how light induces reproduction.

The *external coincidence* model states that gonadotrophin release, for example, occurs when light is coincident with the photoinducible phase of the daily cycle. *Hamner* (1963) exposed photosensitive male House Finches (*Carpodacus mexicanus*) to light-dark cycles of varying length to test this model. The duration of light in Hamner's experiments was always six hours, but the total length of the cycles ranged from 12 to 72 hours. At the end of the experiment, birds kept under 12, 36, and 60- hour regimes had large testes, while birds kept under 24 (the control), 48-, and 72-hours regimes had tests of the normal immature size. The daily photoinducible phase continued to oscillate in birds kept in darkness for as long as 66 hours (the 72-hour regime). The

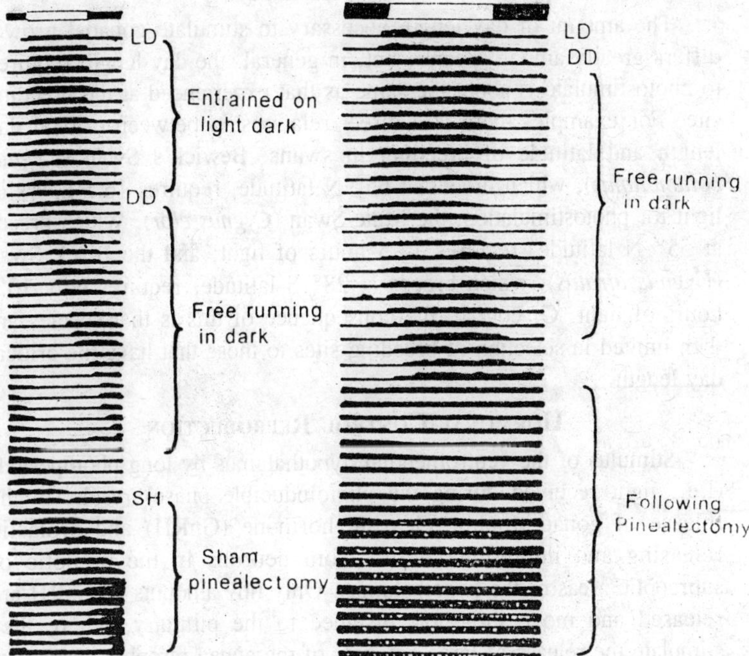

Fig. 6.16. Circadian rhythms of body temperature in House Sparrows (Passer domesticus).

reason that gonadal growth occurred in the 12, 36-, and 60-hours treatments was that the six-hour light period occurred during the photoinducible phase. When the light occurred only during the first half of the cycle, there was no stimulation.

The internal coincidence model assumes that changes in photoperiod will cause changes in the temporal relationship of two or more cireadian rhythms. A specific temporal between the two rhythms induces the physiological process. For example, *Meier* and *Ferrell* (1978) have found that injection of prolactin 12 hours after the daily rise of plasma corticosterone promoted fattening, gonadal growth, and northward-oriented migratory restlessness in White-throated Sparrows (*Zontrichia albicollis*), all characteristic of a spring-breeding bird. In contrast, injection of prolactin 8 hours after the rise in corticosterone in these birds resulted in no fattening or catabolism of fan no gonadal growth, and no migratory restlessness, which is more typical of a midsummer-breeding bird. The two coincidence models are not mutually exclusive, but are both useful in understanding the initiation of reproductive events, because some of the processes seem to be better explained by one model and other processes by the other model.

The amount of day length necessary to stimulate gonadal growth differs greatly among species, but, in general, the day length required to photostimulate is about the same as that experienced at the breeding site. For example, there is a direct relationship between critical day length and latitude of breeding in swans. Bewick's Swan (*Cygnus columbianus*), which breeds at 65° N latitude, requires 16.5 hours of light for photostimulation, the Mute Swan (*Cygnus clor*). Which breeds at 55° N latitude, requires 14.5 hours of light; and the Black Swan (*Cygnus atratus*), which breeds at 28° S latitude, requires only 10.7 hours of light. Of course, the consequence of this is that species are then limited in selection of breeding sites to those that have the critical day length.

Hormonal Control Reproduction

Stimulus of the ventromendial hypothalamus by long photoperiods (i.e., light received during the photoinducible phase) results in the release of gonadotrophin-releasing hormone (GnRH) and prolactin releasing and inhibiting factors from neurons in the prepotic or supraoptic areas of the hypothalamus. Only tiny amounts of GnRH are released and move the short distance to the pituitary, where they stimulate the release of large amounts of the gonad-otrophic hormones, luteinizing hormone (LH) and follicle-stimulating hormone (FSH) into the general circulation. FSH stimulates the development of the gametogenic aspect of the gonads and promotes the production of mature ova and sperm. It also promotes the growth of the steroidogenic interstitial tissue of the gonads, but LH is responsible for stimulating the synthesis of the steroids (androgens and estrogens) and their release into the blood. In the male, the interstitial tissue (*Leydig cells*) secretes testosterone; in the female, the granulose and thecal cells that surround the ovum secrete progesterone and estrogens, respectively. These steroids circulate through the blood to the secondary sex organs (eg., the oviduct of the female or the vas deferens of the male) and are responsible for the growth, vascularity, and secretory nature of these structures during reproduction. They also circulate back to the brain, where they affect the further production of GnRH in a dynamic manner, and also affect other behaviour such as courtship, nest building, singing, and territoriality. Because these changes occur rather rapidly following a period of sexual quiescence, this stage is called the *acceleration phase* of reproduction.

Following a period of gonadal growth, the ovarian follicles mature and begin to secrete less estrogen and more progesterone. Progesterone has a positive effect on LH secretion and causes plasma LH levels to rise, culminating in a preovulatory spike that causes ovulation. The wave of maturing follicles causes plasma progesterone levels to rise each day and LH levels to rise with it, each speaking about 4-6 hours before ovulation. Birds generally lay their eggs at the same time each day, which is a reflection of the circadian rhythm of ovulation.

However, in some birds, notably the domesticated fowl, it takes longer than 24 hours from ovulation to oviposition, and consequently, eggs are laid later each day, until eventually, the timing of the LH surge does not fall within the sensitive period (4-11 hours following the beginning of the dark cycle), causing the bird to miss an ovulation or skip a day's egg production. However, we must remember that daily egg production in all birds depends on the hen's ability to accumulate or mobilize her own resources rapidly enough to produce eggs.

Expulsion of the egg (ovipositor) involves the relaxation of abdominal muscles and muscular contraction of the shell gland, the vagin and the cloaca. Two hormones of the posterior pituitary gland induce oviposition in the laying hen, oxytocin and arginine vasotocin (avian ADH). Both hormones cause contractions of smooth muscle in both birds and in mammals. In chickens, stimulation of the preoptic area of the brain will cause premature expulsion of an egg, via release of posterior pituitary hormones.

The ovulation-oviposition cycle continues until the clutch is complete. How this is determined is not fully understood. High levels of progesterone may eventually inhibit ovulation by negative feedback on GnRH release from the hypothalamus. Visual and tactile cues are also important in the termination of egg laying, but how birds perceive that their clutch is complete remains a mystery. During egg laying, levels of prolactin (secreted by the anterior pituitary) rise and this hormone may also have an negative effect on GnRH release and thereby suppress further ovulation.

Once the clutch is completed, incubation procedes. Most females incubate with greater intensity as the clutch increases in size, perhaps as a result of increasing levels of prolactin during laying. Brood patch development also progresses during laying, as rising levels of prolactin and estmgen and progesterone secreted by the ovary promote defeathering and vascularization of the ventral abdominal area. In phalaropes, in which the male incubates, testosterone and prolactin stimulate the production of a brood patch. Contact with the eggs promotes further increases in plasma prolactin, which in turn promotes more intense incubation efforts. When high levels of prolactin suppress the release of gonadotrophic hormones, the ovaries regress in size and the unovulated, yolky follicles are resorbed.

The role of prolactin in avian reproductive behaviour beyond this point depends on the species. In birds with altricial young, prolactin levels rise somewhat throughout incubation, peak shortly after hatching, and then decline. In birds with precocial young, such as the turkey, prolactin levels drop rather sharply after hatching, presumably because less parental care is required in this species. High levels of prolactin are maintained in adult pigeons and doves for the first week after the young hatch; in these species prolactin stimulates the production of a specia! crop secretion, "pigeon's milk," which is fed to the young.

Termination of Reproduction

To maximize its fitness, a species should have evolved control mechanisms to terminate reproductive activity when it is no longer energetically feasible to produce young and in time to complete its preparation for winter. In many species, the reproductive effort is terminated by a period of *photorefractoriness*, or insensitivity to long photoperiods. Often this occurs when day lengths are still long and, perhaps, even before a summer solstice. But the ecological advantage of such a control is that it allows the young time to grow and mature during a period when food is abundant, and it allows the parents time to complete the postnuptial inolt and to fatten before migrating or over wintering. Through a variety of experiments with male White-crowned Sparrows (*Zonotrichia leucophrys*), *Farner* and *Gwinner* (1980) concluded that it is not possible to induce any of these latter events without previous exposure to long days; thus, it appears that both reproductive and post reproductive events are driven by the same photoinducible stimulus. In species that breed only once per year, individuals that have fledged young enter what, is called an *absolute refractory phase*, in which hey are insensitive to a long photoperiod. This phase is usually short but is followed by a *relative refractory phase* during which individuals remain sexually inactive although they may be responsive to long photoperiods (demonstrated experimentally). The latter state may last for several months, usually through the winter in temperate species, after which the cycle is repeated with the natural increase in photoperiod. Many birds must go though a photorefractory period to be photostimulated again.

We have implied that photorefractoriness occurs in all birds following fledging of young. In fact, some species can produce several broods in a season. These birds start breeding in early spring and delay photorefractoriness until late summer or autumn. In multiple brooded species, external stimuli related to the development of the young of the adequacy of the environment for rearing young must reinitiate the reproductive process. The gonads do not regress completely in these species, and this shortens the period between nestlings. Pigeons and doves continue to produce young as long as climatic conditions allow, irrespective of photoperiod. This group also is known to omit the refractory phase in the reproductive cycle.

There are exceptions to the normal pattern of termination of reproduction. In the reproductive effort is prematurely terminated by nest or mate loss early in the cycle, many species can renest. The speed with which renesting occurs depends on a variety of factors, including the stage of the cycle in which the interruption occurred, the physiological state of the female, and the availability of mates.

Coordination of the Reproductive Cycle with Other Events of the Annual Cycle

All of the above physiological phenomena associated with breeding are energetically expensive, yet they are necessary to produce offspring. For temperate birds, and especially those that migrate, termination of breeding may partly be explained by the demands of the events in the annual cycle that follow reproduction. Some optimal balance of time and energy must be developed to complete the annual cycle.

Following the breeding season birds undergo a postnuptial molt, premigratory or prewinter fattening, and migration. All of these physiological events must be squeezed in between fledging young and the first frosts of winter. Most birds must undergo their annual molt at this time simply because energy demands at other times of the year are too high. For example, high costs of thermoregulation in the winter coupled with diminished food resources preclude having enough energy to molt then. Costs associated with breeding and spring migration obviously rule out a complete molt at these times. This leaves only the period immediately prior to breeding, and some species do undergo partial body molts at this time to acquire their brightly coloured breeding plumage. However, an energy-demanding complete molt prior to breeding would deplete the energy reserve that is required for spring migration and for a successful reproductive season. These constraints leave the post breeding period as the best time to undergo a complete molt. The advantage of a postnuptial molt is that the new set of feathers provides residents with better insulation for winter and provides migrants with new flight feathers to speed their travel south.

The cost of the autumn migration is a further constraint limiting the reproductive period of migrants. Migrants must accumulate extensive fat reserves before leaving the breeding site, and this cannot be accomplished until both reproductive efforts and molting are completed. Birds may use various environmental cues, such as weather or food supply, to judge the efficacy of further reproduction in the face of the energy-demanding events that follow.

7

BREEDING AND NESTING

In reproducing their kind, birds frequently show great ingenuity, whether it's the blackbird nesting in the garden shed, the stork on the chimney pot or the falcon on a sky-scraper. Many have adapted well to a world now dominated by man, but millions of years before *Homo sapiens* first walked the earth birds had already learnt to build nests and rear young in virtually every natural niche on earth. Despite the rigours of having to protect fragile egg in frequently hostile environments, they nest in every continent, from arctic ice to waterless deserts where no man could endure. All lay eggs, but not all make nests. Some are born blind, naked and helpless, but other batch 'ready to go'. Most are good parents, but others show surprising lack of care and a few parasitic species have learnt to hand the entire business of baby care over to foster parents.

Largest Tree Nest in the World

Bald Eagle's – up to 2.9 ml (9.5ft) wide and 6 m (20.0 ft) deep: If we take the popular meaning of nest – a structure made by a bird from natural materials such as twigs and grasses, and containing a cup or cavity in which eggs are laid or incubated – then the largest are undoubtedly made by some of the birds of prey which use the same site year after year. The very largest of these are generally made by the bald eagle (*Haliaeeius leucocephalus*) and the biggest known as 2.9 m (9.5 ft) wide – more than enough for the tallest man in the world to lay across with his arms outstretched – and an incredible 6 m (20 ft) deep. This monotrous fortress at St Petersburg, Florida was almost certainly added to by several pairs, about 3 m (10 ft). The next weighted more than 3,000 kg. (2.9 tons). Another bald eagle nest at Vermilion, Ohio reached 2.59 m (8.5 ft) across and 3.66 m (12 ft) deep after 35 years. Eventually it crashed to the ground during a storm, killing the egglets inside. It had an estimated weight of 1,814 kg. (1.78 tons).

Most huge bird-of-prey nests occur in remote or inaccessible areas where the birds have nested undistributed for centuries. Those of the Australian white-beilled sea-eagle (*Haliaeetus leucogaster*) may be 2-3 m (7-10 ft) across and 4 m (13 ft) deep and traditional nests of the osprey along the Red Sea coast are atleast 1 m (3.25 ft) across and 2 m (6.5 ft) high. The largest nests in Britain are those of the golden eagle (*Aquila thrysaetas*) : in 1954 British naturalist *Seton Gorden* saw one in Scotland which was 4.6 m (15 ft) deep and had been in use for 45 years.

World's Largest Nest-Mounds

Scrub fowls, big footed relatives or the pheasants (*Phasiantidae*), mate for life and a pair inhabits a large territory. It is mostly the male, which works the mound. This begins with the digging of a hole up to 5 m (16 ft) in diameter and 1- 1.5 m (3-4.5 ft) deep. The mound may contain 3,00,000 kg (295 tons) of matter and the birds can move very large objects. A 1 kg (2.2 lb) scrub fowl was once seen to shift a rock of 6.9 kg (15.2 lb). During the winter this hole is filled with vegetation swept up from the ground over a radius of about 45 m (150 ft). When this is moistened by rain the whole is covered by a sandy soil 50 cm (20 in) or more thick. Sealed from the air, by solar heat. When fermentation heat is too much in the spring the birds need to open the mound frequently to let the heat escape and maintain the ideal incubation temperature of 34°C (93.2°F). In midsummer the sun's heat is most important, but this may be too much and then the thickness of soil has to be increased to prevent 'overcooking'. But by autumn the sun's heat is less and the fermentation heat is exhausted so he birds open and flatten the mound daily to let the sun's rays warm the eggs more easily. In this way the birds achieve precise temperature control over several months.

None of the 12 species megapode of Australia. New Guinea, Indonesia and Polynesia tises body heat to incubate eggs. The required heat comes from the decomposition of vegetable matter in the mounds, directly from the sum or even from volcanic upwellings. Where the mound temperature is naturally fairly constant some species leaves the eggs to hatch on their own, but most megapodes employ great skill in maintaining a remarkably constant incubation temperature so that the eggs are not spoiled through chilling or over-heating. The precise way in which they do this is uncertain, but one suggestion is that they gauge the incubation temperature with ultra-sensitive tongues.

In some areas scrub fowls are regarded as rain-prophets as they start to scratch their mounds together at the approach of rain in spring. But they will also begin work if rain falls in the autumn and will attend to mounds through practically the whole year, raking them over for essential temperature regulation and aeration.

Direction solar heat may be more important for the well-studied mallee fowl (*Leipoa ocellata*) of southern Australia as it breeds in dry places where, in the absence of rain, rotting of mound material is very slow. But for those species which live in dense, sunless jungles heat from decomposition is crucial. Yet some moisture is important in every mound to prevent the egg shells cracking.

The number of eggs laid varies from 5 to 35, the great variation being not only between females but also in the same individual from year to year. The interval between the laying of eggs depends on the nutritional state of the female but is often several days. They may be laid over several months but each begins the nine-week incubation immediately so that some chicks may leave the mound before the last eggs are laid.

The Largest Social Nest Sociable Weaver's-up to 300 chambers: The weaver family is well-known is well-known for its 'hanging sock' nests with tubular entrances as long as 70 cm (27.5 in) and as much as 10 cm (4 in) wide. One of the most remarkable is that of the sociable weaver (*Philetairus socius*), of south-west Africa which first constructs a roof of coarse straws in a tree or on a telephone pole and then makes as many as 300 nest chambers below. The ensuring mass can dominate an entire large tree and attract other species. The tiny pygmy falcon (*Polihierax semitorquatus*) is one guest but, although it feeds on small birds, it does not molest its hosts.

Probably the most remarkable of the social-breeding parrots is the South American monk parakeet (*Myiopsitta monachus*) which builds huge colonial twig nests in thetops of trees. Within the main structure each pair has its own nest chamber. In Birds of La Plata (1920), *Hudson* noted that such a clump can 'weight a quarter of a ton and contain enough material to fill a large cart'.

The largest roofed nest hammerhead stork's – up to 2 m (6 ft) wide and 2 m (6.5 ft) deep: More popularly known as the hammerkop, the African hammer-head stork (*Scopus umbretta*) defies accurate classification and is not closely related to the storks. It prefers to build its huge nest of twigs, grass and mud about 12-15 m (40-50 ft) up in a tree. An through the nests are usually 1-2 m (3.25-6.5 ft) across, often of similar depth and take some two months to make, this industrious bird may make several in one season. No one knows why it goes to such great lengths to raise its young.

First a platform is constructed of sticks cemented with mud. Then the wall are raised and roofed over with a metre of thatch which may be decorated with feathers, bones, snake skins and other debris. The whole thing may contain over 10,000 sticks and easily support the weight of a man. The internal chamber, which is about 30-50 cm (12-20 in) in diameter and height, is very carefully shaped and large enough to house both parents and young. The entrance tunnel is 13-18 cm (5-7 in) wide and 40-60 cm (16-24 cm) long and heavily plastered with mud to get in. Where trees are scare the nest may be built on a cliff face or the ground, but man-made structures such as dams are also used.

The three to six young, fed by both parents, spend about seven weeks in the nest before fledging. When both birds feed the young they may leave them for long periods, and presumably the thick nest walls then provide good protection. Even after fledging the young remain near the nest for a month or so roosting in it at night. Many other species are also attracted to the massive nests, whether occupied or not. During construction some nests have been take over by Verreaux's eagle (*Aquadla verreauxii*), and grey Kestrels (*Falce ardostaceus*) and barn owls (*Tyto alba*) often evict the rightful owners from the finished nests. Many smaller birds such as weavers, mynahs and pigeons attach their own nests to the main structure. Other hole-nesting species such as the Egyptian goose (*Alopochen aegyptiacus*) and African pygmy goose (*Nettapus auritus*) soon take over the vacated nests, so overall the hammerkop provides important nest-sites for many birds which might otherwise have to fore-sake the habitat.

Small Builders of Big Nests

The Most extraordinary large nests for small birds are made by oven-birds (*Furnariidae*) (10-26 cm/4-10 in long). That of the rufous-breasted spinetail (*Synallaxis erythrothorax*) is made from thorns, with tunnels to the nest chamber. It is roughly oblong or retort-shaped and as much as 75 cm (30 in) long by 50 cm (20 in) wide. It has a large platform on the side which leads via a tunnel through a tangle of thorns to a thatched nest-chamber lined with downey leaves. That of the rufous-throated thornbird (*Placellodomus rufifrons*) has further chambers added in subsequent seasons and gives the impression of a large colonial nest. It is unlikely that spare chambers are used other than by non-breeding members of a previous brood. Also voluminous is the thornyn nest of the 21 cm (8.3 in) firewood gatherer (*Anumbius annumbi*) of Argentina. It measures about 70 cm × 30 cm (28 in × 12 in) and is made of big sticks with a crooked passage at the top leading down to the nest chamber. But the largest in this varied family is probably the huge, thorny nest of the white-throated cachalote (*Pseudoseisura gutturalis*), being up to 1.5 m (5 ft) in diameter. The enclosed structure has a cavity big enough for an eagle or vulture and strong enough for a man to stand on without damaging it. The brown cachalote (*Pseudoseisura lophotes*) of Paraguay, Uruguay and Argentina makes a nest the size of a barrel. Famous naturalise *W.H Hudson* noted that he could stand on the nests of some of these species and make no impression. Although these huge nests are conspicuous feature of open South American countryside little is known about the breeding because of the impenetrability of the structures.

The longest nest burrow the Rhinoceros Auklet's 8 m (26 ft): Why the 36 cm (14 in) Rhinoceros auklet (*Cerorhinca monocerata*) of the North Pacific should excavate such a long burrow is a mystery. This misnamed bird is actually a puffin and its range is from the coast of Kamchatka and the Kuril Islands and from the west coast of Alaska south to Washington. In winter it is found in Japan and Lower California. Its single egg hatches after about 40 days and the chick fledges after 40-50 days, having been fed on fish.

Strangest Nest-Sites

There are many fascinating nest-sites across the world, but the strangest must include that of the violaceous trogon (*Trogon violaceous*) of Central and South America. This bird takes over a wasp's nest, eats the adult wasps, then digs out the comb to make in nest cavity.

The water thick knee or dikkop (*Burhinus vermiculatus*) of Africa is equally unusual in frequently laying its eggs on the dried droppings of large mammals such as the hippopotamus.

Highest Tree Nest

The Marbled Murrelet's 45 m (148 ft): Kinglets (*Regulus*) and Lewis's woodpecker (*Melanerpes lewis*) nest at 30 m (100 ft) up in trees but the highest nest found so far is that of the marbled murrelet (*Brachyramphus marmoratus*) at 45 m (148 ft). A very strange situation indeed for a 24-25 cm (9.5-10 in) auklet. The single egg is laid in a small cup, made mainly of guano, on a pad of moss in large coniferous trees in remote areas upto 10 km (6 miles) inland. Only five nests of this common seabird have ever been reported. Whereas other auks breed in colonies, often huge, only the marbled and Kittlitz's murrulet (*Brachyramphus brevirostris*) nest in solitary pairs. No one had ever seen the nest of this bird until 7 August 1974 when one was found in a Douglas fir in Big Basin state Park, Santa Cruz Country, California. Kittlitz's murrulet is also exceptional for an auk in that it lays its egg on bare ground above the tree-line and far from the sea.

North American sequoias are the tallest trees in the world and may exceed 90 m (300 ft), but their tops seem to be avoided by birds and there are no records of any birds nesting at such a height.

Smallest Cup Nest in the World

The bee hummingbird's-thimble- sized: There is no doubt that the tiniest cup-shaped nests are made by hummingbirds. These are mostly fixed to twigs by cobwebs and built by the female alone. The narrowest is the thimble-sized cup of the world's smallest bird – the bee humming bird (*Calypte helenae*) of Cuba and the isle of Pines. But this is slightly deeper than that of the vervain hummingbird (*Mellisuga minima*) of Jamaica and Hispaniola, whose nest of lichen, silk and cotton is only about the size of half a walnut shell.

The female humming bird alone incubates the eggs and cares for the young. Except in three or four species, male humming birds do not even know the whereabouts of the nests. Some, such as the hermit humming birds, build hanging nests, attached by cobwebs to the undersides of large leaves, such as palms and ferns, so that the leaf forms the inner wall and they are sheltered from tropical downpours. Others, such as lancebills, metal-tails and hillstars, use cobwebs and glue to suspend their nests from the ceilings of caves or rocky overhangs. The deepest humming bird nest was the only one known of the blue-fronted lancebill (*Doryfera johannae*), which was pendent structure attached by cobwebs to a rocky overhang near the bottom of a 75 m (250 ft) shaft.

Many birds make no nest at all and lay their eggs on bare rock or earth, or even in a tree cavity. Some scrape together a few woodchips or merely make a depression in vegetation or shingle. The (25 cm in) fairy tern (*Sterna nereis*) of Australasia lays its single egg on the rare branch or leaf of a tree, or on coral boulders and cliffs. In the absence of a nest to contain it, the young has strong claws which enable it to cling tightly and even range upside down.

Palm swifts also make tiny nests, one of the smallest being that of the 10.5 cm (4 in) pygmy palm swift (*Tachornis furcula*) of Colombia and Venezuela. The Asian palm swift (*Cypsiurus batasiensis*) and African palm swift (*Cypsiurus parvus*) build any open nests on the insides of palm eggs are glued to the nest with saliva. The nest is made from feathers and fibres and has a small lower rim for the bird to perch on while it incubates vertically.

Most Valuable Nests in the World

The cave swiftlets: Cave swiftlets (*Collocalia*) are best known for providing the Chinese with their esteemed birds' nest soup. While all swifts and swiftlets use saliva to glue their nests together, species of *Collocalia* use saliva as the principle ingredient, though some incorporate feathers, leaves and other materials in varying proportions. Those most prized for soup making are made of pure saliva, and include the little nests of the grey-rumped swiftlet (*Collocalia francica*), which do not require extensive cleaning. The crop of such nests may be both valuable and extensive. In one year alone over 3.5 million nests were exported from Borneo to China. The nest sell for about £ 3 each and it takes two to make a single bowl of soup selling for up to £ 10 a bowl. The nests have no nutritional value and tasteless, but are highly regarded as an aphrodisiac.

The colonies in vast Asian caves my contain several hundred thousand individuals whose nests of dried saliva are often stuck to the roofs and walls of caverns in total darkness up to 400 m (1300 ft) or more from the entrance. Collection of them can be very hazardous, involving ropeways and ladders up to 100 m (330 ft) high. But the swiftlets have no trouble in negotiating the bird-filled blackness because they have developed the faculty of echolocation to a higher degree than any other bird species.

The well-studied edible-nest swiftlet (*Collocalia inexpectata*) has two peaks of maximal breeding activity: October-December and February-April, and the nests take about 30-40 days to build. Even without the cropping by humans, breeding success is poor as they can fall prey to cave crickets which eat the eggs and sometimes the young. Many other nestings fall and are eaten by snakes, while those in houses may be eaten by rats and shrews.

The vast colonies also provide another valuable resource – the droppings (guano) which accumulate on the cave floor and are mined for use as fertilizer. But neither this nor taking the nests endangers the swiftlets' population. Rights to the caves are jealously guarded and nest removal has been carefully controlled for many centuries, even long before the first white man set foot in the area.

Largest Egg of any Living Bird

The Ostrich's – up to 17.8 cm (7 in) × 14 cm (5.5 in): The largest egg of any living bird and the biggest single cell in the animal world today is that of the ostrich (*Struthio camelus*), the world's largest living bird. There is considerable variation among the races but the North African birds generally lay the largest eggs, up to 17.8 cm × 14 cm (7 in × 5.5 in).

As with all species, egg-size is linked to individual female size, heavier individuals producing larger eggs, and is genetically controlled and inherited. Thus exceptional eggs do occur throughout Africa. One from Lake Jipe at the south-west corner of Tsavo (West) National Park in Kenya was 17.1 cm (6.7 in) long, 13.6 cm (5.35 in) across, 49.1 cm (19.3 in) round the long circumference and 43.7 cm (17.2 in) round the short circumference. It weighed 1,974 gm (4.35 lb) fresh weight. This was the largest of 600 eggs weighed and measured in East Africa and considerably larger than any of 100 measured on an ostrich farm at Oudtshoorn in South Africa. Most North African ostrich eggs are about 15.5 cm (6.1 in) long by 13.5 cm (5.3 in) across and weigh about 16.5 kg (3.63 lb).

Ostrich eggs are very strong, with a shell some 1.6 mm (0.063 in) thick, resisting the attentions of most predators, even playful lions, but Egyptian vultures (*Neophron percnopterus*) have learnt to crak them with stones. One egg is equal in volume to some two dozen hens eggs and takes about 40 minutes to boil.

Despite its great size, the ostrich egg represents only about 1% of the female's body weight. Other species lay eggs which represent up to 25% of body weight. Smaller specimens are laid by females breeding for the first time, but the oldest birds sometimes revert to laying smaller eggs. Scarcity of food may also restrict the size of eggs are less successful at producing strong fledglings.

Large as they are, ostrich eggs are much smaller then preserved eggs of the extinct *Aepyornis maximus*.

Largest Egg Proportionate to the Layer

The little spotted Kiwi's-25% of the female's weight: As a proportion of the female's weight, the largest egg is laid by the little spotted kiwi (*Apteryx owenii*) of New Zealand (now known on only three offshore islands). The average 35 cm (113.8 in) female has a body weight of about 1.2 kg (2.6 lb), about 20% heavier than the male, and her eggs weigh 275-370 g (9.7-13 oz), with an average of 310 g (10.9 oz) - about 25% of her body weight. Average dimensions are 108.5 × 71 mm (4.27 × 2.79 in). Eggs of the North Island brown kiwi (*Apteryx australis*) are larger at 330-520 g (11.6 - 18.3 oz), with an average weight of 440 g (15.5 oz) (125.5 × 78.5 mm 4.94 × 2.76 in), but represent just 18-22% of the female's body weight.

Eggshell thickness varies considerably between species and this significantly alters the internal volume. The shell of the larger emu (*Dromaius novaehollandiae*) egg (635 g/22.3 oz, 525 ml/1.05 pt) is about four times and the shell of the ostrich (*Struthio camelus*) egg (1,240 g'43.7 oz, 985 ml/1.97 pt) about eight times the weight of the kiwi eggshell. Total weights, therefore, exaggerate the size differences between the kiwi egg and the eggs of larger ratites, as the weight of the ostrich egg is nearly three times the weight of the kiwi egg, but its internal volume is only about 211, times as great. The average 53 g (1.86 oz) domestic chicken egg and a 435 g (15.3 oz) kiwi egg are both laid by birds weighing about 2.4 kg (5.29 lb). Not surprisingly, kiwi eggs take a long time to incubate 65-85 days, almost entirely by the male.

The little spotted is the smallest of the three species of flightless kiwi. The largest is the Stewart Island race of the brown kiwi (*A. a. lawryi*), which has females of at least 3.5 kg (7.71 lb) and is the only kiwi active by daylight. Kiwis are much smaller than the other ratites because they have no natural predators in New Zealand and therefore size is unimportant in defence. The high-protein diet also makes size is unimportant. As well as worms, this includes woodlice, millipedes, centipedes, slugs, snails, spiders and a wide range of insects, as well as seeds and berries - all highly nutritious.

Captive females have laid up to five eggs in a continuous series with an interval of about 33 days between each. In the wild, clutches are usually 1-2 eggs (rarely 3) and the egg is heavily yolked (61%) like those of other species whose chicks hatch active, open-eyed and fully-feathered.

Even though hen ostrich lays 12-15 of the largest eggs in the world, weighing in total 20-25 kg (44-55 lb), such clutches represent only 20-25% of body weight. Hummingbirds lay two eggs, each of which weighs about 13% of the female's body weight, but the proportion is even greater in the smaller, species.

In total contrast, the smallest of all clutches as a proportion of body weight is that of the emperor penguin (*Aptenodytes forsteri*) whose single-egg clutch represents a mere 1.4% of the female.

Smallest Egg in the World

The bee humming bird's - 6.35 mm (0.25 in) long: In terms of average weight or volume, the question of which hummingbird lays the world's smallest egg is unresolved as comparatively few eggs have been comprehensively and accurately measured, and among these there has been considerable variation. But in terms of length alone the egg of the world's smallest bird – the bee hummingbird (*Mellisuga helenaei*) of Cuba and the Isle of Pines – is the shortest, varying between 6.35 mm (0.25 in) and 11.4 mm (0.45 in) long. Those of the vervain hummingbird (*Mellisuga minima*) of Jamaica and Conave Island, Hispaniola are generally no smaller than 10 mm (0.39 in) long and 0.365 g (0.0129 oz) in weight.

However, abnormally small hummingbird eggs have also been reported for several species. These 'sports' or 'runts' are fairly common throughout the bird world and are generally thought to have been laid prematurely. One exceptionally small example of the Costa's hummingbird (*Calypte costae*) of south-west USA and north-west Mexico measured only 7.36 mm (0.29 in) by 5.33 mm (0.21 in) and contained no yolk. In the same nest at Escondido was a second egg which was slightly incubated and measured 12.7 mm (0.5 in) by 8.4 mm (0.33 in) Amazingly, the finder managed to blow the tiny egg and it is now preserved in the Western Foundation of Vertebrate Zoology at Los Angeles, California. The bird which laid the two eggs was just 8.6 cm (3.4 in) long.

Hummingbirds generally lay two (sometimes one) elongated, white eggs which may be very small to us but represent about 13% of the female's bodyweight. Incubation takes 14-23 days and the nesting period is 18-38 days.

Largest Clutch

Grey *Partridge's – average* 15-19 eggs: The largest single clutches are laid by those species with a high mortality and low average life expectancy. This is particularly marked among the ground-nesting partridges, pheasants and grouse, some species of which frequently lay over 20 eggs. The bobwhite quail (*Colinus virgininianus*) is often said to lay the most eggs, and indeed it produces between 7 and 28, but its average is just 8-15. This is considerably less than the wide-spread grey partridge (*Perdix perdix*), which usually averages at least 15-16, and in Ostrobothia, Finland the average is 19. Within many species clutches become larger with increasing latitude and longer summer days as there is a shorter breeding season with less time for successive broods but more daylight in which to feed a large family. The largest grey partridge clutch to a single hen reported in Britain was 25 in Sussex in 1974. Twenty-four chicks hatched and all were still alive at six weeks. Although it is through that clutch-size in most species is linked to the physical condition and age of the hen, it now seems that the amount of food the parents can collect for the potential brood is more important. There is also evidence that clutch-size is hereditary and that some individual females are either more experienced or more capable than others in caring for large broods.

Hole-nesting birds often lay more eggs than closely related species in more open sites, presumably because the enclosed eggs and young are safer. For example, the blue tit (*Parus caeruleus*), which has adapted so well to the widespread use of nest boxes, generally has the largest clutch of any nidicolous (having young bids that remain in the nest after hatching) species. An average of 11-12 eggs is normal for good habitats in Europe, but individuals may lay up to 19. In tits and many other species there is also some seasonal variation in clutch-size, the larger clutches generally being laid early to benefit from peak food abundance.

Many supposedly large clutches are due to 'dump-nesting' where two or more females have laid in the same nest. This is particularly common among game birds and other *Galliformes* as well as ducks, and the generally unmanageable nest is usually abandoned. This sometimes happens when females have no nest of their own or occasionally practice parasitism. Incubation is very occasionally attempted, though not when the egg pile reaches, intimidating proportions. For example, one North American redhead (*Aythya Americana*) nest contained 87 eggs! Some redheads are entirely parasitic, making no attempt to build a nest and laying all their eggs in the nests of other duck species. Others are partially parasitic and lay eggs in the nests of other ducks, before settling down to raise their own family. Yet others never practice parasitism at all.

Some species, such as anis (*Crotophaga*) nest communally and share the incubation. This is quite distinct from dumpnesting. Up to 29 eggs have been found in one ani nest and the socially dominant pair does most of the breeding. The anis of the Americas are related to the parasitic cuckoos (*Cuculidae*).

Ostriches (*Struthionidase*) have a fascinating system of communal nesting. The cock defends a large territory and acquires a mate who lays her eggs in a scrape. A few days later other hens arrive and also lay in the nest. Surprisingly, the first, or major, hen gets off her nest to let them in, but only she and her mate will incubate - up to 40 eggs! But even an ostrich cannot cover so many eggs and some get pushed to the edge. This was once thought to be a way of regulating the temperature of the eggs, but investigation has shown that the outer eggs get overcooked in the sun.

The major hen is able to recognize her own eggs (perhaps by the pore pattern in the plain white shell) and she rolls those of the minor hens to the edge. The 'rejected' eggs form a frontline defence against predators such as jackals and vultures, which can eat only a few eggs or chicks. This reduces the chances of the major hen's eggs being eaten and presumably strengthens the species as the offspring of the dominant major pair are likely to be more successful than those of the minor birds. But the minor hens gain in that although they have failed to set mates it is likely that at least some of their eggs will hatch.

By removing their eggs as they are laid, birds may be fooled into laying way beyond the normal clutch-size. In this way a hole-nesting common flicker (*Colaptes auratus*), a North American member of the woodpecker family, was once induced to lay 71 eggs in 73 days, also in the woodpecker family, the wryneck (*Jynx torquilla*) was made to lay 48 eggs instead of the usual 5-14. A house sparrow (*Passer domesticus*) l aid 51, mallards (*Anas platyrhunchos*) 80-146 and a bobwhite quail 128. Such stimulated laying is put to good use among domesticated birds such as the common chicken, which will lay for much of the year. And in protected environments, domesticated birds may be exceptionally successful with unusually large clutches. A muscovy duck once hatched 25 ducklings from a clutch of 31.

Many birds with relatively low mortality and high life expectancy lay single eggs. Some of the longest-lived birds, such as the three great albatrosses (*Diomedeidae*) and various large raptors, may breed only once in two years. The single egg laid in the summer produces a chick which is fed through the winter to fledge a year later - the lowest reproductive rate of any bird.

The redlegged partridge (*Alectoris rufa*), on the other hand, has a most unusual method of attaining high reproductivity. It is unique among British birds at least in that one female may lay two clutches in separate nests - one for her mate to incubate and one for herself so that each will raise a brood at the same time. The average clutch size is 10-15 but up to 28 have been recorded. The high rate of egg production is offset by increased losses, for, unlike the grey partridge, the red leg never covers its eggs when left and many are taken by predators. Surprisingly, clutches left for weeks and eventually incubated by the male are hatched as successfully as those incubated immediately.

Most Clutches, Eggs and Fledglings in One Year

The number and size of clutches, and of chicks surviving from each brood, are all governed by seasonal abundance of food. Some species particularly passerines, have a prolonged breeding season and the maximum number of broods raised in the wild is generally six. But there are reports of captive zebra finches (*Poephila guttata*) raising as many as 21 consecutive broods. In the wild this finch is an opportunist breeder, laying in dry parts of Australia at irregular intervals after rainstorms and continuing to breed until the weather deteriorates. But adults of all species are restricted by their own survival needs such as moulting and building up fat reserves for winter, and, for most, late broods do not produce as many surviving young as earlier ones.

Because of their semi-wild state and adaptation to the protecting human environment, feral pigeons (*columba livia*) often enjoy a protracted breeding season and may well hold the record for the number of clutches laid in one year by a free-flying bird, in Britain at least. However, many of their eggs do not produce fledged young. Within Britain, older, more experienced blackbirds (*Turdus merula*) probably fledge as many young as most other birds - often 17 from four broods of 4-5. Birds such as the grey and red legged partridges (*Perdix perdix* and *Alecoris rufa*), which often lay over 20 eggs, generally have only one brood per season and suffer a high mortality rate. Yet the red legged partridge may occasionally fledge more than the blackbird because it has a unique system whereby the male and female raise broods simultaneously.

Another prolific breeder is the moorhen (*Callimula chloropus*), which commonly raises 2-3 broods of 5-11 and is most expert in their care. Predation is high at the beginning of the season but there are many repeat layings as well as 'dump nesting.' Both parents share the incubation and feeding of young. The chicks leave the nest quickly - within 2-3 days - can swim and dive immediately and may even be fed by young of an earlier brood. There may be several special brood nests depending on the number of young. Some have ramps and are built soon after the chicks hatch.

The moorhen is unusual among monogamous birds in that the female plays a dominant, even aggressive, role. The largest females get the pick of the males, but, rather surprisingly, they prefer small males as these need to spend less food to keep healthy and can put on comparatively more fat. Such males need to spend less time feeding and are better placed to concentrate on incubating so that their mates can start more clutches and replace losses.

Though laid singly in the nests of different hosts, the eggs of parasitic species may produce a larger number in a year. Females of several species of African cuckoo, as well as the European cuckoo (*Cuculus canorus*), commonly lay as many as 20-24 eggs in a season.

Fastest and Slowest Egg Laying

A few seconds to 2 hours: The actual laying, or voiding, of an egg from the end of the oviduct (vagina) is made possible by wave-like contractions of the vaginal wall and in most birds takes 1-3 minutes. However, some parasitic species such as cuckoos (Cuculidae), which must lay quickly to minimize chance of detection can lay in just a few seconds. On the other hand, turkeys (Meleagridinae) and geese (Anatidae) may take 1-2 hours.

The interval between the laying of each egg in a clutch also varies. The first egg is often laid as soon as the nest is finished, but some species start before the nest is complete and others delay for a day or two after nest completion. A regular time of day is adhered to for many species. *Songbirds* seem to prefer dawn, but pigeons and doves (Columbidae) like the early afternoon and a few species the evening. Although one egg every 24 hours is common, a three-day interval is not uncommon among birds of prey (Falconiformes) and owls (Strigiformes), for whom varying prey supply is linked to survival. When food is short the older and larger birds get the lion's share and are more likely to survive. But even slower is the masked booby (*Sula dactylatra*) with a seven-day interval between the two eggs. Where food is in short supply from impoverished waters, the booby brood is often reduced to one by sibling murder.

Most variably Coloured/Patterned Egg

The common guillemot's: No two birds' eggs are identical in appearance, though shape and size are remarkably similar within most species. Even in colour and pattern there is little significant variation, though in a few species great variety is a distinct advantage. Of these the common guillemot (*Uria aalge*) is by far the most notable, with a huge variety of egg shades and patterns. The ground colour ranges from white to creamy yellowish, ochreous, blue or deep blue-green, with the most extraordinary variety of markings, inter-lacing lines, sports, biotches or uniform masses of colour ranging from bright red or brown to deep black and greenish black and, occasionally, there are no markings at all. The Brunnich's guillemot (*Uru lomvia*) also has a wide variety of shell markings, but the closely related razorbill (Alea torda) has much less variable eggs.

The guillemot's great egg variation helps to prevent confusion over egg ownership in the species' large, dense colonies on the cliff ledges. It has been clearly shown that guillemots identify their own eggs on the basis of individual combinations of ground colour and marking patterns. Great-tailed grackles (*Quiscalus mexicanus*) may also recognize their eggs in this way among the crowded coconut-palm colonies of Central America.

The single guillemot egg is pear-shaped to help prevent it rolling off the cliff ledge, though many still do. Interestingly, the rolling radius changes from 17 cm (7 in) for fresh eggs to 11 cm (4 in) for fully incubated eggs, but this is a fortuitous outcome of a change in the egg's centre of gravity as the embryo develops, rather than a special adaptation. The large egg (12% of female's body weight) is rested across the feet when incubated. Its shell is thicker at the narrow end, where it is in contact with the rocky nest-ledge, and thinner at the broad end, where the chick emerges. Parents find the right chicks in the crowded colonies through voice identification.

Eggshell is secreted in the uterus and consists largely of proteins and minerals, largely calcium carbonate in the form of calcite. Colour is derived from pigments secreted by cells in the wall of the oviduct, particularly of the uterus. The colours are deposited at different depths in the shell according to the position of the egg in the oviduct at the time of secretion. Much of the ground colour is provided by pigments in the spongy layer of the shell and must therefore be secreted at the upper end of the oviduct, while the blotches, speckles and scrawls on the surface are secreted lower down shortly before laying. The colours are derived from blood haemoglobin and bile pigments. Some shades are achieved by over-lapping of colours. Originally all eggs were probably white as the ancestral reptilian method is to bury them in sand or loose soil. Pale eggs are retained by primitive families such as cormorants (Phalacrocoracidae), pelicans (Pelecanidae) and albatrosses (Diomedeidae) and by more advanced species which nest in holes. Eggs laid away from daylight have no need for cryptic colouring. Hole-nesters, such as titmice (*Paridae*), with speckled eggs, may have taken up the habit after a period of nesting out in the open.

Parasitic species also lay a wide variety of eggs to mimic those of their hosts. The brown-headed cowbird (*Molothrus ater*) of North

America and Mexico is recorded as parasitizing 206 species, some regularly. But the screaming cowbird (*Molothrus rufoaxillaris*) of South America parasitizes just one host – the bay-winged cowbird (*Molothrus badius*).

Although cuckoo species such as the European cuckoo (*Cuculus canorus*) parasitize many different hosts, individual cuckoos generally lay eggs to match just one host and therefore do not produce a wide range of egg patterns and colours. It is believed, that a female cuckoo inherits her egg colour exclusively from her mother and that the egg colouration is not affected by the father's genetic input. She chooses the right nests by seeking out the host species that reared her and is probably attracted by the habitat in which she was raised.

Longest Incubation Periods

Wandering Albatross and Brown Kiwi – up to 85 days: Being warm-blooded, bird embryos must be kept at a constant, relatively high temperature when they leave their mother's body. Thus, except for the megapodes (*Megapodiidae*), which use incubation mounds and parasitic species such as cowbirds (*molothrus*) and cuckoos (Cuculidae), which let other birds incubate their eggs for them, all birds keep their eggs at the proper temperature by covering them so that; their body heat is transferred more or less directly to the developing embryos. The incubation period is strictly defined as the time between the laying of the last egg in a clutch to the hatching of that egg, and among species reliably studied so far the longest periods have been up to 85 days for the brown kiwi (*Apteryx australis*) and wandering albatross (*Diomedea exulans*). But that is an extreme and the incubation ranges of these two species are generally 74-84 and 75-82 days respectively. The royal albatross (*Diomedea epomophora*) has a similar range of 75-81 days, with a tendency towards the higher figure. Generally, the heavier the egg of a species, the longer the incubation: each doubling of egg weight increases incubation time by 16% on average.

Most birds develop a special brood patch for incubation. This comprises 1-3 adjacent abdominal areas which are normally relatively free of feathers all year round, but any down which occurs there, and some marginal contour feathers, are shed as the skin thickens slightly and the density of blood vessels increases.

Sometimes birds will sit on the incomplete clutch but not apply full body heat. The required temperature of 34-39°C (93-102°F), depending on species, is achieved only after a warm-up period, the length of which may be related to tightness of sit and time required for the incubation patch to develop. Some 75% of species aid for a constant temperature of 35°C (95°F).

Most birds cover eggs for 60-80% of the incubation period, regulating the egg temperature according to atmospheric conditions. Periods spent sitting vary greatly from under an hour for many passerines such as the European robin (*Erithacus rubecula*) to several hours in most seabirds, such as gulls and terns (Laridae). Offshore-feeding seabirds such as shearwaters and storm-petrels (Procellariidae) sit for 2-12 days at a stretch and the great albatrosses (Diomedeidae) for 2½ - 3 weeks. But the male emperor penguin's (*Aptenodyies forsteri*) 64-day continuous sitting beats them all. In some species the time spent sitting decreases as the season advances, probably due to rising air temperatures.

Maintenance of correct humidity is also important during incubation, most eggs losing about 15% of their weight before hatching. This is lost through the porous surface, which also allows important ventilation. Turning the eggs, too, is important: some species to this up to 11 times an hour to prevent 'sticking' of membranes and avoid the adverse effects of any temperature gradients in the nest.

In 54% of species sexes share the incubation. For 25% it is the female alone, for just 6% the male alone, and it varies between male, female and both in about 15%. Single birds sit more continuously, but where both sit hatching is not necessarily quicker. Some parents, such as bushtits (*Psaltriparus*) of North and Central America, are assisted in the incubation by adults without nests of their own. Others, such as anis (*Crotophaga*) and acorn wood-peckers (*Melanerpes formicivorus*), have communal ness with several females laying and males and females sharing the incubation. The waxbills (*Estrilda*) are the only species in which the male and female incubate side by side on the nest.

The percentage of egg volume taken up by the yolk food supply at the start of incubation depends upon how advanced the chicks need to be at hatching. For most passerines, which hatch blind, naked and helpless, a 12-15-day incubation is normal, with the yolk taking up only about 20% of the egg.

So-called precocial species (hatching young which are soon able to leave the nest) such as shore-birds, ducks and gamebirds, which hatch in 3-7 weeks, require a larger yolk of about 35% total egg volume. Such chicks emerge from the shell with a full coat of protective down and are soon able to fend for themselves. An embryo consumes the yolk until just before hatching, when the remains of the yolk sac pass into the body of the chick through the umbilical opening and, in some instances, may continue to nourish the bird for several days after hatching, giving the parents or chick time to establish the new feeding routine.

Shortest Incubation Periods

Small passerines-10 days: Ten days seems to be the shortest possible incubation period for a fairly small number of passerines which lay eggs weighing under 1 g (0.035 oz). These include the hawfinch (*Cocothraustes cocothraustes*), blackcap (*Sylvia atricapillai*), lesser whitethroat (*Sylvia curraca*), redpoll (*Acanthis flarnmea*), great-spotted woodpecker (*Picoides major*) and the black-billed cuckoo (*Coccyzus erythropthalmus*). But these birds may also incubate for 11 days or even longer, according to how long the egg was in the oviduct and whether or not it was fully formed when laid.

Many more small birds have 12-14 day incubation periods, their young generally hatching form eggs with relatively small yolks. Birds which hatch in a moon advanced state are sustained by proportionately larger yolks over longer incubation periods.

Faster and Slowest Hatching

30 minutes to 6 days: The actual process of 'escaping' from the egg – hatching – can take anything from 30 minutes or so in small passerines to six days for the larger albatrosses (Diomedeidae). But for most small to medium-sized birds it takes from a few hours to most of a day on average. In most clutches the eggs do not hatch together, but in sequence, reflecting the intervals in laying. Preparation for hatching begins quite early in the incubation. As the embryo's moisture gradually evaporates through the porous eggshell an air pocket gathers at the blunt end of the egg, between the inner and outer shell membranes. The developing chick uses this for breathing over several days prior to hatching, though it still depends on a part of the embryo called the allantois for oxygen exchange.

The actual 'tools' or hatching – the temporary egg tooth on the tip of the upper mandible, and the special hatching muscle – also form early in the incubation, and the eggshell becomes conveniently weaker as it provides minerals for the developing chick's skeleton.

First the embryo reafigns its body to lie along the length of the egg, the best position to force its way out from the blunt end. Convulsive thrusting forces the bill against the shell, and with the aid of the horny egg tooth the shell is soon cracked or dpiped'. After the chick has broken out the hatching muscle withers away and the egg tooth either drops off or is reabsorbed into the bill, according to species. From pipping to full emergence is the hatching period. During this, the chicks of some species are helped by the parents, which may pick at the shell or poke into the cracks. It is said that ostriches crack their eggs with their breastboiies, aiid even drag the chicks out with their bills. Some parents will begin bringing food in response to the chick's peeping even from inside the unbroken shell.

Quickest to Fly

Cabot's Tragopann and Megapodes – within 24 hours of hatching: It would not be right to say these species are the fastest at learning to fly because they seem to be born able to fly without any training or exercising of flight muscles. Most birds are born with down and are said not to be fledged until they have acquired their flist true contour feathers, including the primaries which will propel them in flight. This generally takes at least 10 days and ground-nesting species, whose young leave the nest soon after hatching, are usually much quicker at getting into the air than birds which are born naked and helpless and remain in the nest after hatching. This is taken to the extreme, in the megapodes (Megapodiidae), whose young hatch in special incubation mounds and must fend for themselves immediately. They never see their parents and instead of the usual down they are born with extremely advanced contour-like feathers which enable them to fly and escape from predators almost at once.

Equally advance on hatching is Cabors tragopan (*Tragopan caboti*) of China a member of the pheasant family. Its chicks hatch with a thick coat of coarse, shaggy down, but with primaries so far advanced they are immediately able to flutter up to perches. They also climb well and within a day or two can fly as well as any young passerine. Yet, although incubation is generally long among pheasants, it is not particularly long for this advanced bird, being just 28 days. This species is also unusually arboreal and lives in dense forests with very thick undergrowth which is often saturated. In this habitat a well-developed plumage is a distinct advantage.

Cabot's tragopan is listed as endangered, but reserves have recently been established within its historic range. Only one nest has ever been described from nature and that was 9m (30 ft) up in an old squirrel drey.

The satyr tragopal (*Tragopan satyr*) is also highly precocial at hatching and within two or three days can fly up to an elevated perch to roost under its mother's wings. It too nests in trees, and is widely hunted and trapped with nooses in Nepal, legal protection being little help.

Temminck's tragopan (*Tragopan temmincki* – the Chinese crimson horned pheasant) of the eastern Himalayas can also fly up to elevated perches within two or three days of hatching. Yet the chicks grow slowly, are sensitive to disease and chilling and do not attain full adult male plumage until the second year, the adult female plumage coming first. This tragopan has a wider range and is more secure, but it too is extensively trapped and shot for its feathers and flesh, and much of its forest habitat is being cut for timber or razed for agriculture.

The shortest fledging time for altricial young – those helpless when hatched – is about eight days for some of the warblers (Sylvinae) and finclies (Fringillidae).

Slowest to Fly Great

Albatrosses – 9-12 months: The slowest birds to fledge are the great albatrosses (Diomedeldae), especially the royal (Diomedea epomohora) and the wandering (*Diomedea exulans*), which generally take 9-12 months.

At first the bulky young birds sit very quietly in the nest. They have two successive coats of down and are brooded by a parent for the first three to five weeks, after which they are visited and fed at intervals on regurgitated food. As the time approaches to leave they fidget and flap. Most fly straight from the nest, especially if inland, but they are likely to make abortive flights and land clumsily in unsuitable places. Sometimes they are drawn to village lights, and late-developing young may swim out to sea if they can reach the water. But strong chicks fly well-immediately and never see their parents or birthplace again. When fledging is as long as this the parents can breed only once in two years.

Britain's slowest bird to fledge is the mute swan (*Cygnusolor*), which leaves the nest after a day or two but does not fly for some four months. The cygnets are tended by both parents.

Fastest to Breeding Maturity

Quails – front 5 weeks: The five species of quail in the genus *Coturrtix*, including the common quail (*Colurnix cottirnix*), reach maturity before any other bird – one reason why they have been bred in large numbers for the table. They are able to reproduce from as little as five weeks, through in most quails adult plumage is not attained before 10-12 weeks. Some other bird species are also capable of reproduction while still in immature sub-adult before they are sexually mature.

Most small songbirds breed for the first time-when just under one year old, in their second summer, and many others near the end of their second year. But some individuals within a species mature as year earlier than others.

Although physiologically capable of breeding, some species delay breeding for years as they need to develop their food-finding skills before they are capable of feeding themselves and a family. Hunting species in particular rely very much on experience, so young predatory birds continue to depend on their parents while practising their skills. Some manage this in two or three weeks but the African crowned eagle (*Stephanoaetus coronatus*) continues to receive food from its parents for up to a year even though it can fly.

Slowest to Breeding Maturity

Albatrosses – from 6-10 years old: Despite the fact that the larger albatrosses (Diomedeidae) – notably the royal (*Dioniedea epomophora*) and the wandering (*Diomedea exulans*) – have very long incubation and fledging periods, they still delay for the record period of 6-10 years before breeding for the first time. There are even reports of a first breeding at 12 years old, through the birds are physiologically capable of reproducing before this. And even after all this time first efforts are frequently unsuccessful.

After fledging, the transequatorial migrants set out on long journeys which must include a period of starvation as they cross the tropics. The early years are spent at sea, and they sometimes gather in nurseries where there is a good food supply. As they get older they return to land for increasing periods wandering in search of new nest-sites, though most return to their birthplaces. Further years are spent displaying and excavating nests before they even attempt to breed.

8

STRUCTURE OF EGG

The parts of a newly laid hen's egg are the shell, shell membrane, albumen and yolk. In an egg that has been undisturbed for a short time the yolk floats in the albumen with a whitish disc, the blastoderm about 3.5 mm in diameter, on its upper surface. If the yolk is rotated, its center of gravity is such that it will return to its former position in a few minutes, with the blastoderm on top. The blastoderm is the living part of the egg, from which the embryo and all its membranes are derived. It is already in a fairly advanced stage of development when the egg is laid. The yolk and blastoderm are enclosed within a delicate transparent membrane (*vitelline membrane*) which holds the fluid yolk mass together. We may now consider some details of the structure and composition of the parts of the egg.

The shell is composed of three layers: (1) the inner or mammillary layer, (2) the intermediate sponge layer, and (3) the surface cuticle. The mammillary layer consists of minute spherulitic crystals of calcite about 0.01.015 mm, in diameter, welded together, with conical faces impinging on the shell membrane. The minute air spaces between the conical inner ends of the mammillae communicate with the meshes of the spongy layer, which makes up two thirds of the thickness of the shell, and which is bounded externally by the extremely delicate shell cuticle. It is indented with pores on its outer surface, which are particularly numerous over the region of the air sac. The pores communicate with the meshwork of the spongy layer and thence with the air spaces of the mammillary layer. The colour of the hen's egg is due to pigments localized in the outer part of the spongy layer; they are derivatives of hemoglobin and are secreted by the uterine glands as the shell is being finished. The shell cuticle is a very thin layer of protein containing scattered globules of fat, but is otherwise structureless. It is continuous over the entire surface, including the pores. The entire shell is permeable to gases, and thus allows embryonic respiration and evaporation of water.

The shell membrane consists of two layers, a thick outer layer (40-60 μ) next to the shell and a thinner one (13-17 μ) nest to the albumen. Both are composed of a matted network of fibers which are chemically intermediate in properties between keratin and chitin. The fibers of the inner layer are of the same size (2.3 μ) and cross one another in all directions. Those of the outer layer are variable in size (8-12 μ), the mesh is looser, and there is a star-like condensation of fibers at certain points which are embedded in the calcite of the shell. This union serves to strengthen the shell, which would otherwise be brittle and fragile. At the blunt end of the egg the two layers are separated and form a chamber containing air that enters after the egg is laid.

The physical characteristics of the albumen are too well known to require description. A dense layer immediately nest to he vitelline membrane is prolonged in the form of two spirally coiled opalescent

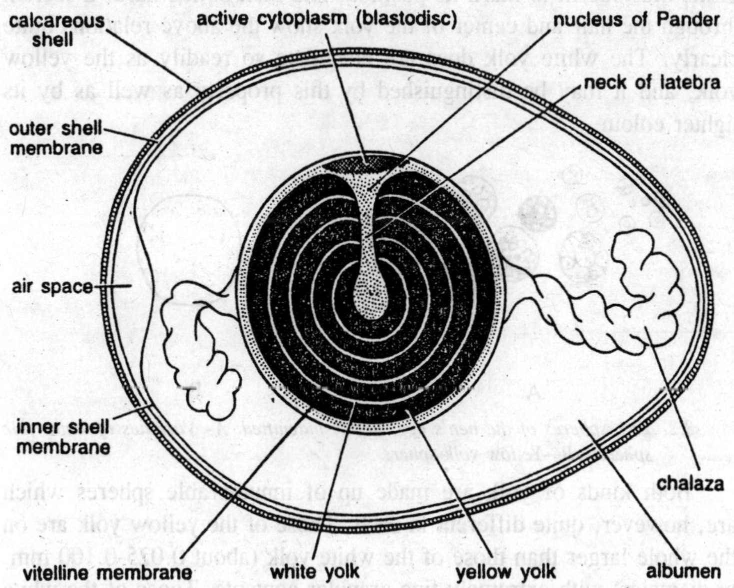

Fig. 8.1. Diagrammatic longitudinal section of a egg.

cords towards the blunt and narrow ends of the egg respectively; these are the chalazae, so called from the Greek for "tubercles" (Romanoff) or "hailstones" (Bartelmez). The two chalazae are twisted in opposite directions. In a hard-boiled egg it is possible to strip off the albumen in concentric spiral layers from left to right from the broad to the small end of the egg.

The yolk and blastoderm are enclosed within the delicate vitelline membrane; the yolk is a highly nutritious food destined to be gradually digested and absorbed by the living cells of the blastoderm and used for the growth of the embryo. It is not of uniform composition throughout, but consists of two main ingredients known as the yellow and the white yolk. The yellow yolk makes up the greater part of the yolk sphere; the main part of the white yolk is a flash-shaped mass, the bulb of which, known as the latebra, is situated near the center of the whole yolk, the neck rising toward the surface and expanding in the form of a disc (nucleus of Pander) situated immediately beneath the blastoderm at its margin this disc is continuous with a thin peripheral layer of white yolk that surrounds the entire mass. In addition there are several thin layers of lighter-coloured yolk concentric to the inner bulb-shaped mass. if an egg be opened, a delicate hair inserted in the blastoderm to mark its position, and then boiled hard, a section through the hair and center of the yolk show the above relations quite clearly. The white yolk does not coagulate so readily as the yellow yolk, and it may be distinguished by this property as well as by its lighter colour.

Fig. 8.2. Yolk spheres of the hen's egg, highly magnified. A—Varieties of white yolk spheres. B—Yellow yolk sphere.

Both kinds of yolk are made up of innumerable spheres which are, however, quite different in each. Those of the yellow yolk are on the whole larger than those of the white yolk (about 0.025-0.100 mm. in diameter) with extremely fine granular contents. Those of the white yolk are smaller and more variable in size, ranging from the finest granules up to about -.07 mm. the larger spheres of the white yolk contain several highly refractive granules of relatively considerable size as compared with those of the yellow spheres and such granules may have secondary inclusions. As we shall see later, the smaller granules of the white yolk extend into the germinal disc (forerunner of the blastoderm) and grade into minute yolk granules contained within the living protoplasm.

The earlier investigators from the time of Schwann regarded the white yolk spheres as actual cells. His especially laid great stress on this interpretation; he believed that they were derived from the cells of the ovarian follicle which migrated into the ovum in the course of oogenesis, that they multiplied like other cells, and took part in the formation of certain embryonic tissues. Subsequently he abandoned this position as untenable. The white yolk spheres are now universally regarded as food matters of a particular sort rather than cells.

Chemical Composition of the Hen's Egg

The yolk and albumen are complex mixtures of many different substances, organic and inorganic, containing all of the compounds necessary for the growth of the embryo. The figures given below are for average amounts; the individual egg is, of course, subject to great variation:

Table 8.1. General Composition of the Yolk

	Amount in grams	*Percent of Total*
Total	18.7	100.00
Water	9.1	48.7
Solids	9.6	51.3
Organic Matter	9.4	50.2
Proteins	3.1	16.6
Lipids	6.1	32.6
Carbohydrates	0.2	1.0
Inorganic Matter	0.2	1.1

The lipids make up the greater part of the solid constituents of the yolk and serve as a major source of food for the embryo. The consist of the true fats (glycerides) (623 per cent), phospholipids (32.8 per cent), sterols (such as cholesterol) (4.9 percent), and traces of cerebrosides, called ovovitellin, which makes up about 77 per cent of the total protein, and ovolivetin (23 per cent), which has a high content of sulfur. The phosphoproteins are the main nutritive proteins utilized by the young of both birds and mammals (Hewitt). The carbohydrates of the yolk consist mainly of free glucose (70 per cent) and of polysaccharides (chiefly mannose and galactose) combined with the phospholipids, phosphoproteins, and cerebrosides. Other organic components include pigments (carotenes, xanthophylls, riboflavin, etc.), vitamins, and enzymes. Of the minerals, phosphorus is the most abundant and occurs mostly in organic compounds, principally lecithin. Calcium, magnesium, chlorine, potassium, and sodium are present in lesser quantities, as are very small amounts of sulfur and iron.

Table 8.2. General composition of the Albumen

	Amount in Grams	*Percent of Total*
	32.9	100.00
Water	28.9	57.9
Solids	4.0	12.1
Organic Matter	3.8	11.5
Proteins	3.5	10.6
Lipids	Trace	-
Carbohydrates	0.3	0.9
Inorganic Matter	0.2	0.6

The proteins re the chief solid constituent of the albumen and consists of ovalbumin (75 per cent), ovomucoid (13 per cent), ovomucin (7 per cent), ovoconalbumin (3 per cent), and ovoglobulin (2 per cent). The second and third named are glycoproteing (i.e., combined with a carbohydrate); the others are simple proteins. The exact nature of the carbohydrates is obscure, but they are polysaccharides and are believed to contain mannose in various combinations with glucosamine or galactose. The only pigment reported for the albumen is riboflavin ("ovoflavin"), which gives it a faint yellowish tinge. Sulfur, potassium, sodium, and chlorine are the most abundant minerals, in the order named; there are lesser amounts of phosphorus, calcium, and magnesium, and traces of iron.

The albumen contributes not only to the nutrition of the embryo, but serves as a protective envelope, shielding the embryo both mechanically (from physical inquiry) and chemically (from bacterial contamination). Chemical protection is afforded by the presence of avidin, a biotin-binding protein which is abundant both in the albumen and in the hen's oviduct from which it is secreted. The albumen also has a lytic action on some kinds of bacteria, which may be due to a discrete substance ("*lysozyme*"). Thus, even if a contaminant should succeed in passing the shell-barrier, it would probably be lysed or its growth would be inhibited by the avidin.

The shell consists of a collagenous matrix impregnated with lime salts: about 95 per cent calcium and magnesium carbonates and phosphates (of which amount the calcium salts constitute 98 per cent); about 5 per cent collagen and water; traces of lipids, iron, and sulfur.

The shell membrane consists of keratin, or a closely allied substance, along with a small amount of water and traces of minerals. The vitelline membrane is believed also to contain a keratin-like material along with mucin or collagen.

Formation of the Egg

The organs of reproduction of the hen are the ovary and oviduct of the left side of the body. Although the right ovary and oviduct are formed in the embryo at the same time as those of the left side, they degenerate more or less completely in the course of development so that only functionless rudiments remain. This would appear to be correlated with the large size of the egg and the delicate nature of the shell, as there is not room for two eggs side by side in the lower part of the body cavity.

The ovary lies at the anterior end of the kidney attached by a fold of the peritoneum (mesovarium) to the dorsal wall of the body cavity. In a laying hen, ova of all sizes are found from microscopic up to the fully formed ovum ready to escape from the follicle. Such an ovary; the gradation in size of the ova will be noticed up to the one fully formed and ready to burst from its capsule. The figure shows a reptured follicle, from where the ovum has escaped. It will be seen that the part of the definitive hen's egg produced in the ovary is the so-called yolk. The blood supply of the very vascular ovary is derived from the dorsal aorta, and the ovarian veins open into the postcaval vein.

The oviduct is a large coiled tube which begins in a wide mouth with fringed borders, the *ostium tubae abdominale* (funnel or infundibulum) opening into the body cavity near the ovary. It is attached by a special mesentery to be dorsal wall of the body cavity, and opens into the cloaca. The following divisions are usually distinguished: (1) the funnel or infundibulum, (2) the albumen-secreting portion or magnum, (3) the isthmus, (4) the uterus or shell gland, (5) the vagina. The albumen-secreting portion includes all of the coiled tube; the isthmus is a short section next to the dilated uterus, and the vagina is the short terminal portion opening into the cloaca.

The formation of an egg takes place as follows: the yolk, or ovum proper, escapes by rupture of the follicle along a preformed band, the stigma, is picked up by the infundibulum, which swallows it, so to speak, and is passed down by peristaltic contractions of the oviduct. The escape of the ovum from the follicle is known as the process of ovulation. During its passage down the oviduct it becomes surrounded by layers of albumen secreted by the oviducal glands. The shell membrane is secreted in the isthmust and the shell in the uterus. The ovum is fertilized in the uppermost part of the oviduct and the cleavage and early stages of formation of the germ layers take place before the egg is laid. The time occupied by the ovum in traversing the various sections of the oviduct is as follows:

The ovum enters the oviduct within 15 minutes after its liberation from the follicle, passes through the funnel in 18 minutes, spends approximately 3 hours in traversing the magnum or albumen-secreting portion, one hour in the isthmus, and 20 to 24 hours in the uterus. Laying normally occurs as soon as the egg is completely formed. The tendency of some hens to lay eggs in "clutches" or groups, instead of laying at the usual daily interval, is due to irregularities in the rate of ovulation and not to the retention of fully formed eggs in the uterus.

Some of the details of these remarkable processes deserve attention: the definite periodicity of ovulation, which occurs at approximately daily intervals, has long been known to be governed in some way by the amount of illumination to which the hen is subjected. Furthermore, if a hen is anesthetized and the oviduct is extirpated so as to remove such possible causes of ovulation as manipulation of the ovarian follicles by muscular activity of the infundibulum, then the liberation of mature ova still continues at the expected intervals. These facts suggest that ovulation is under hormonal control, and indeed. Fraps and his co-workers have successfully induced premature and multiple ovulations by injecting hens with pituitary hormones from the horse luteinizing and follicle-stimulating hormones; gonadotropic hormones from pregnant mares' serum). Another hormone which proved to be highly effective was crystalline progesterone. The release of an ovum could be induced by as much as 17 hours previous to the time of its expected normal ovulation is caused by the sudden release of an appropriate hormone into the blood stream. The source of the rhythm governing its release the identity of the hormone which normally operates have not yet been clarified in birds. However, by analog with the situation in the rat, we may infer that a neural timing factor (localized in the anterior hypothalamus?) acts through the pituitary gland, thus causing the periodic release of increased quantities of gonadotropic hormone sufficient to bring about ovulation (Everett and Sawyer). Light and the sexual hormones are no doubt also involved in the ovulatory cycle, because of their effects on the activity of the pituitary.

The actual expulsion of the ovum from the follicle is accomplished by a contraction of muscular fibers in the follicular wall. The tension thus produced increases the turgidity of the follicle, compresses blood vessels near the stigma so that they "fade out," and causes the stigma to rupture at one of its ends where the stress is greatest.

The upper part of the oviduct, particularly the infundibulum, becomes very active at the time of ovulation. By virtue of its muscular activity, the funnel makes clasping movements, enclosing any object which it encounters, immature as well as mature follicles entirely at random. The funnel does not appear to exert any pressure on the follicles whole grasping them, so that it is doubtful whether such muscular activity is a causative factor in ovulation. The funnel of the oviduct can pick up ova that have escaped into the body cavity, but in some causes ova that escape into the body cavity undergo resorption there.

As soon as the ovum passes through the funnel, it enters the magnum of the oviduct which is lined with secretory goblet cells intermixed with ciliated columnar cells. The albumen is elaborated by the goblet cells as strands of mucinous gel which are then wrapped around the ovum in successive spiral layers as it passes down the oviduct.

Only about 50 percent of the white of the egg is formed by the albumen-secreting portion of the oviduct; this is in the form of a dense layer formed of matted fibers of mucin; the shell membrane is deposited directly on this while the egg is in the isthmus; and the more fluid portion of the albumen constituting 50 per cent or more of its entire bulk enters through the shell membrane while the egg is in the uterus. The uterine secretion is not an albumenous substance, but rather a mineral solution consisting principally of water, potassium and bicarbonate ions, and smaller amounts of sodium and chloride ions. The concentration of potassium ions is unusually high (about ten times that of normal blood serum) and probably related to the heavy demand for potassium by embryos and young animals. The uterine secretion diffuses through the shell membrane, dilutes the thick albumen somewhat, and in turn receives dissolved albumens, resulting at equilibrium in the outer layer of so-called thin albumen.

The chalazae do not appear until the egg has been in the uterus for some time. Contrary to the views of early workers, they are not formed by a special secretory mechanism in the cephalic end of the oviduct but apparently arise by mechanical means. The most plausible explanation is that of Conrad and Phillips: the albumen is laid down throughout the magnum as a homogeneous gel, but as the ovum continues to rotate in its spiral descent through the oviduct, there is a gradual breakdown of the colloidal gel structure of the innermost layer of albumen until it becomes a sol. This conversion into a sol, which is completed at about the time that the egg enters the uterus, permits the ovum to rotate freely within its albumenous envelope. The yolk tends to maintain a constant position (due to the lesser density of the hemisphere which contains the germ spot); but the albumen continues to revolve as the egg turns within the uterus, so that the mucinous fibers of the inner liquefied layer of albumen becomes twisted at each end of the yolk and form the chalazae. Added weight is given to this explanation by removing eggs just as they enter the uterus and incubating them within a rubber "artificial uterus" with a proper amount of artificial uterine fluid; under such conditions, no chalazae are formed unless the rubber "uterus" is rotated. The fact that the line joining the attachments of the chalazae is at right angles to the main axis of the ovum (that passing through the germinal disc) indicates that there must be some antecedent condition that determines the position of the ovum in the oviduct and, therefore, the orientation of the ovum to its albumenous wrapping. This is probably the position of the ovum in the follicle, i.e., the relation of the germinal disc to the stigma, for the follicular orientation is apparently more or less preserved in the oviduct. The question is of considerable importance because as we shall see, the axis of the embryo is later bisected by a plane passing through the chalazac, and is therefore certainly determined at the time that the albumengel is laid down, and Bartelmez even traces it back to the earliest stages of the oocyte.

Abnormal Eggs

These are of two main kinds: those with more than one yolk, and enclosed eggs (*ovum in ovo*). Double-yolked eggs obviously due to the simultaneous, or almost simultaneous, liberation of two yolks, are their incorporation in a single set of egg membranes. The two yolks are usually separate in such cases and are derived, presumably, from separate follicles. But two yolks within a single vitelline membrane have been observed; such are in all probability products of a single follicle. Cases of three yolks with a single shell are extremely rate. The class of enclosed eggs includes those in which there are two shells, one with the other. In some cases the contents of the enclosed and the enclosing eggs are substantially normal, though of course the enclosing shell is abnormally large; in others the enclosed egg may be abnormal as to size (small yolk), or contents (no yolk). In all cases described, the enclosing egg possesses a yolk (Parker). Abnormal eggs of these three classes are of either ovarian or oviducal origin; double-yolked eggs and eggs with abnormal yolks are de to abnormal ovarian conditions; enclosed eggs to abnormal oviducal conditions, or to both ovarian and oviducal abnormalities. Assuming the normal peristalsis of the oviduct to be reversed when a fully formed egg is present, the egg would be carried up the oviduct a greater or less distance and might there meet a second yolk. If the peristalsis became normal again, both would be carried to the uterus and enclosed in a common shell.

Oogenesis

Oogenesis, or the development of ova, may be divided into three very distinct stages. The first stage, or period of multiplication, is embryonic and ends about the time of hatching (in the chick); it is characterized by the small size of the ova and their rapid multiplication by division. The multiplying primitive ova are known as *oogonia*. At the end of this period multiplication ceases and the period of growth begins. The ova, known as *primary oocytes*, become enclosed in follicles; the size of the ovum constantly increases and they yolk is formed. The third period, known as the period of maturation, is characterized by two successive exceedingly unequal divisions of the egg cell, producing two minute cells, the polar bodies, that take up part in the formation of the embryo, but die and degenerate. The process of maturation begins in the fully ripe follicle and is completed after ovulation in the oviduct, while the ovum is being fertilized.

In the young chick all the cell cords and cell nests become converted into primordial follicles. During the egg-laying period there is a continuous process of growth and ripening of the primordial follicles, which takes place successively; the immense majority at any given period remain latent, but all stages of growth of egg follicles may be found in a laying hen.

A primordial follicle consists of the ovum surrounded by a single layer of the cuboidal epithelial cells (granulose or follicle cells); the fibers of the adjacent storma have a concentric arrangement around

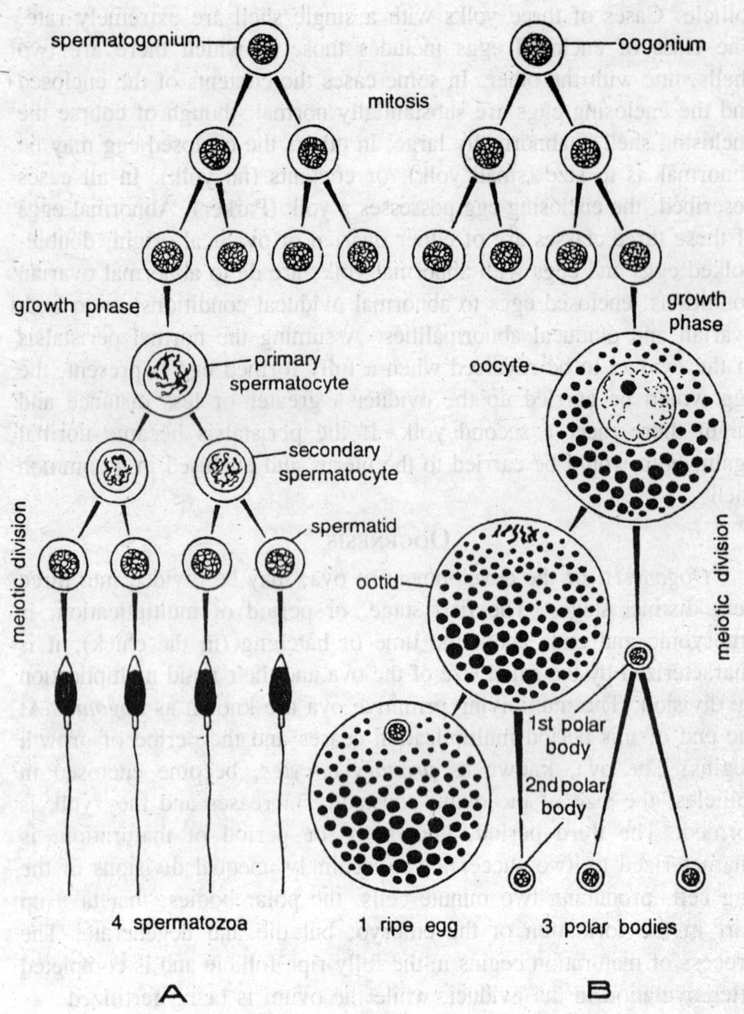

Fig. 8.3. A—Spermatogenesis; B—Oogenesis.

the follicle forming the theca folliculi. The ovum itself is a rounded cell with a large nucleus placed excentrically so as to define a primary axis of the ovum. In the protoplasm on one side of the nucleus is a concentrated mass of protoplasm, the yolk nucleus, from which rays extend, and minute fatty granules.

Holl derives the follicular cells in birds from the storma, but on insufficient grounds. According to D'Hollander, they are derived, like the primitive ova, from the germinal epithelium, in which he agrees with the majority of his predecessors. He states that the period of multiplication of the oogenia ends about the time of hatching that the period of growth of the oocyte begins at about the fourteenth day of incubation (seven days before hatching), and before the formation of the primordial follicle, which begins on the fourth day after hatching. Thus the periods of multiplication and growth overlap.

Although the nucleus is strongly excentric in position in the youngest oocyes, it occupies a more nearly central position in those slightly older. When the ovum is about 0.66 mm. in diameter, its nucleus moves to the surface along the shortest radius and comes to lie almost in contract with the vitelline membrane. It becomes elliptical, and later the outer surface is flattened against the vitelline membrane, the inner surface remaining convex. The point on the surface to which the germinal vesicle migrates is situated away from the surface of the ovary, and thus in the position of the pedicle of the follicle, when the latter projects from the surface of the ovary. This determines the position of the future germ disc. The nucleus increases in size with the growth of the ovum; in the youngest oocytes its diameter is about 9 μ; in the ripe ovum it is flattened and may measure 455 μ in diameter by 72μ in thickness.

While the nucleus is still near the center of the egg a very dense deposit of extremely fine granules is formed around it, and gradually extends out towards the periophery of the cell, but does not involve the peripheral layer of protoplasm. This cluster of granules ("yolk nucleus") is called a "*mitochondrial cloud*" by *Brambell*. The mitochondria swell up and become converted directly into spherules or white yolk. The central aggregation of yolk granules thus formed represents the primordium of the latebra or central mass of the white yolk.

The ovum grows very slowly up to a diameter of about 6 millimeters, and all of the yolk formed during this period belongs to the category of white yolk. Certain of these ova, but only a few at any one time, then suddenly begin to grow at an enormously increased rate, adding about 4 mm. to their diameter every twenty-four hours until the full size of about 40 mm. in diameter is attained. It is during this period that the yellow yolk is laid down in the periphery.

Riddle has studied this period by the ingenious method of feeding the stain Sudan III, which has an especial affinity for fat, to laying hens at definite time intervals. The stain attaches itself to fatty acids of the food which are taken up unchanged by the egg. The consequence is that during any period of Sudan III feeding a red stained layer of yolk is formed: so that it is possible by regulating the dose and interrupting the feedings to obtain ova with alternate bands of stained and unstained yolk. In this way he was able to show that a layer of yellow and of lighter-coloured yolk about 2 mm. in combined thickness on the average is laid down each twenty-four hours.

Later studies have shown that the concentric stratification in colour of the yellow yolk is largely governed by the diet of the hen. If a uniform and well-balanced mash is available at all times, then strata do not appear in the yellow yolk. But if hens are kept on a restricted feeding period (6 hours) or are fed a mash which is poor in the carotinoid pigments (chiefly xanthophylls) which colour the yolk, then the yolk becomes stratified in colour. In view of these facts, it does not appear probable that the concentric lamina of light-coloured yolk are a true "white yolk" as previously described, but rather represent yellow yolk which is lacking in carotinoid pigment.

The germinal vesicle lies in a thickening of the peripheral layer of protoplasm known as the germinal disc or blastodisc, which is continuous, like the remainder of the peripheral protoplasm, in early stages with the protoplasmic reticulum that forms the walls of the yolk vacuoles. The blastodisc increases in extent and thickness, and the peripheral protoplasm disappears over most of the yolk. An inflow of the peripheral protoplasm into the disc appears very probable by analogy with the bony fishes where this process can be studied with great ease.

The method of formation of the neck of the latebra and the so-called *nucleus of Pander*, or peripheral expansion of the neck, follows more or less directly from the preceding account: As the ovum increases in diameter during the period of rapid growth, yellow yolk is deposited all around its circumference except in the region occupied by the blastodisc. Since the blastodisc remains at the ever-changing circumference of the growing ovum, a column which contains no yellow yolk is formed along the radius extending from the central mass of white yolk to the definitive site of the *blastodisc*. The column is known as the *neck of the latebra*. When the ovum is fully grown, the exact boundaries between protoplasmic blastodisc and the yolk are not determinable. The disc itself is charged with small yolk granules which grade off very gradually into the white yolk lying around and beneath the disc.

The ovum is not a perfect sphere, but is ellipsoidal, with its longest axis coinciding with the longest axis of the egg. In addition to this asymmetry of the axes, more yellow yolk is deposited in that half of the ovum which lies opposite the blastodisc than in the half which contains it. Thus, the central mass of the latebra comes to lie somewhat above the true center of the ovum, and the resultant shift in the center of gravity probably accounts for the fact that the yolk tends to float with the blastodisc on top.

The mode of nutrition of the ovum and the formation of the vitelline membrane remain to be considered. The nutrition is conveyed from the highly vascular theca folliculi by way of the follicular cells, or membrane granulosa, to the ovum. The nutriment enters by diffusion; it has been reported that Golgi apparatus is extruded from the follicular cells directly into the ovum and persists in its new environment but there is no evidence of immigration of solid food particles, let alone entire cells, into the growing ovum. Prior to the last stage of yolk formation, a definite membrane is formed between the ovum and the follicular cells, the zona radiata or primordium of the vitelline membrane.

The discussion as to whether the zona radiata is a product of the ovum itself or of the follicular cells seems to be largely academic and will not be summarized here. There seems to be sufficient evidence of a primary true vitelline membrane secreted by the ovum itself, though this may not represent the entire zona radiate of older ova. Yolk is formed probably by a combination of secretion from the follicular epithelium and a diffuse of nutrients from the blood steam through the follicular epithelium and zona radiata, with final synthesis into yolk taking trace with the ovum. The follicular epithelium may be thought of as a selective filter which controls the proportions of ions and food materials which diffuse into the ovum.

9

Fertilization and Early Development

During the growth period the germinal vesicle has increased to an enormous size (455 × 72 μ in an ovum 37 mm. in diameter). It lies in the center of a thickened mass of cytoplasm which, according to *Olsen*, is about ten times the diameter of the nucleus. As seen from the surface, the germinal vesicle appears spherical, but in cross-section it is actually flattened against the vitelline membrane. The margins of the lenticular nucleus are folded into the interior in such a way that sections give an effect of rod-shaped bodies springing from 'the membrane which were doubtfully interpreted as chromosomes by *Holl*. The real chromosomes are however in the center in the form of double rods. The germinal vesicle and its surrounding cytoplasm constitute the germinal disc.

The process of maturation in the hen's egg has been described by *Oslen* as follows: approximately twenty-four hours before ovulation, vacuoles appear in the upper wall of the germinal vesicle, and the membrane starts to break down. The contents of the vesicle then spread out laterally and flatten to form a thin sheet under the vitelline membrane. The chromatin remains in a very limited area near the center of the disintegrating vesicle. The first maturation spindle arises with its long axis at right angles to the surface of the egg, and the first polar body is extruded by a least one hour before ovulation. The first polar body in freshly extruded ova measures approximately 18 μ × 8 μ and lies in a small depression near the center of the germinal disc and just beneath the vitelline membrane. At the time of ovulation the second maturation spindle has formed. Whether the entry of sperm is necessary for the completion of maturation is not clearly demonstrated, but *Olsen* is of the opinion that the second polar body is not extruded until after fertilization.

The wall of the germinal vesicle begins to break down in ovarian eggs of about 18.75 mm. diameter, the full size of the egg of the pigeon being about 25 mm. Part of the fluid contents of the germinal vesicle flows out and forma layer outside the disintegrating wall. The chromosomes and nucleoli form a group near the center of the upper plane surface of the germinal vesicle. The first maturation spindle is formed before ovulation, containing eight quadruple chromosomes (tetrads). The spindle is still in the equatorial plane stage when the ovum is grasped by the mouth of the oviduct. The bulk of the substance of the germinal vesicle soon forms a yolk-free cone extending from the maturation spindle deep into the superficial yolk. The outer end of the spindle is in almost immediate contact with the surface of the ovum. In the late stages of formation of the first polar body each tetrad, or quadruple chromosome, separates into two dyads or double chromosomes, and the members of each pair of dyads separate and approach opposite ends of the spindle (anaphase).

Thus at each end of the spindle there are eight dyads. Those at the outer end then enter a little bud of protoplasm projecting above the surface of the blastodisc, and this bud with the dyads is cut off as the first polar body, which lies in a depression of the blastodisc beneath the vitelline membrane. Eight dyads, therefore, remain within the blastodisc.

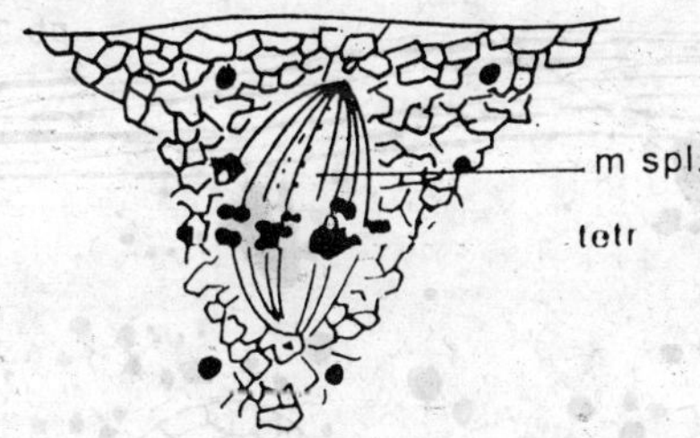

Fig. 9.1. Vertical section of the blastodisc of the pigeon's egg showing the first maturation spindle. m. Spl—First maturation spindle, Tetr.—Tetrad.

A second maturation spindle is then formed almost immediately, apparently without the intervention of a resting stage of the nucleus, and takes a radial position similar to that occupied by the first, with the dyads forming an equatorial plate. Each dyad then divides along the preformed plane of division, and the daughter chromosomes diverge

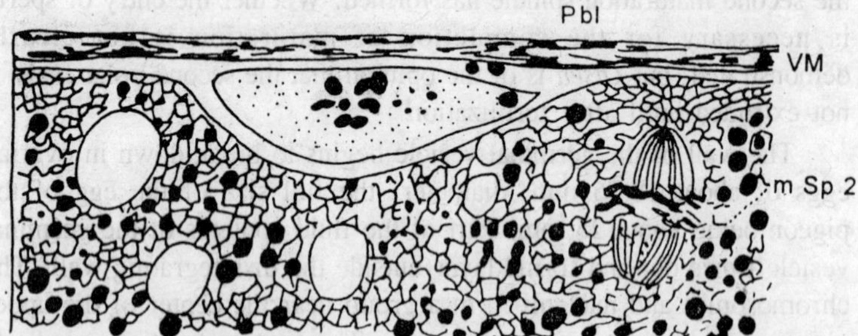

Fig. 9.2. Second maturation spindle and first polar body of the pigeon's egg; a combination of two sections. m Sp 2—Second maturation spindle. Pbl—First polar body. VM—Vitelline membrane.

towards opposite poles of the spindle. The outer end of the second maturation spindle then enters a superficial bud of the protoplasm of the blastodisc similar to that of the first maturation spindle; and this bud together with the contained chromosomes becomes cut of as the second polar body.

The result of these processes of maturation is the formation of three cells, the two polar bodies and the mature egg. The polar bodies are relatively very minute and soon degenerate completely.

After the formation of the second polar body there remain in the egg eight chromosomes, each of which represents one quarter of an original tetrad. These form a small resting nucleus known as the egg nucleus or female pronucleus. It is many times smaller than the original

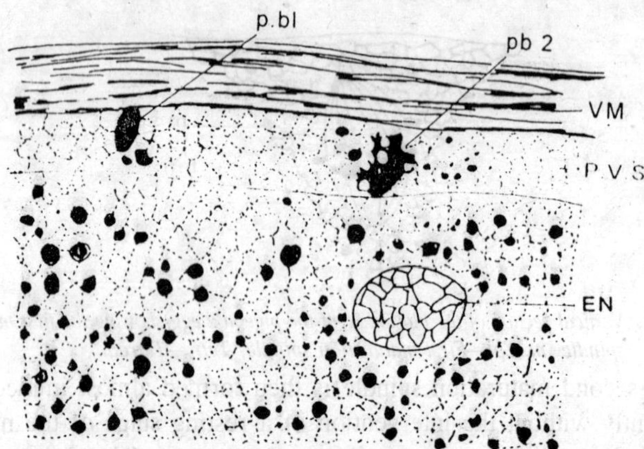

Fig. 9.3. Egg nucleus (female pronucleus) and polar bodies of the pigeon's eggs. EN—Egg nucleus, p.bl—First polar body, pb 2—Second polar body, P.V.S—Perivitellinespace, VM—Vitelline membrane.

germinal vesicle and it rapidly withdraws from the surface of the egg to a deeper position near the center of the blastodisc.

Fertilization

The spermatozoa traverse the entire length of the oviduct and are found in the uppermost portion in a fertile hen. The period of life of the spermatozoa within the oviduct is considerable, as proved by the fact that hens may continue to lay fertile eggs for a period of at least three weeks after isolation from the cock. After the end of the third week the vitality of the spermatozoa is apparently reduced; as eggs laid during the fourth and fifth weeks may exhibit, at the most, abnormal cleavage, which soon ceases. Eggs laid forty days after isolation are certainly unfertilized, and do not develop.

Parthenogenetic cleavage occurs in about 15 per cent of such unfertilized eggs, but lit is of short duration. Evidence of abnormality such as multipolar mitosis is common. The mitotic nuclei apparently contain the diploid number of chromosomes, which suggests that the second polar body may have been retained because of lack of the stimulus of fertilization. By the time that the egg is laid, most of the parthenogenetic cleavage nuclei have become necrotic. Parthenogenetic cleavage also occurs in the pigeon but becomes abortive as soon as the blastoderm reaches late stages of cleavage and before there is any subgerminal cavity.

The ovum enters the infundibulum within fifteen minutes after ovulation and is surrounded there by a fluid containing spermatozoa. According to *Olsen*, the second polar body, comparable in size and appearance to the first, is formed after sperm penetrate the egg. Although probably correct, this conclusion should be accepted with caution, since it is based on inference from the observation that the newly ovulated ovum has only-a single polar body whereas ova taken from the infundibulum have two. As many as three to five sperm may enter the ovum, but only one unites with the female pronucleus. The male pronucleus, which is formed from the head and middle piece of the sperm, is similar both in, ovoid appearance and size ($11.3\ \mu \times 5.6\ \mu$) to the female pronucleus.

The egg of the pigeon varies somewhat from the above account: After the ovum enters the infundibulum, from twelve to twenty-five spermatozoa immediately penetrate the egg membrane (presumably by enzymic action, by analogy with other species) and enter the blastodisc, within which the heads, which represent the nuclei of the spermatozoa, enlarge and become transformed into sperm nuclei. The fate of the middle piece and tail of the sperinatozoon is not known. At the time of entrance of the spermatozoa the first maturation spindle is in process of formation; it lies in the center of a group of granules at the surface of the egg, which is bounded by a non-granular zone of protoplasm, called by Harper the polar ring, in which the sperm nuclei accumulate. External to the polar ring the protoplasm is granular again. The sperm nuclei remain quiescent until maturation is completed, and, when the egg nucleus is reconstituted, one of them, which may be called the male pronucleus is reconstituted, one of them, which may be called the male pronucleus or primary sperm nucleus, moves inwards and comes into contact with the egg nucleus. The opposed faces of the conjugating nuclei become flattened together, until the contours form a single sphere, the first segmentation nucleus, in which a partition separates the original components, the sperm and egg nucleus. The partition apparently disappears. Each gametic nucleus forms an independent group of chromosomes of the same (haploid) number and of homologous types with the exception of the "X" or sex-determining chromosonic which is absent in approximately half of the egg nuclei. The union of the gametic nuclei restores the diploid number of chromosomes typical of the species.

Shortly after its formation, the first segmentation nucleus prepares for division in the usual mitotic way. The first segmentation (or cleavage) spindle thus formed lies near the center of the blastodisc a short distance beneath the surface and its axis is tangential to the surface, or, in, other words, at right angles to the axis of the ovum. The fertilization may be considered to be completed at this stage.

The entrance of several spermatozoa appears to be characteristic of vertebrates with large ova; thus for instance, it has been described in selachians, some amphibians, reptiles and birds. Such a condition is known as *polyspermy*; it is normal in the forms mentioned, but occurs only under abnormal conditions in the great majority of animals. Harper observed that the number of sperm nuclei formed in the pigeon varied from twelve to twenty-five in different cases. Only one of these serves as a functional sperm nucleus; the remainder or supernumerary sperm nuclei migrate, as though repelled, from the center towards the margins and deeper portions of the blastodisc, where they become temporarily active, dividing and furnishing a secondary are of small cells (accessory cleavage) surrounding the true cleavage cells produced by division of the central portion of the disc around the descendants of the segmentation nucleus. It has been supposed by some authors who studied the selachians that the descendants of the supernumerary sperm nuclei from functional nuclei of the so-called periblastic, but this view has been disproved for the hen and for the pigeon in which it can be demonstrated that the supernumerary sperm nuclei have but a brief period of activity, and then degenerate.

Cleavage of the Ovum

The fertilized ovum is morphologically a single cell, with a single nucleus, the first segmentation nucleus. The living protoplasm is aggregated in the blastodisc, and the remainder of the ovum is an inert mass of food material destined to be assimilated by the embryo which arises from the blastodisc. The first step in the development is a series of cell divisions of the usual mitotic type, restricted to the blastodisc, which rapidly becomes multicellular. As the early divisions take place nearly synchronously in all the cells, there is a tendency for the number of the cells to increase in genometrical progression, furnishing 2, 4, 8 and 16 etc., celled stages; but sooner or later the divisions cease to be synchronous. All of the cells of the body are derived from the blastodisc, and the nuclei of all cells trace their lineage back to the first segmentation nucleus. He supernumerary sperm nuclei do not take part in the formation of the embryo.

Cell division is the most conspicuous part of the early development; hence this period is known as the cleavage, or segmentation period. But it should be remembered that cell division is as constant a process in all later embryonic stages.

The type of cleavage exhibited by the bird's egg is known as meroblastic, for the reason that only a part of the ovum is concerned, the germinal disc. This is obviously due to the great amount of yolk.

To understand the form and significance of the cleavage of the bird's egg, it is necessary first of all to gain a clear idea of the structure of the blastodisc and its relations to the yolk. At the time of the first cleavage the blastodisc is round in surface view and about 3 mm. in diameter; the center is white and is surrounded by a darker margin about 0.5 mm. wide. These two zones have been compared to the pellucid and opaque areas of later stages. We shall call the outer zone the *periblastic zone*, or simply *periblast*. In section, the blastodisc is biconvex, but the outer surface which conforms to the contour of the entire egg is much less arched than the inner surface. The disc is everywhere separated from the yellow yolk by a layer of white yolk; on the other hand, there is no sharp separation between the disc and the white yolk. The granules of the latter are largest in the deeper layers and there is a gradual transition from them to the smaller yolk granules with which the disc is thickly charged. It is practically impossible in a section to say where the protoplasm of the disc ceases; it is indeed probable that it extends some distance into the white yolk both beneath and around the margins of the disc. Thus a cone, apparently of protoplasm, extends into the neck of the latebra a considerable distance. In other cases it does not extend so far.

Hen's Egg

The form of cleavage of the hen's is illustrated. The first cleavage appears in surface view as a narrow furrow extending part way across the blastodisc. It occurs just as the egg is entering the isthmus which is about three hours after the estimated time of fertilization. Approximately twenty minutes 'later, while the ends of the first cleavage furrow are still extending towards the periblast, the second division begins. It is a vertical division in each cell like the first, and the two furrows meet the first cleavage furrow at right angles. They may meet the first furrow at about the same point, in which case they form an approximately straight line, or more commonly, they may meet the first cleavage furrow at separate points, in which case the intervening part of the first furrow becomes bent a an angle, forming a cross furrow. The third set of cleavage planes are vertical like the preceding planes, but they tend to be variable otherwise.

Before describing the later cleavage stages, we should note certain important relations of the first four or eight cells. First, these are not complete cells in the sense that they are separate from one another. They are, indeed, areas with separate nuclei marked out by cleavage furrows in a continuous mass of protoplasm. The furrows do not cut through the entire depth of the blastodisc and the cells are therefore connected below by the deeper layer of the protoplasm; nor do the furrows extend into the periblast, and all the cells are therefore united at their margins by the unsegmented ring of periblast. Second, according to several observers, the center of the cleavage, i.e., the place where the first two cleavage furrows cross, is sometimes excentric. It was believed by those who emphasized this point, that the displacement is towards the posterior end of the bastoderm; but *Coste*, for instance, failed to note any excentricity, and Patterson noticed both conditions, and showed that the displacement might even be towards the anterior end of the blastoderm. In the pigeon, according to Blount's observations recorded below, excentricity appears to be exceptional: moreover, the excentric area may bear any relation whatever to the further hind end

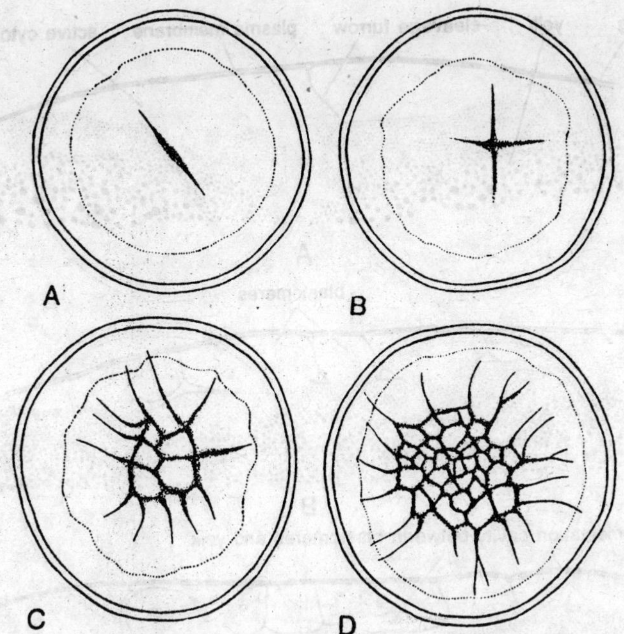

Fig. 9.4. Surface view of germinal disc of hen's egg showing early cleavage. A—Two-cell stage; B—Four-cell stage; C—Twenty-cell stage; D—A late cleavage stage.

of the embryo, so that in the pigeon it will not bear the interpretation that has been placed on it in the hen's egg.

After the third cleavage the ovum leaves the isthmus, and, within four hours after entering the uterus, progresses from the eight to approximately the 256 celled stage. These cleavages in the hen's egg are very irregular, but two classes of furrows may be distinguished in surface view: (1) those that cut off the inner ends of the cells, and (2) those that run in a radial direction. The furrows of the first class produce a group of cells that are bounded on all sides in surface view, but these are, at first, still connected below by the deeper protoplasm. They may be called the central cells. These are bounded by cells that are united in the marginal periblast, and thus lack marginal boundaries as well as deep boundaries; they may be called the marginal cells. The distinction between central and marginal cells is one of great importance which should be clearly grasped.

In the surface views of later cleavages the following points should be noted: (1) the group of central cells increases by the addition of cells cut off from the inner ends of the marginal cells, and by the

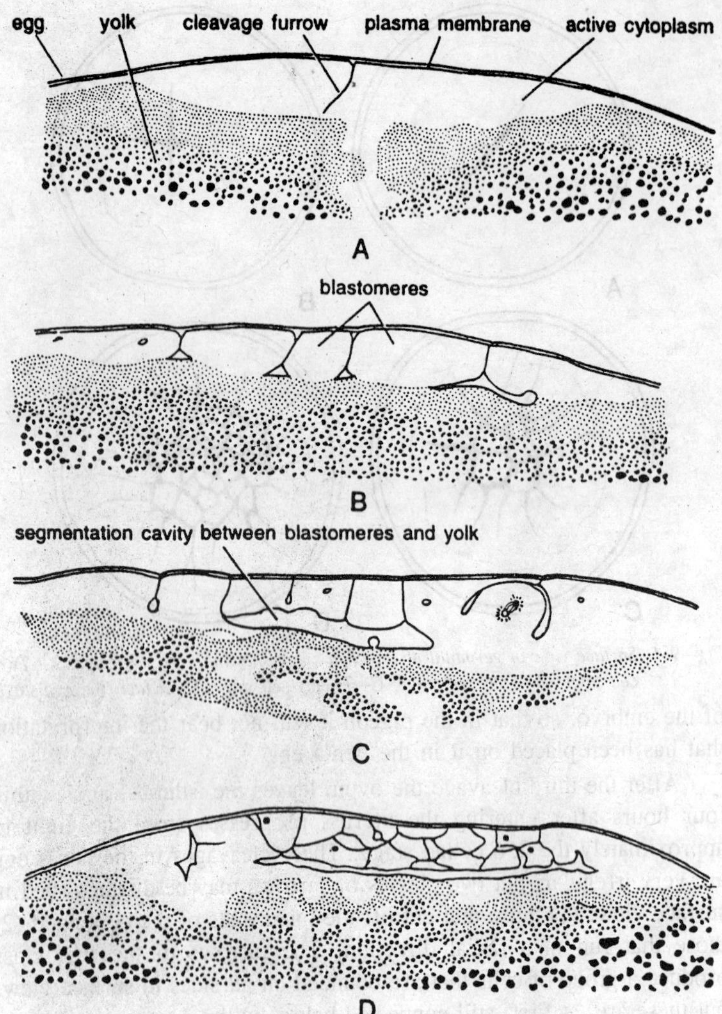

Fig. 9.5. T.S. of germinal disc of hen's egg showing early cleavage.

multiplication of the central cells themselves: (2) the marginal cells increase by the formation of new radial furrows, thus constantly expanding the diameter of the whole bastodisc, which may properly be called the blastoderm now that it is divided into cells. The increase of the central cells is much more rapid than that of the marginal cells, and the cells themselves are much smaller than the marginal cells, both because of their mode of origin and also because of their more rapid multiplication. The area of the central cells is also constantly increasing, with consequent reduction of the marginal zone. Emphasis has been laid by several authors on the excentric position of the smallest cells, and the inference has been drawn that these represent the hinder end of the blastoderm. Similar excentricity in the pigeon's egg is without reference to the furture embryonic axis.

But the surface views do not show what is going on in the deeper parts of the blastoderm. At the eight-celled stage a narrow space appears in the depth of the central portion of the blastoderm approximately between protoplasm and yolk; this is the subgerminal cavity which furnishes a lower boundary to the central cells. It is an area of progressive liquefaction of the yolk, presumably produced by enzymes from the overlying cells, and is probably not homologous to the blastocoele of other species. In later stages it extends peripherally to the inner margin of the periblast, and thus all of the central cells become completely bounded. A new class of cleavage planes then forms in these cells after the thirty-two celled stage, horizontal or parallel to the surface; in this way the central part of the blastoderm becomes two cell layer deep, and later several layers deep. The subgerminal cavity never cuts under the marginal cells, which remain united below and at their margins by the periblast.

In the older accounts of the horizontal cleavages by *Kolliker*, *Duval*, and others these are represented as forming before the subgerminal cavity, thus leaving the deeper cells in continuity with the yolk. Such cells are then supposed to continue budding off cells from their upper surfaces. But this view his been shown to be incorrect by the observations of Blount on the pigeon described below and by Patterson on the hen included above.

Pigeon's Egg

The cleavage of the pigeon's egg, as worked out in detail by Blount, is made the basis of the description of formation of the germinal wall in the absence of any consistent account for the hen's egg. The fundamental features of the cleavage are the same as in the hen's egg, so that the description need not be repeated.

The feature to be particularly emphasized in the cleavage of the pigeon's egg is the occurrence of a secondary or accessory cleavage in the marginal zone or periblast. When the origin of these cells is traced it is found that they arise around the supernumerary sperm nuclei, which accumulated and multiply in the periblast. Another interesting point illustrated by the figures is that the marginal cells have a peripheral wall wherever the accessory cleavage occurs, but between the groups of accessory cleavage cells the marginal cells are continuous with the periblast, as they are everywhere in the hen's egg. In a section of a germinal disc, showing the accessory cleavage it is seen that the peripheral boundary of the marginal cells cuts under the margin for a considerable distance.

The accessory cleavage becomes manifest at the time of appearance of the first cleavage plane, and increases in amount up to about the 32 celled stage, and thereafter gradually decreases until it completely disappears. The peripheral boundaries of the marginal cells disappear at equal pace, and, when the accuracy accessory cleavage is finally wiped out, the marginal cells are everywhere continuous with the periblast, as in the hen's egg. In some eggs the accessory cleavage is much more extensive than in others; indeed, in some it appears to be entirely absent, but this is relatively rare. In the stage shown in Figure for instance, there is usually considerable accessory cleavage; but in this egg there is done. The variation is obviously due to the variable number of supernumerary spermatozoa which enter the ovum.

The question arises whether the disappearance of the cell walls around the sperm nuclei is caused by degeneration of the latter, or is simply a later syncytial condition in the periblast in which the sperm nuclei are embedded. There can be little doubt that the former alternative is correct. While in the stages of the accessory cleavage, sperm nuclei are readily found both in the accessory cleavage cells and also in the unsegmented periblast, they decrease in number as the accessory cleavage planes disappear, and when the latter are entirely lost the periblast is absolutely devoid of nuclei. Fragmentation of the sperm nuclei is a frequent accompaniment of their disappearance.

Thus the accessory cleavage is a secondary and transient feature of the cleavage of the pigeon's egg due to polyspermy. After it has passed, the ovum is in precisely the same condition as the hen's ovum of the same stage of development. In the hen's egg there is a very limited and inconspicuous accessory cleavage around the fewer supernumerary sperm nuclei that occur (Patterson, Olsen). But most of these nuclei in the hen tend to pass to into deeper portions of the disc and there undergo complete fragmentation, producing superifical furrows only rarely.

Another feature brought out by these photographs requires emphasis. The periblastic ring shows no definite outer margin, but beyond the zone of the accessory cleavage there may occur two or three concentric circles variously indicated. Vacuoles, appearances indicate that the periblastic protoplasm extends farther out in the superficial white yolk than is usually believed to be the case; and this suggests an interesting comparison with the teleostean ovum, where the periblastic protoplasm surrounds the entire yolk as a very thin layer. Sections confirm the idea that the periblastic protoplasm has an extension beyond the so-called margin of the blastodisc. Some eggs show a more definite margin than others; it may be that there is a periodic heaping of the periblast at the margins, for which again an analogy may be found in teleosts.

Although the smallest cells may be more or less excentric in the segmented blastoderm of the pigeon, their position bears no constant relation to the further embryonic axis. They may lie in this axis in front of or behind the middle, or to the right or left of it.

At the eight-celled stage a horizontal fissure begins to appear beneath the central cells. Thus marks the full depth of the blastoderm at all stages, and the several-layered condition arises by horizontal cleavages between this and the surface. Comparison of Figures drawn at the same magnification, shows that the depth does not increase by addition of cells cut off from below, as was once supposed to be the case in the bird's ovum. The horizontal fissure not only marks the bull depth of the blastoderm, but it also indicates the site of the subgerminal cavity which arises gradually by accumulation of fluid and liquefied yolk between the cells and the underlying unsegmented protoplasm and yolk. The subgerminal cavity gradually extends towards the margin of the blastoderm, but it is bounded peripherally by the zone of junction between the marginal cells and the periblast.

Origin of the Periblastic Nuclei, Formation of the Germ Wall

Our knowledge of this part of the subject in the hen's egg is very incomplete, and the various accounts are contradictory. The reason for this is the great difficulty of securing a complete series of stages, and of arranging them in proper sequence. There is no exact way of timing the development, so that one has to judge the sequence of the stages, all of which come from the uterus, by reference to the time of laying of the preceding egg, by the degree of formation of the shell, by the size of the cells, and by the appearance of the sections. This is at best only approximate, and the securing of any given stage is largely a matter of chance. In the pigeon, which provides the basis for the following account, the time since the laying of the first egg is a fairly exact criterion of the stages of development of the second egg, so that a complete series may be collected.

The periblastic ring is entirely devoid of nuclei after the supernumerary sperm nuclei have degenerated. The marginal cells become greatly-reduced in size owing to multiplication and continuous production of central cells, and their nuclei thus approach more and more closely to the periblastic ring. The scene then changes; the marginal cells cease to produce central cells; when their nuclei divide the peripheral daughter-nuclei move out into the periblast, which is thus converted into a nucleated syncytium. The periblastic nuclei multiply rapidly and invade all portions of the periblastic ring, which maintains its original connection with the white yolk. Not only do the periblastic nuclei invade the periblastic ring, but some of the also migrate centrally into the protoplasm forming the floor of the subgerminal cavity. They do not, however, reach the center, but leave a nonnucleated subgerminal area, corresponding approximately to the nucleus of Pander, free from nuclei. The subgerminal syncytium may be known as the central periblast to distinguish it from the marginal periblast. They are, of course, continuous. In sections one has the appearance of nuclei in the yolk, for there is no sharp boundary between periblast and yolk. The syncytium, which has received its nuclei from the marginal cells, is the primordium of the germ wall. The periblast probably aids in the liquefaction of the yolk, thus increasing the depth and extent of the subgerminal cavity.

There is a sharp contrast between the segmented blastoderm and the syncytial periblast not only in structure but also as regards fate. The marginal cells constitute a zone of junction between blastoderm and periblast. Thus it will be observed that the large marginal cells on each side are continuous with the periblast, and nuclei are found in the periblast both central and peripheral to the zone of junction. The latter forms a ring around the blastoderm. It persists during the expansion of the blastoderm over the surface of the yolk.

The blastoderm now begins to expand, owing largely, at first, to additions of cells to its margin cut off from the periblast. The central as well as the marginal periblast contributes to the blastoderm, but the former appears to be rapidly used up. The marginal periblast, which is commonly called the germ wall from this stage, on the other hand grows at its periphery while it adds cells to the blastoderm centrally, and thus it moves out in the white yolk, building up the margin of the blastoderm at the same time. The original group of central cells appears to correspond approximately to the pellucid area; the additions from the germ wall would thus constitute the opaque area.

Some phases of these processes are illustrated. In the vertical section, the surface of the germ will next to the blastoderm is indented as though for the formation of superficial cells. Along the steep central margin of the germ wall groups of cells are apparently being cut off the added to he cellular blastoderm. In the horizontal section, the process of cellularization at thé central margin of the germ wall is apparently proceeding rapidly.

The superficial cells thus added to the margin of the cellular blastoderm become continuous with the ectoderm, and the deeper layers later form the yolk sac entoderm which becomes continuous with the embryonic entoderm secondarily. We can thus distinguish a syncytial, more peripheral, and a cellular, more central, portion of the germ wall.

In later stages the central margin of the syneytial part of the germ wall becomes much less steep, owing apparently to active proliferation of cells. This is illustrated. Still later, the external margin extends out peripherally and forms a short projecting shelf, appearing wedge-shaped in section. This we shall call the margin of overgrowth.

Thus we may distinguish the following zones: (1) margin of overgrowth; (2) zone of junction with the yolk (syneytial germ wall); (3) the inner zone of the germ wall, and (4) the original cellular blastoderm (pellucid area).

Origin of the Entoderm

Four main views have been advanced historically as to the method by which the inner germ layer or entoderm is formed. These are: (1) The theory of delamination, namely, that the blastoderm, which is several cells thick at the close of cleavage, splits into two layers - an outer epiblast (which will later segregate into ectoderm and mesoderm) and an inner sheet of primary entoderm (hypoblast); this is the oldest view, promulgated by *Ollacher* (1869). (2) The theory of invagination, i.e., that the primary entoderm arises as an in rolling of the margin of the blastoderm, this view, which was supported by *Haeckel*, *Coette*, *Rauber*, *Duval Patterson* and others, was an attempt to bring the mode of gastrulation in bids into line with lower vertebrates. (3) The theory of multiple ingrowth, advanced by Merbach; according to the view, the epiblast was thrown into many irregular folds, from each of which the entoderm arose by inwardering of single cells or many isolated groups of cells. (4) The view of *Nowack* that the primary entoderm arises as an ingrowth of cells from the germ wall, more particularly from the posterior portion, was adopted in substance by *O. Hertwig* and combined, in part, by Jacobson with the blastoporal feature of the second theory above.

The account of the origin of the entoderm which follows is that which seems most probable in the light of recent work. It is essentially a modernized version of the theory of delamination with emphasis upon the properties and activities of individual cells.

The segmentation of the blastodisc during the period of cleavage results in a disc-shaped aggregate of rounded cells plied one on top of the other, four or five deep. Structurally, the disc is an extremely shallow dome, resting on the yolk at its edge (the germ wall) and separated centrally from the yolk by a narrow, fluid-filled, sub-germinal cavity. On the floor of the latter are occasional scattered cells which may have become detached from the overlying disc or may have been left behind by the ever-expanding germ wall. The cells of the blastoderm show some variation in size and yolk content, but there is no spatial arrangement with respect to these differences. The only visible differentiation is a thickening toward one side of the blastoderm (the future posterior end) where the cells are more numerous.

A gradual assortment of the blastodermal cells then takes place, during which the smaller yolk-poor cells are segregated from the larger yolk rich ones.

It seems probable that the segregation of the yolky cells from the others is a manifestation of negative "tissue affinity" between the ectodermal and entodermal cells as described by Holtfreter. The two kinds of cells may become incompatible after reaching a certain point in their differentiation and then mutually repel each other. The frequent occurrence of yolk- filled flask-shaped cells, with their small ends still in contact with the surface but with the body of the cell "squeezed" toward the interior, is suggestive of such a view.

Meanwhile the blastoderm expands over the yolk and becomes somewhat thinner and more transparent where it overlies the sub-germinal cavity. The central portion (area pellucida) is thus demarcated from the area opera (or germ wall) by virtue of the later's thickness and intimate contact with undigested yolk. The depth of the subgerminal cavity also increases as the blastoderm expands.

As the large yolk-rich hypoblastic cells accumulate toward the lower surface of the blastoderm, the upper yolk-free cells become aligned (perhaps through the aid of a surface coat) into an epithelium of single-cell thickness. The hypoblastic cells, on the other hand, do not organize into a coherent sheet for some time, but remain irregularly distributed one to three deep in the primitive rounded condition. This different in the arrangement of the cells is sufficient in itself to demarcate two layers. Thus, in effect, there is a delamination of epi and entoblast, but not in the sense that a split or space is necessarily formed between the two. Due to the irregular arrangement of the entoblastic cells, small space appear here and there between the two layers, but at many points the separation is only in differences of cellular configuration.

The delamination of the hypoblast begins in the posterior portion of the area pellucida and progresses anteriorly in lesser amount; a point is reached where groups of cell or single cells separate from the epiblast at interrupted loci. Thus, the primary entoblast arises as a continuous layer of cells in the posterior part of the area pellucida, but appears "frayed-out" anteriorly and antero-laterally and occurs only as scattered islands of cells beyond the "frayed" edge.

At the time of laying, the blastoderm shows much variation in the extent to which the hypoblast has formed. The range is from blastoderms in which the separation has barely started and in which the germ wall show's practically no increased thickening posteriorly, to those in which the hypoblast is a separate sheet with considerable anterior spread and in which the germ wall is much thickened posteriorly. Despite this variability, it should be noted that, at the time of laying, the blastoderm is just in the midst of forming the entoblast. The process continues for many hours after incubation begins, but meanwhile other events supervene.

10

Foetal Membranes

Evolution and Homology of Foetal Membranes

The foetal or embryonic membranes of the avian and reptilian embryos are not only interesting from the stand-point of comparative embryology, but they also illustrate in their changes of function and special adaptations to the environment some of the fundamental laws of organic evolution. The foetal membranes as found in the chick embryo are also present in the embryos of mammals, though in the latter they have undergone radical changes, especially in the embryos of placental mammals. It is therefore very desirable that the development of the embryonic membranes of the chick be thoroughly understood, so that their homologues in the embryos of mammals may be identified.

The chick embryo has four different embryonic or foetal membranes: namely, the *yolk sac*, the *allantois*, the *amnion*, and the *chorion* or *serosa*. Of these four, the first two are present in rudimentary form in the frog and other amphibian embryos; however, the last two, namely, the amnion and the serosa, are neogenic structures which were developed first in the reptilian embryo. The birds, having been derived from reptiles, retained these newly-acquired embryonic features in their development. In fact, as indicated above, they have also been handed down to the mammals in a modified condition. At hatching the greater part of the foetal membranes are discarded. The amnion and the serosa are completely eliminated, and the allantois is also discarded to its greater extent. However, the yolk sac is incorporated into the small intestine.

Constriction of the Embryo from the Yolk Sac

The closely apposed ectoderm and somatic mesoderm (somatopleure), as well as the combined entoderm and splanchnic mesoderm (splanchnopleure), extend from the embryo peripherally into the extraembryonic area. The origin of these folds, known as the *limiting body folds*, begins with the formation of the crescent-shaped head fold in embryos of less than twenty hours of incubation. It extends laterally from the subcephalic pocket, turning backward on both sides near the heart of the embryo toward the posterior region in the form of the lateral body folds. Later, when the tail bud is established, the lateral body folds become continuous with the fold around and posterior to it, thus limiting the embryo from the underlying yolk mass by a marginal groove extending from the head fold through the lateral body folds to the tail fold, undercutting and separating the embryo from the yolk mass as it becomes older.

Yolk Sac and Its Relation to the Gut

In chicks of sixteen hours of incubation, i.e., those of the primitive streak stage and slightly older, the gut, or enteron, is represented as a flat, circular cavity beneath the primitive streak. Its roof is formed by splanchnopleure and extends peripherally into the extraembryonic area, while its floor is composed of the non-cellular yolk. In the 24-hour embryo the gut has still the same relationship, with the exception of the small enteric pocket which has developed into the developing, forward-jutting head. This pocket, known as the fore-gut, is the first differentiation of the alimentary canal is completely surrounded by mesoderm or mesenchyme.

In the 48-hour embryo a similar process takes place in the formation of the tail bud, so that a saclike cellular hind-gut is produced. The undifferentiated part of the enteron located between the fore-gut and hind-gut is called the mid-gut. As the embryo grows older and the amniotic head fold, tail fold, and lateral folds, undercut the embryo, thus increasing the length of the fore-gut and hind gut, the mid-gut becomes correspondingly smaller. Eventually the latter is restricted to a small portion of the small intestine posterior to the pancreas, where it leads into the reduced yolk sac by means of the yolk stalk. The embryo consumes the yolk as it grows, and the yolk sac therefore becomes correspondingly smaller, so that two or three days before hatching it has become so diminutive that it is drawn within the tissues of the embryo and shows itself as a protuberance from the small intestine. The splanchnopleure, forming the roof of the enteron in the

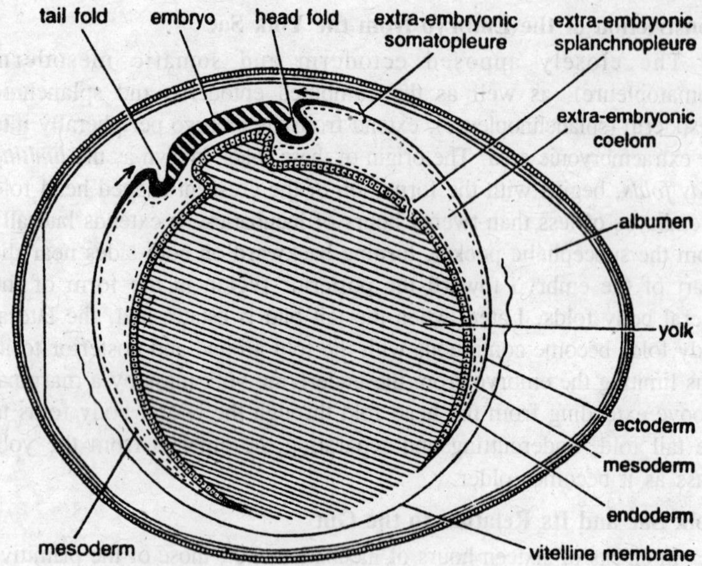

Fig. 10.1. An early chick embryo showing body folds delimiting embryo from extra-embryonic areas.

earliest chick embryos, and forming the complete fore-gut and hind-gut, is the same cellular layer that covers the yolk sac. As the latter diminishes in size, the splanchnopleure follows the yolk sac into the embryo, where it is utilized in the lining of the mid-gut. It appears, therefore, that the yolk sac is really part of the gut, as it was in the frog embryo. It is finally incorporated into the small intestine of the chick, where it is still present several days after hatching.

The yolk is used directly as food by the early embryo. Later it is broken down into diffusible substances digested by enzymes from the entoderm of the yolk sac and picked up by capillaries in the area vasculosa and carried by the vitelline veins to the omphalomesenteric veins, which send it through the liver to the heart, whence it is propelled to all parts of the embryo and to extraembryonic tissues and organs. Since the omphalomesenteric veins, as well as more posteriorly located omphalomesenteric arteries, spread out over the yolk sac in the splanchnic mesoderm, the constriction of the attachment of the embryo to the yolk sac in the formation of the yolk stalk brings the two sets of omphalomesenteric vessels close together.

Amnion and Serosa

The amnion and the serosa are two foetal membranes that have been developed in the evolution of the reptiles and passed on to the

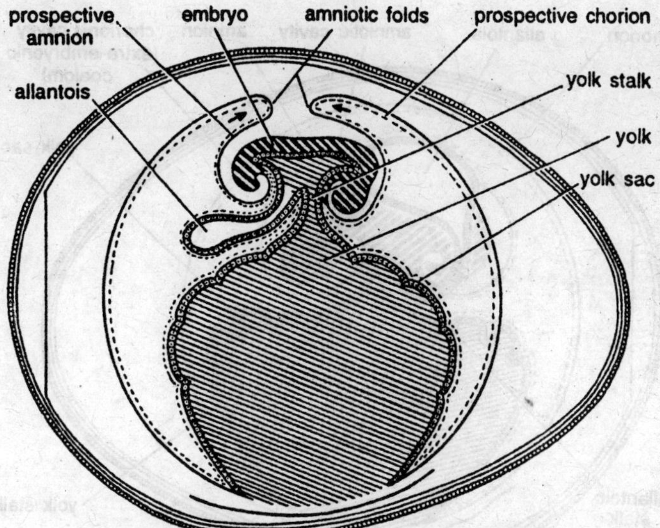

Fig. 10.2. Early stage in the development of the extra-embryonic membranes of chick.

birds and mammals. The amnion is a membrane enveloping the embryo, separating it from its immediate contact with the environment. It acts, therefore, much like a big in which the embryo is contained. Between the embryo and the enveloping amnion is a space (*amniotic cavity*) containing a saline liquid (*amniotic fluid*). Since the reptilian and avian eggs are deposited on dry land, it seems obvious that the amnion and the amniotic fluid have been developed to keep the embryo moist and protect it from desiccation. This original function of the amnion has changed in the mammals, where the amnion is chiefly a protective organ, equalizing and distributing pressure brought against the embryo by physical forces from the environment, and, furthermore, where it serves as a prevention of adhesion by favouring movement of the embryo.

The phylogenetic origin of the amnion is still problematical, though the following theory is sometimes advanced for its origin. The reptilian eggs are more abundantly provided with yolk than are those of the amphibians. It is ssumed, therefore, that due to its weight the reptilian embryo sank into the soft yolk and that the blastodisc around the embryo was thus elevated over it in the form of a crater. In the course of evolution the more of less circular margin of the raised blastodisc grew over the embryo, hiding it form view by covering it with membrane (amnion).

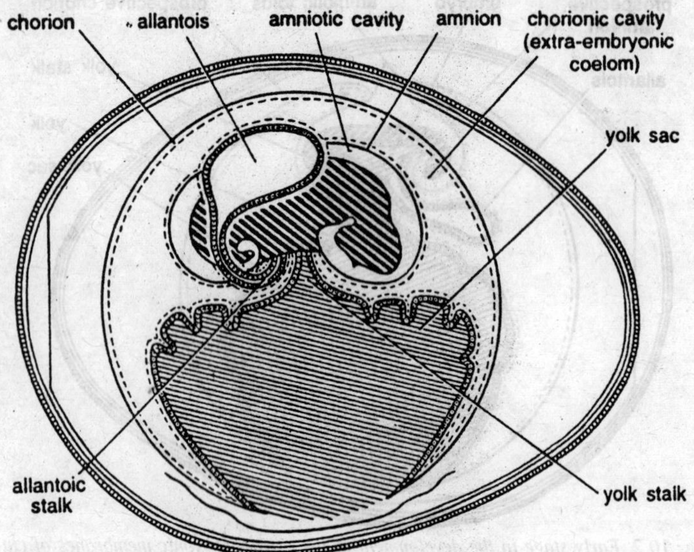

Fig. 10.3. Later stage in the development of the extra-embryonic membranes of the chick.

That this theory is not so fantastic as it appears at first sight is indicated by the actual development of the amnion in the chick embryo. At thirty hours of incubation the large and well-defined head of the embryo just forward over the subcephalic pocket and has sunk into the underlying yolk mass. There is a simultaneous elevation of a blastodermic fold (*amniotic head fold*) immediately in front of the head. The amniotic head fold is crescent-shaped in its initial .stages, its free ends pointing toward the posterior region of the embryo where they will form the lateral amniotic folds in later development.

Shortly after the second day of incubation the amniotic tail fold appears posterior to the tail bud. It grows forward over the embryo in a manner similar to the backward growth of the amniotic head fold. Eventually the two will meet and fuse in the region just slightly posterior to the omphalomesenteric arteries during the fourth day of incubation. The location of the final union of the amniotic folds is marked by a scar called the *seroamniotic connection*.

The amniotic folds are formed from somatopleure, which is composed of ectoderm and somatic mesoderm. Since a fold is composed of an inner and an outer layer, two separate sheets must be produced by the union of the amniotic folds, an inner and an outer one, the former being the amnion and the latter the scrosa. We may compare the amniotic folds of the embryo with an oval crater of a volcano that

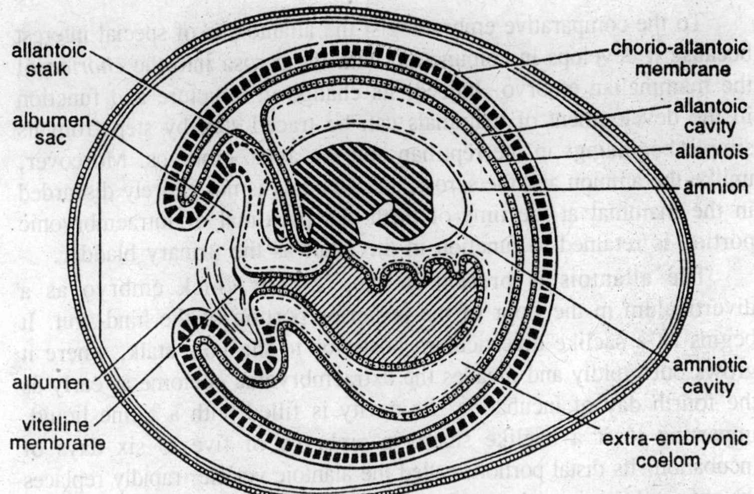

Fig. 10.4. The fully matured extra-embryonic membranes of the chick.

has a well- developed rim on one side and a very small one on the other. The former represents the amniotic head fold and the latter the tail fold, both being connected by the remainder of the rim of the crater, representing the *lateral amniotic folds*. If one assumes further that the wall of the crater is hollow and that it is therefore composed of an inner and an outer surface, one can see immediately that if the rim of the crater should grow and fuse centrally, an outer and an inner sheet would be produced, both covering the central depression of the volcano.

The amnion, representing only the innermost half of the amniotic folds, is a transparent membrane composed of somatopleure, with somatic mesoderm on the outside and ectoderm on the inside. The latter is continuous with the skin ectoderm of the embryo near the yolk stalk and the allantoic stalk (to be discussed later). The serosa, representing the outer half of the amniotic folds, is also composed of somatopleure, having the somatic mesoderm on the inside and ectoderm on the outside. Between the amnion and the serosa is the seroamniotic cavity (*extraembryonic coelome*), which is in direct communication with the coelome within the embryo (*intraembryonic coelome*). The serosa grows around the yolk sac, enveloping it completely at the end of the second week. It expands and adheres to the entire calcareous shell within the shell membrane, so that the embryo with all its foetal membranes is encompassed by it. Its intimate union with the allantois will be discussed in the next paragraph.

Allantois

To the comparative embryologist the allantois is of special interest because it develops in conjunction with the scrosa into the *chorion* of the mammalian embryo. Indeed, its change in structure and function in the development of mammals can be traced step by step from its simple beginnings in the reptilian and the avian embryos. Moreover, unlike the amnion and the scrosa, the allantois is not entirely discarded in the mammal at the time of birth. Its proximal or intraembryonic portion is retained to function in the adult as the urinary bladder.

The allantois is present in the 72-hour chick embryo as a diverticulum in the floor of the posterior portion of the hind- gut. It begins as a saclike diverticulum posterior to the yolk stalk, where it grows out rapidly and invades the extraembryonic coelome as early as the fourth day of incubation. Its cavity is filled with a saline liquid, imparting to it a baglike shape in embryos of five to six days of incubation. Its distal portion, called the alantoic vesicle, rapidly replaces the extraembryonic coelome (*Seroamniotic space*), wedging itself between the amnion and the serosa. The proximal or intraembryonic portion of the allantois consists of a narrow stalk called the allantoic stalk, which, in mammals, is utilized in the formation of the urinary bladder.

The allantois is instrumental in the storage of excretory substances which are given off in development. Being an out- growth of the gut, the allantois must necessarily be composed of splanchnopleure, the same layer which forms the yolk sac. In fact, the splanchnic mesoderm of the allantois also parallels that of the yolk sac in the formation of a complex capillary blood system. It connects with the intraembryonic circulation by means of the paired allantoic arteries and veins. Upon attaining its full size the allantois replaces the entire extraembryonic coelome and extends itself around the entire embryo, apposing itself closely to the somatic mesodermal layer of the serosa. The latter fuses with the splanchnic mesoderm of the allantois, forming the chorio-allantoic blood vessels in this area, and extending the capillary circulation of the allantois in this manner over the entire inner portion of the calcareous, porous shell. The exchange of respiratory gases is easily accomplished through the egg shell, and though the allantois is partly excretory in function and also aids in the absorption of a large portion of the albumen, its main function must be considered respiratory. In later stages of development the allantoic circulation also absorbs calcium from the egg shell, which is used in the embryo for the formation of bone. At the same time this renders the egg shell thin and fragile, thus facilitating its rupture by the chick at the time of hatching.

11

ADVANCED DEVELOPMENT IN BIRDS

Structure of the Blastoderm in Freshly Laid Eggs

There is more or less variation in the progress of development of the hypoblast at the time of laying. These differences, however, are apparent only in sectioned blastoderms; in surface view the blastoderms are similar in appearance, showing only an outer white ring (the area opaca) of even width and a central translucent area (the area pellucida) through which Pander's nucleus and scattered yolk globules can be distinguished. Beneath the pellucid area is the subgerminal cavity bounded marginally by the germ wall; the cavity is somewhat deeper at the posterior end of the blastoderm. The posterior part only of the pellucid area is two-layered. The lower layer or hypoblast (primary entoblast) terminates posteriorly at the germ wall but does not reach the wall either laterally or anteriorly. The hypoblast is a loosely coherent layer of rounded cells, uneven in thickness, continuous posteriorly, but grading out to discontinuous clusters and scattered single cells at its anterior and lateral edges.

The germ wall is slightly thicker in depth at the posterior than at the anterior margin. There is, however, no consistent difference in its breadth at the two regions. Beyond the zone of junction the blastoderm overlaps the yolk a short distance.

The epiblast is thicker in the area pellucida than in the area opeaca. Its cells are more coherent than the underlying entoblast and have assumed for the most part the characteristics of a single-layered epithelium.

Changes Prior to the Formation of the Primitive Streak

With the beginning of incubation the balstoderm resumes development. The changes which take place are the result of (1) mitosis throughout the rapidly growing germ, and (2) orderly cellular movements, both of which occur concurrently. These processes, of course, have been in operation since the first cleavages. The part played by cellular movements, however, becomes increasingly important from this time onward.

The most important change during the first few hours is the continued separation and further differentiation of the *hypoblast*. The cells lose their primitive rounded shape, flatten, and unite to form a continuous layer except at the "frayed-out" anterior edge. These changes in shape, along with a migration forward of the cells, extend the hypoblast toward the germ wall. The process begins at the posterior edge of the hypoblast, progress anteriorly, and is still continuing, during stages of the primitive streak. The hypoblastic epithelium is very thin. The *eipblast*, on the other hand, has now become a definite columnar epithelium with taller cells posteriorly than anteriorly.

The combination of thickened epiblast plus the hypoblast beneath it causes a visible opacity in the posterior portion of the *area pellucida*. In surface view it is seen as an indistinct circular or half-moon shaped area with one edge next to the area opaca. This is the *embryonic shield*. It is the first gross indication of the polarity of the blastoderm, for a line bisecting it will, in general, coincide with the future antero-posterior axis. The embryonic shield is not ordinarily seen in freshly laid eggs but is common in many so-called unicubated blastoderms and appears distinctly after four or five hours of incubation. The entoderm at this stage has the same general crescentic shape and anterior extent as the thickened epiblast which overlies it.

In addition to the flattening and creeping forward of the hypoblast, there are shiftings of cells in the epiblast which are a prelude to the appearance of the primitive streak. If the pellucid are is marked at different points with carbon particles is extensive postero-medial movement of lateral epiblastic cells toward the median posterior quadrant. The cells of the posterior border of the pellucid area move medially, and, if already in the mid-line, move slightly forward.

Primitive Streak

Our knowledge of the mode of origin of the primitive streak progressed slowly during the descriptive era of embryology until suitable experimental techniques could be evolved. Inevitably, concepts arose

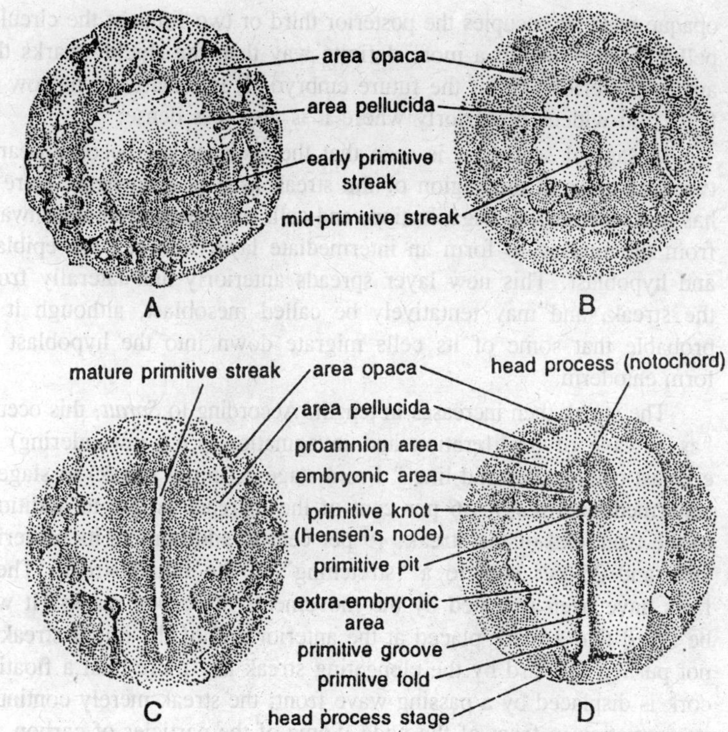

Fig. 11.1. Surface view of chick blastoderm showing development of primitive streak (gastrulation) and head process (start of neurulation). A—Initial streak (stage 2); B—Intermediate streak (stage 3); C—Definitive streak (stage 4); D—Head process stage (stage 5) embryo of 19 to 22 hours of incubation

in the interim (e.g., concrescence) which, although speculative in nature, were widely adopted and even somewhat reluctantly given up as the technique of vital marking revealed the true dynamics of the process. In many cases experiments with vital dyes yielded equivocal results due to the tendency of the dyes to diffuse and fade and the difficulty of preserving the color when blastoderms were prepared for histological examination. Recently, these technical difficulties have been circumvented by marking the blastoderm with particles of carbon, and the results thus obtained, in conjunction with the data of Pasteels and Wetzel, provide the basis for the following account.

The cellular movements in the epiblast, described above, immediately precede and lead to the formation of the primitive streak. After about six to seven hours of incubation the steak appears in the lien of bisection of the embryonic shield as an elongated, slightly opaque band. It occupies the posterior third or two fifths of the circular pellucid area and, in a more definite way than the shield, marks the antero-posterior axis of the future embryo. It is realatively narrow in front and widens posteriorly where it is also less dense.

In sagittal section it is seen that the epiblast has become nearly twice as thick in the region of the streak as it is elsewhere. Here it has lost its epithelial organization, and cells are rapidly moving inward from the surface to form an intermediate layer between the epiblast and hypoblast. This new layer spreads anteriorly and laterally from the streak, and may tentatively be called mesoblast, although it is probable that some of its cells migrate down into the hypoblast to form entoderm.

The streak then increases in length. According to *Spratt*, this occurs "as a wave of proliferation and invagination (i.e., inwandering) of epiblast cells in the mid-line." From stage 2 (initial streak) to stage 3 (intermediate streak), 56 per cent of the increase is due to additions to the front end of the streak, 19 per cent to additions to its posterior end, and 25 per cent to a "stretching" of the initial streak. These facts have been revealed by the movements of carbon marks. It will be noted that a mark placed at the anterior end of the initial streak is not pushed forward by the elongating streak any more than a floating cork is displaced by a passing wave front; the streak merely continues its formation in front of the node. Some of the particles of carbon are carried inward by the inwandering of cells as the streak merely continues its formation in front of the node. Some of the particles of carbon are carried inward by the inwandering of cells as the streak forms, and they then spread anteriorly and laterally with the newly formed mesoblast. At an intermediate stage the streak has reached the center of the pellucid area where the chorda and medullary plate-forming areas of epiblast are located. At this point its anterior end becomes club-shaped and eventually develops a pit, the primitive pit, which corresponds to the neurenteric canal of other vertebrates.

The neurenteric canal is a canal that connects the posterior end of the central canal of the neural tube with the intestine. It arises from the anterior end of the blastopore, and is typically developed in Selachia, Amphibia, reptiles, some birds (e.g., duck, goose, Sterna, etc.). It begins in the primitive pit and extends forward into the head-process. Subsequently the primitive pit becomes surrounded by the medullary folds, and thus opens into the neural canal. An opening is later formed through the entoderm so that the definitive canal connects

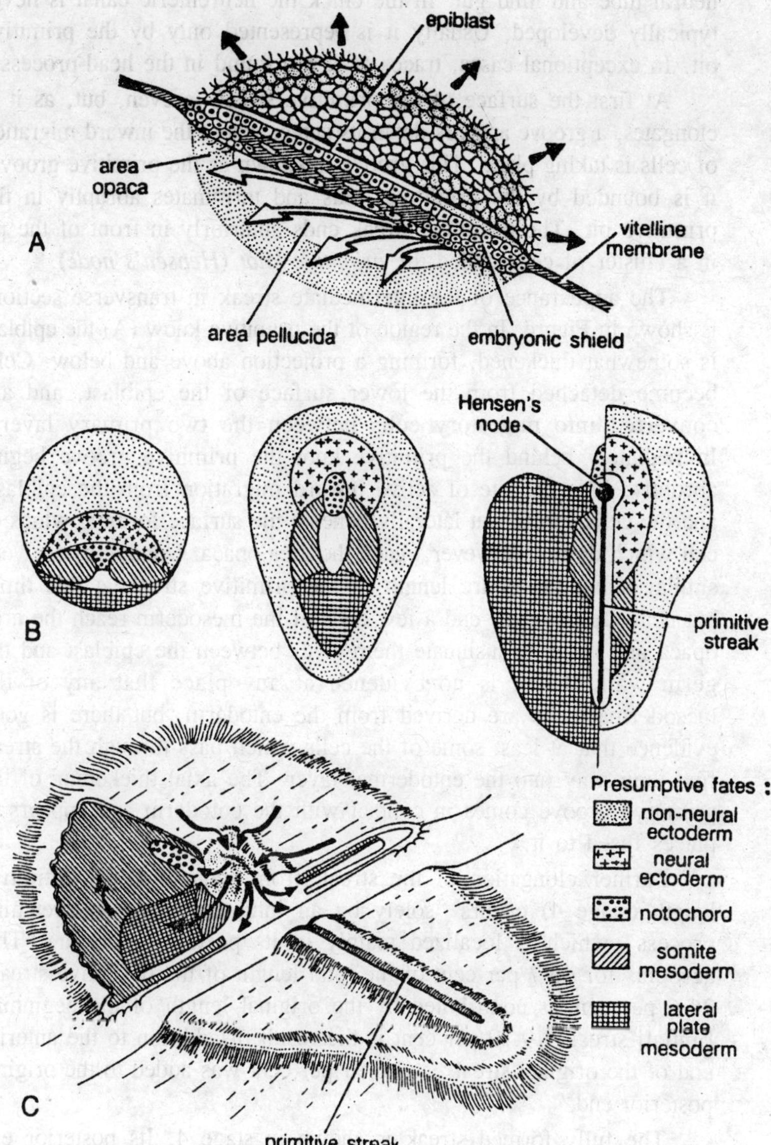

Fig. 11.2. Gastrulation in the avian embryo. A—Early blastoderm, expanding radially; with division into area opaca and area pellucida, the embryonic shield from which cells fan out into the area opaca; B—Fate maps from the beginning of gastrulation to the formation of the primitive streak; C—partly sectioned view of primitive streak stage, showing invagination of endodermal and mesodermal material, with some material at the anterior end of the streak moving anteriorly to form the notochord.

neural tube and hind gut. In the chick the neurenteric canal is never typically developed. Usually it is represented only by the primitive pit. In exceptional cases, traces of it are found in the head-process.

At first the surface of the primitive streak is even, but, as it is elongates, a groove appears down its center where the inward migration of cells is taking place. This groove is known as the primitive groove; it is bounded by the primitive folds and terminates abruptly in the primitive pit. The primitive streak ends anteriorly in front of the pit in a cluster of cells called the *primitive knot* (*Hensen's node*).

The appearance of the intermediate streak in transverse sections is shown in Figure. In the region of the primitive know (A) the epiblast is somewhat thickened, forming a projection above and below. Cells become detached from the lower surface of the epiblast, and are converted into migratory cells between the two primary layers. Immediately behind the primitive knot the primitive groove begins abruptly; it is the site of active inward migration from the epiblast, and the cells spread out laterally beneath the surface forming wings of cell which do not, however, reach the area opaca. Conditions are very similar along the entire length of the primitive streak at this time; but near the posterior end a few cells of the mesoderm reach the area opaca and begin to insinuate themselves between the epiblast and the germ wall. There is no evidence at any place that any of the mesodermal cells are derived from the entoderm, but there is good evidence that at least some of the cells which pass through the streak find their way into the entodermal layer. The axial thickening of the primitive groove comes in contact with the entoderm and appears in places fused to it.

Further elongation of the streak from stage 3 to its definitive length (stage 4) occurs "solely by an intussusceptive or stretching process" which is localized mainly in its posterior portion. "This accounts for 46.7 per cent of the total length of the definitive streak; 26.6 per cent is contributed by the original length of the beginning [initial] streak; 19.79 per cent is the result of addition to the anterior end of the original streak; and 6.91 per cent was added to the original posterior end."

The fully formed streak is shown in stage 4. Its posterior end terminates in an expansion which is not very obvious in surface view, and hence is not usually described; it may be called the primitive plate. In some cases the primitive streak and groove are bifurcated at the posterior end but this condition is by no means typical. Simultaneous with the postero-medial movement of the epiblastic sheet and the "stretching" of the streak, the shape of the pellucid area is itself altered from a circular to pear-shape. The inward migration of the converged epiblastic cells through the primitive groove continues as before and occurs throughout the entire length of the streak including the primitive pit and Hensen's mode.

Formation of Entoderm During Streak Stages

It will be recalled that the hypoblast was in the organizing into a flattened and coherent epithelium and was creeping forward from the posterior part of the pellucid area at the time that the egg was laid. These changes continue during the first few hours of incubation while the primitive streak is forming in the epiblast; in fact, the forward movement of the hypoblast just precedes the anterior differentiation of the streak.

Spratt cites several lines of evidence which suggest a casual influence of the hypoblast upon the development of the streak: (1) the two structures develop at equal pace; (2) when the orientation of the

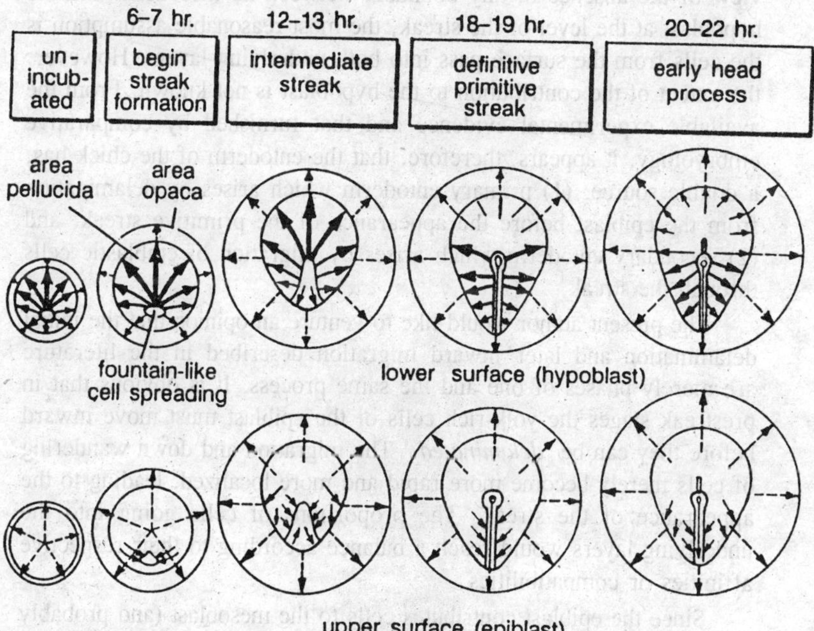

Fig. 11.3. Dye-marking experiments of Spratt and Hass (1960) to illustrate morphogenetic movements of lower surface of blastoderm (hypoblast) in relation to upper surface (epiblast) before and during primitive streak formation.

hypoblastic cells is changed experimentally, the direction of the streak is correspondingly changed; (3) if the hypoblast is removed no streak is formed, etc. Further work is needed, however, to prove whether the suspected relationship is valid.

As the hypoblast forward, some of its cells tend to pile up in a thicker crescent-shaped area (the *Entodermhof* of Wetzel) located behind its fenestrated free edge and ahead of the developing streak. As Rudnick has pointed out, this thickened, almost mesenchymatous, crescent corresponds in general to the germinal crescent which gives rise to the so-called primodial germ cells. The entodermal sheet is not complete throughout the area pellucida until about the twelfth hour of incubation, at which time the streak has almost reached its definitive length.

Although the experimental evidence is meager, it seems probable that the hypoblast receives contributions of cells from the epiblast during the entire period of existence of the primitive streak. When the surface of the epiblast is marked with a vital dye or with carbon, some of the marked cells are found eventually in the entoderm. In view of the absence of any boundary between he mesoderm and the hypoblast at the level of the streak, the most reasonable assumption is the cells from the surface pass into both underlying layers. However, the extent of the contribution to the hypoblast is not known. From the available experimental evidence and that furnished by comparative embryology, it appears, therefore, that the entoderm of the chick has, a double source: (1) primary entoderm which arises by delamination from the epibiast before the appearance of the primitive streak, and (2) secondary entoderm which arises by migration of epiblastic cells through the streak.

The present author would like to venture an opinion that the initial delamination and laιer inward migration described in the literature are merely phases of one and the same process. It is obvious that in prestreak stages the yolk-rich cells of the epiblast must move inward before they can be '*delaminated.*' The migration and down wandering of cells merely become more rapid and more localized, leading to the appearance of the streak. The proportions of cells going into the underlying layers would reach a balance according to their respective affinities or compatibilities.

Since the epiblast contributes cells to the mesoblast (and probably also to the hypoblast), it seems best to use the non-committal terms, "*epiblast*," and "*hypoblast*," until the germ layers are clearly established in front of the streak as indicated by the appearance of the embryo. Therefore, we shall arbitrarily use the more general terminology until the head fold appears (stage 6), after which the epiblast and hypoblast anterior to the node will be called ectoderm and entoderm, respectively. At the level of the streak (and later in the tail bud), however, the three germ layers will still be in the act of forming for several days.

REGRESSION OF THE PRIMITIVE STREAK

Formation of the Head-process

Soon after the streak reaches its definitive length, the first sign of the embryo proper appears as a short mesodermal rod (ca. 0.1 mm. wide × 0.16 mm. long) which extends forward from the anterior border of the primitive knot. This is the head-process or notochord. It is formed by an axial concentration of the chorda-mesoblast just anterior to the node and is continuous anteriorly and laterally with the other cephalic mesoblast which underlies the anterior part of the epiblast. Marking experiments show that the cells from which it is formed have migrated inward through the streak during the latter's period of elongation. Simultaneous with the appearance of the head-process, the entire streak and node begin to move posteriorly, and during the next twenty-four hours the streak shortens until only the node refrains. At the same time the head-process increases in length and other parts of the embryo make their appearance. We shall consider first the structure of the embryo during stages of the formation of the head-process, and then the mode of its elongation and the regression of the streak.

The head-process and primitive streak of a chick embryo at a time when the head-process is still very short. The first section through the head-process is described beyond. B is through the primitive knot, there is a greater accumulation of cells than in the preceding stage and it will be observed that they are now fused with the entoderin, so that the latter no longer appears as a distinct layer. C is through the primitive groove near its anterior end. D is behind the center of the primitive groove, and E is through the primitive plate. It will be observed that the thickened area in the primitive plate where cells are migrating inward is very wide.

It will be noted that the mesoblast is thickest at its apparent place of origin (the streak) and thinks out laterally as it spreads towards the periphery. Mesoblastle cells also creep into the opaque area, and thus it produced a three-layered portion of the latter which corresponds to the future vascular area. The mesoblast migrates out not only from the sides and front of the streak but also from its hind end, that is from the primitive plate, so that the mesoderm extends into the opaque area behind the embryo at a very early stage.

The head-process itself, consists of a thicker central mass of cells with lateral wings; the central part, or primordium of the notochord, is continuous posteriorly with the axis of the primitive streak. The head-process becomes inseparably fused with the entoderm in the mid-line immediately after its formation, and this fusion is continued back along the axis of the primitive streak. The fusion is particularly intimate and persistent at the extreme anterior end of the head-process; behind this point the notochord and entoderm soon separate again in the course of development. But the anterior end of the notochord remains attached to the entoderm for a considerable period after the formation of the head fold. A longitudinal section shows the head-process as a mesodermal appendage to the anterior end of the primitive streak, or the primitive knot.

The embryo arises in front of it around the head-process as a center, the ectoderm of the anterior portion of the blastoderm, under which the head-process forms a median axis, becomes the thickened medullarly plate from which the neural folds are formed the anterior end of the primitive streak marks the hind end of the differentiated portion of the embryo. As the embryo grows in length, the primitive streak decreases and finally disappears, except for remnants which enter with the primitive knot into the tail bud, at the time that the tail fold is formed.

Fate of the Primitive Streak

It was noted previously that the cells which will form the head-process have already migrated inward through the primitive streak, and the first portion of the head-process is molded out of them soon after the streak reaches its definitive length (ca. 1.88 mm). The primitive streak and node then move backwards ("regress") as the head-process increases in length in front of them. This posterior shifting is real, and is most rapid in the anterior half of the streak, as can be shown by marking the node and various parts of the streak and nothing their movement with reference to stationary marks. At the same time the head-process grows in length, its rate and extent of growth paralleling the rate of regression of the streak. Careful measurements show that the tip of the head-process moves forward only shghtiy with reference to stationary marks, and that nearly all of the increase in length occurs by additions to the posterior end of the early head-process. It was formerly thought that the head-process was formed out of the cells of the regressing node but *Spratt's* experiments show that this is not true. The increase in length of the head-process is largely due to proliferation and "stretching" of the cells immediately in front of the node. If the anterior half of the blastoderm, including the node, is served from the posterior half, the notochord, neural plate, and node extend by growth back from the cut surface to form a tail-like appendage. These findings have led *Spratt* to suggest that the cause of regression of the streak is a "pushing" of the node and streak backwards by the growth of the head-process. There is some question, however, whether the node is entirely passive during regression, for Spratt also reports that no regression occurs if the node is excised from the blastoderm. Further study is needed to provide an adequate explanation of this complicated process.

Changes also occur in the epiblast which are correlated with the growth of the head-process and regression of the streak. The whole portion of the epiblast anterior to the level of the node grows at a

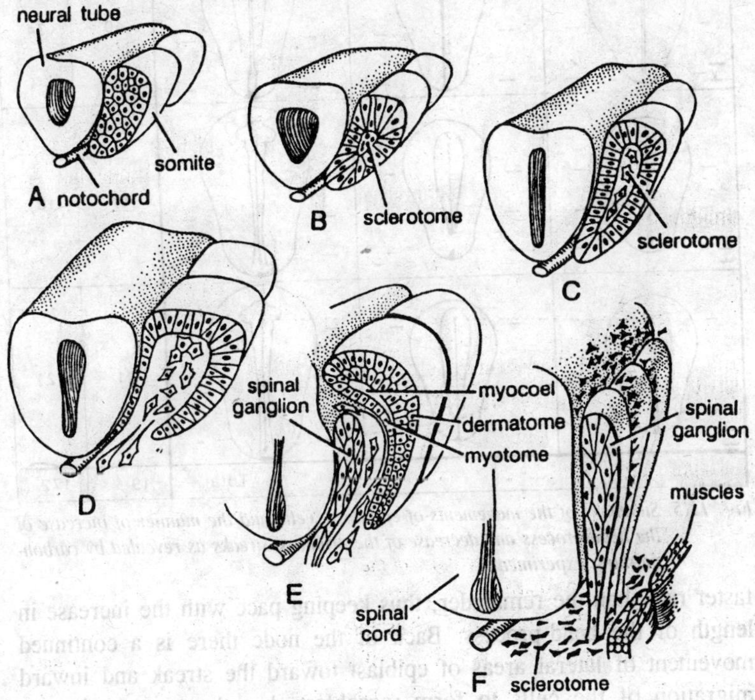

Fig. 11.4. Different steps of somitogenesis.

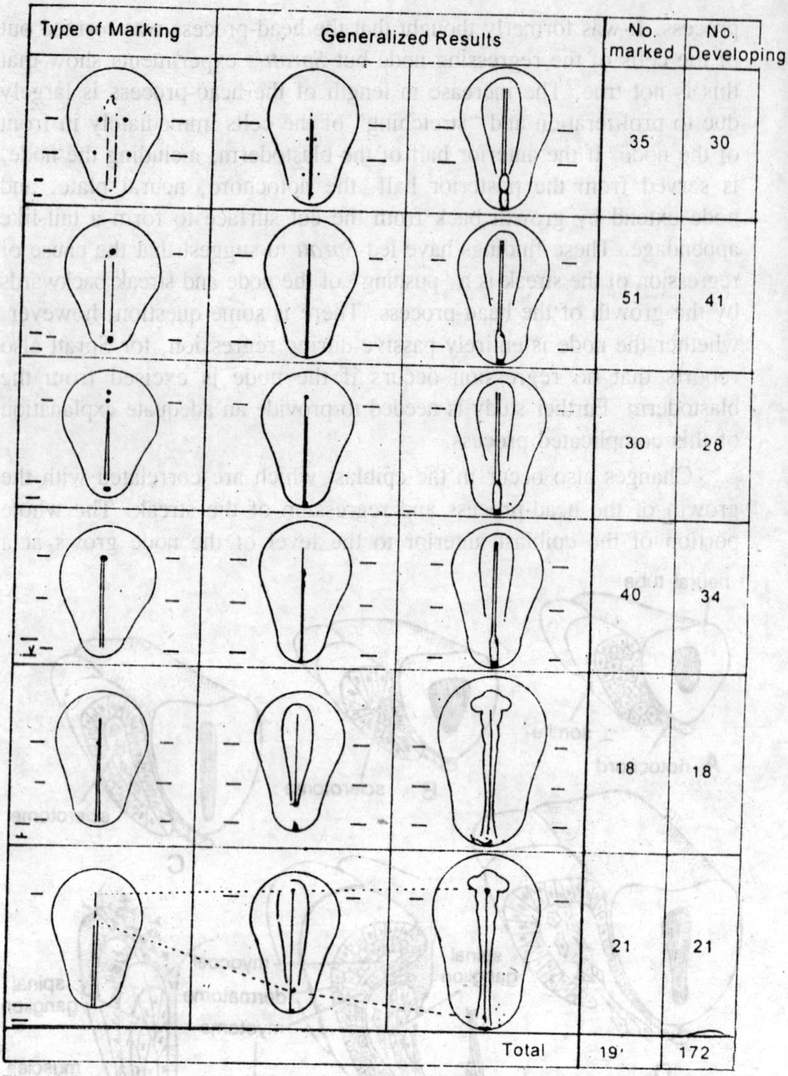

Type of Marking	Generalized Results	No. marked	No. Developing
		35	30
		51	41
		30	28
		40	34
		18	18
		21	21
	Total	19'	172

Fig. 11.5. Summary of the movements of epiblastic cells and the manner of increase of the head-process and decrease of the primitive streaks as revealed by carbon-marking experiments.

faster rate than the remainder, thus keeping pace with the increase in length of the head-process. Back of the node there is a continued movement of lateral areas of epiblast toward the streak and inward migration of the cells to form mesoblast, but the extent of these movements is much less. There is no movement of cells from the surface of the node or through the primitive pit to the interior during regression; the node remains intact until it becomes the major part of the tail bud. Not only the epiblast, but also the mesoblast and hypoblast are apparently displaced back-wards by the regression of the streak.

As the node moves backwards, the primitive streak decreases in actual length. The shortening occurs mainly at the posterior end, where making experiments show that its cells spread out laterally and posteriorly to form embryonic and extraembryonic ectoderm and mesoderm. With the dispersion of the cells, the primitive groove disappears first, and then the streak, at progressively more anterior levels. The shortening continues until only the node and a bit of the streak behind it remain, at which point the tail fold is formed and the primitive knot is incorporated in the tail bud. There is evidence that some of the cells in the streak are consolidated with the node to form the tail bud, since the latter is larger than the original node.

Although evidence is not yet available or the mechanism of shortening of the streak it seems probable that it is result of the slowing and cessation of the medial movements and inward migration of the epiblast. The sequence of events (i.e., disappearance of the groove followed by dispersion of the streak itself) favours this view.

Maps of the Blastoderm During Stages of the Primitive Streak

Organ-presumptive Areas

The active shifting of cells in the epiblast and their migration through the streak to a new location raise the question of their fate in normal developments: to what will each cells or group of cells in the blastoderm give rise, i.e., what is their *prospective value*? Our knowledge of this subject is largely obtained by marking the blastoderm with vital dyes or carbon particles, as described above, and following the movements of the marked areas to their ultimate positions in the body of the embryo. Maps may then be constructed to show the approximate area in the surface of the blastoderm which are destined to take part in the formation of specific organs.

The epiblastic areas of the pre-streak blastoderm, showing the boundaries of the streak at initial and definite stages on the right side, and the extent of the area which is to be moved inward through the streak. On the left side is shown the probable location of prospective organ-forming areas at stage 1 as inferred from marking experiments

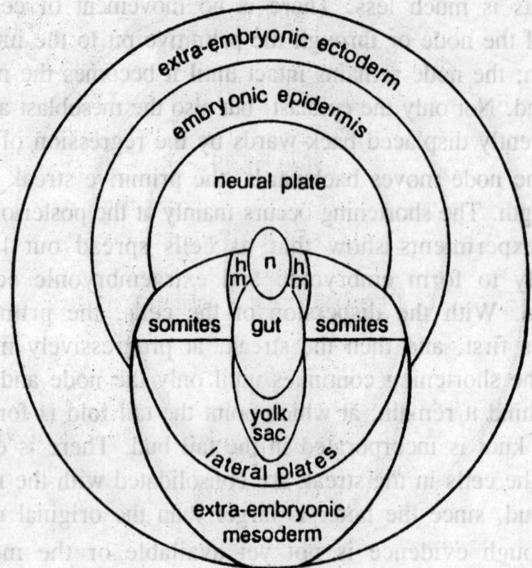

Fig. 11.6. Fate map of the epiblast of a bird which has been prepared by radioactive thymidine marking; hm, presumptive head mesoderm.

on blastoderms at the stage of the definite streak. The actual shapes of the areas and boundaries between them are hypothetical, therefore, in the absence of direct marking experiments at the pre-streak stage. It will be noted that the prospective mesodermal areas are located with respect to the mid-line in the order that they will be moved inward.

A composite map of the prospective organ-forming areas at the stage of the definitive streak. The shapes and size of the areas are ever changing as some of them converge and migrate through the streak and others spread out correspondingly. It will be noted that the principal embryonic areas are concentrated around the node and fore part of the streak. It is this region which under-goes the most growth and elongation and gives rise to the major part of the embryonic axis during the regression of the streak.

Histogenetic Potency

In addition to the prospective value of any unit area of the early blastoderm, each part has a far greater capacity for development than is normally expressed. It is as though there were an untapped reserve potential of ability which is expressed only in case of some unexpected deficiency. For example, developmental areas at certain critical periods may lead to complete or partial twinning. Or, if a lesion is produced

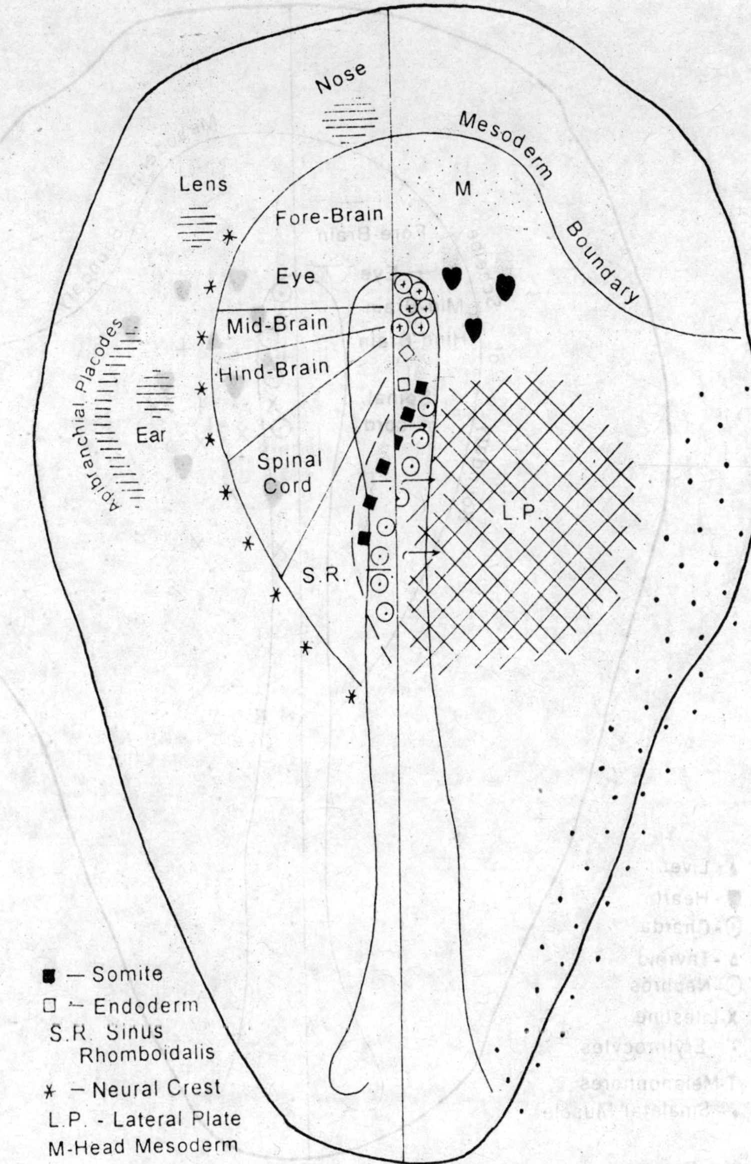

Fig. 11.7. A tentative map of prospective organ-forming areas in the blastoderm of the stage of the definitive primitive streak.

experimentally, then adjacent areas of the blastoderm area able to reconstitute the deficiency so that development may continue normally.

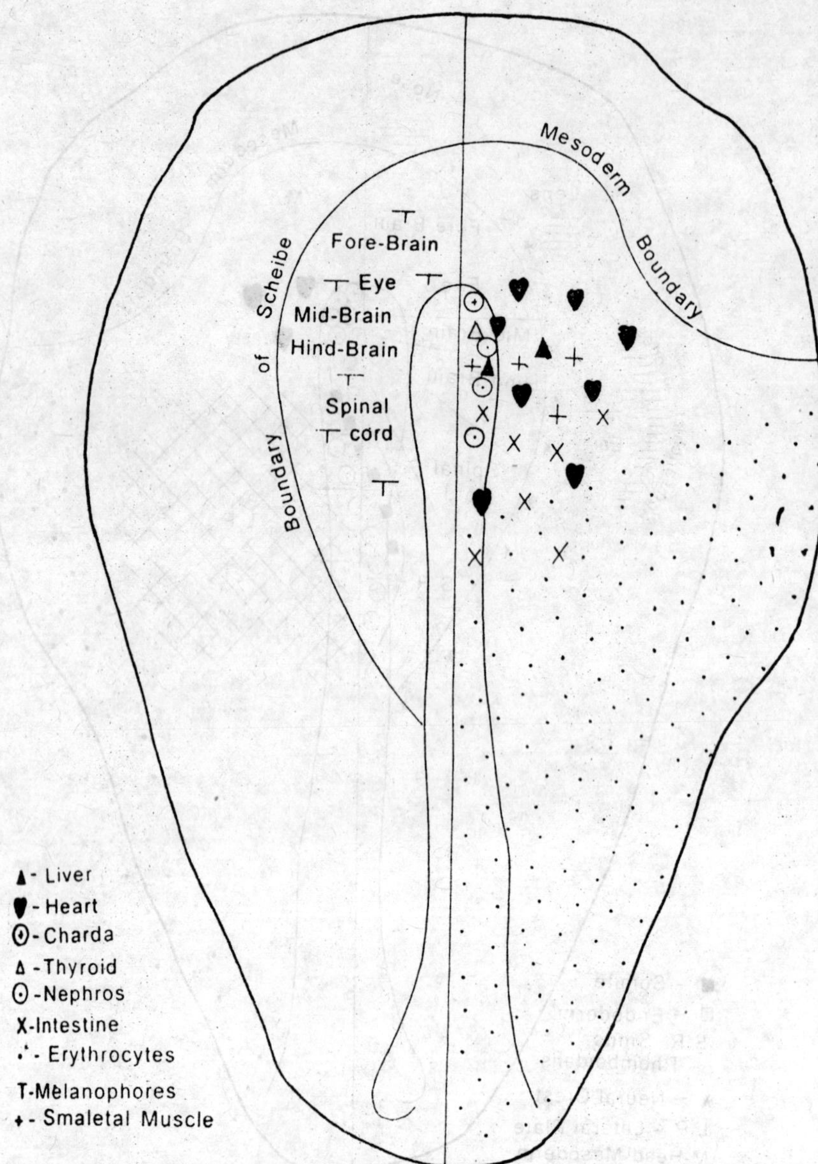

Fig. 11.8. Distribution of histogenetic potencies at the stage of the definitive primitive stage.

This power to develop or *histogenetic potency* can be revealed by removing portions of the blastoderm to other sites for growth such as the chorio-allantoic membrane, the coelomic cavity, or plasma clots, where the cells may differentiate apart from organismic influence (e.g., the effect of neighbouring cells and embryonic fields).

The distribution of organ-forming potencies in the blastoderm at the stage of the definitive streak. When this map is compared with that of prospective values at the same stage it is noted that the ectodernal potencies show the same general axial seriation but that the mesodermal and entodermal potencies are much more closely grouped around the node than in the map of values. The size of any particular area of histogenetic potency, however, is usually greater than the corresponding area of prospective value (e.g., compare the heart-forming area in the two maps). With increasing age the potency of a given

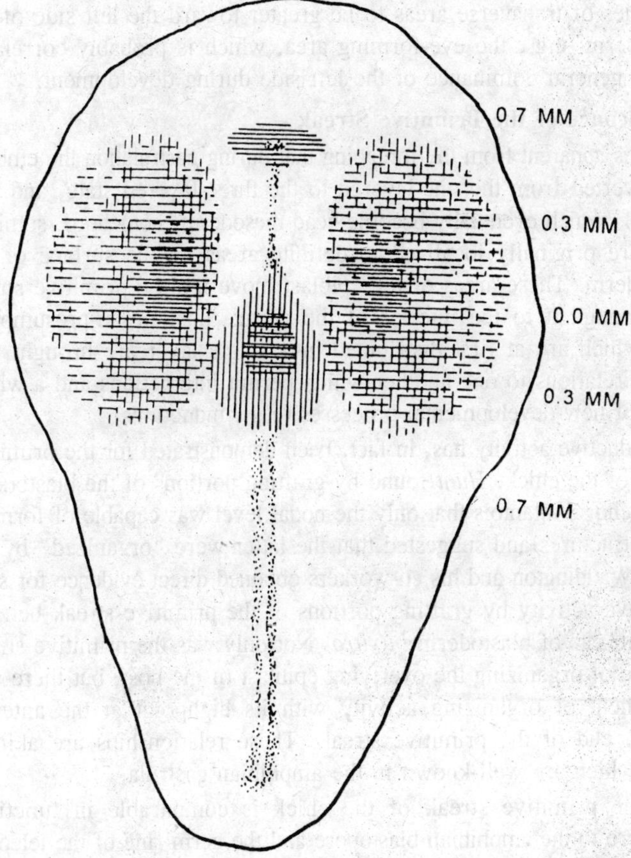

Fig. 11.9. Map of histogenetic potencies at the stage of the head-process.

area becomes progressively more limited until it is equivalent to the prospective value.

By using the method of isolation of parts of the blastoderm, the prospective potencies of the head-process blastoderm of the chick have been thoroughly mapped when this map is compared with that of the potencies of the definitive steak it is noted that there has been considerable lateral and posterior spread of the mesodermal areas during the formation of the head-process. Some areas, such as those of heart and liver-forming potency, which were previously located medially have become bilateral. Each area of potency is an ever changing field which varies in extent and shape throughout development. It intensity is highest at one point and diminishes in·varying degree toward an indefinite edge where it may overlap other areas. There is a tendency for the potencies of transverse areas to be greater toward the left side of the blastoderm (e.g., the eye-forming area, which is probably correlated with a general dominance of the left side during development.

Significance of the Primitive Streak

It is apparent from the foregoing that during gastrulation the embryo is converted from the one-layered to the three-layered state, and that the cells which eventually become head-mesoderm, notochord, somites, etc., are originally localized in definite areas on the surface of the blastoderm. These areas of the epiblast move into he primitive streak and through it to the interior of the germ: thus, organ-presumptive cells which are at first distributed in a single layer are brought into spatial relations to one another which permit interactions and a whole chain of new developmental processes (e.g., inductions).

Inductive activity has, in fact, been demonstrated for the primitive streak of the chick. *Hunt* found by grafting portions of the blastoderm to the chorio-allantois that only the nodal level was capable of forming axial structures and suggested that the latter were "organized" by the node. Waddington and his co-workers obtained direct evidence for such inductive activity by grafting portions of the primitive streak beneath the epiblasts of blastoderm *in vitro*. Not only was the primitive streak capable of organizing the overlying epiblast of the host, but there was a gradient of organizing activity with its highpoint at the anterior (nodal) end of the primitive streak. These relationships are akin to those which are well-known in the amphibian gastrula.

The primitive streak of the chick is comparable in function, therefore to the amphibian blastopore and the germ ring of the teleosts. All three are regions of high activity where outlying areas of cells on the surface are converged and moved inward to form the germ layers and future organs of the embryo. Such homologization was suggested as early as 1876 by Rauber, who considered the primitive streak to be an elongated blastopore. Insofar as *structure* is concerned, there are wide differences: e.g., at no time is there an opening in the primitive streak leading into an archenteron; the primitive streak more nearly resembles the closing amphibian blastopore with apposed lateral lips. However, the differences in morphology are secondary, and are imposed apparently by differences in the amount of yolk within the eggs of different forms.

The node and primitive pit of the definitive streak, being the area of highest morphogenetic activity and the site of inflow of the prospective axial mesoderm, are comparable to the dorsal lip of the amphibian blastopore and the teleostean germ ring at the level of the embryonic shield. If the regressing streak is homologous to a closing blastopore, one would expect that the less active portion (ventral lip) would close first of all, whereas the most active portion (Hensen's node = dorsal lip) would remain functional until the last, spratt's demonstration that the regressing streak is shortened at its posterior end supports such an interpretation. At the close of gastrulation the last of the cells to be moved inward are piled up with the node to form the caudal knot or tail bud from which the remainder of the embryonic axis is competed. The transition from primitive streak to tail bud is almost imperceptible, and the two structures are merely two morphological manifestations of the same phenomenon – the putting in place of prospective organ-forming cells.

Mesoderm of the Opaque Area

We have seen that the prospective mesodermal cells move inward from the surface through the primitive streak, and spread out between the ectoderm and the entoderm to the margin of the pellucid area; the mesoderm then begins to overlap the opaque area at first behind, later at the sides, appearing between the ectoderm and the germ wall. Its peripheral extension; at first it spreads rapidly behind the embryo, but soon extends with equal speed opposite the primitive streak, and thus a considerable portion of the area opaca becomes three-layered, consisting of ectoderm, mesoderm, and germ wall. The contour of the anterior margin of the mesoderm is at first rounded convex anteriorly. Then the anterior-lateral angles of the mesoderm begin to extend forward so that the anterior boundary becomes concave; the lateral horns thus established continue to grow forward and ultimately meet in front of the head they thus bound a mesoderm-free area in front of beneath the head, known as the proaminion, into which the mesoderm does not penetrate until a relatively late stage of development.

Blood islands develop early in the three-layered part of the opaque area; appearing first behind the embryo, they rapidly differentiate forward opposite the sides of the embryo and follow the expansion of the mesoderm. This three-layered portion of the opaque area is known as the vascular area (area vasculosa) after the appearance of the blood islands. It soon acquires a very definite peripheral boundary by the formation of the vena (sinus) terminals at its margin. The two-layered peripheral portion of the opaque area is known as the vitelline area (area vitellina), and here again we distinguish two zones, an outer including the zone of junction, and an inner one.

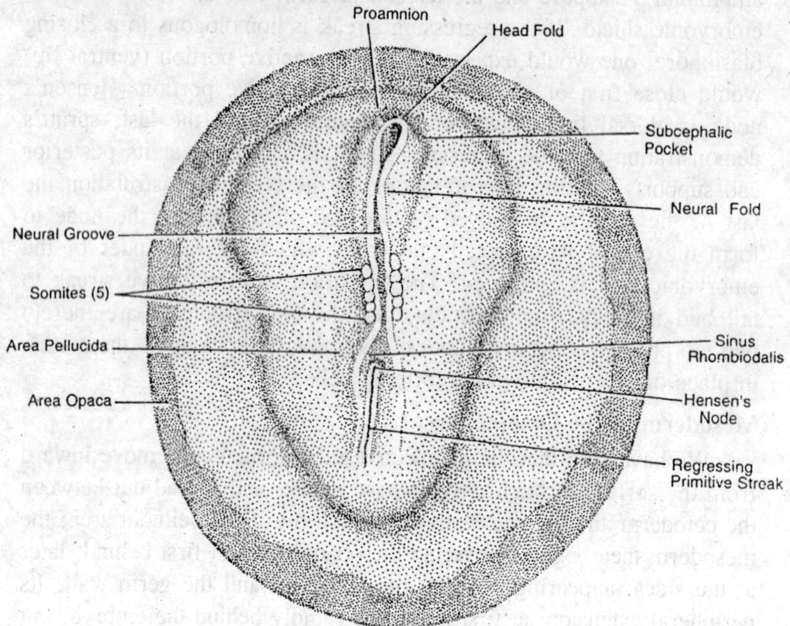

Fig. 11.10. Chick embryo of 25 to 26 hours of incubation showing neural folds, somites (5 pairs), and regressing primitive streak.

The first blood islands are masses of cells laying on the germ wall behind the embryo; the first blood cells (*erythrocytes*) and blood vessels arise from them, hence their name. Soon after their origin the blood islands appear red owing to the formation of hemoglobin. Between the blood islands and the ectoderm is a layer of the mesoderm. If the blood islands be reçkoned as mesoderm we must distinguish two layers of the latter, a deep or vascular (hemagioblastic) layer lying net to the germ wall, and an upper layer next to the ectoderm, which may be called the coelomic mesoderm, inasmuch as the body cavity (*coelom*) develops within it later.

There are two sharply contrasted views concerning the origin of the mesoderm in the area opaca. According to the one point of view it is simply a peripheral extension of the primitive streak mesoderm with which as a matter of fact it is continuous. According to the other point of view, it is split off from the germ wall. One things is perfectly clear, namely, that the mesoderm of the opaque area arises in continuity with the primitive streak mesoderm; the second view would therefore be better expressed as *Ruckert states* it that the primitive streak mesoderm grows in the region of the area opaca at the expense of elements of the germinal wall.

If the cells of the primitive streak mesoderm are compared with the cells of the forming blood islands a sharp contrast will be observed: the mesodermal cells of the area pellucida are devoid of yolk granules; young blood islands on the other hand contain yolk granules of precisely the same character as those of the germ wall, which must have been derived from the latter. If the origin of the blood islands be carefully traced, they are found to be rooted in the protoplasm of the germ wall; and prior to the appearance of the blood islands proper protoplasm and nuclei of the germ wall aggregate superficially in a manner that appears to foreshadow the blood islands. Therefore, either the blood islands are derived from the cells of the germ wall, or cells of the mesoderm growing over the germ wall burrow into the latter, engulf yolk spheres, and reappear in masses as blood islands.

The second alternative is probably right in principle, for several reasons: Patterson and Wetzel prevented the mesoderm of the primitive streak from reaching the germ wall and found that blood vessels did not develop in the absence of streak mesoderm. In addition, when the head fold and anterior end of the embryos were isolated before the appearance of blood islands in the opaque area, the isolate developed its own blood system independently of the blood islands of the opaca (Reagan). This latter observation is supplemented by the multitude of experiments which led to the mapping of histogenetic potencies. It is clear that not only the opaque area but also a large share of the area pehucida and primitive streak itself can give rise to erythrocytes. Furthermore, there is considerable evidence from tissue cultures of

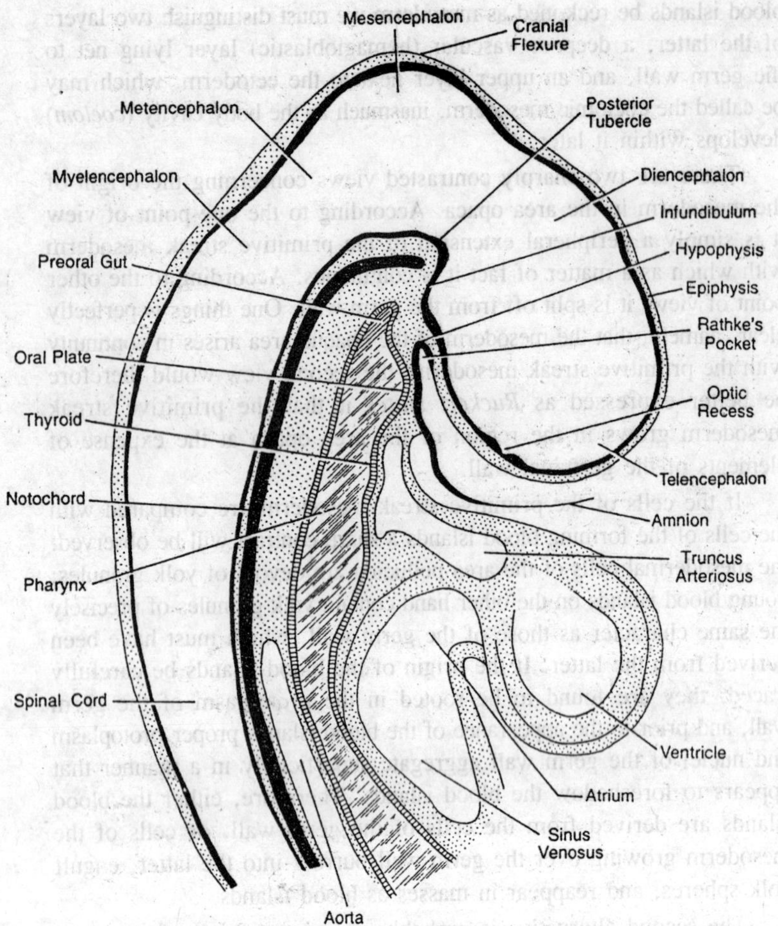

Fig. 11.11. Sagittal section of 48 hour embryo (anterior portion) showing various parts of brain and cranial flexure.

pieces of early blastoderms that the area of erythrocytic potency first moves from a lateral border of the blastoderm and localizes in the area vasculosa. Thus, it can be stated with some assurance that a major part (if not all) of the vascular tissue is derived from mesoderm which has moved inward from the epiblast by way of the primitive streak. Whether the germ wall also contributes to the hemangioblastic layer is an open question.

Another question concerns the origin of the layer of coelomic mesoderm that overlies the blood islands: is it derived from the primitive streak mesoderm, or is it split off from the blood islands? When the latter first appear, in the periphery of the vascular area at least, there is no coclomic mesoderm above them. It appears later, at first not as a coherent layer, but as scattered cells that rapidly unite to form a layer. In many places the microscopical appearances indicate strongly that the cells are split off from the surface of the blood islands; but, as they are usually not far from the edge of the advancing coelomic mesoderm, it may be that they are derived from the latter. Ruckert states, however, that, in the case of some isolated blood islands behind the embryo, a layer of mesoderm is formed over them while they are still isolated. This would render the derivation from the blood islands probable in such cases. It is possible, therefore, that the coelomic mesoderm grows partly, at least, at the expense of the superficial cells of blood islands.

As rapidly as they are formed the various blood islands connect and anastomose with one another forming a vascular network lying between the coelomic mesoderm and the germ wall. This network spreads throughout the vascular area, and appears later inn the pellucid area, and communicates with the blood vessels of the embryo. In the next chapter we shall consider the manner in which the extension takes place, and the origin of the blood vessels and blood cells.

Germ Wall

The germ wall arises, as we have seen, through infiltration of the superficial white yolk by the periblast. These cells multiply and anastomose and form a multinucleated syncytium with the yolk granules in its meshes. By degrees the protoplasm itself takes up the yolk granules, which are gradually digested, and the germ wall thus becomes organized as a coherent layer. It then separates from the underlying yolk. The next period in the history of the germ wall is its differentiation which takes place in the vascular are concomitantly with the formation of the blood island: the vascular mesoderm is formed probably from the streak mesoblast with contributions of yolk globules (if not cells) from the germ wall. The remainder of the germ wall then differentiates into the characteristic entodermal epithelium of the opaque area, which is known as the yolk sac epithelium (entoderm) because it is destined to form the lining of the yolk sac.

After formation of the vascular area the term germ wall must be restricted to the lower layer of the vitelline area, because with in the vascular area the mesoderm and yolk sac entoderm have already differentiated. The development of the germ wall takes place in a centripetal direction; at any period during the overgrowth of the yolk the three stages of the germ wall may be found in the concentric zones. The first stage, that of periblast, is found in the zone of junction (area vitellina external); the second stage, that of organization of the germ wall, is found in the area vitellina interna; and the third stage, that of differentiation, is found at the margin of the area vasculosa. Within the latter area the differentiation is completed.

Advanced Development of Chick

Twenty-four Hours of Incubation

In the average college embryological laboratory it is customary to study chick embryos at definite intervals of incubation, over bridging the gaps between these stages by collateral reading. The 24-hour chick embryo is usually one of the first embryos to be examined in total and serially sectioned preparations. It is therefore desirable to devote some time to the discussion of the chick embryo at that age, and in the following chapters embryos of such ages as are usually preferred for general study will be discussed more thoroughly than others.

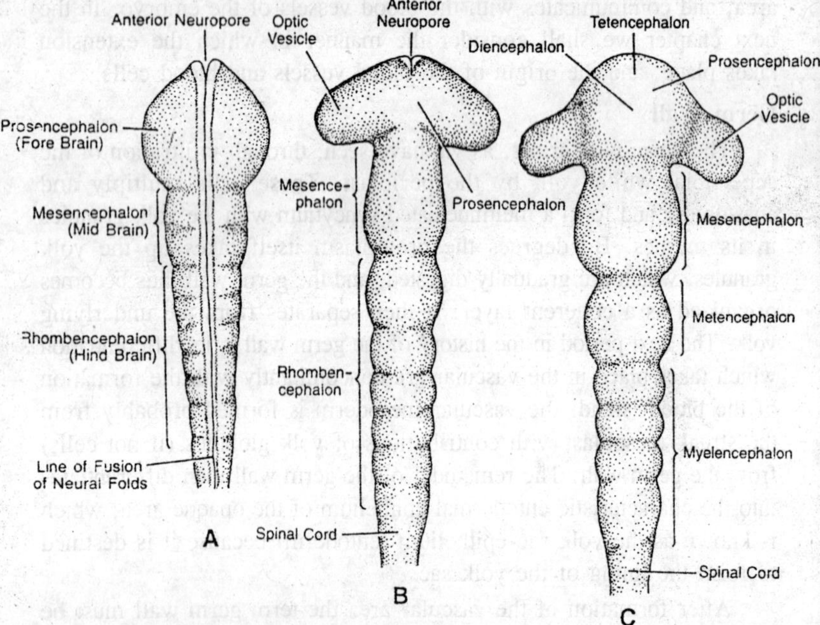

Fig. 11.12. Dorsal view of brain. A—26-27 hour embryo (7-somite stage), B—30 hour embryo (10-somite stage), C—36 hour embryo (14-somite stage).

Neural folds

In the 24-hour chick embryo, the neural folds have approached each other to a variable degree in different regions of the body. Posteriorly they are widely separated, flaring out as they approach Hensen's node and getting lost in the superficial ectoderm on both sides of the anterior portion of the primitive streak. In the head region the neural folds diverge to a lesser degree, but they are well separated and the neural groove is deeper here than in the central and posterior portions. The folds approach each other closest in the area located immediately behind the head and anterior to the first somities, and it is here that they will fuse first to form the neural tube. Viewed from the dorsal aspect in a total preparation, the neural folds appear as two bands, diverging slightly anteriorly and more so posteriorly. As a matter of fact, the neural folds on the anterior tip of the head are curved forward and downward, giving the head a notched appearance.

Enteron

The *enteron* is composed of the pocket-like fore-gut and the open mid and hind-gut. Examined from the dorsal aspect, the opening into the fore gut (*anterior intestinal portal*) can be located behind the crescentic head fold. From the anterior intestinal portal the fore-gut juts forward into the head as a broad flat pocket with single cellular sides, floor and roof.

Mesoderm

The *mesoderm* has spread out considerably between the ectoderm and entoderm and extends far out into the blastodisc, except in the mid-interior region where its absence in front of the head is indicated by the proamnion. In the 24-hour chick the mesoderm has formed from four to five paired somities, located to the right and left of the notochord in the central portion of the embryo. Their organization and relationship to the remainder of the mesoderm can best be observed in transverse sections. The mesoderm can be conveniently divided into three district parts. These are the dorsal or segmental mesoderm represented by the somities; secondly, the non-segmented intermediate mesoderm; and thirdly, the lateral mesoderm consisting of an upper somatic and a lower splanchnic layer. In the early embryo, the somatic layer is always apposed to the ectoderm, and the two in connection are referred to as the *somatopleure*. The splanchnic mesoderm, when in close apposition to the entoderm, forms with it a double layer which is called the *splanchnopleure*. In the peripheral portion of the circular blastodisc, the lateral mesoderm has not as yet differentiated into the somatopleure, and splanchnopleure. Its structure will be discussed in connection with the formation of the blood vascular system.

In addition to these three well-defined divisions of the mesoderm, one may include the mesenchyme, consisting of loose cells which are budded off from the somities in all parts of the body, especially in the head region.

The dorsal or segmental mesoderm produces the mesodermal somities. From the development point of view, it is the most important differentiation of the mesoderm because the somities give rise to several fundamental organic differentiations. They make their appearance as blocks of cells containing a transitory central cavity referred to as the *myocoel.*

The intermediate mesoderm connects the dorsal with the lateral mesoderm. It is not segmented, though it gives rise to the segmented nephrostomes, and later to the segmented *mesonephros*.

The lateral mesoderm is unsegmented, agreeing in this respect with that of all other vertebrate embryos. It is composed of the somatic and splanchnic layers which enclose the coelomic cavity. Since these two sheets of the lateral mesoderm extend from the embryo far out into the extraembryonal area, the coelome must necessarily be very extensive. For descriptive purposes the coelome within the embryo is therefore referred to as the *intra-embryonic coelome*, and that found in the extraembronic area are the *extraembryonic* coelôme. In early embryos, as for example, those studied here, there is no sharp demarkation between the two coelomes.

Near the anterior intestinal portal the paired sheets of the splanchni, mesoderm show conspicuous thickenings as they branch off from the intermediate mesoderm. Moreover, because of the elevation of the gut at the intestinal portal, the two mesodermal sheets are well separated, thus forming a very specious intraembryonic coelome. The thickened portions of the splanchnic mesoderm on either side of the gut initiate the formation of the heart, which will be discussed in more detail in the next chapter. It will be completed and functioning within an additional twenty-four hours of incubation. The spacious part of the coelome, called the *amnicadiac vesicle*, is destined to form the pericardial cavity.

Area opaca vasculosa and vitellina

The total 24-hour chick embryo shows that the area opaca and area pellucida have retained the same fundamental relationship that they had in earlier stages. However, the embryonic area and the growth of the mesoderm have partly obscured the earlier definite outlines of

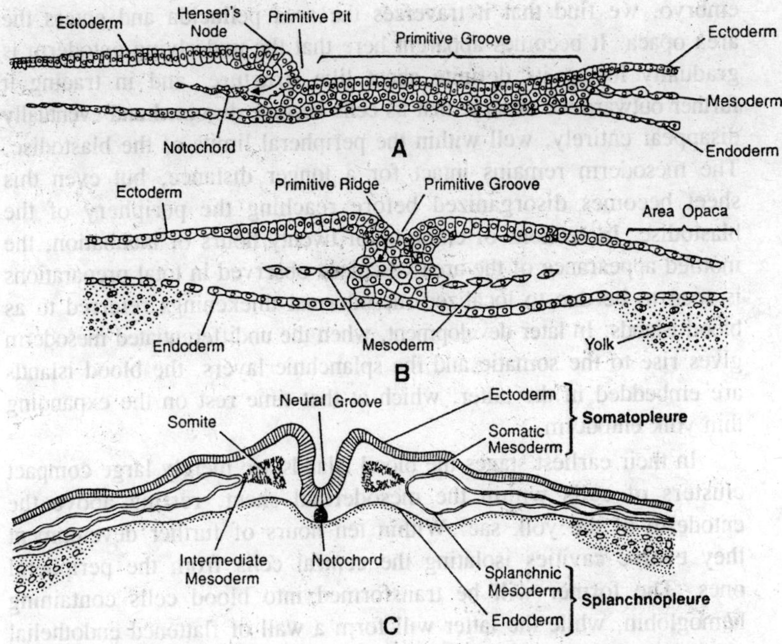

Fig. 11.13. Chick embryo. A—Medial section of a 17 hour embryo showing growing notochord, B—T.S. of a 17 hour embryo showing inward migration of cells, C—T.S. of a 24 hour embryo showing the three germinal layers, notochord, and neural groove.

the area pellucida. This is true to a much greater extent of the area opaca. In its posterior half, closest to the area pellucida and encroaching upon it, it has developed a mottled and blotchy appearance and has differentiated into the so-called *area opaca vasculosa*, which is destined to give rise to a large part of the extra-embryonic vascular system. In further development the area opaca vasculosa, or simply area vasculosa, tends to grow forward, thus encircling the entire embryo in later stages (48 hour check). The area vasculosa does not occupy the entire area opaca. In early embryos it is limited to the portion adjacent to the area pellucida. Beyond the area vasculosa the area opaca does not have a mottled appearance, and this peripheral region is known as the *area opaca vitellina*. A clearer picture of the structure and relationship of these two areas is obtained from the study of transverse sections which extend far out into the extra-embryonal area.

Area vasculosa

Following one of the paired mesodermal sheets as it passes out between the ectoderm and entoderm in the posterior region of the embryo, we find that it traverses the area pellucida and enters the area opaca. It becomes apparent here that the underlying entoderm is gradually losing its definite sheet like structure, and in tracing it further outward we observe that its cells become disjoined and eventually disappear entirely, well within the peripheral limits of the blastodisc. The mesoderm remains intact for a longer distance, but even this sheet becomes disorganized before reaching the periphery of the blastodisc. In sections of embryos of twenty hours of incubation, the mottled appearance of the area vasculosa observed in total preparations is seen to be due to localized mesodermal thickenings referred to as blood islands. In later development, when the undifferentiated mesoderm gives rise to the somatic and the splanchnic layers, the blood islands are embedded in the latter, which at that time rest on the expanding thin yolk entoderm.

In their earliest stages the blood islands are merely large compact clusters of cells within the mesodermal sheet, resting above the entoderm of the yolk sac. Within ten hours of further development they evolve cavities isolating the central cells from the peripheral ones. The former will be transformed into blood cells containing hemoglobin, while the latter will form a wall of flattened endothelial cells around the blood cells. In the meanwhile the latter have multiplied into such large numbers that they touch and ansastomose with each other, thus forming a vascular capillary network containing blood corpuscles. Finally, the cavities within the blood islands become filled with a liquid (plasma) acting as a vehicle for the corpuscles when circulation is later established. In the discussion of the development of the heart in the following chapter, it will be seen how this capillary system becomes connected with the embryo.

Area opaca vitellina

The area opaca vitellina is located beyond the area vasculosa in the peripheral region of the blastodisc. It contains chiefly a surface layer of ectoderm and underlying undifferentiated cells which are more numerous near the area vasculosa than they are in the periphery. It consists of the margin of overgrowth and the germ wall where the cytoplasm of many cells is continuous ventrally with the yolk, and is therefore identical in its general structure with the peripheral layers of the blastula and gastrula, which have been discussed before.

Thirty-Three Hours of Incubation

During the period of incubation from twenty-four to thirty-three hours, the chick embryo undergoes extensive changes in which several permanent anatomical structures begin their differentiation. In a total preparation of the 33-hour chick the most obvious transformation seems to occur in the head region. In the 27-hour chick the neural folds begin to fuse near the future myelencephalon, and within six hours the fundamentals of the vertebrate brain have been laid down. Furthermore, the entire head region has elongated and grown forward over a deep subcephalic pocket, and anterior to the latter the superficial ectoderm of the blastodise is elevated in a crescentic fold (*amniotic head fold*). Within the head region the fore-gut has kept pace with this growth and has elongated considerably, so that the anterior intestinal portal comes to lie relatively further backward. Close to the latter, two blood vessels have been formed which unite anterior to the first somite to form the tubular heart, and postero-laterally they flare out to become continuous with the area vasculosa. Lastly, the fact that the embryo has grown considerably in length is evident by the increase in the number of mesodermal somities.

Neural tube

In the 33-hour chick the neural tube is differentiated into the anterior, more or less dilated portion and the central and posterior, uniformly tubular part, the former giving rise to the brain and the latter to the spinal cord. During an interval of nine hours, from the 24- to the 33-hour embryo, the neural folds unites dorsally, and, proceeding with their fusion forward as well as backward, form the neutral tube, The neural folds do not close simultaneously throughout their entire length; anteriorly they are delayed for a few hours and

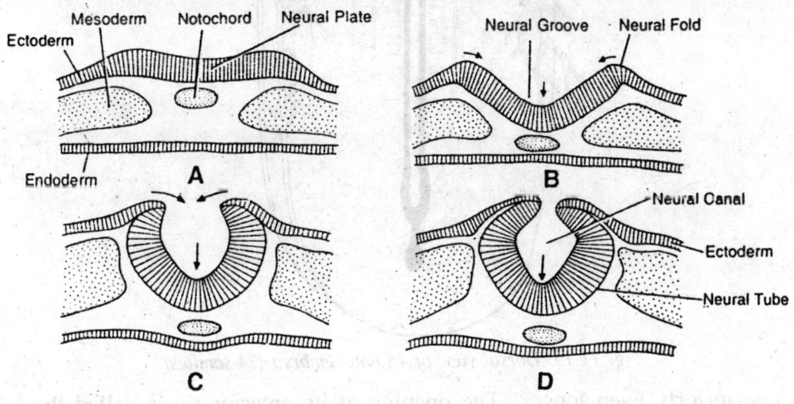

Fig. 11.14. A to D—Stages in the formation of neural tube.

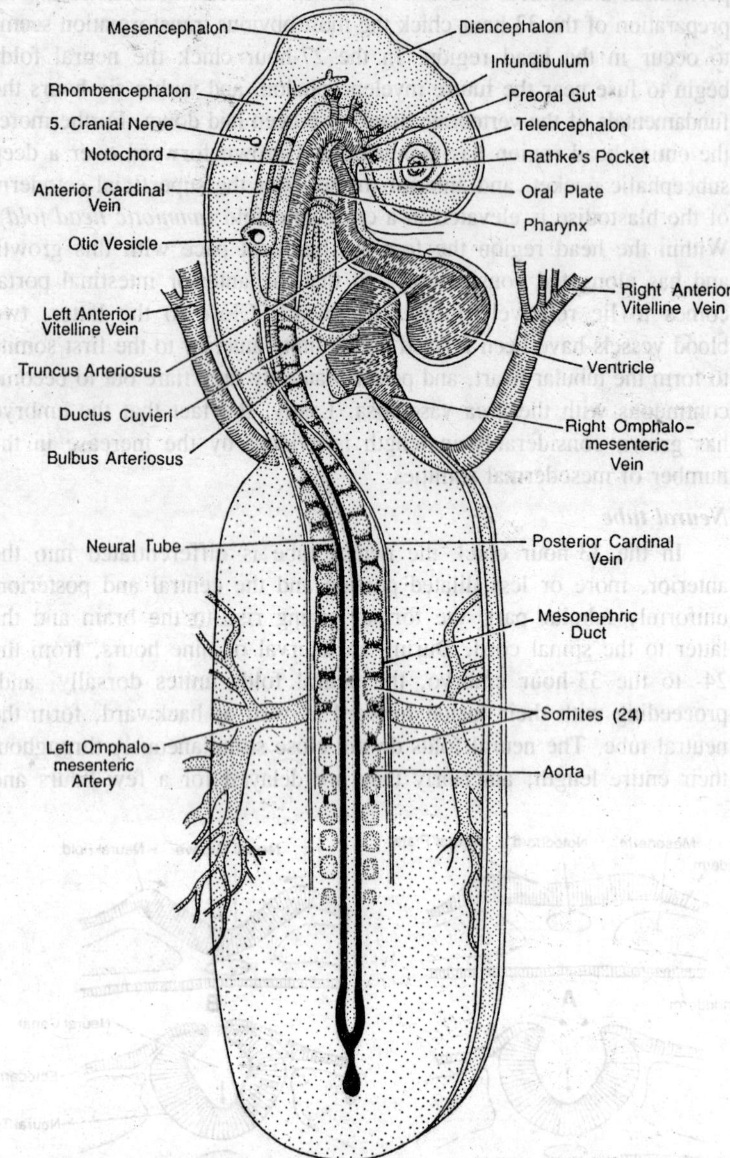

Fig. 11.15. Dorsal view of 48 hour embryo (24-somites).

posteriorly even longer. The opening at its anterior tip is called the *anterior neuropore*; this will close eventually, leaving a scar that is still visible in the 33-hour chick embryo. Posteriorly the fusion of the neural folds is delayed much longer, thus forming a posterior opening to the neural tube referred to as the *posterior neuropore*. Behind the last mesodermal somite the two neural folds diverge, and after having passed the ever-shortening primitive streak, they gradually fade into the superficial ectoderm. In this manner the neural folds encompass a shallow area, called the *sinus rhomboidalis*, which represents the most posterior portion of the materials which will complete the neural tube. Its posterior limit is therefore indicative of the posterior tip of the future spinal cord.

Since the disappearing primitive streak extends into the posterior tip of the sinus rhomboidalis, it has been assumed that the primitive pit may represent an abortive attempt to form a neurentric canal. If one may assume that the neural folds will close over the area of the sinus rhomboidalis and thus form a roof over the primitive pit, and if then the latter would perforate into the enteron, the neurocoel would become continuous with it.

The manner in which the neural folds fuse is similar to that described for the frog embryo. Each fold consists of a single-layered superficial (non-nervous) and a deeper, many-layered (nervous) ectoderm, embodying the bulk of the former neural plate. By the union of the folds the superficial ectoderm unites over the neural tube while the latter detaches itself and sinks into the tissue.

Neural crests

When the two neural folds unite in the mid-dorsal line, loose cells appear between the two ectodermal components of each fold. These cells form two bands (neural crests) on the dorsal right and left sides of the forming neural tube. They are segmented and form the primordial of the dorsal root ganglia of the spinal and of some of the cranial nerves, as well as the ganglia of the autonomic nervous system. Like most other structures, the neural crests appear first in the anterior region of the embryo, and as it grows they are added posteriorly.

Brain

The metameric organization of the brain is indicated early by *neuromeres* in the anterior portions of the neural folds. Before the latter have fused in the head region they shown a vague neuromeric segmentation, consisting of at least eleven neuromeres. It is doubtful whether this is the total number for the entire brain. There are probably more in the anterior part that are not definite enough to be recognized and a number are added to the hind part of the rhornbencephalon.

Shortly after fusion of the neural folds, the three primary brain divisions of the vertebrate brain are differentiated from specific neuromeres. The prosencephalon, of forebrain, takes up the first three, the mesencephalon the next two, and the rhombencephalon the remaining six. Beyond the eleventh neuromere the metameric organization of the neural tube becomes so indefinite that the actual posterior limit of the rhombencephalon cannot be recognized.

With the differentiation of the three primary divisions of the brain, all neuromeric constrictions within the prosencephalon and mesencephalon disappear except those separating these primary divisions from each other. However, most of the neuromeric constructions in the posterior part of the rhombencephalon remain visible for a longer period at least for more than three days.

With the sharp, demarcation of the primary divisions of the brain, the neurocoel has also been divided into certain definite regions. The cavities of the forebrain, midbrain, and hindbrain are the *prosocoel*, *mesocoel* and *rlimbocoel* respectively. The last is continuous with the neural canal of the spinal cord at the posterior part of the rhombencephalon.

The prosencephalon becomes expanded by the lower lateral outgrowths of the sac-like optic vesicles. In the 33-hour chick embryo they are the most conspicuous differentiations of the entire brain, extending outward from the right and left sides of the prosencephalon toward the ectoderm of the head. Their cavities (*opticoels*), which are in free communication with the prosocoel, are actually divisions of it. On the floor of the prosencephalon, immediately posterior to the optic vesicles, is a median depression which forms the infundibulum, a part of which eventually forms the posterior lobe of the pituitary.

The mesencephalon containing the mesocoel, as well as the rhombencephalon with its rhombocoel, shows no other differentiation in the 33-hour chick embryo besides those referred to above.

Enteron

The fore-gut of the 33-hour chick is slightly less than one millimeter in length. It has elongated at the expense of the open mid-gut. The anterior intestinal portal is continually receding posteriorly as a result of the ventral fusion of the lateral walls of the open gut. In this manner the open gut behind the anterior intestinal portal is slowly converted into a closed gut. At the same time the amino-cardiac vesicles, which were located anterior to it in the 33-hour embryo. This fact must be kept in mind in the following discussion of the development of the heart.

Restricted and small as the fore-gut appears to be, it is still possible to distinguish certain features on it. For example, at its anterior ventral side it is directly apposed to the superficial ventral ectoderm of the outer covering of the embryo without any intervening mesoderm. This is the oral plate, which will rupture in proper time to form an opening for the mouth. The oral plate in the chick embryo is homologous to that of the frog embryo, and it is advisable to recall its formation in the latter. The anterior tip of the fore-gut in the 33-hour chick embryo is round in transverse section. It broadens and flattens over the anterior heart region and appears therefore more or less slitlike in transverse section. This part of the fore-gut is destined to become the pharynx. Over the posterior heart region and still further back the fore-gut becomes rounded again, and in due time this part will become the oesophagus.

Mesoderm

Though the organization of the mesoderm has become increasingly more complex, it is not as striking in the structure of the somites as it is in the lateral mesoderm. The somites are bulkier and better defined as compared with those of the 24-hour chick, and in the anterior region they have almost lost their connection with the intermediate mesoderm. Not considering these minor changes, a cross section through the embryo at the level of the sixth or seventh somite will show no radical changes in its organization. The differentiations in the mesoderm of the 33-hour chick are chiefly concerned with the vascular system. Beginning in the 20-hour chick with the formation of the area vasculosa, this system culminates in its completion and function in embryos of forty to forty-four hours of incubation. Of course, there will be changes and additions to this complex system; in fact, an extensive circulatory system (*allantoic*) will be added at the end of the third day of incubation, but this does not alter the fact that a complete blood circulation has been established in the 44-hour chick embryo and that by means of it metabolism is carried on.

In the 33-hour chick two complete circulatory arcs are in process of formation, one within the embryo (intraembryonic) and the other outside of it (extraembryonic). The center of each is the heart.

Heart

The beginning of the heart formation has been alluded to in the preceding chapter. It will be recalled that it consists of the thickening of the splanchnic mesoderm near and posterior to the anterior intestinal portal in the 24-hour chick. In the succeeding three hours this thickened mesodermal portion buds off cells into the narrow space between itself and the entoderm. These are destined to form the endocardium of the heart, and are organized early into short tubes with walls one cell thick around which the thickened splanchnic mesoderm, referred to as the epimyocardium, forms a heavy covering. When, as outlined above, the anterior intestinal portal becomes pushed more posteriorly, the endocardinal tubes with their epimyocardial envelopes approach each other and fuse beneath the newly formed fore-gut. The epimyocardiurn has kept pace with this centrally directed growth and has formed a thick investing covering around the endocardium, thus forming a short, double-walled tube – the primitive heart. Dorsally as well as ventrally it is held in place by the dorsal and the ventral mesocardium respectively, the latter disappearing immediately after it has been formed. The dorsal mesocardium persists for a few hours longer, but it also vanishes, except near the sinus venosus, where the tubular heart begins to dilate and twist upon itself. The epimyocardium give rise to a thinner outer layer, called the epicardium, and a thick myocardium. The large coelomic spaces (amino-cardiac vesicles) which were located at either side of the open gut in the 24-hour chick have now merged ventral to the heart tube. In later development this united coelome will become separated from the general coelome and becomes the *pericardial cavity*. The tubular heart is completed in its simplest form in embryos of twenty-nine to thirty hours of incubation. During the ensuing three or four hours it dilates and bends toward the right side. In these early stages when it is a simple tube, the heart is located immediately in front of the anterior intestinal portal and beneath the rhombencephalon, near the region where the auditory pits will presently form. At first the heart is very sort, less than ½ mm. in length. As it begins to elongate, it is divided anteriorly into two branches which form the two ventral aortic roots, while posteriorly it is continuous with the two *omphalomesenteric veins*. Since in its elongation the heart can neither push forward nor backward on account of the vessels formed there, it is forced to bend upon itself, and it does so by forming a right loop. At this early stage it is possible to locate the positions of the future heart chambers. The sinus venosus and the atrium will develop near the sinoatrial region, located at the union of the two omphalomesenteric veins. The heart flexure, bulging toward the right, will give rise to the ventricle, and is therefore called the ventricular region. At the anterior end, where the two ventral aortic roots leave the heart, is the bulbus arteriosus.

Extraembryonic blood vessels

Immediately in front of the anterior intestinal portal, the posterior part of the heart bifurcates into the right and left omphalomesenteric veins. They connect the heart with the vitelline veins and their complex capillary system of the area vasculosa, whose differentiation has been described before the whence the omphalomesenteric veins will drain the blood when the heart begins to pulsate. In the 33-hour chick great progress has been made in the further development of the area vasculosa, especially in the anastomosis of the blood islands to form a capillary network, and in the differentiation of a circular peripheral vessel called the sinus terminalis. In fact, in the 33-hour chick the pathway for the afferent vitelline circulation of the blood from the area vasculosa through the omphalomesenteric veins into the heart of the embryo has been established. That the blood is not as yet ready for circulation is attributable to the fact that the intraembryonic as well as the efferent extraembryonic circulation has not as yet been completed. This will occur within the next ten hours.

Intraembryonic blood vessels

The divided anterior end of the tubular heart becomes the paired ventral aortae (ventral aortic roots), which pass beneath the anterolateral tip of the fore-gut, where they swing upward, and then pass backward over the fore-gut as the two dorsal aortae (dorsal aortic roots). They are well-defined and are easily identified in transverse sections through the head region of the embryo, but as they pass backward they become less conspicuous and finally become lost as fine capillaries in the tall region. In embryos of thirty-seven to thirty-nine hours of incubation, it is possible to follow these capillaries further until they lose themselves posteriorly in the area vasculosa.

The anterior and posterior cardinal veins are also in the process of development in the 33-hour chick, but they are less striking and less definite in their appearance than the aortae. The anterior cardinals arc located on either side close to the brain, except in the heart region where they are wedged between the dorsal aortae and the body wall on their descent toward the posterior portion of the heart (sinoatrial region). He posterior cardinal veins, being narrower in diameter than the anterior ones, are still more difficult to identify. When present, they are located near the intermediate mesoderm and the ectoderm of the body wall.

While it is not at all difficult to determine that the splanchnic mesoderm gives rise to the heart, the blood and the extra-embryonic blood vessels in the area vasculosa, the source of the intraembryonic blood vessels is not so clear. Apparently they are derived from mesenchyme cells, and they appear in their proper places when needed, leading into the correct, channels and making the right anastomoses.

Forty-Eight Hours of Incubation

External morphology

After forty-eight hours of incubation the chick embryo shows a striking difference in appearance from embryos of earlier stages. Because of twisting (*torsion*) of the anterior part of its body to the right side, it seems to have lost its bilateral symmetry. Furthermore, a sharp bending (*flexure*) of the anterior portion of the head has curved the prosencephalon at right angles to the rhombencephalon. These are the most apparent changes in the examination of the total embryo. However, there are many others: as for example, the increase in the number of somites, the expansion of the area vasculosa, the growth of the heart, and the functioning of the vitelline circulation. Torsion and flexure of the embryo renders the study of the developing organs more difficult. These processes should therefore be well understood and should be kept in mind in the identification and location of specific organs and organ systems.

Changes in portion of the embryo

Though the 33-hour chick appears to be almost perfectly bilaterally symmetrical and appears to be without any curvature in its longitudinal axis, this is not exactly true. Viewed from the side, the prosencephalon is bent slightly downward with the center of rotation located in the midbrain. This is the beginning of the *cranial flexure*, which increases as the embryo grows older. Since the head of the young embryo is raised only slightly above the underlying tissue, a downward flexure of the head would bury it in the yolk in the region of the proamnion. This is avoided by a lateral torsion which begins at the head region. The embryo is twisted to the right, so that the left side is now closet to the yolk and the right side is facing upward. Torsion of the body begins at the tip of the head in embryos of approximately thirty-eight hours of incubation and proceeds backward as far as the eight or ninth smite in the 48-hour chick. At that time the second flexure (*cervical flexure*) can be recognized in the posterior part of the head. It is not very conspicuous at that time, but in later embryos it will be prominent anatomical feature.

Internal morphology

Nervous system

The Brain. On account of the curvature of the head of the embryo, the terms "anterior" and "forward" no longer stand for the same spatial directions as they did in the 24-hour and the 33-hour embryo. In future discussions and descriptions these terms will be used in relation to the anatomical organization of the embryo. Therefore, the most anterior region of the 46-hour chick is the tip of the forebrain and not the center of the midbrain, though, on account of its flexure, the prosencephalon is actually closer by straight line to the tail than is the mesencephalon.

In an embryo of forty-eight hours of incubation the brain and the spinal cord stand out more prominently than other organs. In spite of the flexure of the head and the torsion of the body, no far reaching changes have occurred in the general organization of the brain and spinal cord. There are a number of minor differentiations which will give rise to various important organs in later development, but these are all in their incipient stages. The extent of the three primary brain divisions can easily be ascertained by the two grooves separating the mesencephalon anteriorly from the prosencephalon and posteriorly from the rhombencephalon. The latter is continuous with the spinal cord without showing any definite posterior boundary. The organization in the neurocoel is similar to that of the 33-hour chick, the brain cavities consisting of the prosocoel, mesocoel and rhombocoel being continuous with the central canal of the spinal cord. Posteriorly the neurocoel no longer opens to the outside through the posterior neuropore to the sinus rhomboidails. It is completely enclosed, even in its most posterior aspect where its completion has eliminated every trace of the primitive streak.

A sagittal section through the brain of the 48-hour chick indicates the relative thickness of the different parts. The sides and the floor of the prosencephalon are slightly thicker than its roof. The mesencephalon is uniformly thick throughout its entire length. The rhombencephalon shows are greatest differentiation in that it has acquired a very thin roof, while its floor and especially its sides are thick.

At this early stage the brain seems to be entirely out of proportion to the remainder of the neural tube or spinal cord. It comprises almost one half the entire neural tube. This condition prevails only in the early embryo, and the brain progressively becomes relatively smaller in its development to the adult conditions by pushing the successive divisions of the brain closer together.

Prosencephalon and its differentiations

Beginning with the prosencephalon, one may observe a broad and shallow transverse groove appearing on its median dorsal surface, which, in the 48-hour embryo, has not cut far down toward the ventral side. Eventually it will divide the prosencephalon into the anteriorly located *telecephalon* and the posterior *diencephalons*. At the present stage the demarkation between the two is so faint that it is best to reserve their discussion for embryos of more advanced development.

Eye

The last reference to the differentiation of the paired eyes was made in the discussion of the 33-hour chick. At that time they were hollow, lateral outgrowths (optic vesicles) from the prosencephalon. Within a few hours (37-hour embryo) each optic vesicle constricts at its base where it grows out from the ventro-lateral sides of the prosencephalon and forms the optic stalk. The vesicles proper continue to push out further in a lateral direction toward the outer ectoderm, and where they approach it closes it thickens to form the primordial of the crystalline lenses. Each optic vesicle begins now to invaginate, pushing inward at the lower portion where it is attached to the optic stalk and proceeding upward until the entire optic vesicle is transformed into the optic cup. It resembles a shallow bowl from which a piece of the rim has been broken. The gap thus formed is the choroids fissure, which is located at the lower side of the optic cup near the attachment of the optic stalk.

Concurrently, a similar process has taken place in the formation of the lens. Similar to the invagination of the optic vesicle, the ectodermal thickening in the skin facing the optic cup invaginates. In this way a thick-walled hollow sphere (*lens vesicle*) is formed, opening to the outside by a small aperture. The lens vesicle takes up its position within the optic cup where it is destined to form the crystalline lens. In the 48-hour embryo the lens vesicle is still open to the outside by a tiny pore in the outer ectoderm.

Infundibulum

In chicks of thirty-three or a few more hours of incubation, a shallow depression appears in the mid-ventral line immediately posterior to the optic vesicles. This is the infundibulum. In the 48-hour embryo it is slightly deeper than in the 33-hour chick embryo and it is met by a mid-ventral inward growth of the outer ectoderm known as *Rathk's pocket*. In connection with ectodermal cells proliferated from Rathke's pocket, the infundibulum will form the *hypophysis* or *pituitary body* of the adult.

Optic chiasma and optic recess

Posterior to the infundibulum is a projection called the posterior tubercle (*tuberculum posterius*) which is located near the axial center of the cranial flexure. It projects form the floor of the posterior limit of the midbrain and represents the landmark separating the prosencephalon from the mesencephalon. In front of the infundibulum is the thickened *optic chiasma*, ending in a depression referred to as the optic recess. From here the optic stalks extend in a lateral direction into the optic cups. Anterior to the optic recess the thickness of the prosencephalon is increased, extending for a short distance anteriorly. It diminishes in the most anterior region of the forebrain, which is to give rise to the telencephalon.

Epiphysis

The *epiphysis* cannot as yet be identified as a definite primordium. There is a large bulge in the mid-dorsar region of the prosencephaion, shaping itself later into a more restricted evagination which will eventually develop into the epiphysis or pineal body of the adult. In front of it is a faint transverse depression, referred to as the *velum transversum*, separating the prosencephalon into an anterior telencephalon and a posterior diencephalon.

Mesencephalon

In the 48-hour chick the mesencephalon has undergone very little change when compared with that of the 33-hour embryo. Though there is no difficulty in identifying the midbrain by its central location, by its graceful curve, and by its sharp external demarkation from the forebrain and hindbrain, it exhibits no special organs or landmarks. Its roof, sides, and floor are uniformly thick and enclose the mesocoel which forms the *aqueduct of Sylvius* in the brain of the adult.

Rhombencephalon

The hindbrain or rhombencehalon is the largest of the three primary brain divisions. Its anterior boundary is marked by a groove separating it from the mesencephalon, but its posterior limit is not at all definite merging gradually into the spinal cord. Judging from its later differentiation it is safe to assume that it extends as far back as the level of the second mesodermal somite. Where it joins the midbrain its roof, sides, and floor are uniformly thick, and it exhibits an oval outline in transverse section. Further back the roof becomes very thin. The short anterior portion of the hindbrain with its thick roof constitutes the metencephalon and the remainder the myelencephalon. The latter is further characterized by the persistence of neuromeres, which were a striking feature in the organization of earlier embryos. The spacious cavity of the mesocoel leads into the rhombocoel, of which the large portion will form the fourth ventricle of the hindbrain.

Ear

Though the ear is not a direct differentiation of the hindbrain, its later close association with the myelencephalon makes it desirable to consider its origin at the present time. The beginning of the paired auditory organs shows itself on either side of the mid-dorsal line in the neighbourhood of the tenth neuromere in chicks of thirty-four hours of incubation. Their primordial are laid down as two disk-shaped thickenings in the ectoderm (autidory placodes) which invaginate and detach themselves in the same manner as previously described for the formation of the lens. In chicks of thirty-seven to thirty-eight hours of incubation, in invagination forms a saucer like depression in the auditory placode (*auditory pit*). Pushing further into the tissue of the embryo, the auditory pits take on the shape of sacs (*auditory vesicles*, *otic capsules*), leading to the outside by slitlike openings. These begin to disappear almost entirely in chicks of forty-five hours of incubation and within three hours only a tiny upper pore is still visible, connecting the cavity of the auditory vesicle with the outside. This is probably the old endolymphatic duct, which upon complete later disappearance reappears as a small evagination within the cavity of each vesicles and grows upward, giving rise to the endolymphatic sac in later embryos.

Spinal cord

Without any visible demarkation, the myelencephalon merges into the spinal cord. In its earlier stage, shortly alter the fusion of the neural folds, the central canal is still an elongata oval in transverse section, but it soon becomes compressed laterally as the embryo grows older, assuming in the 48-hour chick the shape of a longitudinal slit. Concurrently, the side of the cord thicken so that its roof and floor appear to be comparatively thin. Two types of cells can be distinguished in the tissue of the nerve cord of the 48-hour chick namely, the original *epithelial* cells augmented by the secondary *germinal cells*. The former have elonged considerably, but they still remain at one end in their original position bordering the central canal. After this differentiation the epithelial cells are referred to as *ependymal* cells which have no nervous function. The smaller germinal cells are wedged between the ependymal cells and give rise to the *neuroblasts* and the *neuroglia cells*. The latter, with the ependymal cells, form the connective tissue of the nerve cord, while the neuroblasts differentiate into the various types of neurons.

Neural crests and ganglia

The is little to be added to the description of the neural crests as given in the precedings chapter. The anterior mesodermal so mites are paralleled in their metameric arrangement by the neural crests. Anteriorly this differentiation is very distinct, but it loses in clearness as one proceeds toward the posterior portion of the embryo, where additional mesodermal somites are still in formation.

In front of the first pair of somites the neural crests extend into the head region, but their metameric regularity is obliterated there. It seems that some of them have fused to form large ganglia for the cranial nerves, of which the fifth, seventh, eighth, ninth, and tenth can be well distinguished in the 48-hour chick. The ganglion of the fifth cranial nerve (*trigeminal*) is located on the side of the anterior portion of the rhombencephalon, midway between the auditory vesicle and the furrow separating the hindbrain from the midbrain (*mesometencephalic furrow*). It is usually referred to as the *Gasserian ganglion*. In front of the auditory vesicle, or auditory capsule, are two ganglia in close apposition so that they cannot be told apart in the 48-hour, chick. These are the *geniculate* and the *acoustic (auditory) ganglion* of the seventh, or facial, and the eighth, or acoustic (auditory), nerve respectively, the ganglia of the ninth (*glossopharyngeal*) and the tenth (*vagus*, *pneumogastric*) cranial nerve make their appearance in close union in the 36-hour chick immediately behind the auditory pit. At forty-eight hours of the incubation they are well-separated, the ninth being located close behind the autitory vesicle and the tenth a short distance further back.

Alimentary system

The Fore-gut. In the 48-hour embryo the fore-gut has attained a length of 1-½ mm. It is only ½ min. longer than that of the 33-hour chick, but it has advanced considerably over the latter in its differentiations. The fore-gut resolves itself into three natural component parts – the preoral, the pharyngeal, and the oesophageal – of which the pharyngeal parts shows the greatest modifications.

Preoral gut

This portion occupied the most anterior part of the fore-gut, pointing toward the infundibulum and being continuous posteriorly with the specious pharynx which it joins at the level of the oral plate. The significance and possible function of the preoral gut is not known. After seventy-two hours of incubation it gradually degenerates. For a time it persists in the roof of the pharynx of later embryos as a blind sac (*Seesel's pocket*), but even that vestige disappears and eliminates the preoral gut entirely from the alimentary canal.

Stomodaeum and the oral plate

The first reference to the oral plate was made in the discussion of the 33-hour embryo. Though its original structure has not undergone any changes, its position in the 48-hour chick has been altered by the cranial flexure and by the rapid growth of the mandibular arches. It should be recalled from the embryology of the frog that the paired *manidibular arches* (first visceral arches) are the primordial of the lower jaw. One should therefore expect that the stomodaeum and the future mouth will form above the between the two mandibular arches. That this is correct. Moreover, the cranial flexure, turning the lower head region inward, assists in the invagination of the outer ectoderm around the oral cavity, is formed as a pocket like in growth toward the pharynx, from which it is separated by the thin oral pate. Its subsequent rupture in the 72-hour chick will connect the pharynx with the outside.

Pharynx

The pharynx is the largest and most spacious division of the fore-gut. It is of great interest to the comparative embryologist because its differentiations have a direct beating on the development of various organs and organ systems, as for example, the vascular and nervous systems, the lower part of the face, the ear, the neck, and certain endocrine glands. The pharynx is the longest division of the fore-gut, and it is wider and more spacious than either the preoral gut or the oesophagus.

The most conspicuous differentiations of the pharynx are the visceral clefts and visceral arches. In a general way they are the same as those of the frog embryo, but their development is slightly different and is modified because the visceral, clefts in bird embryos are never used for respiration as they are in the amphibians and fishes.

Visceral clefts

It does not seem necessary to repeat here the formation of the visceral clefs, since they develop in the same manner. The external visceral furrows grow inward to meet corresponding pharyngeal pouches growing outward, and where the two meet and perforate, a more or less open visceral cleft will be produced. If the term 'cleft' is used in its strictest sense then the chick embryo has only three of them, because the fourth one never breaks through but remains in the incomplete stage of fused visceral furrow and pharyngeal pouch.

The first pair of visceral furrows appears in embryos of thirty-four hours of incubation. Within an additional five or six hours of incubation, the second pair becomes visible posterior to the first. Concurrently, the corresponding pharyngeal pouches have evaginated from the pharynx, so that at the time when the heart begins to function (44-hour embryo), the first two pairs of visceral clefts are almost completed. The perforation of the first is accomplished in the 48-hour chick, but the opening of the second pair is delayed more than twelve hours. The third pair does not open until the fourth day of incubation, and as stated above, the fourth does not open at all. The term "cleft" is really a misnomer for the first pair (hyomandibular clefts), because the opening of the second pair is delayed more than twelve hours. The third pair does not open until the fourth day of incubation, and as stated above, the fourth does not open at all. The term "cleft" is really a misnomer for the first pair (hyomandibular clefts), because the opening is not at all slitlike or cleftlike, being confined to a small aperture on its upper portion. The second and third visceral clefts are more slitlike in structure, but even in these two the clefts do not open throughout their entire length. Indeed, they have two openings each, a small one above and a large one below, separated by a fusion of the clefts a little above their centers.

When it is recalled that the frog embryo has five visceral clefts; it seems that in the volution of the birds and reptiles one of them has been lost. Evidence gathered from the changes occurring in the nervous and vascular systems during, embryology of these types indicates that the fifth has been lost. This evidence is further supported by the presence of certain vestigial organs (*post-branchil bodies*) behind the fourth cleft. It is assumed that the post-branchial bodies represent the abortive pair of fifth pharyngeal pouches.

Moreover, the first visceral, "cleft" never opens in the frog embryo, but does break through in the embryo of the chick. Since the latter never uses its gill clefts for respiration, and since the birds have been evolved through reptiles from amphibians, one should expect that the frog embryo, not that of the chick, would have an open first visceral cleft. This is another striking example of an exception to the so-called biogenetic law.

Thyroid gland

The differentiation of the primordium of the thyroid gland begins in the 34- to 35-hours embryo. It consists of a thickening (*thyroid plate*) in the median ventral wall of the fore-gut. With the development of the pharyngeal pouches, this thickening is localized anterior to and between the second pair of pharyngeal pouches. From forty to forty-four hours of incubation, the thyroid plate changes into a saucer-shaped trough, developing later into a shallow pocket in the 48-hour chick. Its cells are elongate, almost columnar in shape, and are well differentiated from the sŭrrounding entoderm cells.

Laryngotracheal groove and oesophagus

The posterior portion of the pharynx is not so wide nor so strikingly compressed dorsbventrally as is its anterior division. Along the median region of its floor a faint groove appears in the 48-hour embryo. This central longitudinal trough contributes the primordium of the larynx, trachea, and the lungs, and is therefore referred to as the *laryngotracheal groove*. That portion of the fore-gut immediately above the laryngotracheal groove will form the anterior portion of the oesophagus, while the fore-gut immediately posterior to it develop into the osterior oesophageal region.

Mid-gut

The mid-gut is characterized by the lack of a cellular floor, and is usually called the open gut. It begins at the anterior intestinal portal, where it has well-defined lateral walls which diminish in size and tend of flatten out to become continuous with the roof of the open gut as one proceeds posteriorly toward the hind-gut. However, the lateral margins of the closed fore-gut are continued in the mid-gut as lateral folds; they tug the lateral walls inward toward the mid-line, thus forecasting the future complete constriction of the gut from the underlying yolk. Near the anterior intestinal portal, above the junction of the two omphalo-mesenteric veins, two lateral evaginations form a pair of small pockets in the lateral wall of the gut. They are the liver diverticula, which will develop later into the functional liver in close connection with the omphalomesenteric veins by growing together and forming a single use.

Hind-gut

As compared with the origin of the fore-gut, the hind-gut develops in a slightly different manner. It should be recalled that the fore-gut and the head fold developed simultaneously. This is not the case in the formation of the hind-gut begins its development without the external appearance of a fold. Only a faint posterior swelling, the beginning of the *tail bud*, is visible, containing within its tissue the saclike hind-gut which opens into the mid-gut through the *posterior intestinal portal*. The actual tail fold forms in slightly older embryos by the growth of the tail bud and its later projection over the outer ectoderm, much in the same manner as the head fold is formed by the projection of the head over the proamnion anteriorly.

At the most posterior portion of the hind-gut, the entoderm comes into direct contact with the superficial ectoderm in the formation of the *anal plate*. From its homology with that of the frog embryo, this region represents the posterior portion of the former primitive streak. It is placed dorsally at first – not ventrally, as one would expect – because of the delay in the formation of a projecting tail bud which is produced by the deepening of the tail fold, thus carrying the anal plate downward of the ventral side of the embryo.

Vascular system

The uniformity of development processes in the vertebrates is shown more strikingly in the embryology of the vascular system than in any other organ system. The following account should be compared with parallel stages in the frog embryo, and illustrations of the two types should be carefully studied even if the attention of the reader is not specially called to it. It will be seen that the chick "recapitulates" the embryology of the frog very closely. In fact, some parts of the present account will appear to be mere repetition of the development of the circulatory system of the frog embryo and larva.

Heart

In the discussion of the 33-hour chick embryo, the origin of the heart tube was traced from a splanchnic mesodermal tube to the thick-walled primordial heart, which had turned toward the right side in the form of a horsehoe curve. In the succeeding hours, ending with the 48-hour chick, the heart remains essentially a tube, having as yet no valves nor sharp demarcation of heart chambers. However, a great physiological advance has been made in that it has begun to function as a blood pump. Since there are no valves to check the blood from flowing back, it is propelled forward by peristaltic waves. This great change occurs at about forty to forty-four hours of incubation, shortly after the embryo has begun to turn over on its left side. In the 44-hour chick, or sometimes a little earlier, the heart has acquired its rhythmical beat, which was preceded by a two-hour period of spasmodic contractions, starting the heart on its life-long function.

Though the heart is still essentially a tube, it has become more complex in appearance than it was in the 33-hour chick embryo, and if at that time we could assign certain regions of the tube to particular later differentiations, we are able to do so much better now. In the 48-hour chick embryo the heart has grown considerably, and since it is held in place anteriorly by the two ventral aortic roots and posteriorly by the dorsal mesocardium and the omphalomesenteric veins, it increases the length of its curvature by twisting upon itself. In this manner it has formed a complete spiral turn. Posteriorly this turn begins with the sinus vensosus, which is very close to the body of the embryo and is still held in place by a short dorsal mesocadium. The right turn spiral twist is formed chiefly by the thick heart tube, which embodies the atrium and the ventricle. The truncus arteriosus returns in its direction to the body of the embryo in completion of the turn, and is continued there as the paired ventral aortic roots (ventral aortae) within the embryo. The heart, having a right-handed spiral twist, must necessarily have the atrium on the left and the ventricle on the right side.

Aortic arches and aorta

Though the aortic arches as well as the visceral arches and clefts, are paired structures in the chick embryo, it is convenient in their description to refer to them in the singular form. This is done for the sake of clearness and ease of presentation and the singular form will be employed occasionally in the present discussion as well as later accounts. One should always be mindful that all such structures are paired and occur on both the right and left sides of the pharynx.

In the 33-hour chick embryo almost the entire systemic blood circulation was seen to be paired. The two ventral aortic rots were continuous with the two dorsal aortae by a pair of aortic arches. These two aortic arches are not only first in appearance, but also first in their morphological order. In the 48-hour chick the second aortic arch has been added and there may be even a vestige of a third. In this respect the chick embryo differs from that of the frog. In the latter, the first as well as the second aortic arch is never functional. In the chick embryo, functional vessels are formed in both of these arches, though at the end of the fourth day of incubation they will degenerate without leaving a trace.

The paired aortic arches become confluent with the dorsal aortic roots, located dorsolateral of the pharynx. Near the level of the sinus venosus they approach each other and unite into one centrally located dorsal aorta, but they separate again near the level of the posterior intestinal portal and continue backward as paired vessels. Near the eighteenth somite each member of the pair gives off a heavy branch, namely, the omphalomesenteric artery, which divides into the vitelline arteries, and these spread out over the yolk mass through a plexus of capillaries. Since by far the greater amount of blood is thus drained from the aortic, their continuation toward the posterior region of the embryo is in the form of a pair of diminutive vessels leading toward the tail bud.

Anteriorly, near the junction of the first pair of aortic arches and the dorsal aortic roots, the two internal carotid arteries are continued into the large head region to supply the rapidly developing brain with blood.

Cardinal and omphalomesenteric veins

The blood is returned from the head to the heart by the anterior cardinal veins which pass on the right and left side of the brain above the level of the aortae and their descend toward the heart, pouring their blood through the ducts of Cuvier into the sinus venosus. From the posterior part of the body of the embryo, the blood is returned through the posterior cardinal veins, which pass forward parallel to the mesonephric duct and empty their blood also into the ducts of Cuvier. The posterior cardinal veins are considerably thinner than he anterior cardinals, but near their entrance into the ductus Cuvieri hey spread out, forming plexus of smaller vessels and sinuses (not shown in the figures). These plexus of blood vessels may be homologous to the branching-gut of the posterior cardinal veins in the formation of the pronephric capsules in the region of the pronephric kidneys in the frog larva. The omphalomesenteric arteries and veins have also advanced in their development. They now lead the blood-from and to the heart respectively. The transformation of the isolated blood islands into a complex capillary network of delicate blood vessels spread out over the yolk mass has been accomplished within twenty-four hours of development.

Excretory system

Pronephros. The pronephros, which has attained a high degree of prominence in the frog larva, is also present in the chick embryo, but it is doubtful whether it has any functional significance. The paired pronephric tubules are concentrated from the fifth to the sixteenth somite. As a matter of fact, the pronephros does not develop tubules but originates from the intermediate mesoderm as a series of cellular strands which grow upward and outward and then curve toward the posterior direction. These solid strands of cells connect with each other at their free ends and thus form the pronephric ducts. The latter become tubular and resemble that of the frog in structure and location. At the beginning of the third day the pronephros begins to degenerate. The development of the mesonephros has already begun and the pronephric duct will be utilized then as the mesonephric duct. Since the pronephros is never functional, the potential pronephric duct is usually referred to as the mesonephric duct at its very beginning.

Seventy-Two Hours, and Certain Later Stages

External morphology

The more interesting features of chick embryos beyond forty-eight hours of incubation are illustrated, which represent the 60-and 72-hour embryo respectively. Our interest will be centered chiefly on the latter, and intermediate development as far back as the 48-hour chick will be illustrated chiefly on the 60-hour chick embryo.

In a total preparation of the 72-hour chick, one's attention is immediately arrested by the increase of torsion as well as flexure. The slight turn to the right which began in the 37-hour embryo in the anterior part of the body has now involved more than half of the embryo. In fact, torsion has proceeded posteriorly almost to the level of the omphalomesenteric arteries. Only the tail region is still in its original position, and even that will complete its torsion within another twenty-four hours of incubation. The four-day-old chick embryo rests completely on its left side.

Another striking feature observed in the total embryo is the appearance of two additional flexures, one in the region of the tenth to the twelfth somite, known as the *dorsal flexure*, and the other in the tail region, referred to as the *caudal flexure*. In the 33-hour embryo the cranial flexure was observed as the first curvature of the brain. In the 48-hour chick the cervical flexure was added posterior to it, and in the 60-hour chick the dorsal flexure makes its appearance. In the 72-hour chick the caudal flexure has developed in the posterior end of the embryo. Generally speaking, it has now the outline imparting to it the general outline of the mirror image of a question mark.

The curvature of the dorsal flexure has increased considerably in length in the 72-hour chick and has there become continuous with the cervical flexure to form a semicircular outline of the anterior part of the body of the embryo. The effect of this change has transferred the

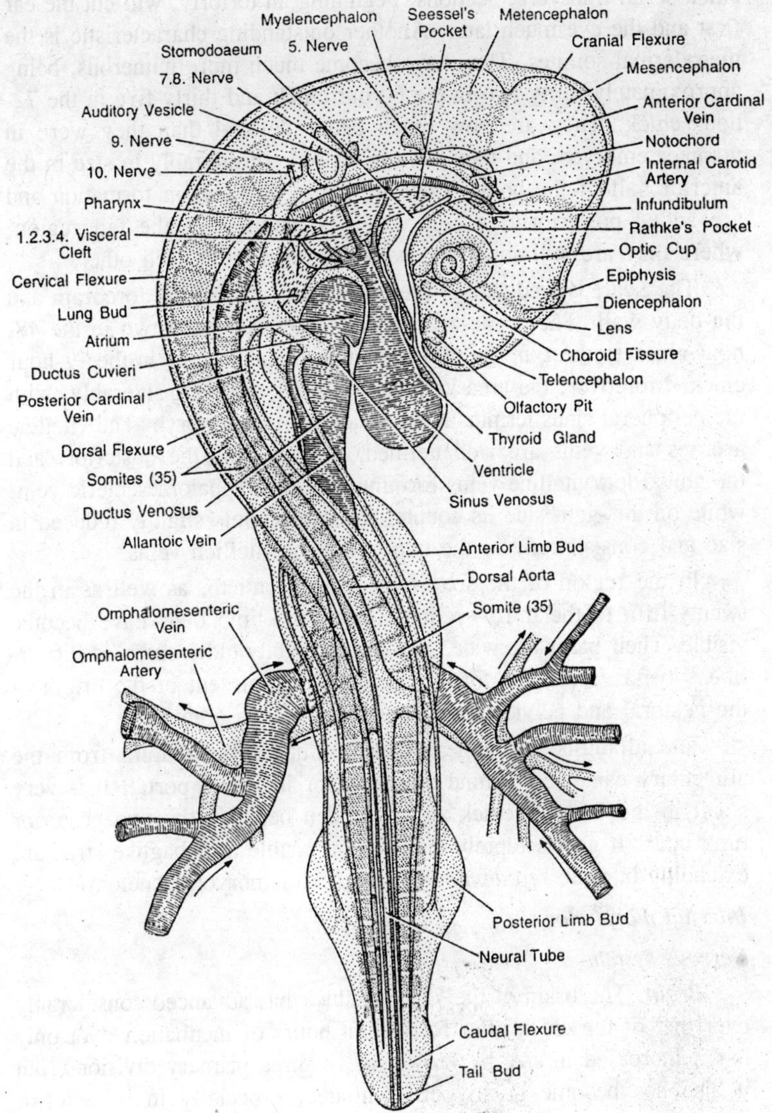

Fig. 11.16. Dorsal view of 72 hour embryo (35-somites).

otic capsules topographically more anteriorly than they were in earlier chicks. A transverse section through the level of the eye will also usually transect the ear in the 60-hour embryo, but in the 72-hour chick serial transverse sections, beginning an teriorly, will cut the ear first and the eye much later. Another outstanding characteristic is the mesodermal somites. They have become much more numerous, being approximately thirty-two in the 60-our chick and thirty-five in the 72-hour chick. They are now much better defined than they were in younger embryos, and they have increased considerably in size in the anterior half of the body. They are apparently still in formation and are added posteriorly, a fact which is manifest in the tail region, where they are still small and well-separated from each other.

The heart is wedged between the lower part of the forebrain and the body wall. The aortic arches have increased from two in the 48-hour chick to three in the 60-hour embryo and to four in the 72-hour chick. Moreover, the area vasculosa has expanded considerably, with the peripheral sinus terminalis far away from the embryo. The vitelline arteries and veins are well defined, the anterior, the posterior, and the united left vitelline veins forming the left omphalomesenteric vein, while on the right side its counterpart has become slightly reduced in size and consists only of the two two right vitellien veins.

In the region of the sixteenth to the twentieth, as well as in the twenty-fifth to the thirty-second somite, the limb buds have become visible. Their bases are wide, forming in slightly older embryos flipper-like appendages. Their form is strongly reminiscent of the origin of the pectoral and pelvic fins in the elasmobranch embryo.

The allantois has appeared as a small diverticulum from the alimentary canal just behind the posterior intestinal portal. It is very small in the 72-hour chick and is hidden between the two posterior limb buds. It grows rapidly and is soon visible as a baglike structure extending into the *seroamniotic cavity* (extraembryonic coelom).

Internal morphology

Nervous system

Brain. The brain of the 72-hour chick has advanced considerably over that of the chick after forty-eight hours of incubation. Not only has it increased in size by growth of its three primary divisions, but it also has become greatly differentiated, especially in its anterior part.

Prosencephalon

The beginning of the separation of the prosencephalon into the diencephalons and the telencephalon has already been pointed out in the 48-hour chick. The faint demarcation between these two parts can easily be observed in the 60-hour embryo, and it has become very obvious in the 72-hour chick. Not only has the telencephalon been separated from the diencephalons by a transverse constriction, but the telencephalon itself has become partly divided by a longitudinal furrow, forming in this manner two rounded anterolateral vesicles called the telencephalic vesicles. They are probably the most important differentiations of the higher vertebrate brain, since they will form the paired *cerebral hemispheres* of the adult. They increase considerably in size, so that they will extend backward over the diencephalons and mesencephalon. The cerebral hermispheres are chiefly the center of intelligence, by means of which the animal is able to learn and profit by past experience.

As the telencephalic vesicles continue to grow, they become progressively more constricted at the point of outgrowth, leaving finally only two small apertures through which the cavities of the left and right telencephalic vesicles (*telocoels*) communicate with the original prosocoel. These apertures are the *foramina of Monro* (*foramina interventricularia*), and the cavity of the left telencephalic vesicle becomes the *first ventricle* of he brain, while the right one becomes the *second ventricle*. These two cavities are usually referred to aş the two lateral ventricles. Through the foramina interventricularia, the lateral ventricles communicate with the small remnant of the original prosocoel and the newly formed *diocoel* of the diencephalons, referred to as the *third ventricle* of the brain. Anteriorly the third ventricle is bounded by the *lamina termainais* and posteriorly it opens into the cavity of the mesencephalon, called the mesocoel, or *aqueduct of Sylvius*. In its earlier stages of development the diencephalons and the telencephalon can be distinguished in the chick embryo as readily as the frog larva. An imaginary line drawn from the posterior tubercle to the *mesodiencephalic constriction* separates the diencephalons from the mesencephalon. Another such line drawn from the optic recess to the *velum transversum* (*dien-telencephalic constriction*) separates the diencephalons from the telelncephalon.

Diencephalon

The differentiations of the diencephalons have been described in the 48-hour chick embryo, and little can be added to that account. Just posterior to the optic recess, the floor of the diencephalons thickens considerably and becomes the location of the optic chiasma. Posterior to the later, the infundibulum has increased its evagination and is directly adjacent to *Rathke's pocket*, with which it is destined to form the *hypophysis*, or *pituitary body*, which functions later as a gland of internal secretion. The roof of the diencephalons remains thin throughout its entire development. Indeed, anterior to the epiphysis it differentiates into a membranous sheet which becomes richly supplied with blood vessels. In later development this membrane becomes convoluted and sinks into the cavity of the third ventricle, and is thus instrumental in furnishing the forebrain with a profuse blood supply. It is known as the *choroid plexus* of the third ventricle. In the 4-day chick the epiphysis changes from its earlier round and wart-like appearance into a slightly elongate outgrowth.

Mesencephalon

The mesencephalon is characterized by its relatively thick walls, which gradually reduce its cavity, the *mesocoel*, to a narrow canal called the *aqueduct of Sylvius*. There is hardly any difference between the mesencephalon of the 48-hour and that of the 72-hour embryo. On its dorsal aspect are the corpora *bigemina*, though in certain Sauropsida (Ophidia) they have developed a transverse furrow and have become the *corpora quadrigemina*. They are the homologue of the corpora bigemina of the frog larva, except that in the case of the snake embryo the two additional bodies containnerve fibers for hearings, while the two anterior ones have the same function as the corpora bigemina in the frog, namely, that of visual sensation. In later development the *crura cerebri* develop in the thickened floor of the midbrain. Their function in the chick is the same as that of the same structures in the frog larva.

Rhombencephalon

Morphologically the rhombencephalon is divided into two parts, namely, the metencephalon and the myelencephalon. The former is separated from the mesencephalon by a deep dorsal and lateral constriction, referred to as the *mesometencephalic constriction*, which forms a narrow connection between these two parts of the primitive brain. Posteriorly it is continuous with the myelencephalonin which the original neuromeric segmentation is still visible. The transition from the metencephalon to the myelencephalon is best observed in its dorsal covering. The roof of the metencephalon is comparatively thick, while that of the myelencephalon is thin – almost membranous. This part of the hindbrain becomes the medulla oblongata, in whose dorsal covering is the choroids plexus of the *fourth ventricle*, which has a similar function as the choroids plexus of the third ventricle, namely, the supply of blood to the brain.

The metencephalon gives rise to the cerebellum. It is large and deeply furrowed in birds. The cerebellum is an association center for muscular co-ordination and for equilibrium.

Cranial nerves

Much has been written about the phylogenetic origin of the cranial nerves and their possible serial homology to spinal nerves, but all the present evidence is neither exact nor weightly enough for the assumption that all cranial nerves of the primitive ancestral vertebrate stock were organized on the metameric plan of spinal nerves. There is no doubt that some of the cranial nerves of the bird, reptile, and mammal have been derived from spinal nerves, as from example the eleventh (*spinal accessory*) and the twelfth (*hypoglossal*). These two nerves are still present in the frog as the first and second spinal nerves respectively. However, in homologizing the other cranial nerves with spinal nerves, we are confronted with certain objections which objections which obscure their derivation considerably.

A typical spinal nerve is composed of two roots – a dorsal, which is an *afferent* or *sensory*, and a ventral, which is an *efferent* or *motor root*. These unite immediately outside the serve cord to form a nerve cable containing both kinds of fibers. The dorsal root of each spinal nerve has a ganglion in which in proper time the ganglionic neroblasts are developed. The neurons for the ventral root are formed in the ventral portion of the neural tube and are multipolar.

The *olfactory nerve* deviates greatly from the typical organization of the spinal nerve. It is purely sensory, and its neuroblasts develop from the epithelium in the center of the olfactory pit. They project their axons toward the ventral side of the forebrain and connect with the cerebral hemispheres there. For this reason it is often called "olfactory tract." The *optic nerve* conforms even less to the plan of the spinal nerves. Here it is the retina which develops the neuroblasts that send the axons toward the central portion of the diencephalons, and it was the retina which was part of the lateral wall of the prosencephalon prior to the formation of the optic vesicles. The retina is therefore truly a part of the brain, and its neurons are comparable to those found in the brain. The auditory nerve is also purely sensory in function.

The *oculomotor*, *trochlear* and *abducens* nerves, on the other hand, are purely motor or efferent in function, and no vestige of a sensory of afferent root is ever present in their formation. There is some evidence that these nerves may represent the motor roots of former spinal nerves, because their centers of origin in the brain are in the gray matter which is continuous with that of the ventral horns of the spinal cord in which the motor neurons of the spinal cord in which the motor neurons of the spinal nerves are located. However, if one considers the exact origin of these nerves, as described below, the case is not quite as clear as it seems.

The *trigeminal facial*, *glossopharyngeal*, and *vagus* nerves agree more closely with the pattern of spinal nerves, since they are mixed in composition and are partly organized from ganglia. Upøn more detailed examination this assumption is rather weighty because the large cranial ganglia are composed of more than one unit, one being derived from neural crest material and the other from the ectoderm of the skin in the form of a placode. Since these four nerves supply the complex area of the visceral arches and the lateral line system in fishes and larval amphibians, it may be possible that their metamerism and fundamental organization have been greatly modified in the evolution from primitive ancestral chordates to modern birds and mammals. These nerves may have been metameric as are those of the present spinal nerves, but may have become aberrant and complex by mutural coalescence, conditioned by anatomical and physiological changes in the development of new organs and organ systems, such of gills, lungs, glands, musculature, skeletal structures, etc.

It will be profitable to review the development and make comparisons with the cranial nerves of the frog. A comparative study of the origin of the nervous system will not only be profitable from the evolutionary point of view, but it will also reveal many features of similarity and will illuminate certain apparent differences between the two types. All the cranial nerves are paired. For the sake of convenience and clearness in the following discussion, reference is usually made to only one member of the pair. The reader should be mindful of the fact that the discussion always applies to both.

Olfactory nerve and olfactory organ

The first indication of an olfactory organ in the chick becomes apparent at sixty hours of incubation. At that time the ectoderm on the anterolateral aspect of the head thickens to form paired olfactory pates. They are homologous to the olfactory placodes described in the development of the nose of the frog larva. The olfactory plates invaginate to form the *olfactory pits*, which by further growth develop into the olfactory sacs. At first their epithelial lining consists of uniform cells, but when in the 4-day chick the nasal sacs push further inward and become deeper, the centrally located cells grow large, while those of the outer ectoderm: The centrally located, larger epithelial cells will be transformed later into neuroblasts which grow with their axons toward the ventral side of the telencephala (cerebral hemispheres), where they connect with the olfactory area of that part of the forebrain. The smaller and more peripherally located ones multiply and grow backward toward the brain, and form the nerve sheaths by overgrowing the developing nerve fibers. In their backward growth the nasal sacs utilize the cells located between them and the fore-gut. Eventually the sacs will reach the anterior portion of the pharynx, which they perforate to establish communication with the oral cavity. The two apertures thus formed are the *posterior nares*. The openings (*anterior nares*) into the olfactory pits are located on the right and left sides of the *nasofrontal process*, which projects below the telencephala.

Optic nerve and Eye

In preceding chapters the development of the optic nerve and the eye have been followed out as far as the 48-hour chick embryo. At the stage the lens is still a hollow vesicle, opening to the outside by a tiny pore called the *lenticular aperture*. In the 60-hour embryo this pore has disappeared, and the lens with its outer thinner and its innermost thicker layer still contains a flattened lenticular cavity which will persist as far as the tenth day of incubation. The two layers of the optic cup become more closely apposed to each other, but hey are still far enough apart in the 72-hour chick embryo to form a shallow remnant of the opticoel. While these changes are in progress, the rim of the optic cup becomes smaller by converging centrally toward the lens, which now becomes located within the diminishing aperture of the optic cup. In this transformation the choroids fissure has become narrower and is continued on the ventral side of the optic stalk as a deep groove. Later on, this groove will harbor the blood vessels leading to the retina and also the visual nerve fibers (axons) which will grow out from the inner layer of cells (retina) of the optic cup. In later development, the groove is entirely eliminated by sinking-deeper into the optic stalk and by overgrowth of its sides, thus encasing the optic nerve and the blood vessels in a sheath which was originally the optic stalk. At about the same time the choroid fissure is also eliminated, so that the optic nerve becomes almost centrally placed on the back of the optic cup, which may now be referred to as the eye-ball.

The outer layer of the optic cup differentiates into a black piginented layer, whose cells absorb light by means of black granules contained in the cells. The mesenchyme cells furnish a hard protective coat, or *sclera*, and a vascular envelop called the *choroids coat*, to the outside of the eyeball; however, the crystalline liquid called the *vitreous humor*, located between the retina and the lens, is probably formed by the cells of the optic cup itself and is therefore believed to be of ectodermal origin. The outer layer of the transparent cornea is continuous with the epidermis of the skin. The iris, which assists in lending the characteristic colour to the eye, is formed from the thin converging portions of the rim of the optic cup.

Oculomotor, trochlearis, and abducens nerves

It seems best to treat this group under one heading because they are purely efferent and motor in function, and because they agree in their specific action by innervating the muscles of the eyeball. Of the three, the third or oculomotor, nerve appears first and may already be identified in the 60-hour chick. However, it can best be observed in its appearance in sections of the 72-hour embryo, where it emerges from the ventral side of the mesencephalon, and, passing forward as far as the optic cup, ends gradually there near the ventrolateral side of the diencephalons. Since the six muscles of the eyeball are not as yet developed at that time, the nerve has no definite terminal branches, but when they do appear the oculomotor will innervate the *superior*, *inferior*, and *internal* rectus as well as the *inferior oblique*.

The fourth cranial, or trochlear, nerve, also called the *patheticus*, and the sixth cranial, or *abducens*, nerve, develop much later than the oculomotor. Both appear shortly after the fifth day of incubation, and trochlear originating in the depression between the mesencephalon and metencephalon, while the abducens arises near the midventral line of the myelencephalon, just below the seventh nerve. The trochlear never innervates the superior *oblique muscle* of the eye and the abducens nerve supplies the *external rectus*.

Trigeminalis

When the neural crests are formed in the early stages of the embryo, they extend along the entire neural tube to the tip of the head. There follows a gradual differentiation and adjustment, especially in the anterior part of the embryo, but even in 33-hour chick these crests can still be observed in the head region as paired condensations of cells extending in the form of paired strands from the tip of the head back to the otic region. These loosely organized strands of neural crest cells, located laterally between the ectoderm and the foregut, make contact with the ectoderm of the skin on their outer borers and organize into massive ganglia. The first and larger one is located just posterior to the first neuromere of the rhombencephalon, and another is located further back, immediately anterior to the otic capsule. The former is the beginning of the *trigeminal ganglion*, also called the *Gasserian ganglion*, and the latter is the ganglion of the seventh nerve, or *geniculate ganglion*. The mass of the Gasserian ganglion is still further increased by the addition of cells which arise as a thickening from the inner portion of the superficial ectoderm in front and above the first visceral cleft. This mass of cells is homologous to the placode of the fifth cranial nerve in the frog embryo.

The trigeminal nerve is a mixed nerve, consisting of motor and sensory fibers, of which the latter arise from the ganglion from bipolar neurones. The ganglion is bipartite in structure, its anterior portion giving rise to the *ophthalmic nerve* which grows forward over the optic cup into the head region. The posterior portion of the ganglion extends downward the branches near the angle of the mouth into the *maxillary* and the *mandibular nerves*, of which the former supplies the maxillary process or upper jaw, and the latter the mandibular arch (first visceral arch) which will form the lower jaw.

Facialis

The seventh and eighth, or facial and acoustic, nerves have a common origin and remain closely associated in early chick embryology. Their ganglia are derived from cranial neural crest cells, and from an ectodermal thickening which is continuous with the auditory placode. However, a small part of the geniculate ganglion is derived from an epibranchial placode which is well-separated from the auditory placode. During the fourth day of incubation, the geniculate ganglion, which gives rise to the seventh or facial nerve, is separated from the acoustico-facialis complex, as described below in the origin of the acoustic nerve. The remainder of the complex forms the *auditory ganglion* which becomes located immediately above the second visceral arch.

Acostic nerve and the ear

The development of the eighth, acoustic or auditory, nerve and the ear are also closely interrelated that it is almost impossible to discuss them apart. In the 72-hour chick embryo the ear has not advanced very far in its differentiations, so that for our present needs not much. However, it is desirable to trace the more general features of the ear from their earliest appearance to their final disposition, and observe how closely this complex organ has been evolved from such primitive beginnings as are present in young vertebrate embryos.

When last mentioned, the otocyst was still attached to the superficial ectoderm by a perforated stalk, ending at the outside in a pore. There was also a short dorsal evagination in the otocyst, which was recognized as the beginning of the emdolymphatic duct. On the ventrolateral aspect of the otoeyst appears now a dense mass of cells which is the material from which the acoustics facialis ganglion will be formed. Upon separation of the otocyst from the superficial ectoderm, this ganglionic mass moves entirely to its ventral side, and after it has united with cranial neural crest cells, it separates into two ganglia, namely, the *geniculate*, which has been discussed above, and the *auditory*, which will give rise to the auditory nerve. While the geniculate ganglion appears as a definite condensed mass, the auditory appears diffuse and stays attached to the otocyst, whence it spreads into the mesenchyme cells that are located between the auditory capsule and the myelencephalon.

Labyrinth or inner ear

The ear harbors not only the sense of hearing but also the sense of equilibrium. Phylengenetically the latter was present before the sense of hearing was added to the inner ear. It is therefore to be expected that in the differentiation of the sense organs from the primitive otocysts the mechanism for the sense of equilibrium should appear first. This occurs in the formation of the semicircular canals which grow out from the otoeyst as flat, pocket like evaginations. Eventually all three pockets are transformed into semicircular canals by separations of their central areas from the otocyst, only their ends remaining attached. After this transformation the otoeyst is referred to as the *utriculus*. Each semicircular canal is supplied with one dilation (*ampulla*) at one end of its attachment to the utriculus. The position of the semicircular in all vertebrates from fishes to mammals is uniform; one is located in the horizontal plane, the second in the vertical plane, and the third also in the vertical plane, at right angles to the second.

During the formation of the semicircular canals, the endolymphatic duct changed from its dorsal position on the otoeyst to a more central and median one. This change is effected by differential growth of cells, and when it is completed the endolymphatic duct is attached to the utriculus between the ampullae of the two vertical semicircular canals. Another differentiation, called the cochlear duct, appears near the utficulus next to the endolymphatic duct, between the ampullae of the two vertical semicircular canals. The entire structure, including the semicircular canals, endolymphatic duct, utriculus, cochlear duct, and cochlea, is now called the *membranous labyrinth*. Later it will become enclosed in a bony envelope, referred to as the bony labyrinth, and between the two the liquid perilymph fills up the narrow space. The combined membranous and bony labyrinth with its perilymph is usually simply referred to as the *labyrinth* or *inner ear*.

The cavities of the membranous labyrinth are also filled with a liquid which is called *endolymph* because it is contained within the cavities. The latter which have been derived from the original cavity of the otocyrt, are lined by a sensory epithelium containing delicate hair like projections in definite areas, as for example in the utriculus, cochleam, and ampullae of the semicircular canals. The sensory areas become connected with the auditory nerve which originates from the ganglionic mass beneath the otocyst. It divides into two branches, of which the dorsal one supplies the utriculus and the three semicircular canals, and the ventral one the chochlea. This is as far as ear development proceeds in the bird. In the mammal the cochlear duct grows out ventrally from the utriculus, coilling into two to four turns which will develop eventually into the cochlea.

Tympanic cavity or middle ear

It has been pointed out before that the first visceral cleft (hyomandibular cleft) is never completely formed in the chick embryo. At its fullest development it consists of only as small opening at the upper region of the first visceral furrow, and even his small aperture disappears shortly after its formation, leaving a depression resembling the original visceral furrow. Viewed from within the pharynx, the closure of the small opening has not diminished the depth of the pharyngeal pouch. Indeed, it seems that it has increased in depth and has pushed itself between the labyrinth and the outer ectorderm or skin of the embryo. Presently there occurs a downward growth of a delicate partition from the dorsal wall of the pharynx, thus adding a minute portion of the pharynx to the distal end of the first pharyngeal pouch. This newly formed chamber becomes the *tympanic cavity* or the *middle* ear, and its connection with the pharynx through the tubular first pharyngeal pouch is the *Eustachian tube*. Later on, a group of cell from the adjacent upper portion of the hyoid arch (second visceral arch) are segregated into the tympanic cavity and transformed into a minute bone called the *columella auris*.

External ear

After completion of the tympanic cavity a groove appears near or at the old location of the original visceral furrow. It grows inward toward the newly formed tympanic cavity in the form of a tubular depression, and remains separated from it by a thin membrane called the *tympanic membrane*. The latter is ectodermal on its outer and entodermal on its inner surface, and between the two is a thin layer of mesoderm cells. The tubular canal from the tympanic membrane to the outside is called the *external auditory meatus*; it constitutes with its opening the *external ear*. The columella auris, mentioned above, is attached by one end to the inner surface of the tympanic membrane, and with the other if fits into the *fenestra ovalis* of the labyrinth. Sound waves striking the tympanic membrane are relayed by the columella auris through the fenestra ovalis to the endolymph of the labyrinth, which transmits them to the cochlear duct of the lagena.

Glossopharyngeus

The ninth, or glossopharyngeal, nerve originates from the *petrosal ganglion*, which is formed by the posterior portion of the otic neural crest segment and the adjacent thickening in the superficial ectoderm, forming the third cranial nerve placode. In the 48-hour and also in the 60-hour chick embryo the *postotic* (*petrosal*) ganglion is still continuous with the *preotic* (*geniculate*) ganglion: however, in the 72-hour embryo the independence of the petrosal ganglion has become quite obvious, and the outgrowth of the glossopharyngeal nerve occurs shortly afterwards between the third and fourth day of incubation. The axons grow from the neuroblasts of the ganglion into the floor of the myelencephalon, and the peripheral portion of the nerve grows downward and divides into two main branches, of which the larger one enters the third, and the smaller one the second, visceral arch. It has been shown above that the region of the first visceral cleft forms part of the external ear. The second visceral arch (hyoid arch), immediately behind this cleft, must necessarily form parts of the mouth, and the third visceral arch parts of the adjacent region of the neck. These parts are innervated by the glossopharyngeal nerve.

Vagus (Pneumogastric)

This is the largest and most complex of cranial nerves. Its main ganglion (*jugular ganglion*) becomes separated from that of the glossopharyngeal nerve. The jugular ganglion is connected with the ventrolateral portion of the myelencephalon by a number of small nerve roots, of which the posterior ones organize a branch that connects with the ganglionic chain of the *autonomic nervous system*. A thick branch from the jugular ganglion connects with the more ventrally located *nodosal ganglion*, from which a branch for the fourth and also one for the fifth visceral arch originates, and, after having supplied these structures, continues posteriorly toward the viscera of the body cavity as the *pneumogastic nerve*, supplying the heart, lungs and stomach. Similar to the nodosal gangion, the jugular ganglion is formed partly by neural crest elements and partly by cells from the thickened superficial ectoderm.

Accessorius and hypoglossus

There is no doubt that the eleventh, or *spinal accessory*, and the twelfth, or *hypoglossal*, never were once upon a time spinal nerves and that they have been added to the cranial nerves by a process of cephalization. They are almost exclusively motor (efferent) in function and therefore represent chiefly the ventral roots of spinal nerves with which they are actually continuous. Both of these nerves appear during the fourth day of incubation and are characterized by the absence of ganglia and the lack of any contribution from the superficial ectoderm. They innervate chiefly regions of the neck.

Spinal nerves and autonomic nervous system

The interrelationship between the spinal nerves and the autonomic nervous system is so close that the two have to be discussed together. The origin of the neural crestş has been described in Chaps. XIII and XIV, so that we shall consider here only the formation of the spinal nerves and their relation to the autonomic system. When in the following discussion the singular form is used in the description of nerves and ganglia, it should be remembered that spinal nerves, like cranial nerves, are also paired and that the discussion is applicable to both members of the pair. Morphologically, each spinal never is composed of two strands known as the dorsal and ventral roots, of which the former contains the spinal ganglion. Furthermore, the nerves originating from the spinal cord are connected with the autonomic nervous system by a communicating strand – the *ramus communicans*. Physiologically, the dorsal root of each spinal nerve is afferent and sensory, and the ventral root efferent and motor. A greater complication in this respect aries with the nerves connected with the autonomic nervous system. The nerve fibers which innervate the somatic peripheral organs and system are referred to as being *somatic sensory* and *somatic motor fibers*. On the other hand, the organs and systems connected with the autonomic nervous system are derived from the splanchnopleure, and nerve fibers of such organs going to or coming from the nerve cord through the spinal nerves are called visceral (*splanchnic*) sensory and visceral (*splanchnic*) motor respectively.

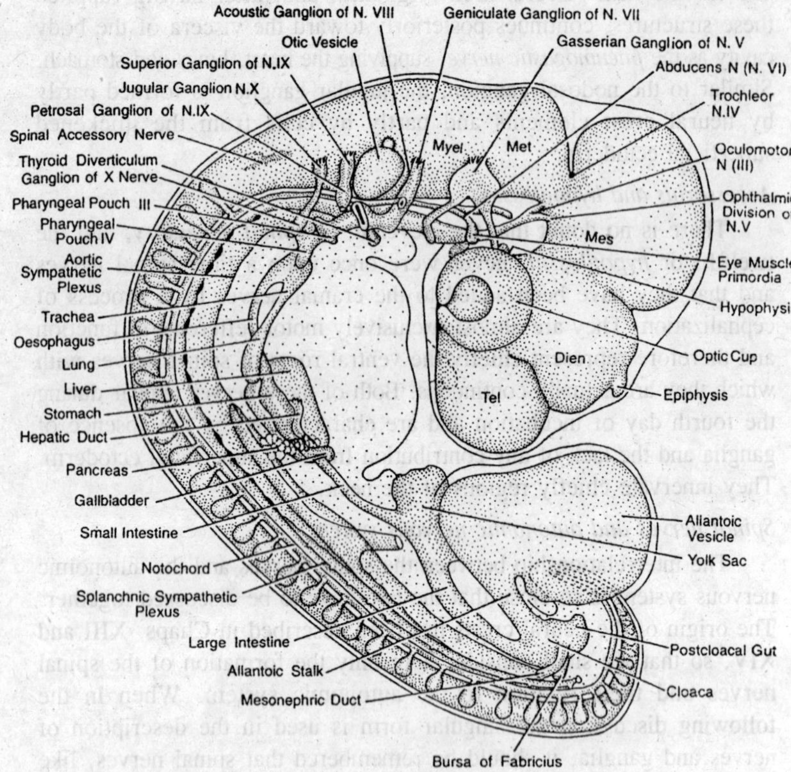

Fig. 11.17. Dorsal view of 96 hour embryo.

The autonomic nervous system is physiologically divided into the sympathetic (*thoracico-lumbar*) and the parasympathetic (*cranio-sacral*) parts. These systems act as mutual checks against each other; they are therefore antagonistic in their action. Nerve fibers from either system are usually innervating the same organ, but while certain fibers may accelerate or tighten muscles or glands, others may decelerate or slacken them. Moreover, the action is not uniform is any one system, but on the whole, the sympathetic system is for acceleration and the parasympathetic for deceleration. In this manner all the organs which function without control do so effectively without the animal becoming aware of their action.

The spinal ganglia contain neuroblasts which send fibers (axones) into the neural tube, and the others (dendrites) into the peripheral somatic or autonomic division of the embryo. The ventral root contains fibers which are derived from neuroblasts within the ventral portion of the horns of the neural tube. Never fibers grow into the myotomes and others organs and structures when they are still closely located near the neural tube. However, peripheral nerves actually grow along definite pathways to establish proper connections.

The autonomic nervous system with its paired sympathetic ganglia originates during the fourth day by strands of cells which are derived from the neural tube and the neural crest material. These strands extend in metameric order from the neural crests to the sides of the aorta, where they establish terminal thickenings that will later form the sympathetic ganglia. The latter become united by connections between the ganglia to form the characteristic sympathetic chains of the adult. Anteriorly the chains are connected with the sympathetic system of the cervical region, and the paired *pneumogastric* or vagus nerves.

Alimentary canal and its derivatives

Growth of the enteron

In embryos of less than one somite, the alimentary canal is an open gut, with the cellar entodermal roof above and the non-cellular yolk floor below. When the head fold appears, the entoderm follows by pushing into it, to differentiate the fore-guts. Similarly, the hind-gut is established by the growth of the entoderm into the tail bud. The elevated head and tail are undercut by the subcephalic and the *subcaudal pockets* respectively, and the two are continuous with the lateral body folds, which constrict the embryo on both sides from the underlying blastodise. There is a progressive undercutting on all sides, shaping the contour of the embryo and limiting the open gut to two small areas, one over the yolk stalk and the other over the allantoic stalk. The body folds which accomplish this constriction converge on the ventral side of the embryo, surroundings the yolk stalk and allantoic stalk on all sides. In this manner a new stalk is formed, referred to as the *unbilical cord.*

As the embryo grows in size, the yolk sac diminishes accordingly, so that shortly before hatching it has become depleted and is small enough to be withdrawn into the alimentary canal. On the other hand, the allantois remains large and completely functional almost to the day of hatching. Shortly before emergence the chick begins to use its lungs for respiration, thus relieving the allantois of this function. At the same time the vascular system establishes its pulmonary circuit, resulting in a progressive diminution of respiratory function in the allantois. The latter now begins to dry up, its attachment to the body

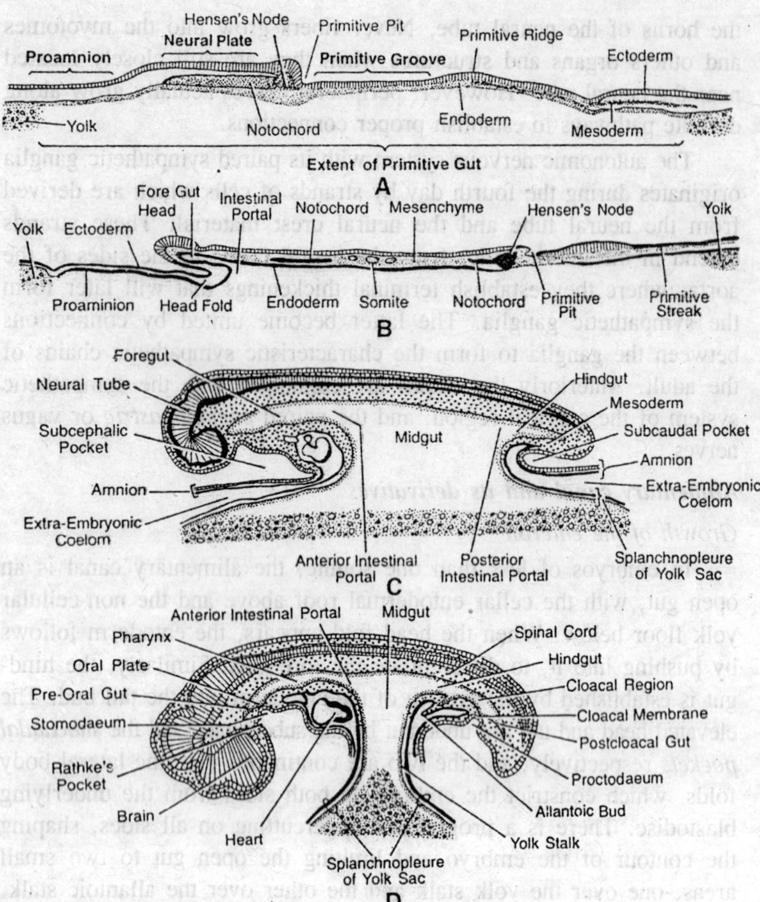

Fig. 11.18. Development of alimentary canal. A—M.L.S of 18 hour embryo showing primitive gut, B—M.L.S. of 24 hour embryo showing head fold and foregut, C—M.L.S. of 60 hour embryo showing hindgut, D—M.L.S. of about 96 hour embryo showing almost fully formed simple gut.

(*umbilicus*) is severed, and the chick is ready to pick its way through the calcareous shell.

Mesenteries

As the embryo becomes constricted from the underlying yolk, its alimentary canal becomes more or less tubular, except in the restricted areas of the umbilicus where it still remains open. Moreover, its various portions become differentiated and assume their permanent position in the body cavity. During these changes the gut moves away from its original location immediately beneath the notochord and becomes suspended by the *dorsal mesentery*, composed of splanchnic mesoderm, which is a reflected portion of the somatic mesoderm. Since the splanchnic mesoderm extends also over the yolk sac and the allantois, a ventral mesentery must necessarily be formed when the yolk stalk becomes progressively smaller and constricted, thus leaving the closed gut attached to the ventral body wall by a second mesentery. Eventually this ventral mesentery disappears, with the resulting union of the two lateral coelomic cavities. Only in the region of the liver, the hind-gut, and the oesophagus does the ventral mesentery remain. As a matter of fact, the liver diverticulum growing out from the alimentary canal in the 48-hour embryo is caught between the two approaching sheets of the splanchnic mesoderm and is permanently held in place by them.

With the exception of the stomodaeal and the proctodael portions, the entire alimentary canal is differentiated from the entoderm, which, in the adult, still forms its lining. Moreover, all glands and organs which are formed by outgrowths from the undifferentiated enteron retain their entodermal heritage in a similar manner. To the original entodermal layer are added mesenchyme cells which form the muscular layers, and the outer covering of the canal with all its derivatives is furnished by the splanchnic mesoderm.

Fore-gut

The entire alimentary canal is conveniently divided into the fore-gut, mid-gut, and hind-gut, of which the fore-gut extends from the mouth to the pancreas. The mouth forms in the 60-hour embryo by the rupture of the oral plate, which is located between the two mauidibular arches. During this process the superficial ectoderm is drawn inward so that the oral cavity becomes lined by it anterior to the pharynx. The transition between the ectoderm and entoderm is soon lost and has become imperceptible in the 72-hour chick.

Pharynx and visceral arches

The mouth is followed by the pharynx, which is chiefly characterized by the paired pharyngeal pouches. These have been discussed quite thoroughly in the preceding chapters, and very little need be added here to complete the account. Of the four pharyngeal pouches developed in the embryo, only three pairs form apertures to the outside. The fourth, or last one, never opens but remains a pouch from whose posterodorsal border the *posibranchial bodies* are developed. These bodies contain tissue which resembles that given off for the organization of the *thymus gland* by the third and fourth pairs of pharyngeal pouches. They also contain cells similar to the *epithelioid bodies* given off by the third pharyngeal pouches. However, the postbranchial bodies never enter into the formation of the thymus gland.

The visceral arches separating the pharyngeal pouches are short, stubby columns which spread out fanwise from the level of the truncus arteriosus to the paired dorsal aortae. They are covered on the outside by ectoderm and toward the pharynx by entoderm, and since the pharyngeal pouches are considerably deeper than the visceral furrows, the contribution of the entoderm is much greater than that of the ectoderm. The core of each visceral arch consists of mesenchyme, which differentiates into the bronchial blood vessel (aortic arch) and skeletal support. The bronchial skeleton is composed at first of cartilage, but later this is replaced by bone in certain visceral arches, resulting

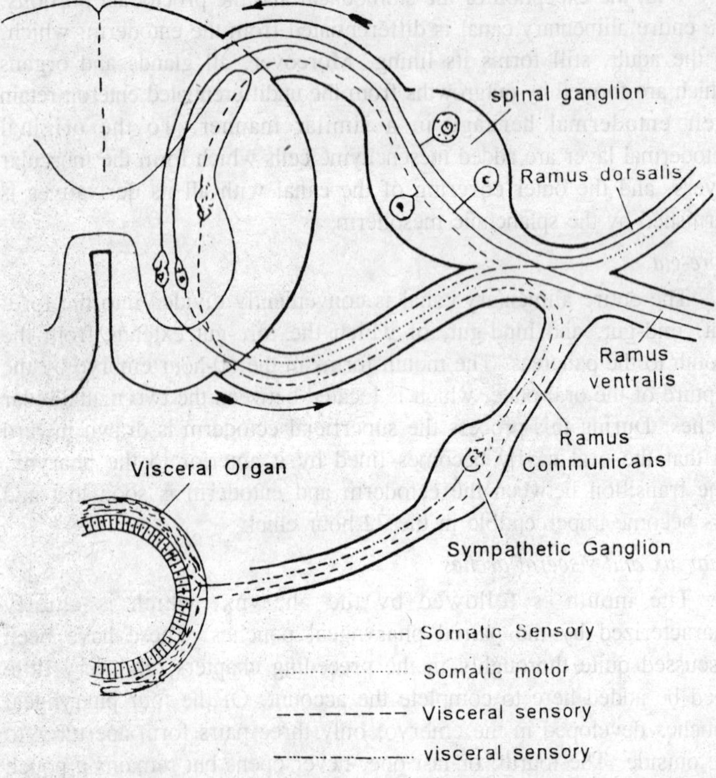

Fig. 11.19. A spinal nerve and its components.

in the partial ossification of the *columella auris* of the middle ear, and some of the bony elements for the mandible or jaw. Furthermore, each arch is supplied by one or more nerves, as outlined above in the discussion of the cranial nerves.

The first pair of visceral arches, or the mandibular arches, project downward on both sides, with the mouth opening between them. During the fifth day of incubation they unite ventrally to form the lower jaw. The upper jaw is formed later by the approach of the two *maxillary processes* which are derived from the uppermost portion of the mandibular arches, and the *frontal process*, which is located centrally and projects downward toward the mouth.

Thyroid gland

The thyroid gland appears as a shallow depression in the 48-hour embryo between the second pair of pharyngeal pouches. As its grows down-ward it becomes constricted at its origin in the floor of the pharynx. In the 72-hour chick it has become vesicular, and shortly afterwards, in the 4-day embryo, it becomes entirely detached from the alimentary canal. After elimination of its cavity it begins to differentiate into its characteristic glandular form. Early during the fifth day of incubation, the same region of the pharynx which gave rise to the thyroid gland develops the *tongue*.

The origin of the thyroid glad in the chick is to strikingly like that of the frog that there seems to be a close relationship between the two. Indeed, this relationship can be carried back to amphioxius, in which the endostyle (hypopharyngeal groove) is apparently homologous to the thyroid gland of vertebrates. The ammocoetes larva of the lampreys bridges this gap since it has an endostyle in its larval form which becomes constricted off and functions as a thyroid gland in the adult.

Pulmonary apparatus

In the posterior part of the pharyntx, where it becomes transitional with the oesophagus, another depression is formed in the center of the floor, called the *laryngotracheal groove*. At first it is very narrow, but it soon deepens, becoming saclike, and as it pushes away from the pharynx it is converted into an elongate diverticulum, divided into two lobes at its distal end. This diverticulum represents the beginning of the pulmonary apparatus, consisting in this early condition of an embryonic *larynx*, *trachea*, and *lung buds*. The appearance of the laryngotracheal groove may be observed shortly after the second day of indubation, and in the 72-hour chick the two lung buds are well differentiated. The opening leading from the pharynx into the newly formed larynx is the glottis. To the students of comparative anatomy the origin of the lungs is significant because it occurs in the same manner as the development of the swirnbladder in certain present day ganoid fishes.

Immediately behind the pharynx the alimentary canal is continued through the short oesophagus into the stomach. These portions of the canal undergo little change in younger embryos and we shall not consider them. We shall therefore eliminate them from further discussion and consider now the glands that are developed posterior to the stomach.

Liver

The liver was first mentioned in the discussion of the 48-hour chick embryo, where this gland appears as two depressions in the wall of the entoderm near the anterior intestinal portal. One of the two depressions is located slightly higher than the other, and when the anterior intestinal portal grows backward, as outlined above, one of these depressions or pockets becomes located above and the other one below the union of the omphalomesenteric veins (*ductus venosus*). To be more exact, the upper diverticulum becomes located slightly ahead of the lower one, but both continue to grow forward into the ventral mesentery so that in the 60-hour embryo the liver has reached the level of the sinus venosus. During this time the two primary diverticula have rebranched into a profuse network of liver tissue surrounding the entire ductus venosus. The bile duct is formed by the fusion of two liver diverticula which takes place, when the embryo in its forward growth pushes the intestinal portal further back. The resulting single (*ductus choledochus*) will remain to act as bile duct in the adult.

Pancreas

This gland appears during the third and fourth day of incubation near the liver diverticulum. It develops from three rudiments, one from the dorsal part of the gut, directly opposite the outgrowth of the liver, and two from the ventral part, slightly lateral to the liver. It is difficult to distinguish these pancreatic primordia from that of the liver because their cellular structure is identical. The ventral pancreative diverticula are so close to that of the liver that they enter the intestine through the ductus choledochus of the liver. In later embryology each gland will have its separate duct; as a matter of fact, the adult chick has two or three pancreatic ducts. The pancreative primordial grow

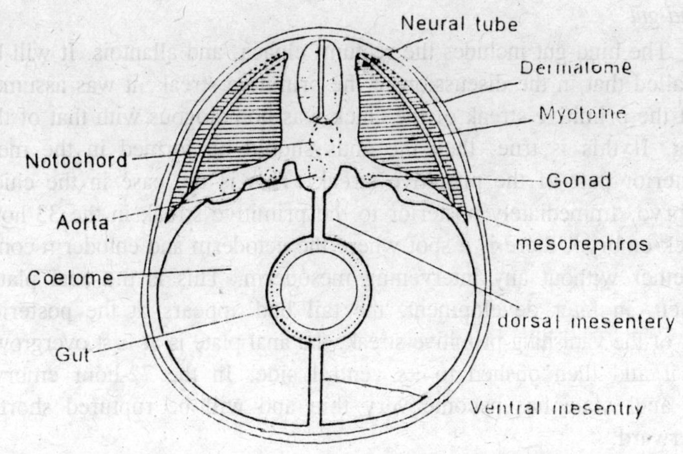

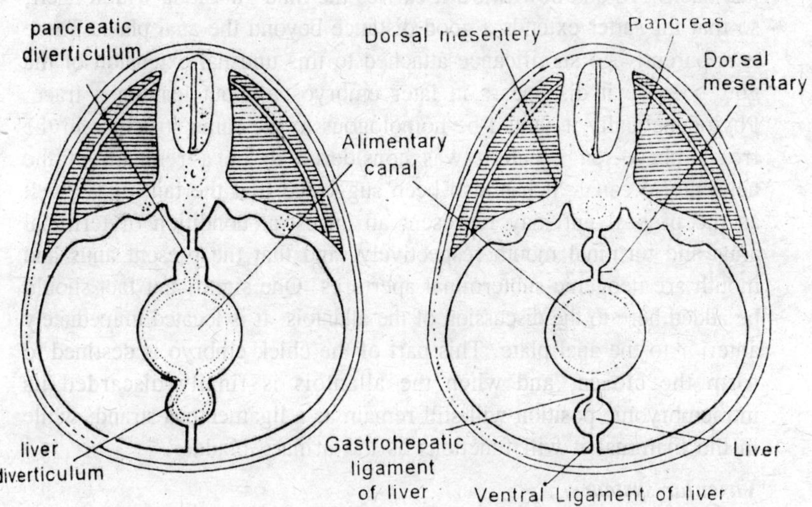

Fig. 11.20. The dorsal and ventral mesenteries and their relation to the gut, liver and pancreas.

into the dorsal mesentery while the liver is held in place by the ventral one.

Mid-gut

Posterior to the pancreas the alimentary canal is still open and is continuous with the yolk sac. The latter must be considered part of the alimentary canal because it is finally incorporated into it, as outlined above.

Hind-gut

The hind-gut includes the rectum, cloaca, and allantois. It will be recalled that in the discussion of the primitive streak, it was assumed that the primitive streak of the chick was homologous with that of the frog. If this is true, then the anus should be formed in the most posterior part of the primitive streak. This is the case in the chick embryo. Immediately posterior to the primitive streak in the 33-hour chick embryo, there is a spot where the ectoderm and entoderm come together without any intervening mesoderm. This is the anal plate. When, in later development, the tail bud appears at the posterior end of the vanishing primitive streak, the anal plate is at first overgrown by it and then pushed to its ventral side. In the 72-hour embryo the anal plate has become very thin and will be ruptured shortly afterward.

The growth of the tail but take place at a rapid rate, and as it just backward and downward it carries the hind-gut along within itself, so that the latter extends a good distance beyond the anal plate. There is apparently no significance attached to this unusual extension of the gut, because it disappears in later embryos without leaving a trace. Phylogenetically it should be homologous to the same structure in the frog embryo, in which it was considered to be a remnant of the neurenteric canal. It has also been suggested that the tail gut as well as the preoral gut may represent an ancestral condition of terminal anus and terminal mouth respectively, and that the present anus and mouth are neogenic subterminal apertures. One significant fact should be added here to the discussion of the allantois. It is located immediately anterior to the anal plate. This part of the chick embryo is destined to form the cloaca, and when the allantois is finally discarded its intraembryonic position will still remain as a ligamentous strand, while in the mammal it will functions as the urinary bladder.

Vascular system

The entire vascular system of the embryonic chick may be divided into an *intraembrayonic* and an *extraembryonic* system, of which the latter may again be classified into the *vitelline* and the *allantoic* circulation. However, such distinctions are arbitrary and conventional, because these subdivisions are merely integrated parts of one great system. We shall consider the intraembryonic circulation first, but in doing so we shall have occasion now and then to enter the domain of the vitelline as well as the allantoic circulation.

Heart

The development of the heart has been followed as far as the 48-hour chick, and through it has increased in size and also changed in form in the 72-hour embryo, its fundamental plan and structure have been very little modified. The most obvious external transformations of the heart, viewed from its posterior and its progressive changes from its simple, curved tubular form in the 33-hour embryo to the four-day chick can be followed there.

In the four-day embryo the sinus venosus anteroventrally into the atrium, which is separated from it by a faint constriction. Posteriorly the sinus venosus leads into the ductus venosus, which has been formed by the union of the bases of the two omphalomesenteric veins. The atrium has a slight central, longitudinal depression, indicating its future division into a smaller right and a larger left auricle. The atrium leads into the muscular ventricle through the *atrioventricular* aperture, and the ventricle projects forward and upward, tapering off into the *bulbus* and *truncus arteriosus*.

The valves of the heart are still absent in these early embryos. The blood is therefore still propelled by peristaltic waves which prevent the blood from regurgitation.

Aortic arches

In younger embryos, as for example in those of thirty to thirty-seven hours of incubation, it is possible to identify two ventral aortae, or aortic roots, beneath the pharynx which are continued dorsally as the paired dorsal aortae or dorsal aortic roots. Even in the 48-hour embryo it is not difficult to identify two paired ventral vessels leading away from the truncus arteriosus. In the 60- and 72-hour chicks these two branches have been reduced to such minima that it is difficult to identify them as separate units. It appears that the truncus arteriosus splits up immediately into the paired aortic arches.

To the first and second pair of aortic arches which were seen to be present in the 48-hour chick embryo, the 60-hour chick has added the third, and the 72-hour embryo the fourth pair. Indeed, the first aortic arches are in the process of atrophy by the time the fourth pair has been completely formed; and while the fifth and sixth pair are added on the fourth day of incubation, the second pair also degenerates. At no time during the developed of the early are there ever more than three pairs of functional aortic arches present.

In the chick embryo the ultimate fate of the aortic arches differs slightly from that of those in the frog larva. In both animals the most

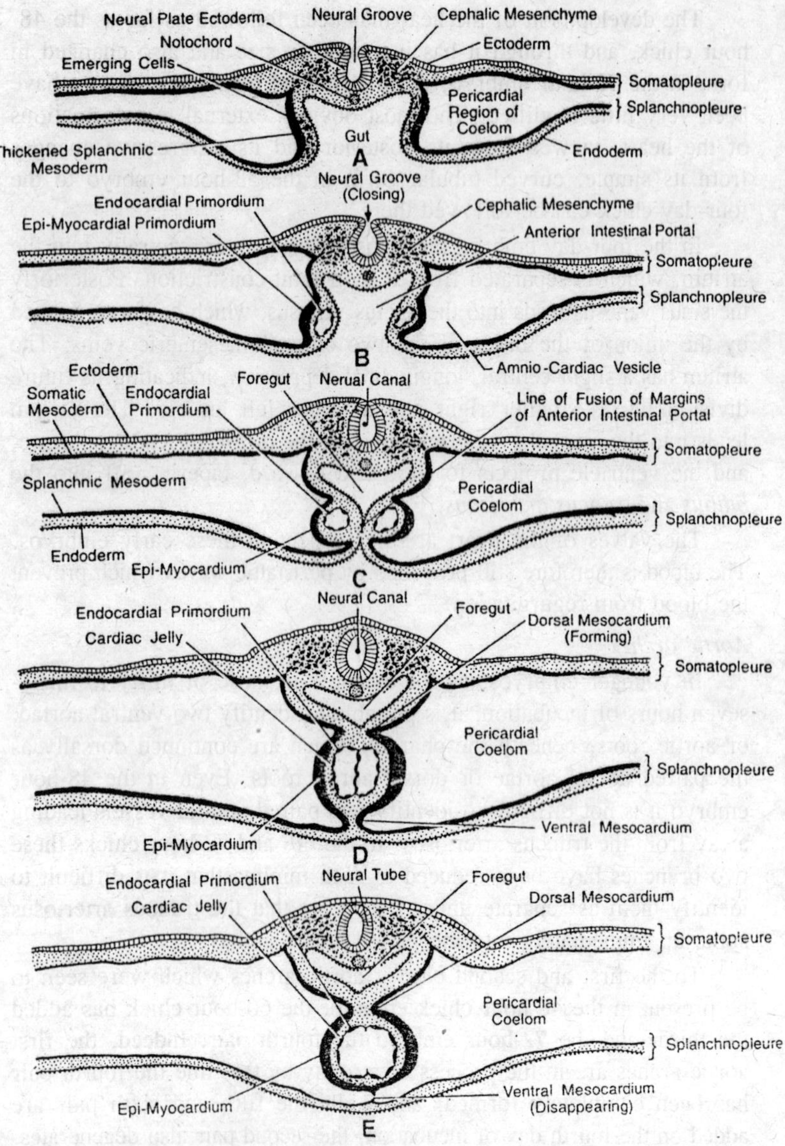

Fig. 11.21. Development of heart. T.S. through the pericardial regions of embryos at various stages. A—25 hour embryo, B—26 hour embryo, C—27 hour embryo, D—28 hour embryo, E—29 hour embryo.

anterior two pairs are eliminated and the dorsal connections between the third and fourth arches disappear also, leaving the two ventral aortae as the external, and the third arches plus the anterior portions of the two dorsal aortae as the internal, carotid arteries. The fourth pair is represented by its right member in the formation of the arch of the systemic aorta (*dorsal* or *abdominal aorta*), while its left counterpart persists in this proximal portion as the *Left subclavian artery*. The left subclavian artery in the birds has a second root from the carotid atery, and the original root of the fourth arch is eventually lost; it is therefore absent in the adult. The fifth and sixth are so closely united that the fifth seems to be a mere loop on the sixth.

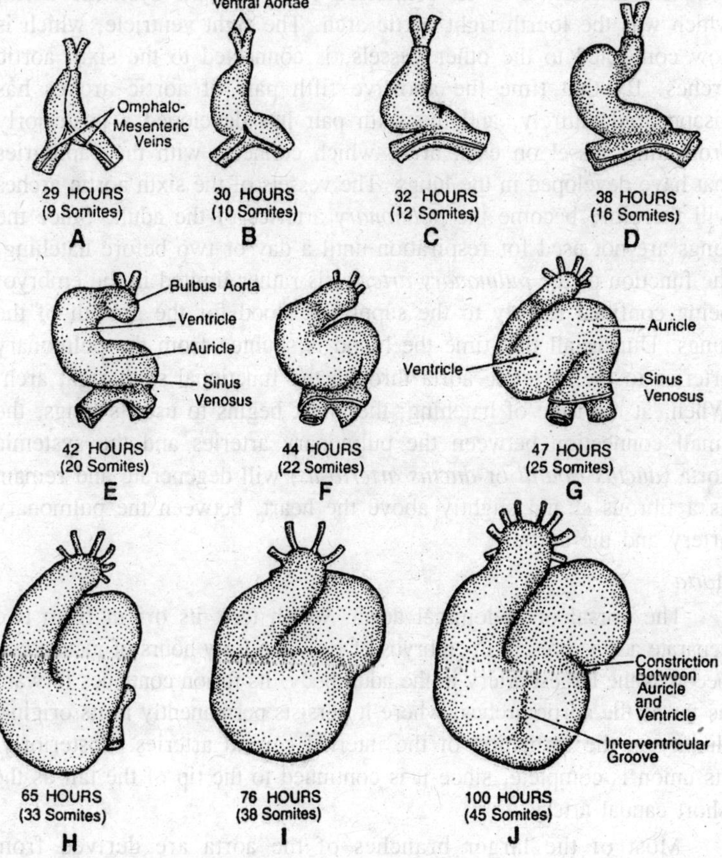

Fig. 11.22. Development of heart. Ventral views of the heart at various stages to show its change of shape and regional differentiation.

They have common origins ventrauy and enter the dorsal aortic roots also as untied vessels. The connection of the united fifth and sixth arches into the posteriorly directed left root of the aorta is also obliterated. However, the root of the combined fifth and sixth arches remains and will be changed in function, as explained in the next paragraph.

Toward the end of the first week of incubation, a septum appears in the truncus arteriosus which is continued into the bulbus and finally into the ventricle, thus dividing the latter into a right and a left ventricle, and the bulbus and truncus into two vessels, one leading away from the right and the other from the left ventricle. The left ventricle is from then on connected only with the systemic aorta, which was the fourth right aortic arch. The right ventricle, which is now connected to the other vessels, is connected to the sixth aortic arches. By that time the abortive fifth pair of aortic arches has disappeared entirely, and the sixth pair has developed a posteriorly protruding vessel on each arch, which connects with the capillaries that have developed in the lungs. The vessels of the sixth aortic arches will therefore become the *pulmonary* arteries of the adult. Since the lungs are not used for respiration until a day or two before hatching, the function of the *pulmonary arteries* is rather limited in the embryo, being confined merely to the supply of blood for the growth of the lungs. During all that time the blood is shunted from the pulmonary arteries to the systemic aorta through the functional sixth right arch. When, at the time of hatching, the chick begins to use its lungs, the small connection between the pulmonary arteries and the systemic aorta (*ductus Botalli* or *ductus arteriosus*) will degenerate and remain as a fibrous strand slightly above the heart, between the pulmonary artery and the aorta.

Aorta

The dorsal or abdominal aorta, which took its origin from two separate aortae present in embryos of less than forty hours of incubation, becomes the largest artery in the adult body. Its fusion continues forward as far as the aortic arches, where it persists permanently in its original duality in the formation of the internal carotid arteries. Posteriorly, its union is complete, since it is continued to the tip of the tail as the short caudal artery.

Most of the larger branches of the aorta are derived from intersomitic segmented vessels, which are still present in the adult in the form of paired intercostals arteries. In this manner the *subclavian*, *renal*, *spermatic*, *ovarian*, *posterior mesenteric*, and *sciatic arteries* are formed, of which the last gives rise to the allantoic arteries. Even the two large omphalomesenteric arteries are said to be of similar origin.

Cardinal veins

The cardinal veins are as prominent in the venous circulation of the chick embryo as the aorta is in the arterial circulation. They are paired vessels consisting of two anterior and two posterior veins which enter the sinus venosus through the ducts of Cuvier. These ducts are situated and held in place in the anterior region of the *lateral mesocardium*, which was formed by the fusion of the two omphalomesenteric veins and the somatic mesoderm. It may be of interest here to digress for a moment and point out that the lateral mescardium, in conjunction with the dorsal mesocardium and the ventral mesentery, constitutes the septum transversum. The latter is located immediately behind the heart and gives rise to the muscular *diaphragm* in the mammals, which divides the general body cavity into the thoracic and the abdominal cavity.

The anterior cardinal veins, or internal jugular veins, empty through the ducts of Cuvier into the sinus venosus. When the atrium becomes divided into a smaller left and a larger right auricle, that part of the sinus venosus which is connected with the two ductus Cuvieri becomes incorporated into the right auricle. Thus it happens that the two jugular veins flow into this heart chamber. Later on the two ducts of Cuvier become the anterior (superior) vena cava. The posterior cardinal veins require out special attention with regard to their modification, though these changes do not occur in early embryos of the ages that are usually studied in the college laboratory. However, they are of great interest to the comparative embryologist and anatomist, because they are instrumental in the formation of the posterior (inferior) vena cava, which is the largest vein in the adult body of birds as well as of mammals.

Just prior to the third day of incubation the posterior cardinal veins are paralleled by the subcardinals, which develop on either side of the embryo beneath the larger posterior cardinal veins, and slightly to one side of the mesonephroi. The subcardinals are really the anterior paired continuations of the single caudal vein, which bifurcates and passes along the kidneys to enter the posterior cardinals just prior to their entry into the ducts of Curvier. At the time of their appearance the posterior cardinal veins develop a profuse vascular network, growing into the tissue of the mesonephroi, while the subeardinals send out fine branches to make connections with this capillary system. In this manner a renalportal system is formed by means of which the blood drained from the body by the posterior cardinal veins is filtered through the kidneys and is received by the subcardinals, which send it forward into the anterior end of the posterior cardinal veins, whence it reaches the heart.

It is well to remember here that the posterior cardinal veins lay the foundation of the venous system of the adult by sending into the body wall their segmented intersomitic branches, similar to those of the aorta. The large veins that parallel the arteries of the adult are merely modified metameric vessels of the original posterior cardinal venous system.

Posterior vena cava

Toward the fourth day of incubation a short vessel is organized from small blood cavities (*sinusoids*) in the dorsal part of the right lobe of the liver. To this is added another short piece derived from small cavities that developed in the thickened dorsal mesentery near the anterior portion of the liver. These two elements form the anterior part of the posterior vena cava, which connects with the ductus venosus located within the liver.

In later development the vena cava grows from the right side of the liver backward toward the right mesonephros, where it connects with the anterior portion of the right subeardinal vein. After approximately one week of incubation the anterior portions of the posterior cardinal veins degenerate, so that their blood enters the ductus Cuvieri directly through the subeardinal veins. This venous modification persists during the existence of the mesonephros, but when the latter atrophies and the metanephroi, or permanent kidneys, make their appearance, the posterior remnants of the cardinal veins unite and fuse with the subcardinals on both sides. The posterior vena cava is finally made up from its anterior portion in the liver and ductus venosus, the right subeardinal vein, some renal veins which connected the posterior cardinals and subeardinals, the posterior united cardinals, and the caudal veins.

Vitelline circulation

Allusions to the fate of the vitelline circulation and also in the discussion of the alimentary canal in the present chapter. This vitelline venous circulation becomes confluent in the ductus venosus, which enters and is continuous with the sinus venosus. The ductus venosus represents the united omphalomesenteric veins. They drain the blood from the right and left sides of the area vasculosa through lateral vitelline veins which connect with the sinus terminlis. After the third day of incubation a posterior and an anterior vitelline vein are added to the left omphalomesenteric vein, so that this vessel carrics more blood than its mate on the right side. The anterior vitelline vein is organized from two anterior vitelline vessels which are still separated from each other in the 48-hour chick. They have become partly fused in the 60-hour embryo and continue to do so throughout their entire length, except near the body of the embryo where the right anterior vitellien vein remains as a small spur.

The two omphalomesenteric veins undergo radical changes by partial fusion, by transverse connections dorsal and ventral to the fore-gut, and by elimination of short parts, thus utilizing in restricted regions only sections of one or the other of the two veins. In this manner those two veins become united into one as far as the yolk stalk. At the same time the single vein becomes twisted around the fore-gut. The omphalomesenteric vein is later incorporated into the hepatic-portal vein, which is formed independently in the dorsal mesentery, becoming confluent with the omphalomesenteric vein near the pancreas. In the seven-day embryo the ductus venosus becomes obstructed by the in growth of liver tissue and ceases to be a direct passage for the blood from the omphalomesenteric vein to the sinus venosus. From then on the blood from the yolk sac enters the liver through the posterior remnant of the omphalomesenteric vein, which is now called the hepatic-portal vein. It ramifies through the liver, and leaves by two vessels referred to as the hepatic veins.

The two omphalomesenteric arteries do not change appreciably in later stages of development. Similar to the omphalomesenteric veins, they unit into one artery which leaves the dorsal aorta between the posterior limbs, near the twenty-third somite, and spreads out over the yolk mass. It is still present in the adult as the anterior mesenteric artery. The coeliac and the posterior mesenteric artery develop as independent outgrowths from the dorsal aorta, slightly more posteriorly.

Allantoic circulation

During the third day of incubation just prior to the appearance of the allantois itself, the lateral body walls of the embryo develop the umbilical or allantoic veins. When the allantois begins to differentiate from the cloacal region of the alimentary canal, it develops a protuse capillary system which becomes connected with the two umbilical arteries. The latter are branches of the iliac arteries which supply the developing posterior limb buds. The two allanotic veins extend forward and enter the ducts of Cuvier near the sinus venosus. During the fourth day of incubation the right umbilical vein begins to atrophy. The left one, which becomes correspondingly larger, develops at its distal end a branch which passes the blood through the liver directly into the ductus venosus, and from there into the heart. Its primary connection to the ductus Cuvieri is then entirely lost, so that from then on all the blood returning from the allantois to the heart has to pass through the liver. At the time of hatching, when the allantois is lost, the umbilical arteries become greatly reduced in size, supplying a small area near the cloacal region of the alimentary canâl from which the allantois extended into the seroamniotic cavity in the embryo. The umbilical vein also remains functional in the adult chick, where it assumes a minor function remaining as a small vessel leading from the body wall to the left hepatic vein.

Lymphatic system

The lymphatic system is another phase of the circulatory system which develops comparatively late in the chick embryo. It appears toward the end of the first week of incubation at two centers, one in the pelvic region and, slightly later, a much larger one in the anterior part of the body at the base of the neck. The two become connected by the organization of lymphatic spaces within the mesenchyme, and by their confluence form the lyrnph channels.

Lymph is a body fluid composed of plasma and white corpuscles, or lymphocytes. The entire system is rather loosely organized so that lymphocytes are able to pass through the walls of the lymph vessels and return in other places of the body. Likewise, the plasma may pass through the walls and be returned to the system again. The walls of the lymphatics are composed of a thin, mostly simple squamous endothelium, except in localized plexuals or lymph sacs and in the heavier contractile tubes called lymph hearts.

All the lymphatic vessels finally empty into the venous system through the *thoracic ducts* as the junction of the subclavian and jugular veins.

Excretory system

Three different types of kidneys are found in the vertebrates: namely, the pronephros, the mesonephros, and the metanephros. Of these the pronephros is present in adult cyclostomes, the mesonephros in adult fishes and amphibians, and the metanephros in adult reptiles, birds and mammals. It is highly probable that fishes have been derived from a type of primitive chordate of which the modern cyclostomes are an aberrant remnant, and that this ancestral stock was equipped with the pronephros. Again, reptiles have been derived from fishes through amphibian ancestry, and birds have been evolved from reptiles. It is therefore not at all surprising to see in the embryology of the reptiles and birds a complete "recapitulation" of the development of these three types of kidneys. In the chick the first kidney to appear is the pronephros, followed by the mesonephros, which in turn is replaced by the metanephros. These kidneys appear in all higher vertebrates in their orderly, phylogenetic succession.

Pronephros

In the following discussion the singular form is applied to the kidneys or to their ducts and tubules. This is done to avoid ambiguity and clumsiness of expression. It should always be borne in mind that the kidney system consists of paired organs.

The pronephros begins to appear in chick embryo of thirty-three to thirty-four hours of incubation. It develops from the intermediate mesoderm, which is really the kidney-building or nephrogenous tissue. It is therefore equivalent to the uppermost portion of the lateral mesoderm, described in the frog embryo. It will be recalled that in the amphibian embryo this part of the lateral mesoderm becomes isolated to form the pronephros.

In the chick the pronephros never develops hollow pronephric tubules. They appear as solid strands of cells in the intermediate mesoderm, one end of which remains attached to the lateral mesoderm, the other growing outward toward the superficial ectoderm. When they have reached a point halfway between the latter and their origin from the lateral mesoderm, they turn backward at an angle of ninety degrees, so that all of these strands become joined and confluent with each other from the fifth to the sixteenth somite. Beyond the latter the nephrotome forms a hollows duct (*pronephric duct* or *segmental duct*) which continues as far as the thirty-third somite, where it enters the alimentary canal.

It is obvious that in the chick embryo the pronephros cannot be functional, because its "tubules" are not hollow. Neither do they have nephrostomes, though attempts to form such openings are indicated by a notched appearance of the strands near their origin bordering the coelome. It appears, therefore, that the pronephros represents an earlier phylogenetic condition of the bird embryo. That the pronephric duct is hollow beyond the sixteenth somite is probably due to the fact that the succeeding kidney (mesonephros) has hollow tubules and uses this duct to transmit its excretory products, and instead of forming another duct, uses the pronephric duct for this purpose. It is for this reason that the pronephric duct becomes automatically the *mesonephric* or *Wolffian duct* with the arrival of the next kidney.

Mesonephros

The mesonephros develops before the pronephros has disappeared; in fact, it encroaches upon the latter by forming mesonephric tubules from the thirteenth to the thirtieth somite. The mesonephric tubules are much like those of the pronephric "tubules", except that they are actually hollow and that they connect with the mesonephric duct on one end and develop cuplike outgrowths called *Bowman's capsules*, or *renal capsules*, on the other. A small artery, branching off from the aorta, leads into each capsule and breaks up into a *glomerulus*. The renal capsule with the glomerulus is called a *renal corpuscle* or a *Malpighian corpuscle*.

Some of the more anteriorly located mesonephric tubules still have nephrostomes leading into the coelome, similar to the pronephric tubules described in the from embryo. However, the more posteriorly located ones lose the nephrostomes and rely exclusively on the glomeruli for removal of nitrogenous wastes and water. At its highest development the mesonephros is confined chiefly to the region limited by the twentieth and thirtieth somites. In this area the simple metameric organization of mesonephric tubules becomes obliterated by the formation of several more tubules in each segment, and these again bud off primary, secondary, and tertiary tubules, which evaginate into the Wolffian duct to act as *collecting tubules* for the urine. Thus the mesonephros, or *Wolffian body*, has increased considerably in size and bulk, and has assumed a definite, elongate shape. In a little over one week of development the mesonephros has been completed, and it remains functional almost to the end of incubation.

Nitrogenous wastes are removed from the blood by extracting them in the glomeruli. Apparently not all wastes are removed in this manner. After leaving the glomeruli, the blood is again broken up into capillaries surrounding the so-called *secretory portion* of the mesonephric tubule, where more waste and water are removed. From here the excretions are carried into the collecting tubules and sent into the Wolffian (mesonephric) duct. The blood is thus filtered through the kidney and enters the subcardial vein, whence it is transported to the heart.

The blood supply from the aorta to the glomeruli is gradually decreased with the development of the renal-portal system. In is later stages the blood to the mesonephros is chiefly supplied by the posteiror cardinal vein, filtering through the mesonephros and entering the subeardinal vein.

Metanephros

This kidney also develops while the mesonephros is still functional, but it is fully developed at the time of hatching, so that the young chick is equipped with the functional metanephros. This kidney develops from a very limited region, localized to the nephrotomes between the thirty-first and thirty-third somites. The tubules which constitute the metanephros are somewhat like those of the preceding kidney. The Wolffian duct is no longer utilized for the transportation of urine. Instead, a new tube, the ureter, grows out at the base of the Wolffian duct near the cloaca, and as it grows forward it sends out pocket like evaginations (*collecting tubules*) which unite with the *excretory tubules* formed by the nephrotomes. Other elements associated with the ureters in its forward growth form the renal corpuscles and secretory tubules. The ureters of both sides of the embryo lead independently into the cloaca. The mesonephric ducts, or Wolffian ducts, which are also separated from each other, lead into the cloaca slightly anterior to the ureters.

Reproductive system

In their earliest stages of development the gonads are paired organs in the chick embryo. This condition prevails throughout the life of the male. In the female, however, the right ovary degenerates completely, leaving only the left as the functional sex gland. As in the discussion of the excretory system, the singular form will be used in the description of the development of the gonads.

Genital ridge and germ cells

The first indication of the presence of sexual development can be observed in the late 4-day chick. There is a slight swelling of the peritoneal epithelium, located between the mesonephros and the dorsal mesentery, for about seven somites immediately behind the omphalomesenteric arteries. This swelling, known as the *genital ridge*, is covered by epithelial cells (*germinal epithelium*), and contains mesenchyme cells, and the primordial germ cells which are conspicuous by their larger size. The latter are found in the germ wall of the blastodisc at the late primitive streak stage. They remain there until the blood circulation has been established, which they enter the blood stream to be transported all over the body of the embryo. Many of them are lost, but there are some that will finally arrive near the dorsal mesentery where they have the blood stream by amoeboid movement to take their place in the genital ridge.

Testis

With the growth and protrusion of the mesonephros into the coelome, the genital ridge becomes covered by peritoneal epithelium and located on that side of the mesonephros which faces the mesentery. In fact the genital ridge becomes now incorporated into the mesonephric protrusion and the two are jointly referred to as the *urinogenital* ridge. This intimate union with the kidney is further increased by proliferation of the epithelial cells closest to the mesonephros. In this region the primitive testis forms strands (*rete cords*) which grow toward the capsules of the renal corpuscles and eventually connect with the mesonephric tubules.

At the same time the mesenchyme cells have differentiated into connective tissue (stroma) which permeates the developing testis. The stroma becomes invaded by another growth of cellular strands (*sexual cords*) which grow inward from the periphery of the young testis and are composed of germinal epithelium containing numerous germ cells. In later development the sexual cords differentiate into the *semiferous tubules* and establish connection with the rete cords, which will also become tubular and form the *rete testis*. Eventually the mesonephros will also its excretory function in the region of the gonad and degenerate except in its mesonephric tubules, which have made connection with the rete cord. These tubules retain their connection with the testis and are known as the *vasaa efferentia*. Together with the mesonephric duct (Wolffian duct) in this region, which will be converted into the *vasa deferens*, they constitute the *epididymis*. Some mesonephric tubules remain without connection and do not act as vasa efferentia. These constitute the *paradidymis*.

In its final transformation to the compact glandular testis, the genital ridge shortens and pushes away from the mesonephros and the dorsal wall of the coelome. In this manner the testis becomes suspended by the *mesorchium*, which is a mesentery formed by the splanchnic mesoderm. Within this mesodermal sheet the entire gonad becomes surrounded by a layer of compact connective tissue cells forming the *tunica albuginea*.

Ovary

The ovary develops in the same manner as the testis in its earlier stages, except that the one on the left side becomes increasingly larger and the right one eventually degenerates entirely, thus leaving only the left one as the functional ovary in the adult. The developing ovary also forms rete cords and sexual cords containing germ cells. They even establish connection with each other, but they disappear almost completely shortly after they have been formed. Moreover, these cellular strands are so rudimentary that there is no connection with the mesonephros. The mature ovary has therefore no ducts or tubules that lead away from it.

After one week or a few days more, the young ovary enters a second period of cellular proliferation in its peripheral region, producing again strandlike projections of germinal epithelium and germ cells into the stroma. Since these strands begin in the cortical layer they are called *cortical cords*. Small nests of cells separate from these cords to form the ovarian follicles, each containing one oocyte with an enveloping follicular layer of smaller cells.

The oviduct, or Mullerian duct, appears as a band of cells on the outer side of the Wolffian duct. It remains open at its anterior end (*ostium tubae* or *infundibulum*) and is connected with the cloaca at its posterior termination. The ostium tubae represents probably the nephrostome of a mesomephric tubule. The Mullerian duct appears in both sexes. In the males it disappears shortly after its formation. Furthermore, the right Mullerian duct disappears also, probably the right ovary atrophies.

The ovary is suspended by the mesovarium, a mesentery which is homologous to the mesorchium in the male. The degenerating mesonephros leaves two remnants to its organization near the ovarian region: namely, the *epoopheron*, homologous to the epididymis, and the *paroopheron*, which is homologous to the paradidymis in the male.

12

Migration in Birds

Any movement between two areas is called *migration*. As a rule, it is a response of an animal population to changes in environmental conditions. Birds are more uniformly migratory than any other group of animals. Nearly all orders of birds include species which perform migrations; in other vertebrates and in the lower groups of animals the migratory habit occurs in species scattered through a smaller proportion of orders. Among birds there are two common kinds of migration, *daily* and *seasonal*. A daily migration is a movement to and from a familiar place such as a roosting area. A seasonal migration, on the other hand, involves a passage at one season from a place of hatching and a return at another season to the same general area. This section of the book is concerned entirely with seasonal migration.

For centuries the phenomenon of migration has been primarily associated with birds; indeed, judging by the references to the subject in the earliest literature, migration was first observed in birds. Since civilization developed in a temperate region of the world where migratory movements are especially pronounced, it is hardly surprising that bird migration has long received attention. Man could not help noticing the flocks of birds in the spring and fall, the seasonal disappearance of some species and reappearance of others; nor could he help being interested in what he saw and eager to investigate what he could not understand.

Today there is an enormous literature on bird migration, based on extensive studies in Europe and North America. And yet the causes and processes of migration are ñot fully known. The rood of the problem is that bird migration, whether it occurs by day or night, is "an unseen movement". One must investigate its mechanisms indirectly through laboratory research on physiological and environmental influences; the analysis of migrant birds mist-netted or otherwise captured, of birds killed during migration by television towers and other man-made hazards, and of returns from banded birds; mathematical calculations based on kinds and numbers of birds observed through a telescope as they fly across the face of the moon; correlation of meteorological data with known migratory activity; deductions derived from direct field observations, radar surveillance, and tracking by radiotelemetry; and experiments on homing and direction-finding. The following pages present briefly some of the important facts and concepts of migration and suggest a few studies that students may undertake in conjunction with class work.

Causes of Migration

All modern birds-even those incapable of flight are descended from volant stock. Early in their history birds had the power of flight and presumably could migrate with facility. Today many species in the temperate regions of the world are strongly migratory, exhibiting mass movements away from both poles as day-length, temperature, and food supply diminish, then reversing the movements at the season when there is a general augmentation of these environmental factors. Such migrations are more evident in the temperate region of the Northern, or Continental, Hemisphere since more species are involved.

Because the north-south migrations of the Northern Hemisphere include many well known and conspicuous birds which seem to move in the same general way, there has been a tendency to conclude that migration, like bird flight, has developed along the same line in all species, with deviations for adaptive purposes. A study of the migration phenomenon in all groups of birds soon shows the fallacy of this reasoning. One finds that:

1. Some species migrate as a result of seasonal alteration in rainfall and drought.
2. Some species migrate in directions other than north-south.
3. In certain species, some populations migrate while others do not.
4. In some population, some individuals migrate while others do not.
5. Some individuals migrate in some years but not in others.
6. Some species migrate irrespective of day-length, as in tropical lands.
7. Some species migrate when the temperature is mild and the food supply ample, and others when the opposite conditions are true.

The only conclusion one can safely reach after considering the above peculiarities is that there is no one line along which migration in all birds developed and that there must be different causes of migration in different groups of birds.

A number of authorities have sought cause of migration in historical factors. Three of the several causes suggested bear mention. (1) Bird migration, at least in the Northern Hemisphere, was initiated by the effects of the ice Age (Pleistocene). Prior to the coming of the great glaciers to the polar regions, birds lived the year round in the northern Hemisphere where they originated. Though forced to retreat with the advance of the glaciers, they nevertheless continued to return to nest in the summer because of an innate attachment to their homeland. Objections to this suggestion are several. Many of the birds which are today typical migrants were in existence before the Pleistocene and there is no reason to suppose that they were not already migrating before the glaciers advanced. The retreat from the glaciers does not account for migrations in directions other than north-south, nor does it account for migrations of birds in tropical regions that were never glaciated. (2) Birds migrate in the fall because of the oncoming shortage of food during the winter in their breeding areas. Not that they "know' of the impending lack of food; it is the fact of the food shortage that has caused fall migration to evolve among species which, owing to the shortage, would fail to survive if hey stayed for the winter. Birds return in the spring because the northern areas provide more favorable and less crowded conditions for nesting and rearing families. (3) Intraspecific and interspecific competition for food, territory, nest sites, and so on may have been important factors initiating migration. When, as suggested by *Cox*, individuals among normally sedentary species could benefit by moving into adjacent areas where the season was favorable and competition reduced, they did so if the hazards of moving did not exceed the gains in their survival and reproduction.

Unquestionably, certain historical factors and various factors prevailing today such as day-length, air temperature, and food supply have influenced migration indirectly by affecting the environment, but no one factor can account for migration or has played the principal role in establishing migration. In view of the current diversity of migratory movements, it is evident that migration has evolved independently in different bird populations through selective pressure. When any resident population experienced and unfavorable situation during a seasonal period in the area it occupied and could gain an advantage by shifting to another area for that period, it gradually developed a migratory pattern, probably with a genetic basis.

Preparation and Stimulus for Migration

Migration is synchronized with the annual seasonal changes, but it will not take place until the bird is internally prepared and outwardly responsive to a stimulus. Before migrating, a bird must be ready to meet the energy requirements for prolonged flight. It accomplishes this by eating amounts of food in excess of its daily needs and thereby storing energy in the form of subcutaneous fat. At the same time, the bird must become predisposed to migrate by developing a condition commonly called *migratory restlessness*.

In the spring, the physiological process leading toward this state is influenced by the pituitary gland whose activity at this time is stimulated by the total effects of day-length; in the fall, the bird reaches a similar metabolic state during a period when the pituitary is "refractory". When the bird has attained the necessary physiological and behavioral conditions, an outside stimulus is required to trigger migratory behavior. The stimulus is probably some meteorological factor, or combination of factors, such as a change in the temperature of the air, the direction and velocity of the wind, or the onset or passage of a cold front. Normally an adult migratory bird goes through the special metabolic cycle twice a year, once before the journey to the nesting area and once before the journey away from it. If the bird does not reach the necessary physiological and behavioral condition, it cannot migrate. Furthermore, if the external stimulus for migration is absent, the bird will tend not to migrate even though physiologically and behaviorally capable. For a summary of knowledge concerning the nature and mechanisms of periodic preparation and stimulus for migration.

Diurnal and Nocturnal Migrations

Migrations proceed by day or night. Many birds-e.g., loons, geese, ducks, gulls, terns, and shore birds-travel by day or night, apparently indifferent to daylight or darkness. But this is not the case with many other birds. Herons, hawks, eagles, falcons, crows, hummingbirds, swifts, and swallows migrate only during the day, while nearly all passerine birds (excepting crows, swallows, and a few others) migrate primarily during the night from after sunset until dawn. At least two explanations have been advanced for the development of nocturnal migration. (1) movement by night affords birds, which normally live in thick vegetational cover and rarely take long flights away from it, the protection of darkness against their diurnal predators. (2) Movement by night affords birds the opportunity of using all the daylight hours for feeding, thereby enabling them to build up sufficient energy resources for sustained long-distance flights.

Effects of Weather on Migration

Normal weather alternates between fair and inclement conditions. The movements of the vast majority of migrants show a close correlation with these conditions which are largely governed by barometric pressure patterns, temperature, and wind directions. To understand how migration takes place with relation to whether, the student must first be acquainted with a few basic facts about weather elements and their sequence over a ground area.

Perpetually sweeping across the continent in an average easterly direction are air masses that vary in velocity, depending on the season and numerous other factors, from 500 to 700 miles a day. In these masses, which may be visualized as roughly circular, are centers of low barometric pressure ("lows"), with generally warmer, more moist air, and centers of high pressure ("highs") with cooler, drier air, within the lows the air circulates counterclockwise; within the highs, air circulates clockwise. Where the lows and highs adjoin there are boundaries called "front". The front of an oncoming high is the cold front; of an oncoming low, the warm front. The area of generally low pressure between the cold and warm fronts is called the warm sector. Any weather map appearing in daily newspapers will show the lines of equal barometric pressure (isobars) as roughly concentric circles around lows and highs, and cold and warm fronts as heavy lines with marks indicating the direction they face. Areas where there has been precipitation are shaded.

Migration in the spring usually takes place with warm weather. Studies of spring migratory movements in eastern United States and Canada show that movements begin at the onset of warm fronts, when barometric pressure is dropping and warm moist air from the Gulf of Mexico and Caribbean Sea is flowing in from a southerly direction. As each low (with mild temperature and southerly winds) passes, movements proceed in full force. On the approach of cold frints, the movements usually slow down-though they may occasionally be heavy, as when a cold front advances against a western flank of warm air. When cold fronts arrive, movements stop. Not until the highs have passed will movements begin again.

Migration in the fall usually takes place with cold weather. In the Chicago area, migratory movements in September and October start immediately after the passage of cold fronts when there is a flow of continental polar air from a northerly direction. Movements then proceed in full force until the first part of each low passes; thereafter the movements decrease somewhat in intensity and may even cases altogether as the next cold fronts approach.

Many species are reluctant to initiate migration under an overcast. Air temperature is probably the principal factor is starting migration; wind direction or air flow is a decidedly critical factor in regulating migratory movement. Most movements take place when the wind is favorable – i.e., blowing in the direction of flight – and after migrants have been held back for long intervals by such weather conditions as fog, rain, and headwinds. In the spring the weather that ordinarily accompanies cold fronts is especially obstructive to movements, forcing migrants to take to the ground without delay.

The arrival of any migration movement in an area is more often controlled by the weather at the point of departure than during its course. Thus at the height of the migration season, when the weather appears suitable in his area, the student will not always observe migration movement because inclement weather at the point of departure or some intervening point has arrested the flight.

The study of weather maps in conjunction with observations on movements is very useful. By means of weather maps one can frequently anticipate a migration movement in a given area. For instance, if during the height of spring migration the map indicates a cold front moving in from the northwest, one may expect its arrival to stop and hold numerous transients in the area. Weather maps also assist in explaining the failure of a migration movement to appear. If there is no pronounced migration movement in an area for a long period, even though the season and weather are favorable, maps may reveal that a pressure area along the migration route has become quasistationary, either "damming up" migrants (in case the pressure area is unfavorable to movement), or (in case it is favorable) allowing migrants to move along from day to day without massing in conspicuous waves.

Exceptional weather conditions with unusually high winds often deflect migrants from their usual routes and at he same time carry many non-migrating birds from their regular ranges. The hurricanes or heavy northeast storms that occasionally move north along the eastern Atlantic seaboard, by the counterclockwise direction of their winds, force many south-bound migrants and sea birds far inland. As a result, ducks, geese, and gulls are reported in great abundance in places where they do not ordinarily occur, and such sea birds as petrels show up far inland. Two very severe northeast storms in December, 1927, and January, 1996, bore spectacular numbers of Eurasian Lapwings (*Vanellus vanellus*) over the North Atlantic from their migration route in western Europe to the vicinity of Newfoundland. The student will find instructive the paper by Bagg showing in detail, with a series of weather maps how the great storms brought the lapwings to North America.

Regularity of Migratory Travel

Despite the effects of weather on migration, migratory travel over a period of years is regular on the average. This is apparent to a student observing bird populations from year to year in any given area of North America north of Mexico.

If one keeps records for several years of the days when common summer-resident species first arrive in the spring, and computes average dates of arrival of each species, he can eventually predict within a few days when these species will appear. Similarly, by keeping records of departure of transient spring species – i.e., dates when species going through the area are last seen – he will know approximately when these species depart each year.

There is much less regularity in the arrival and departure of transient species in the fall, thus the securing of records is difficult. Fall migration is more prolonged. Slight variations in weather conditions have stronger effects. Cool late-summer weather, for instance, may induce species to arrive surprisingly early and warm weather may cause them to linger very long. Keeping track of early and late individuals is complicated by the fact that many species are customarily silent in the fall and have inconspicuous plumage. While it is possible to obtain average dates of arrival and departure, fall dates are apt to be much less useful and meaningful on account of the great discrepancy in annual dates and the problems of finding early and late individuals.

In conterminous United States, north of the southern tier of states and in Canada, there are two so-called *migration waves*. The first, in the early spring, is made up of "hardy" birds – many fringillids and a species or two from various other bird groups; in the second, a month later, there is a preponderance of insect – eating birds – various species of flycatchers, vireos, warbles, and other groups. The migratory movement has a wave effect in that the total population of birds rises and recedes. Thus soon after the first few individuals, called *stragglers*, make their appearance, the population steadily approaches maximum density, which may prevail for a day or more. There after the population dwindles until only those birds which stay for the summer are left. Migration waves also occur in the fall but the migration movements are more prolonged and the crests much less apparent.

In the spring, the migration population of any one species, provided it is large in the area studied, will show the wave effect. Almost invariably the species makes its initial appearance with a straggler or two. A few days to a week or more later the population begins to increase and later decreases in the manner described for groups of species. Such a population wave, as it moves northward in the spring, may be many miles in width. The author of this book took a trip southward from Minnesota through Iowa and Missouri in late March, before the Robins (*Turdus migratorius*) had appeared commonly in Minnesota. He recorded an occasional Robin in northern Iowa; great numbers through central and southern Iowa; and a steady decrease in numbers through northern Missouri until in central Missouri there were only scattered individuals, presumably the birds that were to become summer residents there. He estimated the width of the migration wave to be roughly 225 miles.

In making the first spring and fall studies of birds, the student should pay special at attention to the local movements of transient species. He should note the dates each species is seen, make counts or estimates of the number of individuals of each species observed on each date, and keep a record of weather conditions. This information will give him a proper conception of the length of time each species remains in the area, the way a species population rises and recedes giving the wave effect, and some of the relationships of weather conditions to population trends.

Irregular Migrations

The many cases of movements among bird populations, which either do not conform to the usual seasonal migration pattern or are not sufficiently well understood to seem a part of the pattern, are loosely classified as *irregular migrations*.

In certain permanent-resident species there may be mass movements of particular populations with some periodicity. The Blue Jay (*Cyonocitta cristata*), especially in the northern part of its range, shows some migratory movement. Each fall, small numbers usually move south past hawk Mountain in Pennsylvania; in 1939 there was an exceptionally heavy migration (over 7,000 individuals counted), which may have been due to a shortage of beechnuts and acorns in northern forests. In northwestern Oklahoma, the Bobwhite (*Colinus virginianus*) shows a distinct seasonal population shift by moving from summer habitats in the uplands to pass the winter in bottomlands and dunes where there is better cover. Their movements, involving distances up to 26 miles, are apparently heavier during severe winters.

Populations of species which are permanent residents may on occasion show a mass movement- *invasion* or *irruption* without periodicity. Now and then there is a winter when considerable numbers of Snowy Owls (*Nyctea scandiaca*) leave the Arctic and invade southern Canada and northern conterminous United States. The cause of this behavior is sometimes attributed to a sharp reduction in the lemming on which the Snowy Owl preys to a large extent. Crossbills (*Laxia* spp.) and Evening Grosbeaks (*Hesperiphona vesperttina*), normally residents of the Coniferous Forest Biotic Community, occasionally appear in flock as far south as Florida, presumably due to a failure of their food supply. Sometimes invasions involve mainly young birds. At Cedar Grove, Wisconsin, on the west shore of lake Michigan, *Mueller* and *Barger* reported a southern invasion of Goshawks (*Accipiter gentiles*) in the years 1961 through 1963. Most of the birds that they trapped and examined were apparently hatched in 1961 shortly after a decrease in snowshoe hares and grouse, their principal prey. *Mueller* and *Berger* hypothesized that these young birds had come south after being displaced by adults already well established in a range that could not support large wintering populations of the species.

Young of numerous species, after attaining full growth, often wander in the late summer and fall for great distances. The movement, called *juvenile wandering*, is explosive in that the birds move in all directions from the hatching area. Among the species particularly noted for this behavior are egrets, herons, and gulls. Some young egrets and herons actually travel several hundred miles north of their place of hatching in the south. At the conclusion of the breeding season in the big colony of Herring Gulls (*Larus argentatus*) at kent Island, New Brunswick, an impressive number of immature birds go northward along the coast, although the majority seem to take a southerly direction. Many first-year herring Gulls, reared in colonies on islands in the Great lakes, proceed in late December to the coast of Georgia, Florida, and the Gulf of Mexico, and quite a few reach the coast of Mexico; second-year and older herring Gulls tend to remain on the shores of the Great lakes within 300 miles of their colonies. Juvenil Sooty Terns (*Sterna fuscata*) from the large nesting colony on the Dry Tortugas, islands lying directly west of key West, Florida, move across the Atlantic to the Gulf of Guinea, West Africa, and do not straggle back to the western Atlantic until they approach breeding age; the adults, after nesting, tend to confine their dispersal to the Gulf of Mexico and the Caribbean. For the extensive wandering of young birds, the most plausible explanation is that they cannot compete sufficiently well with older birds for food and must therefore keep moving until they find an adequate supply for themselves.

Reverse Migration

Migratory movements may be reversed, proceeding in a direction opposite the one expected for the season. A good example of ***reverse migration*** occurs in the fall on Nantucket Island, Massachusetts, and Block Island, Rhode Island, where many nocturnal migrants (mostly passerines representing well over species) sometimes pass rapidly through during the daytime and leave in a north or northwestward direction for the mainland, into the wind. *Baird* and *Nisbet* interpret the movement to be the result of south-bound migrants, carried toward the Atlantic Coast by strong northwest winds, attempting to fly back and redetermine or regain their preferred lanes of passage overland.

Another example with a different interpretation comes in the spring from Point Pelee, a peninsula projecting nine miles southward into western lake Erie from Ontario, and from Pelee Island that lies about eight and one-half miles southwest of Point Pelee and nearer the Ohio mainland. Time and again many small land birds have been seen returning southward over lake Erie from the tip of Point Pelee. *Lewis* reported such a movement in mid-May at Pelee Island. Here for several hours he watched large number of birds representing 35 species (mostly passerine) streaming southward into a headwind. The movements are not based solely on visible evidence; they have actually been proven. Birds, banded at Point Pelee prior to starting south, were later recovered at Pelee Island and on the Ohio mainland. The participants in these reverse flights may be birds which, during the preceding night, overshot their destination or were swept past it in high winds and, consequently, are attempting to return to it.

Rate of Migratory Travel

Most passerine birds fly at ground-seeds averaging 18 to 25 miles per hour (mph). Stronger fliers such as ducks, hawks, falcons, shore birds, and swifts attain much greater speeds. Any bird can accelerate its speed in special circumstances as when frightened or diving earthward. In general, the normal, unhurried, cruising speed of a bird is much slower than suggested by published records, most of which, until recently, were estimated by observers in automobiles or airplanes moving parallel to the birds line of flight.

Schnell, using Doppler radar equipment similar to that operated by law enforcement agencies in determining speed of automobiles measured the ground flight-speeds of 17 species of birds in northern Michigan. He recorded on windless days two speeds of the Spotted Sandpiper (*Actitis macularia*) at 25 mph; four speeds of the Eastern Kingbird (*Tyrannus tyrannus*) at 21 mph and one at 13 mph; three speeds of the Cedar Waxwing (*Bombycilla cedrorum*) at 21,23 and 29 mph; three speeds of the Red-winged Blackbird (*Agelaius phoeniceus*) one at 17 mph and two at 23 mph. Had the wind been blowing, the speeds might well have been slower for birds flying into it and faster for birds flying with it. Strong winds can significantly affect flight-speed as Schnell proved with the 267 speeds of the Herring Gull (*Larus argentatus*) that he recorded in different wind velocities. Speeds, he found, averaged 25 mph in winds less than 6 mph, but averaged 18 mph (extremes 7 and 39 mph) into winds of 6 to 15 mph and 34 mph extremes of 21 and 49 mph) with the same winds.

During migration, according to radar surveillance by *Bellorse*, birds appear to reduce their flight-speed somewhat proportionately to the increase in favorable wind speed. Apparently they adjust their flight efforts in relation to the degree of wind assistance or resistance. Thus the ground-speeds of migrants tend to remain fairly constant despite variations in wind-speed whereas the ground-speeds of birds in the daily activity flights, as shown by Schnell, are definitely influenced by winds.

Many of the stronger flying birds show great ability for fast migratory travel. *McCabe*, in an airplane going at an air-speed of 90 miles per hour, was overtaken by two flocks of sandpipers flying at an estimated air-speed of 110 mph. *Spears* once estimated the average ground-speed of the Oldsquaw (*Clangula hyemalis*) at 61.5 mph and the air-speed at 50.5 mph.

Birds homing to their breeding sites, after displaced at great distances away, demonstrate impressive ability for sustained speed for many hours. A female Purple martin (*Progne subis*), taken from her colony at the University of Michigan Biological Station in northern

Lower Michigan and released in Ann Arbor, Michigan, 234 miles to the south, at 10:40 PM, was back feeding her young at 7:15 AM, having made the return flight in not more than 8.6 hours at an average speed of 27.2 miles per hour (Southern, 1959). A Manx Sheawater (*Puffinus puffinus*) removed from its nesting burrow on Skokholm off the west coast of Wales and released in Boston, Massachusetts, reached its burrow after at least 3,200 miles in 12 days and some 13 hours, or an average of 250 miles a day (Mazzeo, 1953). Another sea bird, a Leach's Petrel (*Oceanodroma leucorhoa*), averaged about 300 miles a day for nine days from its point of release at Prestwick, Scotland, back to its nesting burrow on New Brunswick's Kent Island in the Bay of Fundy. Of the 18 Laysan Albatrosses (*Diomedea immutabilis*), taken from their nests on Midway island - one of the Hawaiian Leewards in the north - central Pacific - and released at widely scattered points in the northern Pacific, 14 returned, one from the Philippines, a distance of 4,120 miles in approximately 32 days, and one from Whidby Island off the coast of Washington, a distance of 3,200 miles in 10.1 days at an average speed of 317 miles a day. Presumably, not one of these birds homing to its breeding site had the fat reserves for energy that migrants acquire prior to their long journeys.

There is much additional evidence, obtained by other means, of the bird's ability for sustained speed during long distances of migration. *Cochran*, *Montgomery*, and *Graber*, using radiotelemetry, tracked migrating *Hylocichla* thrushes nearly all night from Illinois northward into Michigan, Wisconsin, and Minnesota. Although they found considerable variation, most flights were at air-speeds - i.e., speeds with relation to the winds aloft - between 25 and 35 mph. These were usually less than ground-speeds - speeds with relation to the earth - and thus suggested that the birds were aided by favorable winds. One of the most remarkable records of a long, sustained flight is that of a banded Ruddy Turnstone (*Aremaria interpres*) released by Max C. Thompson at St. George Island, one of the Pribilofs in the Bering Sea, on August 27, 1965, and shot four days later, on August 31, at French Frigate Shoals in the Hawaiian Leeward Islands. Assuming that this individual covered 2,300 miles between St. George Island and French Frigate Shoals in a steady bee-line flight, its average speed was 575 miles a day.

Recently, radar studies have provided many reliable estimates of the rate at which migratory birds travel. *W.R.P. Bourne* assessed the air-speed of Lapwings (*Vanellus vanellus*) in their flights during June over the southern North Sea to England at 35 knots (40 mph). *Lee*, at the Isle of Lewis in the Hebrides, Scotland, showed that the air-speed of Wheatears (*Oenanthe oenanthe*) from Iceland approximated 20 knots (23 mph); Redwings (*Turdus iliacus*), from 30 to 35 knots (34.5 to 40 mph); and Grey lag Geese (*Anser anser*), from 53 to 55 knots (61 to 63 mph). *Bergman* and *Donner* demonstrated that the still-air-speed for the Oldsquaw (*Clangula hyemalis*) at low altitudes over the Gulf of Finland was 40 knots (46 mph) and for the Common Scoter (*Oidemia nigra*), 45 knots (52 mph). Once the birds reached a higher altitude inland, their speed increased by about 10 percent. After recording air-speeds of passerine birds off the coast of Norflok, England, for a whole year, *Tedd* and *Lack*, on analyzing the results, found evidence of a seasonal difference: in the spring, the speed averaged 27 knots (31 mph), 4 knots faster than in the fall. At Cape Cod, *Massachusetts*, *nisbet* and *Drury* found another seasonal difference in that the directions of migration in the spring were much less diverse than in the fall, thereby suggesting much less time lost in passage.

In the late fall, long-distance migrating ducks commonly pass from breeding area to winter quarter in a short series of mass movements, each of which carries them many hundreds of miles in one continuous flight. They start each flight immediately after the passage of a cold front when temperature has dropped and the sky is clear, but they may overtake bad weather as they proceed. Sometimes, owing to the triggering effect of extremely low temperatures resulting from a strong flow of polar air, the mass movements are spectacular both in numbers of birds involved and distances covered. *Bellrose* documented one such migration in 1955 that moved with unusual rapidity from the Great Plains of Canada to the marshes of southern Louisiana. The exodus began from Canada on October 31; early on November 1 the flight was in full force through the Dakotas; and on November 2 the vanguards had reached northern Tennessee and Arkansas shortly after sunrise and Louisiana later in the day. Many thousands of ducks made the flight from Canada to southern Louisiana, a distance of 1,200 to 2,000 miles, in two days, or roughly 35 to 50 hours, at an average speed of 40 miles, in two days, or roughly 35 to 50 hours, at an average speed of 40 miles per hour. No doubt some of he birds covered the distance without stopping, accomplishing their migration in one flight.

In undertaking long-distance migrations, many small land birds tend to begin with short flights and complete them with longer flights. Indirect evidence of this procedure was reported by *Caldwell*, *odum*, and *Marshall*, after comparing the fat reserves of six species of ropical-wintering North American passerines killed during fall migration by television towers, one near the Florida Gulf Coast and the other in central Michigan. All the birds killed by the Florida tower showed significantly greater amounts of fat, strongly suggesting that these migrants began with low to moderate fat reserves that allowed only short flights and then increased their reserves until they had acquired a maximum amount for the long, non-stop flights such as across the Gulf of Mexico. European birds migrating south across Africa building up fat reserves of 30 to 40 percent of their body weight by the time they set out across the Sahara.

By making longer flights as they near their destinations, birds gradually speed up their migrations. *Cooke* provided evidence for this acceleration when he analyzed migration dates of North American species, mostly passerines. Approaching their northern nesting areas. "Sixteen species," he wrote, "maintain a daily average of 40 miles from southern Minnesota to southern Manitoba, and from this point 12 species travel to from southern Minnesota to southern Manitoba, and from this point 12 species travel to Lake Athabasca at an average of 72 miles a day, 5 others to Great Slave lake at 116 miles a day, and more to Alaska at 150 miles a day".

From all these studies and reports, several generalizations on the rate of migratory travel emerge. Strong winds can affect ground-speed of birds in their daily activity flights but not in migration. Birds make long, sustained flights, usually at increasingly higher speeds at higher altitudes. Spring migration proceeds at a greater rate with less time loss than fall migration. Larger birds such as ducks accomplish their migrations in a short series of a few mass movements, occasionally in one non-stop mass movement. Small land birds, however, tend to begin their migrations in many short flights, gradually building fat reserves for long, non-stop flights, thereby accelerating their migrations.

Mortality in Migration

Migrating is dangerous for all birds. In their long flights over land or water they are likely to meet disaster through vagaries of the weather. When forced to land by cold fronts, frequently they must accept environments where, because of inadequate cover, they are easy victims of predators.

While migrations are adjusted to the normal alternation of fair and inclement weather during spring and fall, sudden and unseasonable changes in the weather occasionally have serious effects, once, during fall migration in the vicinity of Lake Huron, untold numbers of birds crossing this huge lake were forced into the water and drowned because of a very quick drop in temperature and exceptionally heavy snowfall. After the storm, one observe reported an estimated 5,000 dead birds washed up on a one-mile stretch of shore. In their flights north in the spring, birds are sometimes caught in severe storms and killed by becoming first exhausted and then being exposed to excessively low temperature coupled with heavy rain or wet snow. After a blinding march snowstorm in Minnesota as many as 75,000 Lapland Longspurs (*Calcorius lapponicus*) were found dead on the ice of two lakes, each of which covered only a square mile.

Man has created awesome hazards for migrating birds by erecting lighthouses with strong light beams and by illuminating various tall structures such as the Washington Monument in the District of Columbia and the Empire State Building in new York City. During nights in the spring and fall when migration is proceeding at a low elevation because of an un-surmountable cloud layer, passing birds are attracted by the brightness and, approaching it, soon become blinded and fly into its source, killing themselves. Under certain circumstances, even street lights can be a hazard. Vast numbers of parulid warblers, driven ashore on the Texas coast by a northeast storm while migrating northward across the Gulf of Mexico during a night in early May, met their death by flying into street lights. In a part on Padre Island, James counted more than 900 dead birds under just one light pole plus an estimated 100 on the adjacent pavement. There were nine other light poles in the vicinity with similar tolls.

Airport ceilometers indirectly cause mortality among small, nocturnal migrants. These instruments, which are used to determine the cloud ceiling, direct a narrow, extremely brilliant beam of light straight upward, at night when the clouds are low, they produce a bright spot on the cloud ceiling that can be seen for a considerable distance. On mornings following a heavy, nocturnal migration, numbers of birds varying from three to over a thousand have been found dead near spots where ceilometers are used. Three ornithologists, *Howell*, *Laskey*, and *Tanner*, who have investigated many of these accidents, explain these cause as follows: When there is a pronounced migration and a low ceiling, the beam attracts the migrants. After circling through the bright light, many circle back to fly in and about it. While in the beam their bodies reflect light attracting still other migrants. Blinded by the light, the birds die by collision, either with each other, with the ground, or (rarely) with building.

A direct cause of mortality among small, nocturnal migrants are television towers erected to heights 900 to 1,000 feet or more and, as is often the case, situated on hills of bluffs where they reach even greater heights above the local terrain. Each tower is supported by guy wires and has a system of steady, flashing red lights, mandatory on all tall structures that are potential hazards to airplanes.

When migrants are flying under a low ceiling, they are attracted to a television tower because of its lighted area and become reluctant to leave. Just as birds, released at night in a lighted room with doors and windows open, continue to fly about in the room rather than escape into the darkness, the migrants fly through the tower framework and circle out to the edge of the lighted area, then return toward the light. Mortality results when the birds strike the dark guy wires while circling. The above observation and explanations come from *Graber*. For examples of the extent of avian mortality around television towers, see the papers by *Tordoff* and *Mengel* and *Stoddard* and *Norris*.

Altitudes of Migratory Flight

The recent analysis of migratory flight by means of radar shows not only that birds move at altitudes averaging higher than formerly believed, but also that their altitude varies widely depending on the circumstances.

Nisbet, studying radar heights of nocturnal fall migrants above Cape Cod, Massachusetts, and the outlying ocean, found that the most frequent height was usually between 1,500 and 2,500 feet. About 90 percent of the birds, probably small passerines, were below 5,000 feet. On some nights they were lower than 2,500 feet, while on others they were up to 6,000 or even 8,000 feet.

The presence or absence of cloud cover may determine the altitude chosen by birds. *Bellrose* and *Graber* discovered, during their radar studies of nocturnal migrants in central Illinois, that birds are prone to migrate at higher altitudes when the skies are overcast than when they are clear. If the clouds are not too high, the birds apparently attempt to surmount them; but if the clouds are too high, they usually continue to fly, sometimes in the clouds, although usually immediately under them. When the birds are flying under an overcast, and consequently, at much lower altitude, they can usually be heard from the ground.

Birds fly higher by night than by day. *Lack* first noted this tendency, by radar, among migrants crossing the southern north Sea between England and the Continent. Later, *Eastwood* and *Rider* at the Bushy

Hill station in England proved that the tendency is significant. From their considerable data they were able to show that 80 percent of the birds fly below 5,000 feet at night and 80 percent below 3,500 during the day. They further demonstrated that migrating birds, in a 24 hour day, have a tendency to fly at the lowest altitudes in the afternoon and the highest just before midnight. From radar studies and tape recordings off call notes in Illinois, *Graber* has concluded that migrants reduce their altitude after midnight to 1,500 feet or less, although they continue their flight until daylight. After their descent to lower altitude, they increase their calling. This helps to explain why nocturnal migrants can be heard more frequently as dawn approaches than earlier in the night.

There are seasonal variations in altitudes. *Bellrose* and *Garber* found that migrating birds in Illinois fly higher during the fall than during the spring, possibly because the winds during the fall are more favorable for southward migration at higher altitudes. *Eastwood* and *Rider*, on the other hand, found the reverse to be the case in England. They suggest as one reason for this seasonal difference that flocks of fall migrants include many young birds whose flight capabilities are inferior to those of adults and which are, consequently, unable to achieve the higher altitudes of the more mature spring migrants.

Birds migrate higher over land than sea. Common Scoters (*Oidemia nigra*) and Oldsquaws (*Clangula hyemalis*), in their spring passage over southern Finland and the Gulf of Finland, were noted by *Bergman* and *Donner* to fly at altitudes that averaged 3,400 feet over land and ranged from 300 to 1,000 feet above water. Passerine migrants, in passing from sea to land in England, wee shown by *Eastwood* and *Rider* to make a similarly significant though not as great change in altitude, climbing from a median height of 1,700 feet to a median height of 2,200 feet.

Birds have long been known to reach very high altitudes during flight. Direct observation from aircraft proved that large birds can fly over the highest mountain ranges – for example, the Himalayas between central Russia and India. The yellow-billed Chough (*Pyrrhocorax graculus*) was actually found on Mt. Everest at an elevation of 27,000 feet. The use of radar in determining heights of migration shows that while most birds rarely exceed 8,000 to 10,000 feet, a small proportion of migrants, particularly the stronger fliers, nonetheless attain great heights, in some cases astonishing. In his radar studies of migrants at Cape Cod, Massachusetts, *Nisbet* recorded a number of birds on several dates in September and October, usually before midnight, or before and after sunrise, at altitudes between 8,000 and 15,000 feet and a few birds as high as 20,000 feet. These may have been sandpipers and plovers, flying over the ocean, toward the Lesser Antilles and eastern South America. Using an especially powerful and accurate height-finder at Norflok in southeast England, *Lack* observed at sunrise on 16 dates in September a thin scattering of birds extending fairly uniformly up to least 15,000 feet. On seven of these mornings he noted that the greatest height was 19,000 feet and on two mornings it was 21,000 feet. Probably the highest migrants were small shore birds such as the Dunlin (*Erolia alpina*) which had left Scandinavia the night before.

Bearing in mind that the oxygen content of the air at 18,000 feet is 50 percent less than the air at sea level, one wonders whether high-flying birds suffer "altitude sickness." When a man sets out to climb a lofty mountain he acclimates himself gradually over a period of days, but birds take off and reach a comparable elevation in a matter of a few hours. Do birds have special adaptations that enable them to avoid altitude sickness? The answer may come someday from experimental studies of bird flight in pressure chambers.

Course of Migration and Migration Routes

Many species breeding in North America north of Mexico have their winter ranges far south and southeast; in southern Mexico, Central America, and South America. To reach their winter ranges, most of these species proceed at night from their breeding ranges to southern United States in broad fronts without notable regard to topographical features. Radar and other observations confirm that their movements trend southeast- towards their winter ranges. This direction, coming as it does it in the wake of a cold front, is with the wind and, therefore, beneficial to the migrants. In the spring, the direction trends northwest, in reverse, and again with the wind since the movements take place with the onset of a warm front. Many species, however, do not exactly retrace their course in the spring, but fly instead somewhat to the west of their fall passage. Evidence of this elliptical course-going to southern United States one way and coming back another- is borne out by kills at television towers. Certain species are well represented in the spring migration but seldom or not at all in the fall, and vice versa.

Owing to the narrowing of the North American continent southward and the intervention of the Gulf of Mexico and Caribbean Sea, all species moving southeastward through the United States toward their wintering ranges in southern Mexico, Central America, and South America converge on special routes. There are five altogether. Certain species use mainly one route, others two or three; no species is known to use more than three. The routes are as follows:

Route 1 : From the coasts of Newfoundland, Nova Scotia, New England, and New Jersey southward over the Atlantic Ocean to the Lesser Antilles and the northeastern coast of South America. A few shore birds use this route.

Route 2 : From Florida southward over the Bahamas, Hispaniola, Puerto Rico, and the Lesser Antilles to South America. The few birds which frequent this route are seldom far from land as there are many small islands along the way.

Route 3 : From Florida southward over Cuba and Jamaica across 400 miles of the Caribbean Sea to South America.

Route 4 : From the shores of the Gulf states across the Gulf of Mexico to the Yucatan Paninsula and southern Mexico. This is route most frequently used by the many species of birds from eastern United States and Canada.

Route 5 : From Texas, New Mexico, Arizona, and California through northern Mexico. The majority of birds from western conterminous United States, western Canada, and Alaska use the western side of this route.

Species vary greatly in their course of migration and use of routes. A few species move south over one route and return by another; a few species move eastward or westward before going south; and a few species have spectacularly long routes that take them as far south as southern South America. Among a few species which breed in western United States- e.g., the Western Kingbird (*Tyrannus verticalis*) and the Scissor- tailed Flycatcher (*Muscivora forficate*)- some individuals in the fall move eastward across the Gulf states to winter in Florida whereas most of the population moves directly south into Mexico.

To illustrate the wide variation in migratory movements and the choice of routes, the migration of six species are described below:

The American Golden Plover (*Pluvialis dominica*) passes eastward from its breeding range to the Atlantic Coast, where it turns southward over Route 1. Once in South America, it flies directly across the continent to its winter range. It returns, however, by another route, coming up across northwestern South America and the Gulf of Mexico and reaching the United States along the coast of Texas and Louisiana. From there it continues up the Mississippi Valley and through central Canada to its breeding range.

The Blackpoll warbler (Dendroica striata) shows a remarkable convergence in its southward migration. From its vast transcontinental breeding range it converges on the Atlantic coastal plain as far north as Virginia and from there proceeds to Florida where it lives for South America over Routes 2 and 3. It returns to Florida by the same routes but from there fans out northward to its breeding range.

The Mourning Warbler (*Oporornis Philadelphia*) shows a similar convergence. From its breeding range of more modest extent it converges on southern Texas, then goes southward along the eastern portion of Route 5 through eastern Mexico and Central America to its winter range. It returns via the same part of Route 5 and fans out from Texas northward.

The American Redstart (*Setophaga ruticilla*) shows little convergence. Instead, it passes southward more or less directly over a broad front of nearly 2,500 miles, eventually using Routes 2,3, and 4. It returns the same way.

The Bobolink (*Dolichonux oryzivorus*) migrates am exceptionally long distance, averaging farther than any other passerine species. From its transcontinental breeding range, it converges southward to leave the United States over Routes 3 and 4. Once in South America, it continues directly overland to its winter range in extreme southern Brazil, southeastern Bolivia, Paraguay, and northern Argentina. It returns the same way.

The Connecticut Warbler (*Oporornis agilis*) migrates in an eccentric manner. From its breeding range it flies directly eastward to New England, then to South America along the Atlantic coastal plain and eventually Route 3. From its winter range in South America it returns over Route 3 to Florida, but from there it passes diagonally to the Mississippi Valley and northward to its breeding range.

Altitudinal Migration

Some bird populations of high mountains in both temperate and tropical regions move down to the lower slopes and valleys when winter sets in at higher elevations. In the descent of a few hundred feet they accomplish what many other populations do in their latitudinal migrations of many hundreds of miles.

Several observers have noticed that mountain birds tend to move to higher slopes after the nesting season. Probably many are young birds which, after getting their growth, always show a great tendency to move about. The reason for this may be the agonistic behavior of their elders, but more than likely it is another example of juvenile wandering.

Distances in Migratory Travel

Extremes in distances traveled by migration birds are represented on the one hand by high- mountain species, which merely pass up or down slopes of several hundred to a few thousand feet, and on the other hand by the Arctic Tern (*Sterna paradisaea*). It makes the longest flight of any bird, migration thousand of mile from the Arctic, where a part of the population breeds, to its wintering area adjacent to the pack ice around Antarctica. This species nests as far north as the northern tip of Greenland at 83 degrees North Latitude and has been recorded as far south as 74 degrees South Latitude. Most of the individuals from Greenland, Canada, and northeastern United States undertake the passage by flying across the North Atlantic to the continental shelf of western Europe, and the south over the coastal waters of West Africa and finally across the Antarctic Ocean. They return by the same route.

While a few species breeding in conterminous United States, Canada, and Alaska go as far south as central and southern South America, the majority migrate no farther than northern South America. In fact, many species in northern conterminous United States, Canada, and Alaska move only to the southern states. There appears to be no correlation between the distances traveled by birds and their size, flying abilities, or habits. A number of small species journey to Mexico and Central America, outdistancing a great many species which to all appearance shave much greater capacities for travel. Still to be explained is why certain species have developed long migration routes, while other species, sometimes closely related, have routes that are half the length or less. It has been postulated that the long migration of certain species to northern latitudes for nesting is to take advantage of increased daylight and the consequent shortening of the period in which the young are confined to the nest. No satisfactory theory has yet been advanced to account for the arduous passage of such birds as the Bobolink (*Dolichnyx oryxivorus*) across the tropics from the northern to the southern temperate region, or the Arctic Tern from one polar region to the other.

When a migratory species has an extensive breeding range that includes parts of northern conterminous United States, Canada, and Alaska, the more northern populations of that species move farther south for the winter than the other populations do. For example, among the several subspecies of the Fox Sparrow (*Passerella iliaca*) breeding along the Pacific Coast from Alaska to Puget Sound, the subspecies nesting farthest north have been found wintering in southern California, passing by other subspecies, which either do not migrate at all or move long to central or northern California. Apparently the more northern breeding populations of a widespread species acquire a stronger migratory habit then the populations breeding in more southern areas that have milder, year- round climate.

In some species there may be sexual differences in the extent of the migration. Howell found that females in the eastern race of the Yellow- belied Sapsucker (*Sphyrapicus varius*) outnumber the males in the southern part of the winter range by about three and one- half to one.

Flight Lanes and Concentrations

In North America migratory movement is continent- wide. There are probably no areas over which birds do not pass in their latitudinal migrations. Prairies, forests, mountains, lakes, and inland extensions of the oceans fail to stop or divert migration altogether. Even so, as diurnal migrants move northward or southward across Canada and the conterminous United States, many species tend to favor or be influenced by certain topographic features which trend in a north- south direction, some species fly along ridges; others follow, the coasts, large rivers and chains of lakes. A great many species go through valleys, move along peninsulas, or pass from island to island across large bodies of water. In both Canada and the United States there are many places where the topography is such as to cause narrow flight lanes in which migratory movement is especially conspicuous.

Particularly in the fall, hawks and a few other large birds follow the crests of north- south ridges, riding on the updrafts as they proceed southward. The traffic in these lanes is unusually heavy on clear, windy days following the passage of a cold front, because there is considerable wind deflected upward, thus making these lanes advantageous to travel. One of the best known places is the Kittatinny Ridge in eastern Pennsylvania. At one point, Hawk Mountain where the ridge becomes suddenly high and slender, the birds are brought together and closer to the ground. As a result of this narrowing of the flight lane observers at Hawk Mountain have been able to count over 22,000 hawks moving by in a single season.

Large bodies of water constitute barriers to day- migration birds and thus cause flight lanes to curve around them. The Great Lakes are a good example. In the fall, south- bound hawks approaching their north shores from western Quebec and southern Ontario take the shortest courses around them that geography and air movements will allow. If the birds are migration in great numbers, as on the second days after cold fronts when there are steady westerly winds and ample sunlight producing thermals, large numbers can be seen in continuous passage at such points as Port Credit on the northwest shore of Lake Ontario, Port Stanley on the north side of Lake Erie, Cedar Grove on the west side of Lake Michigan, and Duluth at he western most extension of Lake Superior.

Peninsulas projecting into large bodies of water that lie athwart the direction of migration may become funnels for land birds in diurnal passage. Hawks moving northward in the spring through Michigan to Canada converge in large numbers on the northern tip of Lower Michigan at the Straits of Mackinac. Here, if the weather is rainy and windless, they settle on trees and other perches. With the advent of the next clear day and a favoring wind, the hawks begin to spiral higher and higher until one bird peels out and heads northward over the Straits with the others following. Small numbers of north- bound Blue Jays (Cyanocitta cristata), in order to get across Lake Mendota at Madison, Wisconsin, converge first at Picnic Point and then spiral upward until "barely visible to the naked eye" before crossing the 1.7 miles of open water to Fox Bluff on the north shore. Cape May, the southern tip of New Jersey between the Atlantic Ocean and Delaware Bay, is noted for its hordes of land migrants, large and small, which gather from August through November when northerly winds are strong. Some of the migrants held up here those which regularly follow the Atlantic Coast southward, but many are birds which have been drifted by wind southeastward from their usual flight lines. Frequently, migrants at Cape May may be seen in the day flying north and northwestward into the wind as they skirt Delaware Bay before continuing their journey. Similar concentrations may be observed at Cape Charles, a south- pointing peninsula separating the waters of Chesapeake bay from the Atlantic.

Night migrants do not follow topographically determined flight lanes to any significant degree. Instead, as radar surveillance shows, birds migrate at night without regard to what lies below.

In the spring, land migrants returning to the United States from across the Gulf of Mexico vary in their manner of arrival in accordance with weather conditions. Of the weather is mild and the wind favorable, birds bound for more northern destinations continue inland from the Gulf for considerable distances before coming to land. The coastal area thus appears to be an ornithological "hiatus". But if a cold front with strong northerly winds moves in over the area while migration is in progress, migrants are forced to come down to the first land reached, with the result that the coastal area is flooded with birds that linger here until the weather again becomes favorable. A somewhat similar situation occurs during spring migration at point Pelee. Here, since it is the nearest land, north- bound small land birds, on meeting a cold front from the north while they are over Lake Erie are forced to descend and remain until the cold abates. At such times Point Pelee swarms with birds.

Flocking During Migration

During migration bird species show wide differences in flocking habit. A number of diurnal migrants, notably many hawks and other predators, are little inclined to move in groups, preferring to travel solitarily. But the majority of migrants, diurnal or nocturnal, exhibit the flocking habit.

Certain species migrate in flocks strictly of their own kind. These are usually birds whose flight-speed, feeding habits, or roosting preferences are so individual as to make them incompatible traveling companions. The Common Nigthawk (*Chordelies minor*) and Chimney Swift (*Chaetura pelagica*) are good examples of birds which migrate in their own company. Neither waxwings nor crossbills will migrate with other birds, but Cedar and Bohemian Waxwings (*Bombycilla cedrorum* and *B. Garrulus*) have been seen in the same flocks and so have Red and White-winged Crossbills (*Loxia curvirostra* and *L. leucoptera*). Some of he larger birds - e.g. pelicans, cormorants, storks, swans, geese, and cranes - noted for V-shaped or linear flock formations likewise tend to travel in unmixed groups.

The majority of species traveling in flocks, whether unmixed or mixed, give call notes. This is especially true of nocturnal migrants; some species such as *Hylocichla* thrushes utter calls heard only in night migration; other species such as the Bobolink and Dickcissel (*Spiza Americana*) give calls that are the same as ones heard in the day time on their breeding grounds. If the calls are distinctive as in the case of he Bobolink and Dickcissel, it is possible to identify the species, but the calls of most species are faint chips and lisps that sound more or less the same to the human ear.

Unmixed or mixed flocks of some species of smaller birds – e.g., certain sandpipers and plovers – fly in compact formations, all individuals in the flock simultaneously performing almost identical maneuvers. Many more species of smaller birds, including the majority of passerines, travel in flocks that are loosely formed, though still cohesive, the individuals proceeding in the same direction. At night, the cohesion of flocks is probably maintained by call notes. At the same time, the call notes serve to space out individuals in each flock so that they will not collide with one another.

No flock in migrants, appears to have a persisting leader. The direction taken by a flock, as suggested by Hamilton, represents a compromise by each individual to the directional preference of the other individuals of the flock. At night, call notes convey directional information form one individual to the other. When a nocturnal flock shifts its direction or lowers its altitude, or when it is disoriented for one reason. Or another, all its members greatly increase their rate of calling.

Whether or not flocks remain intact for the duration of migration has not been determined. Nor is it known for certain whether flocks remain together during the winter. In all probability, most flocks, if hey are comprised of common, widely distributed species, changes from day to day during migration and in the winter split up into smaller groups, or combine with other flocks to form larger groups.

Flocking during migration is undoubtedly advantageous to the individuals concerned. Just as flocking among resident birds provides group protection against predation or increases the success in finding and exploiting food sources, flocking in migration greatly facilitates the attainment of destination. Younger birds traveling with more seasoned adults benefit from their experience. As another advantage, Hamilton suggests that groups of birds on an average determine their direction with greater accuracy than single individuals. Thus flocking assists any migrant that goes a long distance, or any migrant required to pinpoint its destination on a small land area in mid-ocean. Hamilton cites as examples: (1) The Broad-winged and Swainson's Hawks (*Buteo platypterrus* and *B. Swainsoni*). Both of these North American species travel in large flocks to winter in South America. By contrast, the Red-tailed Hawk (*B. jamaicensis*) and certain other buteos, which rarely leave the North American continent, seldom move in appreciable groups. (2) The Long-tailed Cuckoo (*Urodynamis taitensis*). After breeding in New Zealand, this species gathers in large flocks for the exceedingly long, non-stop passage to winter quarters on tiny islands in the west-central Pacific. By contrast, the Yellow-billed and Black – billed Cuckoos (*Coccyzus americanus* and *C. erthropthalmus*) of North America for the winter, migrate solitarily.

V-shaped formations help to conserve energy by creating favorable air currents for all individuals in the flock except the leader. When fatigued, the leader drops back and is replaced by another bird in the flock. An alternate advantage hypothesized by *Hamilton* is the V-shaped structure serves as a means of communication, enabling the individuals to profit fully from the collective direction-finding of the group. By flying in parallel alignment, each individual moves in the same direction as the leader. If, as in flocks of gees traveling in poor visibility, difficulties in establishing direction arise, the leadership changes frequently in order that collective "judgment" may prevail in maintaining the proper course. Sometimes the V-structure gives way temporarily to a crescent from; forward flight remains in the same direction but is slowed until a new leader takes over and the V-shape is resumed.

Unmixed or mixed flocks may contain only immature individuals, only adults, or only adults of one sex; or they may contain individuals of the all ages and both sexes. Flocks of geese and cranes may be comprised of one family or several families.

During the fall migration the adults may precede the immature birds, the birds-of-the-year. *Hagar* reported that adult Hudsonian Godwits (*Limosa haemastica*) withdraw from their nesting grounds in central and northwestern subarctic Canada in late July; the immatures follow a month later. Among passerine species there is convincing evidence assembled by *Murray* and *Jehl* from several thousand migrants, mist-netted in the fall at island Beach, New Jersey, and analyzed as to age, that adults and immatures travel at approximately the same time. However, in the case of the Least Flycatcher (*Empidonax minimus*), *Hussell*, *Davis*, and *Montgomerie* concluded from an analysis of 182 individuals trapped in the late summer at Long Point, Ontario, that most of the adults migrate in advance of the immatures: the adults during the second half of July and first half of August; the majority of immatures from the second week of August to the end of September.

In the spring migration many of the first flocks of certain species coming north have a preponderance of adult males which reach the breeding grounds and establish territories before the rest of the population arrives. *A. A. Allen* once carefully studied the spring migration of Red-winged Blackbirds (*Agelaius phoeniceus*) at Ithaca, New York. Since the males and females have distinct plumages and birds hatched the previous year (i.e., the immature birds) differ sufficiently in color from the adults, he was able to analyze flocks and work out a migration schedule according to age and sex. While his findings may not hold for all Red-wing population, it is presented below as a useful guide and basis for comparison.

Migrant adult males .... March 13-April 21
Resident adult males .... March 25-April 10
Migrant females and immature males .... March 29-April 24
Resident adult females .... April 10-May 1
Resident immature males.......................... May 6-June 1
Resident immature females .... May 10-June 11

In watching spring migration in his own area, the student will find that not all species follow such a schedule. In fact, males and females of quite a few species migrate together. Only rarely, however, do females precede males.

Direction-Feeding

How migrating birds determine their direction when migrating or homing by day or night over areas unfamiliar to them is one of the most fascinating aspects of migration. Before considering the subject of direction-finding in migration, it is worthwhile to review some of the problems associated with homing in birds. The basic means by which birds orient themselves, whether migrating or homing, are much the same.

A great many experiments have demonstrated the remarkable ability of wild birds to return to their eggs or young after being removed great distances and released. Years ago *Watson* tested the homing ability of Sooty and Noddy Terns (*Sterna fuscata* and *Anous stolidus*) which nest on the Dry Tortugas, the islands in the Gulf of Mexico west of Florida. These species come to the tortugas from tropical seas and are seldom seen farther north. Two nesting Sooty Terns and three Noddy Terns were captured, marked, and transported northward in a ship to a point off Cape Hatteras, about 1,000 miles by sea from the Tortugas. Here they were released. Just five days later the two Sooty Terns were back on their nests; one of the Noddy Terns showed up after a few more days. Some of the more recent experiments demonstrating the sustained speed of homing flight by the Purple martin,

Manx Shearwater, leach's Petrel, and Laysan Albatross attest at the same time to their precision in direction-finding.

The inducement of birds to home is not necessarily provided by their eggs or young; it can be the breeding area or home range. Breeding Brown-headed Cowbirds (*Molothrus ater*), which are brood parasites, will home from maximum distances of 250 to 380 miles. An adult female Bobolink (*Dolichonyx oryzivorus*), escaping from captivity in September at Berkeley, California, was recaptured the following June at Kenmare, North Dakota, where it was originally trapped as a breeding bird. Six hundred and sixty Golden-crowned and White-crowned Sparrows (*Zonotrichia atricapilla* and *Z. leucophrys*), captured while wintering in the San Jose area of California, were immediately carried by plane to Laurel, Maryland, and released. Fifteen were known to have come back the following winter. In the interim they had presumably found their way in the spring to the nesting grounds in northwestern Canada and Alaska, then returned to California in normal migration.

Homing flights are more or less routine with homing pigeons which are Common Pigeons (*Columba livia*) specially bred for racing. Their precision and speed of return to the home loft is developed by training and experience. Sometimes the experience of only one flight to the home loft is sufficient to determine the proper direction for successive flights. In his work on homing pigeons, *Matthews* found that certain individuals, trained to maintain a given direction, can adhere to that direction over unfamiliar terrain and that certain other individuals can fly straight towards the home loft from unfamiliar territory regardless of the direction of the home loft. In the course of their training, pigeons must be made familiar with the area around the loft so that they will have a broad or reasonable target.

Although homing has been amply demonstrated in both wild birds and racing pigeons, the perplexing question remains: How do homing birds finding their way? In seeking an answer, *Griffin* and *Hock* attempted to determine how displaced and released nesting birds find their way by following them in an airplane and watching their behavior. For their experiment they selected the Gannet (*Morus bassanus*), a marine bird which rarely occur inland; being large and white, it was easy to follow. Taking 17 individuals from their nests on an island off the Gaspe Peninsula, Quebec, they carried them to a point in northern Maine, 100 miles from salt water and 215 miles from the home island. There they released nine of the birds (the others were used as controls) and, from an airplane, traced their flights from 25 to 230 miles. The investigators were careful to keep the plane 1,500 feet or more away from the birds so as not to frighten them. The experimental birds flew in all directions with no significant tendency to head directly toward their nests. Their flight paths were generally gradual curves. The first birds to reach the coast within the first few hours were the first to get back to their nests. Altogether 62.5 percent of these birds eventually reached their nests. In from one to four days.

The result of Griffin and Hock's work on the Gannets suggests that the ability of birds to home-that is, to return to a known or familiar site such as a nesting area-is dependent on random searching. In a strange territory birds keep circling and exploring by trial and error until they find familiar landmarks within familiar territory. However, the concept of random searching as a means by which all birds find their way cannot be reconciled with the rapid homing exemplified by Sooty Terns and other species already mentioned. Many birds, if not all, obviously have an ability to find their way by orienting themselves - determining their position with respect to their environment - and by following directional cues or navigating.

In taking up the subject of the means by which birds orient themselves and navigate, it is well to consider first the question whether or not birds inherit at least part of their ability to find their way. *Rowan* at Edmonton, Alberta, caught young Common Crows (*Corvus brachyrhyncos*) in the late summer and kept them in captivity. In November, when winter conditions had begun to set in and all adult Common Crows had left for their winter range in Kansas and Oklahoma, he banded the captive birds and released them. Altogether 54 individuals were set free, and in the next few days he received reports of recoveries. Apparently some of the birds had not traveled very far, but those which had gone an appreciable distance were headed toward their winter range. *Schuz* at Rossitten on the Baltic Coast of eastern Prussia tried similar banding experiments with White storks (*Cionia ciconia*). In the middle of September, after all the local population had departed, he released 73 young banded birds. Most of them traveled eastward toward the Black Sea, paralleling the normal flight line for the local population, though some of the birds flew in a more southerly direction and three went southwestward to Itlay. *Perdeck*, over a period of four years, caught and banded over 11,000 fall-migrating Starlings (*Sturnus vulgaris*) in Holland and released them in Switzerland. Recoveries totaling 354 later showed that the juveniles took their ancestral direction southwest, paralleling the normal route, to a new winter area, whereas the adults soon separated and veered westward toward their ancestral winter range. From these experiments alone, it seems clear that at least some birds must have an innate ability to follow the normal migratory route or one parallel to it. How the birds "know" when they have flown far enough is yet to be determined.

Granting that migrating birds have an innate ability to find their way does not deny that some birds acquire their ability by experience. Young Indigo Buntings (Passerina cyanea), hand-raised in various conditions of isolation, apparently do not attain the accuracy of orientation typical of adult buntings and thus seem to depend, at least partly, on some kind of experience. Young geese and cranes, which migrate in families or groups of families, probably learn the migration routes by following their elders. They no doubt "memorize" features of the landscape when they migrate by day as they often do. But whether or not birds inherit or acquire their ability to find their way, the fact remains that they must depend on cues other than landscape features to orient themselves and navigate when traveling at night, over the sea, or above or in a heavy overcast. What are the cues?

The first break-through came in the early 1950's when it was proved that the sun is a cue to orientation and even a guide in navigation. At Wilhelmshaven, Germany, *Kramer* placed a small, circular cage high in the center of a circular pavilion that was completely enclosed except for six windows, each high enough to give only a view of the sky from the cage. *Kramer* put a hand-reared Starling in the cage at the time in the spring when it would normally migrate, and from below the cage he recorded the direction in which the bird, in its migratory restlessness, showed a tendency to flutter. The bird fluttered persistently in the normal direction of spring migration

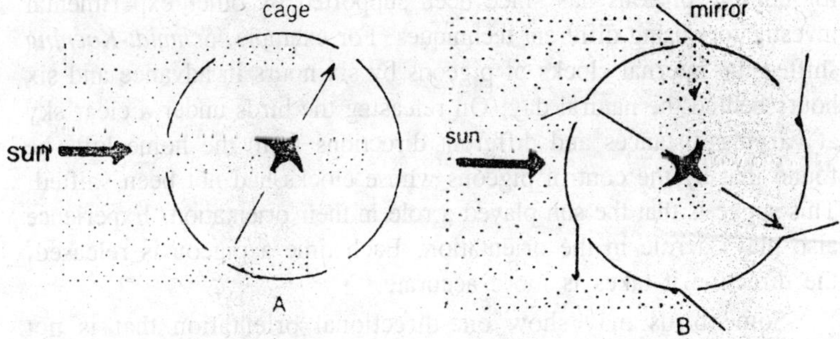

Fig. 12.1. Kramer's experiment with starlings to show that day migration use sun s a compass.

if the sun was shining but not if the sky was heavily overcast. When, by an ingenious use of mirrors at direction in order to maintain the same angle as before. *Kramer* and his associates soon demonstrated in subsequent experiments that birds have some sort of "internal clock" that enables them to compensate for the sun's daily "movement" across the sky and thus can hold the same direction of flight despite the sun's steadily changing position.

Hoffmann experimented further on the internal clock as a basis for orientation by the sun. He trained caged Starlings to seek a food reward at a particular time of day and always in the same direction. Then he tested them without rewards at the time they had come to expect and at other times. The birds, he found, could allow for the daily movement of the sun. Having proved this, he subjected the trained birds to a regime of light and darkness that shifted their internal clocks six hours ahead or six hours behind the natural day outside. Later he exposed the birds to the natural day. The birds responded by shifting their directions accordingly by 90 degrees, counterclockwise if the clocks were set ahead, clockwise if hey were set behind. These and later tests showed that the birds did not orient themselves by the elevation or altitude of the sun in the sky but by its azimuth or position with relation to compass direction. The birds thus determined direction by what is called "sun compass orientation."

Soon after *Kramer* reported his initial experiments with Starlings, *Matthews*, found that homing pigeons, which are non-migratory, use the sun as a guide. When he released pigeons in unfamiliar territory under clear skies, they headed in the direction of home. If the sky was overcast, they failed to do so. The concept of the sun as a compass for homing pigeons has since been supported by other experimental investigators using different techniques. For example, *Schmidt-Koening* shifted the internal clocks of pigeons by six hours in advance and six hours behind the natural day. On releasing the birds under a clear sky at varying distances and different directions from the home loft, he found that by the control pigeons whose clocks had not been shifted. This suggests that the sun played a role in their orientation. Experience also plays a role in the orientation. Each time a pigeon is released, the direction it takes is more accurate.

Some birds may show one-directional orientation that is not necessarily related to migration or homing. *Matthews*, experimenting with non-migratory mallards (*Anas platyrhynchos*) at Slimbridge, England, discovered that when birds of any age were displaced during a clear day for any distance in any direction at any season, they demonstrated a strong tendency to fly in one direction, namely, northwest. The flights were always short and seemed to be guided by the sun, but since they had no discernible purpose other than possible escape, Matthews called the behavior "nonsense orientation." He believed that it might be innate or perhaps developed at an early age. Other birds may show the same phenomenon. Migratory Mallards wintering in Illinois, one being trapped and released during a clear day or night at points far east and west of their winter-home lakes, consistently flew northward regardless of the direction of their home-lakes. Common Terns (*Sterna hirundo*), displaced from their breeding colony on Penikese Island off Cape Cod, Massachusetts, on a clear day, flew southeast, irrespective of where they were released or the direction of Penikese Island.

Adelie Penguins (*Pygoscelis adeliae*), when displaced from their breeding colonies at Cape Crozier on the coast of Antarctica to the featureless expanse of compacted snow in the interior, oriented themselves by the sun, departed in one direction, and ultimately reached their nest sites. The investigators, *J. T. Emlen* and *Penney*, used breeding males, some of whose internal clocks had been artificially shifted in advance. Releasing them individually from three groups, each at widely separated points, they observed that the birds headed straight for the coast on courses which were essentially parallel without any convergence toward Cape Crozier. The birds seemed to have no information on their location at release with respect to their home colonies. They took their courses from the sun and, as shown by the breakdown in orientation among those birds whose clocks had been shifted, maintained their courses by referring to the sun's azimuth. If heavy clouds obscured the sun and eliminated all shadows, their orientation soon deteriorated. Emlen and Penny considered such one-directional courses to be fixed and to be maintained by an inherent time sense; they likened the procedure to nonsense orientation as described in waterfowl and other birds, but believed that it might be escape orientation with survival value by steering the penguins to off-coast feeding areas whence they would be guided, perhaps in part by familiar landmarks, to their home colonies. Later experiments by the two investigators confirmed their original findings and conclusions.

A few years following Kramer's initial discovery that migratory restlessness in caged Starlings was directed toward the sun, Sauer and his wife, undertook experiments in Germany to determine by what means nocturnal migrants find their way. The *Sauers* used three species of sylviid warblers, reared in captivity without ever having seen the natural sky. During the period when the species would normally migrate, the *Sauers* put each bird in a rotatable circular cage and exposed it to the night sky. Under a clear, starry sky, even when their cages were turned periodically, the test birds fluttered persistently in the direction that the species takes at the season of the experiments; under heavily overcast skies the birds fluttered randomly in various directions, obviously disoriented. Then the *Sauers* placed the cage in a small planetarium with a starry sky, adjusted to the local time and latitude. The birds fluttered in the direction appropriate to that season depicted. There seemed to be no doubt that these birds obtained their information for direction from the starry sky.

The *Sauers* carried their experiments further. Placing the birds under skies representing the non-migratory seasons, they noticed that some of the birds were completely disoriented. From these experiments and others, *Sauer* concluded that birds do not rely on the stars themselves for direction but on the azimuth and altitude of the starry sky. This bicoordinate system would give birds the necessary information on their location since azimuth or hour angle would denote longitude and altitude would indicate latitude.

Working with mist-netted Indigo Buntings in the United States, *S. T. Emlen* repeated many of he Saurers' experiments and made still other well-controlled tests under planetarium skies. The results confirmed some of the *Sauers'* studies but differed sharply from the others. *Emlen* found no evidence that the buntings relied on a bicoordinate celestial system for orientation but rather made use of the numerous stars, particularly "the constant, two-dimensional spatial relationships" existing between them. He believed that no single star, with the possible exception of Polaris (the North Star) could give the birds sufficient information for direction. It is the configuration or patterning of the bright stars in the constellations such as Ursa Major (the Big Dipper) that gives the cues. While *Emlen* could not determine with nay certainty which patterns were of special importance or essential to orientation, the evidence seemed to point to the northern astral sky, especially the area within 35 degree of Polaris.

What prompts birds to take the appropriate seasonal direction? Seeking an answer to this question, *S. T. Emlen* induced physiological readiness for spring and fall migration in two groups of Indigo Buntings and then tested them simultaneously under the spring sky of planetarium.

The group conditioned for spring migration oriented northward; the group in condition for fall migration took the opposite direction. This clearly suggested to Emlen that the internal physiological changes in Indigo Buntings, rather than differences in external stimuli (e.g., in the night sky), are responsible for their direction in spring and fall.

Practically all the experiments on the responses of homing and migrating birds to the sun and stars have demonstrated that when skies are heavily overcast the birds show disorientation. The consequent implication is that birds cannot find their way when celestial cues are obscured. Very recent studies however, indicate that this may be untrue. *Keeton* has shown that homing pigeons, while using the sun as a compass when available, can navigate accurately under total overcast and even without familiar landmarks, radar studies reveal that birds migrate successfully when there is a heavy overcast. If the cloud layer is too high to surmount, birds will fly under it or even in it. This being the case, how do birds orient themselves without celestial cues and, if they are flying at night or in a cloud layer, without celestial cues and, if they are flying at night or in a cloud layer, without being able to see landmarks or topographical features familiar to them? The cue may be wind direction.

Nisbet once theorized that the birds might use wind-more specifically atmospheric or wind turbulence – in orientation. In central Illinois, *Bellrose*, with his associates, has gathered ample experimental evidence to show that Blue-winged Teal (*Anas discors*), a long-distance migrant that commonly winters in northwestern South America, does indeed use the turbulent structure of the wind for direction. The species migrates by day or night, and radar surveillance and visual sightings by Bellroes confirm its ability to migrate under overcast skies. In the fall and early winter, Bellrose used both hand-raised immature teal that he released at various points up to 100 miles distant from their home pens and wild immature teal, trapped during migration, that he held in pens and released from 10 to 40 days after other Blue-winged Teal had left the region. All his experimental birds were banded. The hand-reared birds had never flown over the area and none of the birds had ever viewed the landscape along the standard migration routes southward. When released under both clear and overcast skies, nearly all the birds tended to start in the same direction – with the wind. Analyzing his data from visual sightings and banding recoveries and drawing upon his knowledge of waterfowl movements from radar studies and airplane tracking, Bellrose concluded that Blue-winged Teal, and probably other species of waterfowl as well, prefer landscape features for orientation, but, if unavailable, they resort to celestial cues. Both being unavailable, they use wind direction, perhaps referring at the outset of flight to landscape cues for information on the sector of the compass from which the wind its blowing.

The present knowledge of direction-finding, the highlights of which are briefly reviewed in the foregoing paragraphs, points all too clearly to the danger of generalizing on the means of orientation and navigation in migration. Different groups of birds in their adaptations to different modes of existences may well have developed correspondingly different means of finding their way from one place to another in accordance with the prevailing ecological condition. It is unlikely that any species orients itself entirely by one cue. A one-directional orientation may suffice for some birds while a bicoordinate system of navigation may be necessary for others. Direction-finding, though appearing to be basically inherent, may actually prove through eventual research to be acquired chiefly by experience. In all probability, direction-finding in strongly migratory birds is a highly complex procedure involving physiological and behavioral responses to not one but several environmental factors - celestial bodies, wind, and perhaps others presently considered as having no relationship to the problem.

Aids and Additional Suggestions for the Study of Migration

Books by the following authors contain good, highly readable information on such aspects of migration as probable origin, routes, distances traveled, relation to weather and season: *G. M. Allen*, *Chapman*, *Dorst*, *Griscom*, *Hochbaum*, *Lincoln*, *Thomson*, *Wetmore*.

For general information pertaining to migration movements in conterminous united States the student is referred to the guides by *Pettingill*. The introduction to the chapters on each state contains a description of the principal migration concentrations in the state and, in most cases, a series of inclusive dates when one may expect to observe peak flights of the majority of waterfowl, shore birds, and land birds. If there are places in the state where one may observe hawk flights or especially heavy concentrations of migrating birds, they are indicated in the body of the chapter.

Of great value and interest to any student following migration in his own area of conterminous United States or southern Canada are the annual first and fourth numbers of *Audubon Field Notes*. The first number each year, published in February, contains a country-wide summary and regional reports of the preceding fall migration; the fourth number, published in August, contains similar coverage of the preceding spring migration. The vast amount of information in these numbers is gathered through the cooperative effort of many observers. Any student who is able to identify birds is urged to send in reports of his observations to the particular regional editor handling data from his region.

Study of Nocturnal Migration

There are at least five field methods of studying nocturnal migration. (1) By observations of movements across the face of the moon. The principal equipment needed is a telescope with a power of 15 or greater. For methods and procedures, consult *Lowery* and *Nisbet* and for the application of accumulated data. (2) By radio-tracking. The equipment needed includes a transmitter and receiver. For general information on the type of equipment required, consult *Sclater*, *Cochran* and *Lord*, and *Southern*. For information on a transmitter adapted to small migrants, as well as an example of methods and procedures in radio-tracking small migrants. (3) By radar survillance. This requires the use of a special facility operated by skilled technicians. (4) By tape-recording. Besides a tape recorder, this requires a parabolic reflector, microphone, and amplifier. (5) By the study of migrants killed at television towers or migrants killed as a result of airport ceilometers or other man-made interferences with migration.

Of the five listed methods, the most practical for the beginning student is the study of migrants killed at television towers. It requires no special equipment. Practically every city or large community has on its outskirts one or more television towers the almost certainly take a toll of nocturnal migrants. Much as these kills are regretted, they nonetheless provide rewarding material for the study of many aspects of migration locally.

An early-morning search of the ground under a television tower and its guy wircs following a night during which migration proceeded at low altitude will usually yield birds of many species. If the student chooses to make such a search as often as these accidents occur through the migration season and on successive seasons, keeping a careful record with dates of the number of individuals of each species killed, he will obtain a true sampling of the nocturnal migratory activity in the area of the tower. He may also discover the presence of species not heretofore reported, or even suspected, in the area because they have always passed through at night unseen.

Given the time necessary, the student may collect specimens for making one or more special studies such as t he following:

1. Succession of sexes and age groups in different species: whether males precede females and adults precede immatures, or *vice versa*.
2. Geographic variation in a wide-ranging species migrating through a particular area: whether the color and measurements of individuals reveal one or more populations or subspecies.
3. Molt with relation to migration: whether certain species are in stages of molt and, if so, which feather tracts are involved. Normally birds do not molt the remiges and their primary coverts during migration, but the rest of the alar tract and all the other tracts may be in the process of molt, depending on the species or the sex and/or stage of maturity of individuals in each species.
4. Weight with relation to the length of night-flight: whether the birds are quit heavy, having been killed soon after take-off, or quite light, having been killed after a long flight.
5. Fat condition with relation to stage of migration and duration of night-flight: whether the birds are quite obese, indicating that their migration was well under way with long night-flights, or quite lean, indicating that their migration was just beginning with short night-flights.

Before collecting any specimens, the student must obtain both a federal and a state (or provincial) collecting permit authorizing him to take dead birds "for salvage."

Collect the specimens after a kill as early in the morning as possible since the carcasses not only decompose rapidly but are soon molested by insects or eaten by house cats, crows, gulls, and other creatures that inevitably find the ground around a television tower a promising source of food. Weigh each specimen without too much delay as the body begins losing weight shortly after death. Mark the weight on a tag and attach it to a leg. Seal all specimens collected in plastic bags to avoid their dehydration, mark with the date, time of day, and place of collection, and put at once in a deep-freezer for study and analysis later.

Study of Diurnal Migration

Whenever opportunity permits, the student should watch the diurnal movements of migrants in his own area. He will soon discover how greatly birds are influenced in their daytime movements by the terrain, vegetation, and waterways. He is almost certain to note that passerine migrants, although continually searching for food, follow much the same course and in the same direction. If the birds inhabit trees or shrubs, they choose paths in which these grow and avoid, when possible, crossing wide stretches of water and open country. For an idea of how much detailed information one can obtain in a local study and some of the procedures to follow, the student is referred to the classic work by *Ball*, in which he reported on six fall migrations on a small point of land of the great Gaspe Peninsula, Quebec.

13

Selective Studies

Ratites and Tinamous

Ratites, the giants among birds, and their small relatives, the tinamous, are the living representatives of the order Struthioniformes, though the tinamous are sometimes placed in a separate order. All species are restricted to southern continents, which has encouraged the view that they represent a primitive group that did not penetrate the Northern Hemisphere. Recent discoveries of ratite fossils in Europe, however, indicate that they may have once been wide ranging. Members of this order—the ostrich, rheas, cassowaries, emu, and kiwis—show that birds can evolve into large flightless vertebrates comparable with the large herbivorous mammals.

An Unkeeled Breastbone

The order contains six living families (or five if the emu is placed with the cassowaries): Struthionidae, represented by the ostrich of Africa, the world's largest bird; Tinamidae, about 45 species of tinamous in South and Central America; Rheidae, two species of rhea in South America; Casuariidae, the cassowaries, three species in New Guinea and Australia; Dromaiidae, the emu of Australia; and Apterygidae, three species of kiwi in New Zealand. In the historical past the Diornithidae, with at least 12 species of moas, inhabited New Zealand, and individuals may have survived into the nineteenth century. The final date of extinction of another family, the Aepyornithidae (elephantbirds), confined to Madagascar, was about 1650.

All "true" ratites are flightless, and they have a flat sternum (breastbone) without the keellike prominence of most flying birds. (The

Latin word ratis means "raft"). The tinamous have a keeled sternum, and also have the ability to fly, but they resemble the other Struthioniformes in many unusual anatomical characters such as the structure of the palate. Their plumage is loose compared with the feathers of most other birds. Cassowaries and the emu have plumage that hangs like hair from their bodies; each feather has two shafts of equal length. The ostrich, rheas, tinamous, and kiwis have feathers with one main shaft, but the barbules, if present, do not interlock closely so the birds appear shaggy.

The Ostrich: A King with His Harem

Ratites are running birds. They gain a mechanical advantage in having long, thin legs to support the body's weight well above the ground, in a similar way to the ungulates (horses, cows, and their relatives). The number of toes has been reduced in the course of ratite evolution. Most birds have four toes—in ratites, the kiwis, moas, and some tinamous have four toes; the emu, rheas, and many tinamous have three toes; and the ostrich has only two toes. In the ostrich, unlike in most ratites, males are larger than females; males grow to 2.75 meters (9 feet) tall, females to 1.9 meters (61/4 feet) tall. The ostrich's wide range once included the Middle East, North Africa, and Africa south of the tropical rainforests, but it is now extinct in the Middle East and most of North Africa. Many southern African populations are confined to national parks.

Ostriches use their huge wings in courtship, and each cock builds a nest to which he attracts a hen. She lays her eggs there and becomes the major hen. Other hens (minor hens) also lay eggs there, but only the major hen and the cock incubate. She selectively keeps her own eggs in the nest, discarding some of those laid by other hens. Eventually 60 or more eggs may be laid in or around the nest but only about 20 are incubated. The major hen incubates by day and the cock takes over at night during the incubation period of 39 to 42 days. Both sexes guard the chicks, which may remain as a family for 12 months. Nests are usually spaced about 2 kilometers ($1^{1}/_{4}$ miles) apart, but in dense bush they may be closer than that, and on the plains, they may be more widely spaced.

Large concentrations of ostriches occur daily around water or where food is abundant, and immatures are found in flocks of up to 100 birds. The ostrich's diet is a selection of fruits, seeds, succulent leaves, and the growing pails of shrubs, herbs, and grasses. They also take small vertebrates.

Fig. 13.1. Struthio camelus (Ostrich).

The South American Families

The two representative families of ratites in South America, the rheas and the tinamous, total 47 species and inhabit a variety of habitats from forest, to the high antiplano (puna) of the Andes.

Rheas

Rheas are sometimes called South American ostriches. The greater rhea *Rhea americana* stands about 1.5 meters (5 feet) tall and weighs 20 to 25 kilograms (44 to 55 pounds). The lesser rhea *Pterocnemia pennata* is smaller. Both species have gray or gray-brown plumage, with large wings that cover the body like a cloak. When they run rheas sometimes spread their wings, which then act as sails, but the birds are unable to fly.

The original distribution of the two species was unusual. The greater rhea lived on the plains from northeastern Brazil to central Argentina, but its range has been dissected by agricultural development. The lesser rhea has two separate populations: one on the pampas (grasslands) of Patagonia, known as Darwin's rhea; and the other in the high Andes of southern Peru and northern Chile, the puna rhea.

Rhea males fight for territories, and once a male has established his domain he builds a nest, a scrape on the ground lined with leaves and grass. To this he attracts females, often as a small flock. Each female lays an egg in the nest, returning to do so every two or three days until the male, responding to the size of the clutch, drives them away and begins to incubate. Before and after the females lay in the nest, however, they lay eggs on the ground in the vicinity, some of which the male rolls beneath him; the others rot. Once he sits, the female flock goes off to attend another male and may serve half a dozen nests in a season. The cock leads the chicks, which grow quickly and are of adult size in about six months but do not breed until they are two years old.

Tinamous

The 45 species of tinamou vary from the size of a quail to that of a large domestic fowl. While they show close relationships to other Struthioniformes in their anatomy, their eggwhite proteins, and the structure of their genes, they differ in some conspicuous ways. Many, perhaps all, species can fly, although they seldom do so; they usually escape predators by stealing away through cover or freezing. Most species have three toes, a common ratite number, but some have four. Members of the genus *Tinamus* roost in trees; all other tinamous roost on the ground. In *Tinamus* species the back of the tarsus is roughened to give the birds a good grip on the branch when at rest.

Many species feed on vegetable matter, but some (for example, *Nothoprocta* species) take much animal food, and the red-winged tinamou *Rhynchotus rufescens* digs for roots and termites. In some species (such as the ornate tinamou *Nothoprocta ornata*) a single male and female establish the nest, but in most a male associate with several females at nesting. Tinamous nest on the ground, lining a depression with grass and leaves, and like most ratites the male undertakes the incubation (19 days for *Eudromia*) and looks after the family. Tinamous are found in many habitats, including rainforest and the high and barren Andes. On the open tablelands the martineta tinamou *Eudromia elegans* lives in flocks of up to a hundred. Tinamous are diverse and abundant, an impressive achievement considering that they are now thought likely to be close to the ancestral stock of all ratites.

Emu and Cassowaries

The Australian emu Dromaius novaehollandiae lives a nomadic existence, continually moving to keep in touch with its food—not that the food moves, but rather that abundances of flowers, fruits, seeds, insects, and the young shoots on which it feeds appear in random sequence in the Australian deserts. Emus, standing 2 meters ($6^1/_2$ feet) tall and weighing up to 45 kilograms (100 pounds), move over vast distances, usually as monogamous pairs, stopping when they find abundant food and moving again when it is exhausted. Only when the male undertakes the eight weeks of incubation is it impossible for him to move to find food. During incubation he does not eat, drink, or defecate, living instead on the fat reserves he has built up in the previous six months. If conditions have not allowed the pair to store fat before the winter breeding season, they do not breed, or if eggs are laid the male may desert them before they hatch. The male guards the chicks and leads them for their first seven months and sometimes longer. The female may remain nearby, or move far away in search of food, or mate with another male. Seldom do the pair re-form for a second season.

Emus live throughout southern Australia, not just in deserts. They become less common in the north, although a few birds can be found as far north as Darwin and Cape York. Their numbers, currently estimated at about 500,000, can rise or fall rapidly in correlation with wet and dry seasons. They are common in coastal scrub, in eucalypt woodland, and on saltbush plains. A few venture into alpine heath, and many are still present in farming areas provided some bush land remains.

Cassowaries favour jungle. Three species live in New Guinea, and one of these, the double-wattled cassowary *Casuarius casuarius*, also lives in the tropical rainforests of far northeastern Queensland, Australia. In New Guinea the original distribution of the three species is uncertain because humans have transported them and released them beyond their natural range. It is likely that the double-wattled cassowary favoured mid-level rain forest, the one-wattled cassowary *C. unappendiculatus* low-level rainforest, and the dwarf cassowary (or moruk) *C. bennetti* the highlands, perhaps even the montane grasslands. Several islands around New Guinea have cassowary populations, usually of one species—for example, the double-wattled cassowary on Ceram and the moruk on New Britain. The double-wattled cassowary stands 1.5 meters (5 feet) tall and may weigh more than 55 kilograms (120 pounds). Its glossy black plumage grows after the first year; before that the young birds are clad in a sober gray. All species have throat wattles, brilliant red and blue in adults but less colourful in immatures. The moruk does not have a distinct casque, but a casque adorns the heads of the other two species. Cassowaries depend on forest fruits for food— fruits from more than 75 species of tree in northern Queensland. Individuals seem to maintain a territory of 1 to 5 square kilometers ($^1/_3$ to 2 square miles), moving around it to gather fruit as different trees ripen. The territory is occupied by pairs during the winter breeding season, and the clutch of six to eight eggs is incubated for about two months by the male, who also looks after the young chicks Cassowaries are not abundant anywhere, and their survival will be imperiled if the diversity of the forests in which they live is reduced by logging.

Kiwis, The Burrowing Ratites

Three species of kiwi remain in New Zealand: the brown kiwi *Apteryx australis* is the largest, 55 centimeters (21 inches) long, with females weighing 3.5 kilograms ($7^3/_4$ pounds); the great spotted kiwi *A. haastii*, intermediate in size; and the little spotted kiwi *A. owenii*, 35 centimeters (14 inches) long, weighing 1.2 kilograms ($2^1/_2$ pounds). The brown kiwi is still found on North, South and Stewart Islands, the great spotted only on South Island, and the little spotted on Kapiti Island, where it was introduced in 1913.

Kiwis are nocturnal, feeding on invertebrates which they find mainly by scent, probing with their long and sensitive bills. Pairs form during the late winter/spring breeding season, and the male excavates a burrow in which the female deposits one to three white eggs. Each egg is equivalent to 25 percent of the female's body weight, proportionately the largest egg laid by any bird. The eggs are incubated by the male for 78 to 82 days, and the chicks appear to be independent almost from the time they emerge from the burrow.

The call of the male brown kiwi is a shrill whistle with a long ascending phrase and a short descending one at the end giving rise to the name "kiwi". Females have a hoarse, low cry. Two anatomical features set kiwis apart from other ratites. Firstly, the wings—small in the emu and cassowaries—are vestigial in kiwis. Secondly, female kiwis have paired, functional ovaries—in most birds usually only the left is functional, and the right is absent altogether. All species live in native podocarp (southern conifer) forest, but the brown kiwi has survived in farmland and in pine forest, although it is still unclear if such populations are self-sustaining outside these natural forests.

PENGUINS

Penguins form a distinct group of highly specialized, social, flightless pelagic seabirds, widely distributed throughout the cooler waters of the southern oceans. The greatest concentrations and largest number of species occur in the sub-antarctic between latitudes 45° and 60°S, with the greatest diversity of species in the New Zealand area and around the Falkland Islands. Only two species are restricted to south of latitude 60°S in the Antarctic. Penguins are absent from the Northern Hemisphere, although the Galapagos penguin *Spheniscus mendiculus* sometimes ranges slightly north of the Equator. Other species inhabit the mainland coasts and offshore islands of Australia, New Zealand, Patagonia, Tierra del Fuego extending northward to Peru, and offshore islands of southwestern Africa. Although most penguins inhabit regions free of terrestrial predators, at sea they must contend with such efficient aquatic predators as carnivorous leopard seals and killer whales. In some areas, skilled aerial predators such as skuas take substantial numbers of chicks and eggs.

Underwater Swimmers

Penguins have remained essentially unchanged for at least 45 million years. Although flightless, they evolved from flying birds. The most aquatic of all birds, some species may spend up to three-quarters of their life in the sea, coming ashore only to breed and molt. Many are migratory. With wings that have evolved into stiffened, flattened, paddle-like flippers, penguins are supreme swimmers. The only other birds that swim underwater using their wings rather than feet are auks and their allies (the Northern Hemisphere counterparts of penguins) and diving petrels. While penguins can attain speeds of up to 24 kilometers per hour (15 miles per hour) during brief stints, they generally swim at 5 to 10 kilometers per hour (3 to 6 miles per hour). They are by far the most accomplished of avian divers. The emperor penguin *Aptenodytes forsteri* can dive to 540 meters (1,772 feet) and remain submerged for more than 20 minutes. Even much smaller species such as the gentoo penguin *Pygoscelis papua* dive to depths exceeding 150 meters (500 feet). Penguins feed on fish, krill, and other small invertebrates, and cephalods (squid), which are captured and consumed underwater.

All penguins are faced with thermoregulatory challenges: the polar penguins must conserve heat, whereas the temperate and tropical species have to shed excess heat. Thus the well-insulated south polar penguins generally have relatively smaller appendages, and feathering may extend well down on the bill. Conversely the tropical penguins have larger appendages and bare skin about the face which, when flushed, provides a mechanism for dissipating excess heat. No other group of birds is forced to endure air temperatures ranging from -60°C (-75°F) during the dark Antarctic winter to more than 40°C (105°F) at the Equator. Penguins depend on the insulative quality of their overlapping feathers to maintain their body temperature, the dense waterproof layer effectively trapping warm air. During the annual molt, when all feathers are lost simultaneously, a penguin is not waterproof and must come ashore or onto the ice. Molting birds cannot enter the sea to feed and therefore during the molt period of three to six weeks the fasting birds may lose a third or more of their body weight.

Like most seabirds, penguins tend to be rather long-lived, although juvenile mortality may be high. In the breeding season most species are highly territorial, but the emperor penguin forms large "huddles" during the winter. Some species do not become accomplished breeders until their tenth year. Upon hatching, the chicks are down-covered but are dependent on the adults for warmth and protection. Chicks are fed via regurgitation, and in surface colonies the parents recognize their young by voice.

The Six Genera

The two largest and most colourful species, the king and emperor penguins, are both included in the genus Aptenodytes. Unlike other penguins which typically produce two-egg clutches, both lay a single egg which is incubated on top of the feet and covered by a muscular fold of abdominal skin. The emperor penguin is unique in that it breeds during the height of the dark Antarctic winter; only the males incubate for the entire incubation period of 62 to 67 days; and colonies are typically located on the annual fast ice, thus the emperor penguin is the only bird (under normal conditions) never to set foot on solid ground. The fasting period of 110 to 115 days endured by incubating males is the longest for any bird.

The smaller but more colourful king penguin *A. patagonicus*, of subantarctic regions, weighs nearly 20 kilograms (44 pounds) and is

Fig. 13.2. Rockhopper penguin.

capable of producing only two chicks in a three-year period. The chicks spend the winter in large groups known as creches where they are fed sporadically, and many perish. The chicks require nine to thirteen months to fledge, the longest fledging period of any bird. Formerly exploited for their oil, most king penguin colonies have recovered since being given legal protection.

The Adelie, gentoo, and chinstrap penguins are collectively referred to as the long-tailed penguins. The most familiar of penguins, the Adelie penguin *Pygoscelis adeliae* is essentially restricted to the Antarctic, where a minimum of $2^1/_2$ million pairs breed. The chinstrap penguin *P. antarctica* occurs in an area known as the Scotia Arc, extending from the tip of the Antarctic Peninsula and including the South Shetland, South Orkney, and South Sandwich islands, and South Georgia. The gentoo penguin *P. papua* inhabits mainly the subantarctic although some breed along the north coast of the Antarctic Peninsula.

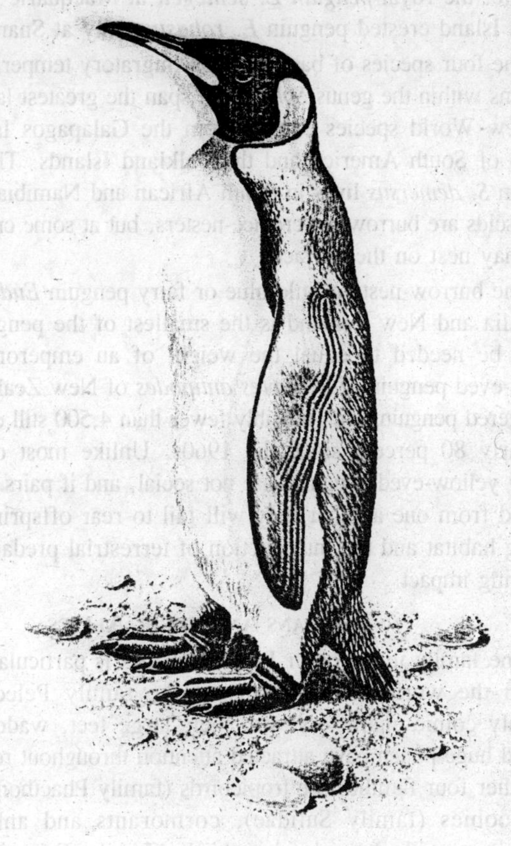

Fig. 13.3. King penguin.

All three species nest during the southern spring and summer, October to February The migratory Adelie penguin winters in the pack ice, whereas wintering chinstraps favour open water. Some gentoo penguin populations remain near their colonies year round, but others disperse widely.

The six species of thick-billed crested penguins (genus *Eudyptes*) are essentially circumpolar throughout the subantarctic, and adults are characterized by prominent orange or yellow crests. All species lay dissimilar-sized two-egg clutches, and although some (at least three species) may hatch out two chicks, none is capable of fledging both young. Several species have very restricted breeding ranges—for example, the royal *penguin E. schlegeli* at Macquarie Island, and the Snares Island crested penguin *E. robustus* only at Snares Island.

The four species of basically non-migratory temperate and tropical penguins within the genus *Spheniscus* span the greatest latitudinal range: the New World species extend from the Galapagos Islands south to the tip of South America and the Falkland Islands. The black-footed penguin *S. demersus* lives in South African and Namibian waters. Most spheniscids are burrow- or crevice-nesters, but at some crowded colonies they may nest on the surface.

The burrow-nesting little blue or fairy penguin *Eudyptula minor* of Australia and New Zealand is the smallest of the penguins—up to 30 would be needed to equal the weight of an emperor penguin. The yellow-eyed penguin *Megadyptes antipodes* of New Zealand is the most endangered penguin, with possibly fewer than 4,500 still extant, a decline of nearly 80 percent since the 1960s. Unlike most other penguins, nesting yellow-eyed penguins are not social, and if pairs are not visually isolated from one another they will fail to rear offspring. The loss of nesting habitat and the introduction of terrestrial predators have had a damaging impact.

Pelicans and their Allies

One family in the order Pelecaniformes is particularly well known around the world—the pelicans of the family Pelecanidae. These ungainly comic characters with their large feet, waddling gait, long bill and huge pouch have attracted attention throughout recorded history. The other four families are tropicbirds (family Phaethonitidae), gannets and boobies (family Sulidae), cormorants and anhingas (family Phalacrocoracidae), and frigatebirds (family Frigatidae). The one characteristic that unites these diverse families is their totipalmate feet: all four toes are connected by a web. The most familiar feature of the group is probably the large naked throat (gular) sac, which can be spectacular in pelicans and male frigatebirds, but is entirely absent in the tropicbirds.

Nesting in Colonies

While primarily marine birds, pelecaniforms are found in all types of water environments from the open ocean and sea coasts to lakes, swamps, and rivers. Pelicans and cormorants may switch between fresh water and salt water during the year. For example, the American white pelican *Pelecanus erythrorhynchos* nests inland and migrates to coastal waters during the non-breeding season. Most species inhabit tropical and temperate regions, but several species of gannets and cormorants live in Antarctic and subantarctic waters.

Pelecaniforms commonly live more than 20 years, and many return faithfully to the same nest site each year, mating with the same individual. All species are colonial to some extent, nesting with members of their own type, in isolated places such as on islands. Cormorants and gannets often build their nests within a few inches of each other. Aggressive interactions between neighbours are frequent in these dense colonies as each pair defends a space around their own nest. In contrast, masked booby colonies are often loose associations of birds nesting 6 to 60 meters (20 to 200 feet) apart. Frequently, a single colony will have two or three, or more, different pelecaniform species nesting in it.

In all species, both parents share incubation and chick-rearing duties. An individual's shift of sitting on the egg(s) varies from a few hours to more than a week, according to the nesting locale and the species. When the mate returns from feeding, the pair may go through a brief greeting display, allowing mate recognition and reinforcing the pair bond. If the incubating bird does not relinquish its duties, the returning bird, seemingly impatient to begin, may sit beside the bird on the nest and begin gently pushing it off. Incubation takes four to seven weeks depending on the species, and the adults either wrap the eggs in their large webbed feet or tuck them into the breast feathers to provide warmth. They do not have a brood patch. Chicks hatch naked in all pelecaniforms except the tropicbirds, whose single chick is covered by thick, fluffy grayish to white down when it hatches. Chicks must be carefully shaded from the hot sun during the day and kept warm at night. After two to three weeks, chicks are covered with down. By four to six weeks, they are often left alone while both parents forage for food. Adults regurgitate meals directly into the chicks' mouths—birdwatchers may wonder how any of the chicks get fed, when three nestling pelicans all have their long bills jammed into one parent's throat. Pelecaniform birds feed primarily on fish, but squid and other invertebrates and even other birds' eggs and small chicks may be eaten. In years when food is plentiful, more than one chick may be raised in species that lay more than one egg.

The air-sac system, which enables birds to have a continuous supply of oxygenated air passing through the lungs both when breathing out and when breathing in, is very extensive in many pelecaniforms. It also branches extensively across the chest and lower neck, making this area feel soft and cushioned to the touch. This padding may provide a shock absorber to species that dive into the water from the air (tropicbirds, pelicans, gannets, and boobies) and may provide extra buoyancy.

Tropicbirds

Tropicbirds differ in many characteristics and behaviours from other pelecaniforms, while sharing the defining character of the order: totipalmate feet, in which four toes (instead of three toes as in many other species) are connected by webs. They are widely distributed in tropical and subtropical seas, occurring in the Caribbean, Atlantic, Pacific, and Indian oceans, and are not seen on land during the non-breeding season. The three species (genus *Phaeton*) are similar in appearance, being white, with some black on the head, back, and primaries. They all have two long central tail feathers.

Amazingly, tropicbirds cannot walk—their legs are located too far back on the body—and to move on land they push forward with both feet and plop on the belly. They perform their courtship rituals in the air, flying around in groups of two to twelve or more, squawking loudly. A pair will land and push their way into their potential nest site, a hole in a cliff or under a bush, where they sit and squawk at each other, somehow deciding whether or not to form a pair. Tropicbirds are often referred to as boatswain birds, presumably because their harsh call is reminiscent of a boatswain's yell. They are plunge divers, diving into the water from varying heights to catch their fish or squid prey.

Pelicans

All seven species of these fascinating birds have the characteristic pouch, long bill, and long neck. The adults of five species are primarily white, with some black in the primary and secondary feathers. The gray or spot-billed pelican *Pelecanus philippensis* is light gray with some black primaries. The brown pelican *P. occidentalis* has a very complicated sequence of annual adult plumage changes: it is silver gray on the back, with a black belly, white head, and white neck, but at different times of the year, depending on the breeding stage, the neck is chocolate brown and/or the head is yellow, and the pouch varies in colour.

Most pelicans nest near and feed in fresh water, although all species are able to feed in either fresh or salt water. The brown pelican is the only marine species and is the only one to dive from

Fig. 13.4. Brown pelican.

varying heights into the water to catch a meal. The other species all feed as they sit on the surface, dipping down into the water with their bill and extensible pouch. Groups of pelicans will herd fish into shallow water where they are more easily caught. Brown pelicans especially are known to scavenge for meals around fishing piers and boats, unfortunately contributing to their decline in many places as they easily become entangled in fishing line which later snags on rocks or trees.

Adult pelicans are essentially voiceless, and courtship involves the use of "body language" (visual displays) rather than vocalization. Males pick a nest site in the colony—pink-backed *P. rufescens* and spot-billed pelicans mainly in trees; Australian *P. conspicillatus*, great white *P. onocrotalus*, Dalmatian *P. crispus*, and American white pelicans on the ground, and brown pelicans either in trees or on the ground—where they display by posturing, primarily with the head and neck, as females fly over. When a female is attracted, the two go through a series of coordinated displays. Once mated, the male brings nest material to the female who builds the nest. The number of birds in a colony ranges from as few as five pairs to several thousand. A large pelican colony is very noisy because chicks do have a voice and use it loudly to beg for food from their parents.

Gannets and Boobies

The three species of gannets live primarily in temperate regions, while the six species of boobies range throughout the tropical and subtropical regions of the world. Most boobies and gannets have a white head, neck, and underside, and are white with varying degrees of brown or black on the back. Colours of the soft parts of the bill and feet vary from bright sky-blue in the blue-footed booby *Sula nebouxii* to vivid red in the red-footed booby *S. sula*. Plumages are similar in both sexes, except the eastern Pacific subspecies of brown booby *S. leucogaster*, in which females have brown heads that match the body, and males have lighter brown to white heads. Male gannets are larger than females, but the reverse is true for boobies.

Fig. 13.5. Blue-footed booby.

It is thought that the name "booby" is derived from the Spanish word *bobo* meaning clown or stupid fellow. Courtship can involve much parading around, lifting of the head up high, mutual preening, fencing with bills, and tossing of heads. When seen, it does make the booby's name seem appropriate. Only Abbott's *Papasula abbotti* and red-footed boobies nest in trees, building a nest of twigs which may be lined with some leafy vegetation. The others lay their egg(s) on bare ground or build a nest of twigs, debris, or dirt.

Gannets and boobies dive like missiles, often from amazing heights, into the water to capture fish and squid, feeding alone or in flocks. Sometimes gannets may even pursue fish underwater, moving with powerful feet and half-opened wings. A few boobies are reported to be kleptoparasitic, chasing other boobies until they regurgitate, then stealing the meal.

Cormorants and Anhingas

Most of the 28 species of cormorants (also known as shags) and four species of anhinga (or darters) live in tropical and temperate areas, but some inhabit colder Antarctic and Arctic waters. Some species are solely freshwater, others solely marine, and some are found in both habitats. One member of the family, the Galapagos cormorant *Nannopterum harrisi*, cannot fly. It hops in and out of the water, scrambling up rock ledges to roost or get to its nest site on predator-free islands. Tree-nesting species construct nests of twigs, whereas species that nest on rock islands or cliff ledges use seaweed, or even guano and old bones, to build their nests. Cormorants form some of the largest and densest seabird colonies in the world which, as might be expected, produce great quantities of excreta. This guano is mined in some areas of the world for fertilizer.

Most cormorants and anhingas are black and may have an iridescent green or blue sheen, while others have striking white markings. Their diet is mostly fish but includes smaller amounts of squid, crustaceans, frogs, tadpoles, and insect larvae. They generally pursue their food by swimming underwater. The legs and feet, placed far back on the body, may not make walking easy but they make great propellers. The fish-catching ability of cormorants has been exploited by humans since the sixth century AD, and a few fishermen in Asia still keep trained flocks of cormorants. A collar is tied around the neck of each bird to prevent it from swallowing fish; then with a long line attached, the fishermen let the birds dive and catch fish, pulling them back to the boat and taking the fish when they resurface.

Frigatebirds

The five species of frigate bird range widely over tropical oceans during the non-nesting season and nest on isolated islands. All five are very similar in size and appearance: adult males are all black, except for the Christmas frigatebird *Fregeta andrewsi* and the lesser frigatebird *F. ariel* which have some white on the ventral side. Females are the larger sex, and all have some white markings on the underside, except the Ascension frigatebird *F. aquila* which is dark. Males pick out a nest site and sit in groups with other males, all with the large red gular sac expanded like a huge red balloon. When a female flies over, the males begin bill-clattering, whinnying, and fluttering the wings. Females land and display with various males until a pair determines they are "compatible". The male then begins bringing nest material to the female, frequently stealing twigs from unwatchful neighbours. A single egg is laid.

Frigatebirds probably have the longest chick-rearing period of any bird. The young begin to fly at five to six months but return to the nest to be fed until they are up to a year old. Flying juveniles are often seen "playing" with sticks or other items around the colony. One will dip down, picking up a stick from the ground, and others will pursue it, agilely coming at the young bird from all directions trying to grab the stick. The bird drops the stick. which may be picked up by another juvenile, often before it hits the ground, and the chase is on again. They are no doubt learning an important skill for catching their own meals.

Walking is impractical for frigatebirds because they have very short legs and small feet, and the very long tail drags if they land on the ground. Some ornithologists have suggested that they do not sit on the water because their feathers are not well waterproofed. With their large wings (wingspan up to 2.5 meters, or 8 feet), small feet, and small body, they do have a very difficult time taking off from water, getting the wings at the correct angle for flapping and eventual flying. Frigatebirds therefore feed on the wing, grabbing fish or squid from near the surface of the water or catching flying fish. With their huge wing area and light weight, they have the lowest wingloading of any bird measured and can remain in the air for days. They also have incredible maneuverability and often chase and harrass other birds, particularly boobies, causing them to regurgitate and then stealing the meal.

Threats to Survival

The severest threats to pelecaniforms are caused by humans: disturbance of nesting colonies, and destruction of nesting habitat. The taking of birds for food causes the loss of many individuals. Predators such as rats, cats, and pigs introduced to islands continue to destroy breeding colonies ground-nesters are particularly susceptible. Organochlorine pesticides such as DDT, which cause pelicans and other fish-eating birds to lay thin-shelled eggs that crush during incubation, are legally restricted, but the organophosphate pesticides now used are also highly toxic to birds. Oil spills and other water pollution cause local mortality. Pelicans are the most endangered of pelecaniforms, probably because they live in close proximity to humans. Safe nesting habitats and unpolluted food sources are critical to their survival.

Pigeons and Sandgrouse

There are two quite different families of birds within this order, and They may not even be closely related. Pigeons and doves of the family Columbidae are basically seed-and fruit-eating, tree-dwelling, terrestrial birds, occurring throughout the world except in the high Arctic and classified in more than 300 species. Less well known are the 16 species of sandgrouse of the family Pteroclididae, which are desert-dwellers of Africa and Eurasia. Scientists argue frequently about whether they are related to pigeons at all, some suggesting they are

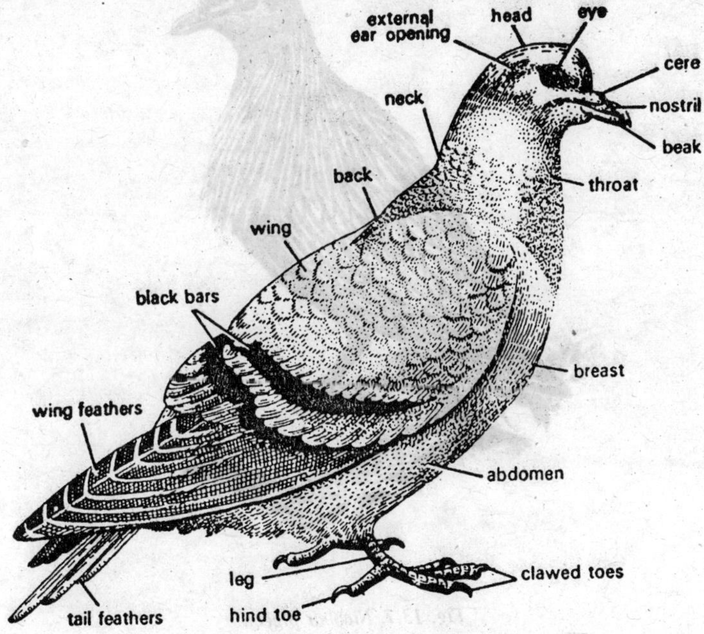

Fig. 13.6. Pigeon (Columba livia). External features.

waders (Charadriiformes), others that they should form their own order. A third family, Raphidae, now extinct, consisted of the dodo and two related species of the Mascarene Islands in the Indian Ocean.

Sandgrouse

Sandgrouse are medium-sized birds, specialized for a life in the deserts and semi-arid regions of Africa and Eurasia. They have dull, well-camouflaged brown, gray or khaki-coloured plumage and are compact and streamlined, with small heads and short necks. The tops of their feet are densely clothed in feathers. Males and females have different plumages. Their adult feathers are similar to those of pigeons; and like pigeons (and unlike most other birds) they can drink by sucking, although less expertly than pigeons—they have to raise their heads to swallow. They differ from pigeons, however, in several important ways: they cannot produce crop milk; they have a pair of large functional ceca (pouches, or blind tubes, forming the beginning of the large intestine); they have a different syrinx or voice-box; and they have oil-glands that produce an oil which is used to preen the feathers.

Fig. 13.7. Nicobar pigeon.

They are very strong and fast fliers, the Namaqua sandgrouse *Pterocles namaqua* of the deserts of southern Africa being able to outpace a falcon in level flight. They need to drink regularly and may have to commute over 60 kilometers (37 miles) to water. A typical species is the pin-tailed sandgrouse *P. alchata* of North Africa, Spain, the Middle East, and Central Asia west of the Caspian Sea. Flocks of at least 50,000 have been recorded at waterholes in Turkey. In the breeding season, March to May, they break up into pairs, then gradually congregate again in flocks after the young fledge in September.

Fig. 13.8. Pin-tailed sandgrouse.

Sandgrouse nest on the ground, and the young leave the nest a few hours after hatching. The chicks take every opportunity to shield themselves from the hot sun and even shelter under their parents while moving. As a protection against predators they half-bury themselves in the sand under the shade of bushes. Sandgrouse have a unique way of watering their young: the male flies to a waterhole and wades in with his feathers lifted; the central feathers soak up water, then the male returns to his family where the chicks drink from his wet feathers.

Pigeons and Doves

About three-quarters of the 304 species of pigeons and doves live in tropical and subtropical regions. The term "pigeon" is used for larger species, and "dove" for the smaller, more delicately built ones. They are medium-sized to small birds which feed on seeds and fruits. Most are tree-dwelling, yet some of the common species feed in huge

Fig. 13.9. Superb fruit dove.

nocks on the ground. The plumage is soft and dense, and the feathers have characteristically thick shafts and fluffy bases. They have no, or very small, oilglands—instead, special plumes disintegrate to produce powder that cleanses and lubricates the plumage. The most specialized feature of the family is the ability to produce crop milk: when the birds are breeding, special glands in the crops of both male and female enlarge and secrete a thick milky substance which is fed to the young.

The sexes are usually similar in appearance, but some species have different male and female plumages. Pigeons and doves have characteristic sexual and advertising displays, such as bowing, and special display flights. Their calls are usually pleasant cooing notes. All species build flimsy nests of a few sticks in trees, or on the ground or on ledges. One or two plain white eggs are laid, and the chicks are cared for by both sexes; they leave the nest in 7 to 28 days, depending on the species.

The common street pigeon or rock dove *Columba livia* has adapted well to agriculture and towns. It originally occurred in Eurasia and North Africa, where it nested colonially on cliffs, but it has easily made the transition from cliffs to buildings and now occurs in almost all the world's cities. But this rather drab species gives no indication of the diversity and brilliance of plumage in the family. For instance, the snow pigeon *C. leuconota* from the high plateaus of the Himalaya mountains is a striking white, black, and gray, and the Seychelles blue pigeon *Alectroenas pulcherrima* is deep metallic blue with silver-gray foreparts and a red head with naked wattles.

But perhaps the most beautiful are the 47 species of fruit dove (genus *Ptilinopus*) of the Indo-Pacific region. These smallish plump pigeons are spectacularly coloured with bright greens, brilliant reds and oranges, purples and pinks, blues and golds. They live high in the canopy of the rainforests, and some species are found only on single islands in the Pacific Ocean. Fiji, for example, has three very specialized species collectively called golden doves: the orange dove *P. victor* is fiery orange; the golden dove *P. luteovirens* is metallic greenish-gold; and the yellow-headed dove *P. layardi* is green with shining gold fringes to the feathers. Fruit doves eat only the fruits of rainforest trees and have specialized digestive systems—features they share with the 36 species of imperial pigeons (larger birds, in the genus *Ducula*) which have the same distribution. Most birds take grit that lodges in the crop and helps grind up food, but fruit doves and imperial pigeons do not take grit and have a thin gizzard with horny knobs which gently strips the flesh from the seeds. The seeds are defecated whole and so these birds act as important dispersers for rainforest trees.

The New Guinea rainforests are the home of some spectacular birds such as the three species of crowned pigeon in the genus *Goura*. The size of small turkeys, they are the largest pigeons and are characterized by big filmy crests and subtle purple and gray plumage. They forage in small groups on the forest floor and, despite their size, nest up to 15 meters (50 feet) in trees. Elsewhere in the Pacific and Indian oceans pigeons have adapted well to life on islands. They have evolved into many distinctive species, and several frequently fly long distances between the islands in their range. The white and black Torresian imperial pigeon *Ducula spillorrhoa* migrates from New Guinea to northern Australia in August and breeds in huge colonies, mostly on the offshore islands of the Great Barrier Reef. While there, flocks of several thousand birds fly to the rainforests of the mainland every day to feed; in March they return to New Guinea.

In Asia and Africa, the aptly named green pigeons (genus Treron) replace the fruit doves and imperial pigeons as the arboreal fruit-eating species in the tropical forests. They lack the specialized gut, however, and grind up the seeds of the fruits they eat. Elsewhere, in Eurasia and the Americas, the various pigeons are less specialized and less spectacularly plumaged. Many pigeons are gregarious and form small to large flocks. Flocks of up to 100,000 wood pigeons *Columba palumbus* have been recorded in Germany, and the eared dove *Zenaida auriculata* of South America breeds in huge colonies of tens of thousands of birds. The flock pigeon *Phaps histrionica* of semi-arid north and central Australia occasionally irrupts in huge nocks of thousands of birds; nineteenth-century explorers described the noise of the flocks as deafening, like "the roar of distant thunder".

Driven to Extinction

Nothing symbolizes human treatment of wildlife and the need for conservation better than the tragic extermination of the dodo *Raphus cucullatus*. It was discovered in 1507 and exterminated by 1680. The dodo of Mauritius was one of three species of massive, flightless, highly aberrant birds on the remote Mascarene Islands, east of Madagascar in the Indian Ocean. Presumably, they derived from pigeon-like ancestors that flew to the islands.

The strange dodo was ash gray with a reddish tinge to its black bill and weighed about 23 kilograms (50 pounds). Its wings were reduced to useless stubs and it had no defense against, or means of escape from, the seafarers who killed it for food, sport, and because they thought it abominably ugly. The pigs, cats, rats, and monkeys that were introduced to the islands may have contributed to its extinction, but basically it fell victim to human persecution.

The very similar white solitaire *R. solitarius* of neighbouring Reunion Island was wiped out in the same way by about 1750, but the Rodriguez solitaire *Pezophaps solitaria* managed to survive until perhaps 1800. There are few accounts of the behaviour and biology of these species and, indeed, few specimens in museums. They supposedly laid one egg each year, were vegetarian, used their stubby wings for fighting, and were agile runners despite their size and gross proportions.

Like the dodo, the North American passenger pigeon *Ectopistes migratorius* was hunted to extinction. But unlike the dodo, the passenger pigeon was found over much of a continent and was incredibly abundant, possibly the most numerous bird in the world. When white people first came to North America there may have been three to five thousand million or more of the species.

Passenger pigeons underwent irregular migrations within their huge range and were not abundant every year. In good years, however, flocks reached staggering proportions. In 1871 one flock seen over Wisconsin occupied 2,000 square kilometers (850 square miles) and contained 136 million birds; in 1810 a single flock of two and a quarter billion birds was seen in Kentucky; and in Ontario a flight of birds moving north from the United States in 1866 was 480 kilometers (300 miles) long and 1.6 kilometers (1 mile) wide and continued for 14 hours. Possibly there were three billion birds in it.

Forest clearing obviously hastened the decline of this species, but the passenger pigeon was exterminated by relentless slaughter just as the bison almost was. Birds were shot, trapped, and poisoned in millions; at one nesting colony in Michigan alone 25,000 birds were killed daily for market during the breeding season of 1874. Over 700,000 a month! Even the commonest bird in the world could not sustain such obscene carnage indefinitely. By the 1880s the species was close to extinction, and the last passenger pigeon died in Cincinnati Zoo on September 1,1914. Thus passed one of the greatest wildlife spectacles witnessed by modem man.

The dodo, the solitaire, and the passenger pigeon have not been the only species in this order to suffer extinction. The Mauritius blue pigeon *Alectroenas nitidissisma*, Norfolk Island dove *Gallicolumba norfolciensis*, tanna ground dove *G. ferruginea*, bonin wood pigeon *Columba versicolor*, and the silverbanded black pigeon *C. jouyi* have all been exterminated. The small, beautiful, Solomon Islands crowned pigeon *Microgoura meeki* is probably extinct, and many other species, perhaps all those or the small islands of the Pacific where forests are being cleared, are endangered. For such an inoffensive group of birds, pigeons have suffered badly at the hands of humans.

Parrots

Probably no group of birds is more widely known to the general public than the parrots. Indeed, one species—the budgerigar from inland Australia—rivals goldfish as the most popular pet animal in the world. The popularity of keeping parrots as pets dates from early recorded history: rose-ringed parakeets were known to the ancient Egyptians, and it was probably Alexander the Great who introduced tame parrots from the Far East to Europe. Today, the international trade in live parrots has reached alarming proportions, and there is virtually no city or town without a pet shop selling budgerigars, cockatiels, or lovebirds.

Bright Birds in Bold Plumage

Parrots belong to a very distinct order of ancient lineage and are strongly differentiated from other groups of birds. Some distinguishing features are obvious to even a casual observer; most prominent is the short blunt bill with a down curved upper mandible fitting neatly over a broad, upcurved lower mandible. This unique design enables parrots to crush the seeds and nuts that constitute the diet of most species.

Another conspicuous characteristic is the typical parrot foot, with two toes pointing forward and two turned backward. Parrots show remarkable dexterity, using their feet for climbing or for holding food up to the bill. The skull is broad and relatively large, with a spacious brain cavity. The extremely muscular tongue is thick and prehensile, and in lorikeets of the subfamily Loriinae it is tipped with elongated papillae for harvesting pollen and nectar from blossoms.

Parrots are renowned for the generally brilliant colouration of their plumage. There are plain or dull-coloured parrots, such as the two *Coracopsis* species from Madagascar, but these are few. Green

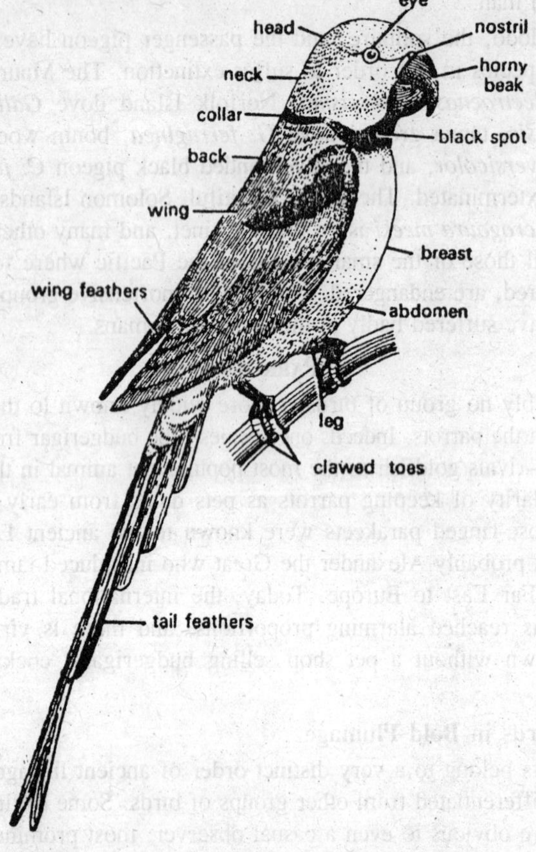

Fig. 13.10. Psittacula (Parrot).

predominates in most species, and is effective as camouflage amidst foliage in the rainforest canopy where many species live. Bold markings, mainly of red, yellow, and blue, are prevalent on the head or wings, and many species have brightly-coloured rumps. Unusual plumage patterns are present in the spectacular *Anodorhynchus* and *Cyanopsitta* macaws from South America and some *Vini* lories from the Pacific Islands, all of which are entirely or almost entirely blue, while bright yellow predominates in the plumage of the golden conure *Aratinga guarouba* from Brazil, and the regent parrot *Polytelis anthopeplus* and yellow rosella *Platycercus flaveolus* from Australia. Some *Ara* macaws from Central and South America are almost entirely red, as are some lories from the Indonesian archipelago.

The sexes generally are alike, though females may be appreciably duller, but the eclectus parrot *Eclectus roratus* of Australia. is notable in that the bright green males are strikingly different from the predominantly red females.

Variations on a Theme

Despite the homogeneity of their basic features, parrots come in all shapes and sizes. Tails may be long and pointed, as in the long-tailed parakeet *Psittacula longicauda* from Malaysia and the princess parrot *Polytelis alexandrae* from Australia, or short and squarish as in the short-tailed parrot *Graydidascalus brachyurus* and some *Touit* parrotlets from South America, or there may be ornate feathers as in the Papuan lory *Charmosyna papou* from New Guinea or the *Prioniturus* racket-tailed parrots from Indonesia and the Philippines. Wings can be narrow and pointed, as in the swift parrot *Lathamus discolour* and the cockatiel *Nymphicus hollandicus* from Australia, or broad and rounded, as in the *Amazona* parrots from South America. Prominent erectile head-crests distinguish the cockatoos, which are placed in the separate family Cacatuidae. Other parrots may have elongated feathers on their crowns or hindnecks.

Even in the characteristic bill there are variations in shape, which represent modifications for different feeding habits. A curved, less elongated upper mandible enables the slender-billed corella *Cacatua tenuirostris* of Australia to dig up roots and corms, while similarly-shaped bills of the slender-billed conure *Enicognathus leptorhynchus* of South America and the red-capped parrot *Purpureicephalus spurius* of Australia seem to be ideal for extracting seeds from large nuts. Parrots that feed extensively on pollen, nectar, or soft fruits tend to have narrow, protruding bills.

Distribution and Habitats

Parrots live mainly in the Southern Hemisphere, and are most prevalent in tropical regions. Once the Carolina parakeet *Conuropsis carolinensis* of North America became extinct in the early part of this century, the northernmost species became the slaty-headed parakeet *Psittacula himalayana*, in eastern Afghanistan. The most southerly parrot is the Austral conure *Enicognathus ferrugineus*, which reaches Tierra del Fuego. The strongest representation of parrot species is in Australasia and South America, with 52 species recorded from Australia and 71 from Brazil, but in South America there is a marked uniformity of types. There are parrots in Asia, mainly on the Indian subcontinent, and in Africa, but representation in these regions is surprisingly low. The most widely distributed species is the rose-ringed parakeet *Psittacula krameri*, which occurs in Asia and northern Africa and has been introduced to parts of the Middle East and Southeast Asia. Most of the species with restricted ranges are confined to quite small islands. With a total area of some 21 square kilometers (8 square miles), the Antipodes Islands south of New Zealand are inhabited by two *Cyanoramphus* parrots; one of these, the Antipodes green parakeet *C. unicolour*, is endemic.

Parrots are particularly plentiful in lowland tropical rainforest, although in Australia and parts of South America open country is preferred by many species. While some species, especially those restricted to rainforest, show little capacity to withstand interference with their habitat, others have adapted remarkably well to the human impact and are commonly seen in parks, gardens, or even trees lining city streets. In Australia the galah *Eolophus roseicapillus* is plentiful in many towns and cities, while in downtown Sao Paulo, Brazil's largest city, small flocks of plain parakeets *Brotogeris tirica* can be seen in parks surrounded by towering buildings.

Parrots tend to be less common at higher altitudes, and species that occur there normally are absent from or are rare in neighbouring lowlands.

Distinctive highland forms include the Johnstone's lorikeet *Trichoglossus johnstoniae* in the Philippines, the Derbyan parakeet *Psittacula derbiana* in Tibet, and the yellow-faced parrot *Poicephalus flavifrons* in Ethiopia. Possibly the most interesting of highland parrots is the kea *Nestor notabilis* from the Southern Alps of New Zealand; it is a species that has been much maligned because of its alleged sheep-killing habits.

Familiar and Unfamiliar Species

Parrots are difficult to observe in the wild. Most are predominantly green and live in the rainforest canopy, so sightings usually are little more than momentary glimpses of screeching flocks flashing overhead. Species that inhabit open country or are plentiful near human habitation are conspicuous, and there is much more information on their habits. We know a great deal, for example, about the habits of species such as the eastern rosella *Platycercus eximius* and red-rumped parrot *Psephotus haematonotus* in Australia, Meyers parrot *Poicephalus meyeri* in Africa, and the monk parakeet *Myiopsitta monachus* in South America, but virtually nothing about many forest-dwelling species in New Guinea, Central Africa, and South America.

The Australian night parrot *Pezoporus occidentalis* is nocturnal, and there are reports of some normally diurnal species being active on moonlit nights. Migration of swift parrots and *Neophema* species across Bass Strait, in southern Australia, usually takes place at night. In most parrots, patterns of daily activity are typical of birds in tropical regions: peak periods in the morning and toward evening, and low activity during the heat of the day. Many parrots are gregarious. Pairs and family parties come together to form flocks, which in arid areas may build up to enormous sizes after breeding has been brought on by favourable conditions. At such times, massive flocks of little corellas *Cacatua saguinea* and budgerigars darken the skies of inland Australia.

The flight of most parrots, especially the smaller ones, is swift and direct. Some have a characteristically undulating flight produced by wing beats being interspersed with brief periods of gliding. In the larger species it is variable; macaws are fairly fast fliers and their wing beats are shallow, but the buoyant flight of *Probosciger* and *Calyptorhynchus* cockatoos is conspicuously slow and labored. The kakapo *Strigops habroptilus* is the only flightless parrot.

The distinctly metallic call-notes of most parrots are harsh and unmelodic, generally being based on a simple syllable or combination of syllables. Variation comes primarily from the timing of repetition. Larger species normally have raucous, low-pitched calls, while small parrots give highpitched notes. The mimicry of captive parrots is well known, so it is surprising that there are very few convincing reports of wild birds imitating other species.

Food and Feeding

Most parrots eat seeds and fruits foraged from treetops or on the ground. Lories and lorikeets of the subfamily Loriinae are strictly arboreal, and feed on pollen, nectar, and soft fruits. Insects are often found in crop and stomach contents; woodboring larvae are an important food item for some of the black cockatoos from Australia. Mystery still surrounds the diet of *Micropsitta* pygmy parrots, which seem to take lichen from the trunks and branches of trees, but at times they have been observed foraging for termites.

When feeding, a parrot makes full use of its hooked bill; while climbing among foliage it often uses the bill to grasp a branch onto which it then steps. Many species use a foot as a "hand" to hold food up to the bill, and with the bill they expertly extract kernels from seeds and discard the husks.

Breeding Behaviour

The age at which parrots reach sexual maturity varies, but in general it is three or four years in larger species and one or two years in small birds. As far as can be ascertained from observations, most species are monogamous and the majority remain paired for long periods, perhaps for life. Notable exceptions are the kea, which is polygamous, and the kakapo, a lek-display species with males almost certainly taking no part in incubation or care of the young. Pairs and family groups are usually discernible within flocks. Courtship displays are simple, with bowing, wing-drooping, wing-flicking, tail-wagging, foot-raising, and dilation of the eye pupils being the more common actions.

Parrots usually nest in hollows in trees or holes excavated in termite mounds, occasionally in holes in banks, or in crevices among rocks and cliff-faces. The ground and night parrots from Australia and some populations of *Cyanoramphus* parakeets on New Zealand islands nest on the ground, usually under or in grass tussocks. Monk parrots from South America gather twigs to build a huge communal nest in a tree, and each pair has its own breeding chamber.

Eggs are normally laid every other day, and clutches vary from two to four or five, sometimes up to eight for small parrots. Incubation starts with or immediately after the laying of the second egg, but there is mounting evidence that this can vary individually. Generally the female alone incubates. The duration of incubation for small parrots is from 17 to 23 days, but for the large macaws it can be up to five weeks. Newly-hatched chicks are blind and naked or have sparse dorsal down, which in most species is white.

Young parrots develop slowly, and remain in the nest for three to four weeks in the case of the smallest species, and up to three or four months for the large macaws. After leaving the nest, young birds are fed by their parents for a brief time while learning to fend for themselves; young black cockatoos are fed by their parents for up to four months after leaving the nest.

Juveniles generally resemble females or are duller than either adult sex. There are species, such as the crimson rosella *Platycercus elegans* from Australia and some *Psittacula* species, that have a distinct juvenile plumage. A striking difference between adults and juveniles occurs in the vulturine parrot *Gypopsitta vulturina* from Brazil: in adults the bare head is sparsely covered with inconspicuous "bristles", but in juveniles the head is well covered with pale green feathers. The time taken for juveniles to attain adult plumage varies greatly between species; it may be within months of leaving the nest, or up to three or four years.

Conservation of Parrots

Ten extinct species of parrot are represented by specimens in museums, while others are known from subfossil material or reports in the writings of early explorers. Probably the best known of these extinct species is the Carolina parakeet; the last living bird died in the Cincinnati Zoo on February 21, 1918. Even for this species the causes of extinction will never be fully understood, but the loss is a warning that should be heeded if parrots are to be protected from the serious threats they now face in virtually all parts of their range. Habitat destruction is by far the most serious threat, especially the clearing of tropical forest. Of special concern are parrots confined to small islands, where the habitat is finite and cannot be extended.

Parrots are among the world's most endangered birds, in part because of the live-bird trade. Methods of capture are wasteful and often inhumane, and the levels of trapping are having severe impacts on populations already suffering from loss of habitat.

Owls, Frogmouths and Nightjars

The Strigiformes (owls) and Caprimulgiformes (frogmouths, night jars, and their allies), are both well-defined groups, and even for people with little ornithological training the members of each are instantly recognizable. The two orders share many characteristics and are thought to be distantly related. Both are crepuscular (twilight-active) and nocturnal (night-active). Their soft plumage is typically in "dead-leaf" and "mottled-bark" colours and patterns, which are most refined in night jars and frogmouths. Immobility and posture add to the effectiveness of their camouflage. With flattened feathers, bill tilted skyward, and eyes closed to a slit, a disturbed frogmouth is indistinguishable from the broken branch of a tree. So cryptic are the night jars as they crouch, roosting on the ground, that photographs of them become "find-the-hidden-bird" puzzles. The owls also flatten their plumage when slightly disturbed but with their longer legs and wider eyes they are more obvious; they roost in more hidden places and flush more readily than many of the caprimulgiforms.

Adapted to Dim Light

These birds are more often heard than seen; their distinctive calls, described as startling, strange, or weirdly beautiful, often carry across the countryside. Their calls and mysterious nocturnal habits have been the basis for much superstition, from shrieking ghosts to the ancient belief that the night jars steal milk from goats, hence one of their common names, goatsucker. In fact, they flit around goats and other livestock in pursuit of the insects attracted to them.

Life in dim light has led to some remarkable sensory adaptations: large eyes with good vision in poor light; and, in total darkness, navigation by echolocation (oil birds) and hunting by exceptional hearing (barn owls).

They all have rather large heads. Most species have large eyes: forward-facing in the owls for increased binocular vision; more laterally placed in the caprimulgiforms. Their eyes are specialized for vision in poor light, with more rods (light-sensitive elements) than diurnal (day-active) birds. Nevertheless, most species appear to need some light before they are able to hunt. While most species habitually hunt in poor light, they can see well by day and some occasionally hunt in daylight (for example, the barn owl *Tyto alba*, the burrowing owl *Athene cunnicularia*, and the barking owl *Ninox connivens*); the northern hawk-owl *Surnia ulula* is largely diurnal.

The remarkable barn owls (genus *Tyto*), with rather small eyes, have the most exceptional hearing. They are able to catch prey in total darkness, guided by sound alone. They and several other owls have facial masks to catch sound, and some have asymmetrical ear openings. Either the external feathering or the skull itself is modified so that sounds reach one ear at a slightly different time to the other; by turning its head the owl can locate the source or a low sound, such as a mouse chewing grain, very precisely. Oilbirds also have a remarkable adaptation for night navigation. They nest and roost gregariously, deep in caves. At night a mass of birds navigates through the cave by making audible (to humans) clicks and using the echoes that return to their ears to guide them from the cave; once outside they cease clicking.

Most species have soft, loose plumage, with frayed trailing edges to the flight feathers of their wings and tail, for noiseless hunting flight. Exceptions are the fishing owls (genus *Scotopelia*) of Africa and the oilbirds, which are hunters of fish and gatherers of fruit, respectively, presumably with little need for silent flight; both have firmer feathers.

The two groups differ most obviously in their bill and feet. The owls have a sharp, hooked bill and strong legs and feet, with sharp curved talons for their predatory lifestyle. The night jars and their allies have a broad flattened bill, an enormous gape, and small, weak feet and legs. Both orders have reversible outer toes and can perch with two toes forward, two back. The barn owls and the caprimulgiforms have a serrated edge on the talon of their middle toe, perhaps as an aid to grooming.

Owls

Currently, the owls are split into two families. All have rather long, broad wings.

Barn owls

Members of the family Tytonidae are medium-sized owls with heart-shaped faces, inner toes as long as their middle toes, and long bare legs. The bay owls (genus *Phodilius*) are currently placed in this family but may resemble barn owls (genus *Tyto*) only superficially.

Hawk-owls or True owls

The family Strigidae are small to large owls with rounded heads, large eyes, stout, sometimes feathered legs, and the inner toe shorter than the middle toe. Some show little sign of a mask; others are partially masked; and some have a full, rounded mask. Several species have two tufts of erectile feathers or "ears" which they can raise in emotion and which may help with concealment by disguising the owl's outline. One species, the maned owl *Jubula lettii* of west Africa and the Congo, has voluminous crown and nape feathers.

The female of most owl species is larger than the male, sometimes considerably so: female Tasmanian masked owls *Tyto novaehollandiae* weigh an average of 965 grams (34 ounces), males a mere 525 grams ($18^1/_2$ ounces). But, in some of the *Ninox* species, it is the male that is larger: for example, the female barking owl weighs 510 grams (18 ounces), the male 680 grams (24 ounces).

Nightjars and their Allies

The Caprimulgiformes are divided into five families.

Oilbird

The oilbird *Steatornis caripensis* is the sole member of the family Steatornithidae. It has a fan-like tail, long broad wings, and is dark brown with white spots and black bars. Adult size is about 30 centimeters (12 inches). In common with the other caprimulgiforms, it has a strong hook-tipped bill, a wide gape surrounded by bristles, and large eyes.

Frogmouths

Members of the family Podargidae are the largest of the caprimulgiforms. They have been described as the most grotesque of birds, with a great flat shaggy head dominating the body, which taper from it. The massive bill, surrounded by large tufts of facial bristles, as wide as it is long and heavily ossified (hardened like bone), acts as a heavy snap-trap. Their legs are short and weak.

Potoos

The potoos (family Nyctibiidae) resemble frogmouths in their arboreal roosting habit and colour pattern. Yet their broad, weakly ossified bill, which is surrounded by relatively few bristles, and their aerial hawking behaviour, ally them with the night jars.

Owlet-nightjars

These birds (family Aegothelidae) are somewhere between a night jar and an owl in appearance, but their closest relatives are the frogmouths. They have a broad flat bill almost hidden by bristles. Their feet are slightly stronger than those of the other caprimulgiforms, and their legs longer, perhaps because they run about more.

Nightjars

The nightjars (family Caprimulgidae) are a large group and comprise about half of the species in the Caprimulgiformes. They have long pointed wings and swift flight, a wide gape, stubby bill, and brightly coloured mouth (usually pink), shown in threat. Their legs and feet are weak, much reduced, and rarely used. The night jars are fairly uniform in appearance, but variations on the basic form include the standard-winged night jar *Macrodipteryx vexillaria* and pennant-winged night jar *M. longipennis*, which have extraordinary trailing feathers used in courtship, and the longtailed nightjar *Caprimulgus climacurus* with a long gradated tail; these three live in Africa. In North America, members of the subfamily Chordeilinae are called nighthawks.

Distribution and Habitats

Owls are cosmopolitan in distribution. They occur on all continents except Antarctica and are absent from some oceanic islands. *Strix* and *Otus* are widespread genera, the latter mostly in tropical areas; they do not occur in the Australia-Papua New Guinea region, where they are replaced by the genus *Ninox*. Some species such as the barn owl and the short-eared owl *Asio flammeus* are among the most widely distributed of all birds. In contrast, the Palau owl *Pyrrcglaux podargina* is found only on the Palau islands in the western Pacific Ocean. Habitat destruction and introduced animals have taken their toll and pushed some of these island owls toward extinction.

The majority of owl species inhabit woodlands and forest edges. A few species prefer treeless habitats: for example, the snowy owl *Nyctea scandiaca* of Arctic tundra regions, and the elf owl *Micrathene*

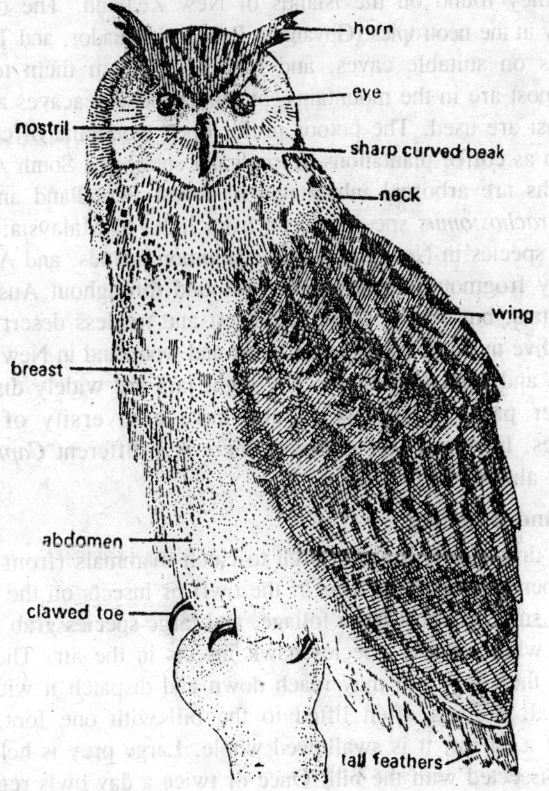

Fig. 13.11. Bubo bubo (Owl).

whitneyi of the southwestern deserts of the USA. Some, long-legged, species are terrestrial and live in flat grasslands (the grass owl *Tyto capensis* of Africa, and India to Australia) or marshes (the marsh owl *Asio capensis* of Africa), or among rocks. Various species can be found in most habitats, from tundra and desert to rainforest and swampland, from wilderness to the suburbs; the great horned owl *Bubo virginiatus* occurs in most habitats of North America. Some are more specific in their habitat requirements than others: the northern hawk owl lives in the northern conifer forests (taiga) of North America and Eurasia; the white-throated owl *Otus albogularis* is found in the cloud forests of the Andes; and the Peruvian screech owl *O. robaratus* likes habitat with mesquite and large cacti in arid parts of Peru.

The night jars and their allies have a similar distribution to owls but are not found at such high latitudes or on as many small islands. Nor are they found on the islands of New Zealand. The oilbird is found only in the neotropics (Guyana to Peru and Ecuador, and Trinidad); it depends on suitable caves, and ranges out from them to forage locally—most are in the mountains, but in Trinidad seacaves along the rocky coast are used. The potoos prefer open woodland of cultivated areas such as coffee plantations in tropical Central and South America. Frogmouths are arboreal inhabitants of forest, woodland and forest edge: *Batrachostomus* species occur from India to Malaysia; and the *Podargus* species in New Guinea, the Solomon Islands, and Australia. The tawny frogmouth *P. strigoides* is found throughout Australia in most habitats, but avoids dense rainforest and treeless desert. Owlet-night jars live in rainforest or open forest and woodland in New Guinea, Australia, and New Caledonia. The night jars are widely distributed in warmer parts of the world and have a diversity of habitat preferences. In Africa, for example, there is a different *Caprimulgus* species in almost every habitat.

Feeding and Breeding

Owls drop down from a perch to catch mammals (from mice to hares, depending upon the size of the owl) or insects on the ground. They also snatch insects from foliage, and large species grab arboreal mammals while smaller species hawk insects in the air. They catch prey with their feet and may reach down and dispatch it with a few bites. Small prey is often lifted to the bill with one foot, in the manner of a parrot; it is swallowed whole. Large prey is held in the feet and dissected with the bill. Once or twice a day owls regurgitate a pellet containing the fur, most bones, chitinous insect remains, and other indigestible parts of their prey.

The caprimulgiforms do not produce a pellet. Oilbirds hover to pluck a variety of fruits and seeds, which they locate by sight and scent. Frogmouths pounce from a perch to catch non-flying animal prey in their massive gape and heavy bill; they batter prey to soften it before swallowing it whole. Owlet-night jars take some insects and frogs on the ground and dart out to snatch termites, moths and other insects from the air. Most aerial of all are the fast flying night jars and nighthawks which commonly trawl, openmouthed, for airborne insects.

Since they are more often heard than seen, it is not surprising that many of these birds are named for the calls they make. All owls call, especially as the breeding season approaches. They have a variety of shrieks, hoots, and barks, which are typical of individual species. Several owls sing quite musically. Some screech-owls (genus *Otus*) duet, the male and female each taking turns to complete their section of a song. Caprimulgiforms also have a variety of far-carrying calls: low drumming in frogmouths; churring in owlet-night jars; and various other screams and shrieks, hence the name "night jar". However, some like the whip poor-will *Caprimulgus vociferus* of North America, make quite melodious whistles, and one African species, the fiery-necked night jar *C. pectoralis*, sings "Good Lord, deliver us".

Owls nest in a hole in a tree or cliff, an old building, or the old stick nest of a crow or raptor. The burrowing owl takes over a gopher hole, eagle owls sometimes dig a nest cavity in the side of an anthill, and the snowy owl nests on the open ground in a scrape to which it adds a little lining. A woodpecker hole, drilled in a cactus, is used by the the elf owl. Some caprimulgiforms build a nest. Regurgitated fruit, which sets firm, forms the oilbird's nest, which is built in recesses in the cave and added to each season. Frogmouths build a flimsy nest of sticks on a horizontal branch (*Podargus* species) or use a pad of down from the birds themselves, plus spider webs and lichen (*Batrachostomus* species). Owlet-night jars nest in a hollow in a tree or occasionally a bank; potoos use a depression on a branch; night jars and nighthawks nest unceremoniously on bare ground or occasionally on an epiphyte.

Perhaps because they are nocturnal, many species do not seem to have elaborate courtship displays. The male owls feed the females during courtship. During the breeding season, the second primary in each wing of the male standard-winged night jar projects about 35 centimeters (14 inches) beyond its neighbours and is shown to effect in slow aerial breeding displays. The bird nips them off after the displays cease.

Some owl species lay a similar-sized clutch of eggs each year during a regular breeding season (for example, two to three eggs for *Ninox* species); other vary the start of breeding and the clutch size quite dramatically according to seasonal conditions. The snowy owl lays up to 14 eggs in a year when its lemming prey is abundant, but two to four when prey is scarce. Incubation takes between four and five weeks depending upon the species, and the young must be brooded for a few weeks. The male forages and the female incubates, then both parents feed the young by offering them food. The nestlings often leave the nest to perch nearby when still downy, and in some species the family may stay together for several months.

The caprimulgiforms have a clutch of one to four eggs. Because the risk of predation is high, some ground-nesting nightjars have short incubation times (17 or 18 days in the Northern Hemisphere, but longer in Australia) and the young are semiprecocial—within hours they can totter around. They stay with their parents until migration. Oilbirds feed their nestlings on regurgitated oily fruit for 120 days, until they reach adult size. They have long been collected by South American Indians for their fat, used for cooking and in lamps.

Typically, owls and caprimulgiforrns are solitary; the gregarious oil birds are an exception. In both orders some species are resident, others partially or totally migratory. For example, some European populations of *Otus* owls migrate to Africa for the winter. Most temperate-zone species of night jar spend winter in the tropics and some tropical species are partial or total migrants. Rather than departing the North American winter, however, each year the common poorwill *Phalaenoptilus nuttallii* hibernates, clinging to the sides of a rock crevice. Its heart rate and respiration drop to almost unmeasurable levels, and its temperature falls from about 41°C (105°F) to about 19°C (66°F). It is one of the very few birds that hibernate regularly.

SWIFTS AND HUMMINGBIRDS

Swifts, crested swifts, and hummingbirds are generally classified as three families (Apodidae, Hemiprocnidae, and Trochilidae, respectively) in the order Apodiformes. They share some anatomical features, particularly the relative length of the bones of the wing, which is related to their rapid wing beats and night behaviour. The connection between swifts and crested swifts seems clear, but the inclusion of the very dissimilar hummingbirds in this order has often been challenged. Any communality of ancestry is indeed old.

Swifts

Swifts, with their narrow swept-back wings, have a well-deserved reputation for being among the fastest flying birds. They range in size from the pygmy swiftlet *Collocalia troglodytes* of the Philippines and pygmy palm swift *Micropanyptila furcata* of Venezuela, which weigh less than 6 grams (1/4 ounce), up to the white-naped swift *Streptoprocne semicollaris* of Mexico and purple needletail *Hirundapus celebensis* of the Philippines, both of which approach 200 grams (7 ounces). All are predominantly dark brown or sooty, with some areas of white or gray, and they have short legs with strong claws. All swifts pursue and capture their food, mostly insects, on the wing and stay aloft throughout the day, perching only at their overnight roosts. Sometimes the food ball or bolus taken to a nestling will contain mainly swarming insects such as termites, mayflies or aphids, as well as winged ants, wasps, and bees. At other times up to 60 different kinds of insects and spiders and several hundred individual prey items can be found in a single bolus.

Although most numerous in the tropical areas of the world the 80 or so species of swifts are widely distributed and even occur in Scandinavia, Siberia, and Alaska. The common swift *Apus apus* and alpine swift *A. melba* of Europe, the white-throated needletail *Hirundapus caudacutus* of Siberia and the chimney swift *Chaetura pelagica* of eastern North America all make long migration flights, often over stretches of ocean, to Southern Hemisphere wintering grounds. Even on the breeding grounds some swifts regularly spend the night on the wing.

Many swifts use secretions of their salivary glands in nest building. (Members of the New World subfamily Cypseloidinae do not do this, however, and their nests of mosses, ferns, and other plant material are placed near or behind waterfalls). The salivary glands enlarge during the breeding season to produce a sticky material which, in the genus *Chaetura*, is used to glue together small sticks to form the nest and also to attach it to the vertical wall of a hollow-tree nesting site; while in flight, the birds break dead twigs from the tops of trees. The use of saliva in nest building is most highly developed in some of the smaller cave-inhabiting swifts, known as cave swiftlets, of Southeast Asia, where saliva makes up the bulk of the nest. It is sometimes mixed with plant material and feathers (black nests) or forms the entire nest (white nests). These nests are collected by men who climb rickety bamboo scaffolding or vine ladders to reach the high ceilings of caves where tens of thousands of these swiftlets nest. Although white nests are considered the most valuable, as the main ingredient of bird's nest soup, both white and black nests are harvested and have become a major economic resource in that part of the world. Harvesting is controlled to protect the birds and keep this a renewable resource. Occasionally swiftlets, as well as other species of swifts, nest in close association with humans and use buildings and bridges as nest sites; chimney swifts now nest more commonly in chimneys than in hollow trees.

Researchers have found that several species of swifts and their nestlings are able to survive short periods of inclement weather by entering a semi-torpid state with a lowered body temperature. There are anecdotal accounts of what appears to be true hibernation in the chimney swift, but this needs further study.

Some cave swiftlets (genus *Aerodramus*) can nest and roost in total darkness deep in caves, sometimes more than a kilometer from any light. These birds make a series of audible clicks or rattle calls, and the returning echoes enable them to navigate within a cave and locate their own nest or roost site. (The only other bird that uses echolocation is the oilbird *Steatornis caripensis* of northern South America and Trinidad.) Non-echo locating swiftlets nest in the twilight zone and near the entrance of caves where there is still sufficient light for visual flight.

Both sexes participate in nest building, incubation, and provisioning of the chicks; incubation requires 19 to 23 days, and the nestling period may last as long as six to eight weeks. For species that nest in colonies there often is much social activity in the form of grouped flights and vocalizing. Their calls vary, from short sharp chips to long-drawn-out buzzy screes or screams.

Crested Swifts

The four species of crested swifts (genus *Hemiprocne*) are distributed from peninsular India eastward through Malaysia and the Philippines. All have frontal feathered crests, various degrees of forked tails, and patches of brighter colours. They are far less aerial in their behaviour than the true swifts, in that often they alternate between perching on prominent treetops and making graceful flights in pursuit of flying insects. Nowhere as abundant as swifts, crested swifts tend to be more solitary and sparsely distributed. Their nest is tiny, consisting of a small cup of plant material and lichens barely large enough to hold the single egg; it is fastened to a small lateral twig, and the brooding bird straddles the nest and supports itself on the underlying branch. Because their nests are typically high in the outer branches of large trees, many aspects of the breeding biology of crested swifts remain to be studied.

Hummingbirds

Hummingbirds are known for their small size, bright iridescent colours, and hovering flight. This diverse New World family, with 320 species in 112 genera, is most abundant in the warm tropical areas of Central and South America, but some are also found from Alaska to Tierra del Fuego and from lowland rainforest to high plateaus in the Andes. The average weight of these tiny birds is between 3.5 and 9 grams (less than 1/30unce)—the bee hummingbird is perhaps the smallest living species of bird, at about 2.5 grams ($^1/_{10}$ ounce)—but a few are larger, the giant hummingbird *Patagona gigas* being almost 20 grams ($^2/_3$ ounce).

The shape of the bill clearly reflects the type of flowers each species visits for nectar and insects. Hummingbird foraging takes two major forms: territoriality, in which floral nectar sources are vigorously defended; and trap-line foraging, where rich but more widely dispersed sources of nectar are regularly visited. The tongues of hummingbirds are brush-tipped to aid in nectar acquisition, but insects provide a needed source of protein and are a major component of their diet.

The extremely rapid wing beat (22 to 78 beats per second), coupled with a rotation of the outer hand portion of the wing and a powered upstroke, permits hummingbirds to hover adroitly in front of flowers during foraging. They also make vigorous acrobatic flights during territorial chases, and some species make elaborate aerial courtship displays. Longer flights to follow seasonal flowering patterns are also undertaken, and some species migrate over several thousand kilometers from nesting areas in temperate zones to wintering grounds in the tropics. During its migration, the ruby-throated hummingbird *Archilochus colubris* flies 1,000 kilometers (620 miles) across the Gulf of Mexico.

The breeding season of most species is keyed to the local flowering cycle, although it avoids seasons of intense rain. In most species the female alone builds the nest and incubates the eggs. Nests are typically small cups of plant material held together with spider web and sometimes adorned with moss or lichen. Bulkier nests, sometimes attached to the underside of a leaf, are typical of the hermit hummingbirds and some cave-nesting species.

INDEX

N

O

P